FRAGMENTARY
REPUBLICAN LATIN

I

LCL 294

FRAGMENTARY REPUBLICAN LATIN

ENNIUS

TESTIMONIA
EPIC FRAGMENTS

EDITED AND TRANSLATED BY

SANDER M. GOLDBERG

GESINE MANUWALD

HARVARD UNIVERSITY PRESS

CAMBRIDGE, MASSACHUSETTS

LONDON, ENGLAND

2018

First published 2018

LOEB CLASSICAL LIBRARY® is a registered trademark
of the President and Fellows of Harvard College

Library of Congress Control Number 2017940159
CIP data available from the Library of Congress

ISBN 978-0-674-99701-1

*Composed in ZephGreek and ZephText by
Technologies 'N Typography, Merrimac, Massachusetts.
Printed on acid-free paper and bound by
Maple Press, York, Pennsylvania*

CONTENTS

SERIES INTRODUCTION

AIMS AND OBJECTIVES OF
THE EDITION

Fragments of ancient texts have been collected since the early days of modern scholarship; the antiquarian and positivist tendencies of the nineteenth century especially encouraged such efforts and led to a proliferation of editions. In the early twentieth century, the four volumes published from 1935 to 1940 by E. H. Warmington in the Loeb Classical Library under the title *Remains of Old Latin* (*ROL*) were for their time a remarkable achievement; this collection provides an edition of the fragments of important early Republican poets as well as some inscriptions, together with the first translation into a modern language and concise notes.[1] Yet now, more than three-

---

[1] See reviews: vol. 1: C. J. Fordyce, *CR* 49 (1935): 188; A. Klotz, *PhW* 58, 23/24 (1938): 645–49; N. Terzaghi, *Leonardo* 9 (1938): 352–53—vol. 2: C. J. Fordyce, *CR* 51 (1937): 71–72; A. L. Keith, *CW* 30 (1937): 240; A. Klotz, *PhW* 58.5 (1938): 124–27; N. Terzaghi, *Leonardo* 9 (1938): 352–53—vol. 3: C. J. Fordyce, *CR* 53 (1939): 187–88; A. Klotz, *PhW* 59 (1939): 1048–51; A. Rostagni, *RFIC* 17 (1939): 289; N. Terzaghi, *Leonardo* 10 (1939): 319; B. L. Ullman, *CPh* 35 (1940): 217–18; M. Hammond, *CW* 35 (1941): 6–7; R. G. Kent, *CJ* 36 (1941): 559–63; E. B. Stevens,

quarters of a century later, the methodology, textual reconstructions, and coverage of *ROL* seem increasingly out of date. Hence the plan was developed for a substantial revision and rearrangement of the existing volumes, extending the subset to include more authors and more literary genres that survive in fragmentary form from the Republican period.

To indicate this new perspective and to avoid the difficult question of defining "old" and the problematic term "archaic," the title of the subseries was changed to *Fragmentary Republican Latin* (*FRL*). The new set is still not entirely comprehensive, but it will include all remains of Ennius; all remains of Pacuvius and Accius as well as tragic *incerta*; all remains of Livius Andronicus, Naevius, and Caecilius Statius as well as comic and dramatic *incerta*; the fragments of the *togata*, Atellana, and mime; all remains of Lucilius as well as fragments of political invective and popular verse; most testimonia and fragments from Roman Republican orators; most testimonia and fragments from Roman Republican historians; a selection of lyric, elegiac, and hexameter poetry; as well as selected inscriptions, including the Twelve Tables. Volumes covering all this material are in preparation by different editors and will appear successively over the next few years. Fragmentary works by authors of whom complete pieces are also extant are not part of this collection; thus, fragments

AJPh 65 (1944): 206–8—vol. 4: M. Hammond, *CW* 35 (1941): 6–7; H. M. Hoenigswald, *Language* 18 (1942): 65–66; H. Mattingly, *CR* 56 (1942): 34–35; A. Degrassi, *Gnomon* 23 (1951): 355–56; A. Rostagni, *RFIC* 29 (1951): 370–71.

by Varro, Cato, and of course Cicero are not represented in *FRL*.

The study of fragments requires particular awareness (on the part of both editors and readers) of the limits of our knowledge and of the kinds of inference that can be reliably drawn from the available evidence as well as some familiarity with the technical side of the discipline. The lack of context (e.g., other works by the same author, by contemporaries, by predecessors, the responses of audiences, etc.),[2] which can impede the study even of complete works, is especially limiting for the analysis of fragmentary ones.

Also, while it is reasonable to suppose that complete and fragmentary representatives of a single genre are in some ways similar, one cannot presuppose identical structure, style, or content. So, for instance, in the presentation of Greek myths, each tragedy probably offered a slightly different version within a general, fixed framework.[3] In most cases, therefore, while a number of assumptions can be made about fragmentary works, often by eliminating impossible or improbable options, it is hardly possible to "reconstruct" these works fully. Earlier scholars (especially in the nineteenth century) often attempted to do so, but their approach was based on the assumption of a much closer correspondence between Greek and Roman literature as well as between different versions of a story than is now accepted. More generally, scholars often tried to

[2] See Sommerstein 2010, 62.
[3] Ibid., 64–65.

reconstruct what has not been preserved rather than to concentrate on the existing evidence. With the greater methodological awareness of more recent times, reconstructing the plots of lost works has fallen from favor.

This new edition, while building on the achievements of predecessors, takes account of these developments. Its presentation of the fragments is based on the insights and established methodologies of twenty-first-century scholarship, even as it seeks to avoid conveying false certainties or promoting unprovable interpretations.

EDITORIAL PROBLEMS AND SOLUTIONS

The title *Fragmentary Republican Latin* is meant to be suitably broad, since the series aims to present not only verbatim fragments of the respective authors and literary genres but also *testimonia* on the life and works of writers and on individual works as well as paraphrases and indirect comments where appropriate.[4]

For extracts of literary texts transmitted in the secondary tradition, the identification of what can be called a "fragment" is not always clear, and there is also the mediating factor of the quoting author. It is therefore often difficult to decide whether a piece of evidence is a "fragment," where it begins and ends, and whether it has been reproduced literally. In the case of poetry, meter often helps, but given the flexibility of metrical structures in Republican verse and the frequent quotation of incom-

[4] On these different types of evidence with reference to incomplete works of historiography, see Brunt 1980.

plete lines, even that is not always a safe guide. Equally, even if the quoting author claims to reproduce the actual words, the claim may not be true, especially if the quotation is from memory (as can be seen, for instance, by comparing Cicero's quotations from Plautus and Terence with the extant complete texts). Further, quoting authors have their own agendas: they may cite passages that were of minor importance in the original context and/or give them a different interpretation than they originally had. Vague references such as "Ennius says" often mean "a character in Ennius' works says," and such notes can introduce both literal quotations and paraphrases. All these different types of evidence are presented in *Fragmentary Republican Latin*. What is thought likely to be a verbatim quotation is printed as a "fragment"; anything else is identified as a *testimonium* or an indirect quotation.

Assessments of Republican writers by contemporary or later ancient authors provide important additional information (presented here among the *testimonia* and in the contexts of fragments). Again, these cannot be taken at face value, since they are obviously influenced by the authors' own prejudices and those of their time, as shown, for example, by the rehabilitation of early writers in the second century AD.

Therefore, in the case of fragments[5] editors must not only decide which text to adopt for the fragments themselves but also whether to print them apart from the transmitting context or within that context (and if so, how much of the context to provide), in which order to print them

---

[5] On general issues connected with editing fragments, see Most 1997; Manuwald 2015.

(e.g., according to an assumed structure of the work or the chronology of quotations), to what extent potential meanings (and speakers in dramas) are indicated, and where to place fragments that are not explicitly attributed to a particular work in the transmission but can almost certainly be assigned to a specific piece. Editors must recognize that an entirely neutral presentation is impossible even if they believe they are merely presenting what is transmitted without drawing inferences.[6]

Most of these issues could conceivably have been avoided if *Fragmentary Republican Latin* had moved from traditional print to an online edition exploiting the opportunities provided by the digital medium (and not simply making the print volumes, like the rest of the Loeb Classical Library, available online).[7] Such a structure might be thought to eliminate the need to decide on a single option for arranging fragments (with introductory texts and cross-references), permitting the presentation of multiple versions, and empowering users to make their own decisions about arrangement and thus to be more aware of their implications. Still, even if editors try to be self-effacing, they must still enter the texts and establish the options (for instance, by deciding which versions to print in the main text and in the critical apparatus, or by ordering fragments "according to assumed plot"). Different presentations would not remove the fundamental diffi-

[6] For considerations concerning arranging the fragments of Ennius' *Annals*, see Elliott 2013.

[7] See the review of the digital Loeb Classical Library by Helma Dik, *CJ* 110 (2015): 493–500. For developments in this area see Clivaz et al. 2012.

culty: it is impossible to edit fragments without making decisions that impose a particular view on the text.

Editors of *Fragmentary Republican Latin* have nevertheless made an effort to be as neutral and open as possible; they strive to avoid basing the presentation of texts on unsupported assumptions, and they explain their arrangements of texts and choice of readings in introductions and notes or via the English translations.

EDITORIAL PRACTICE

Since dozens of ancient authors supply the quotations on which our knowledge of fragmentary texts is based, editors of those texts do not normally return to the manuscripts and research the transmission for each quoting author. They instead rely on the best available edition of each source. This principle, reinforced by the recent advances in the editing of the majority of the source authors, has, with few exceptions, been applied to the volumes of *FRL*. The standard editions of all source authors used are listed in the bibliography (and identified in the context of each quotation where necessary), so that the origin of each text is clear.

Source texts are typically printed as they appear in the respective editions, but their apparatus is not reproduced in full: those editions should be consulted for textual details and information about the manuscripts. Textual notes are given only where major changes to the transmission have been made or readings are controversial or bear on the interpretation of the fragments.

The readings of the text of the fragments themselves represent the views of the *FRL* editors and may differ from those in the source editions. When the fragment printed is the product of significant editorial intervention, this is noted: emendations affecting the meaning or metrical shape of a fragment are recorded together with noteworthy variants (though fuller reports can be found in more specialist editions of the fragmentary authors or the source editions). The correction of mere spelling variations and obvious errors in the manuscripts are generally not noted.

What can be identified clearly as a literal fragment has typically been set off from the surrounding text in a separate line or paragraph. Paraphrases and *testimonia* are printed as continuous texts, with individual words singled out by quotation marks where appropriate.

The English translations seek to stay as close to the Latin texts as possible (serving as guides to the original versions on the facing page), but obviously also try to present readable English. However, the style of the grammarians who quote a number of fragments is often clumsy and lacunose, which affects the English rendering. In the case of fragments that are incomplete sentences, the English too can only be incomplete. This also means that occasionally several translations (or rather, interpretations) are possible (depending on the grammatical analysis and the relevant supplements); this is indicated by the provision of various versions separated by a forward slash or by discussion in the notes. Some fragments are too corrupt to be translated at all or in their entirety. In those cases, a translation can only be conjectural: this is signaled by question marks in parentheses in the translation and/or by notes indicating the probable meaning of a line.

For transmitting authors whose works have been translated elsewhere in the Loeb collection, these English versions provided an important point of reference and are sometimes adopted with little or no variation. In the case of the fragments themselves, Warmington's renderings have been an inspiration throughout.

TECHNICAL POINTS

In line with the objectives of the Loeb series, these volumes aim to present reliable Latin texts and accurate English translations (as far as possible in the case of fragments), with little technical annotation.

Textual notes do not record mere spelling differences in the manuscripts or variants that do not make sense. More significant changes to the text are indicated in the textual notes and attributed to their author or a general "edd.," if they are generally accepted. Since for this edition no specific work on the manuscripts has been done and no full list of sigla for the manuscripts of each quoting author is provided, manuscript readings are denoted by "cod."/"codd."; for further details individual editions of the quoting authors should be consulted.

Numerous versions of a single fragment have sometimes accumulated over time: previous editors may have chosen differently among the transmitted readings or introduced their own conjectures, differed in their views of the beginning and the end of fragments, on the metrical shape of verses, and in their opinions on the position of fragments in the original work. In this edition, the origin of the printed version of the text is provided. Other transmitted versions that make sense or conjectures that have been important in the history of scholarship are recorded

in the textual notes, but this edition does not list all con-
jectures. Those may be found in the editions with fuller
apparatus criticus recorded in the bibliographies and in
the introductions to each volume.

An effort has been made to avoid cluttering the printed
texts, Latin and English, with editorial sigla, but the fol-
lowing specialized brackets have been used where neces-
sary: ‹text added by editor›; {text deleted by editor}; [ex-
planation added by editor]. Expansions of Latin ellipses in
the English translations are indicated only in problematic
cases.

All fragments are presented in the context in which
they are transmitted.

Fragments quoted several times in ancient authors are
presented in the context of the most meaningful quota-
tion. Other contexts that add further information may also
be printed; the rest are listed as references.

Where a well-established or recently revised system
for numbering fragments is available, it has been adopted
(with concordances to other widely used systems at the
end of each volume); in some cases a new system has been
developed. The adoption of existing numbering systems
in the majority of cases means that different principles
of ordering are in use across the collection: according to
the chronology of quoting authors or to the assumed posi-
tion of the fragments in the original work. The respective
methods are made clear in individual introductions.

Indications of a potential context or meaning for a frag-
ment are provided before the text when judged to be help-
ful. Purely conjectural suggestions are indicated by a ques-
tion mark. For dramatic fragments, speakers are identified

where there is sufficient evidence (the name followed by a colon before the text of the fragment). No comments are provided when the sense of a fragment is self-evident. Issues affecting a work as a whole are addressed in the introduction to that work, which may also discuss the possible order of fragments or their meaning in a wider context and provide a list of fragments not attributed to the particular poet and/or work in the transmission, but possibly belonging to it.

Detailed information necessary for understanding a fragment and its context is presented in notes. Explanations of individual words and the structure of a passage are sometimes inserted in square brackets within the translations for ease of reference. The latter applies particularly to excerpts from grammarians and lexicographers, who often discuss the precise form or meaning of a word.

General *testimonia* on life and works of authors are assembled in a separate section preceding the respective collection of fragments (referred to by T + number in introductions and notes). *Testimonia* on individual pieces providing information about the content of a particular work (or section thereof) are placed before the fragments of that work (and indicated by t + number).

References to secondary literature are kept to a minimum in annotations. A select bibliography for each ancient author or literary genre and references to particular works of scholarship may be found in the introduction to each volume, author, or work.

Abbreviations of the names of ancient authors and of the titles of works follow the *Oxford Classical Dictionary* (4th ed., 2012); authors and works not included in the

OCD have been assigned an abbreviation in similar style. General abbreviations are also based on the *OCD*. Abbreviations for journal titles follow *L'Année philologique.*

The names of editors of standard editions of the fragmentary texts collected in these volumes are abbreviated throughout; in references to editions of other texts, editors' names are spelled out for the sake of clarity. Important earlier collections of Roman Republican fragments are abbreviated as follows (for full details see the Bibliography): *FPL = Fragmenta Poetarum Latinorum*; *FRHist = The Fragments of the Roman Historians*; R. = Ribbeck; Sk. = Skutsch; *TrRF = Tragicorum Romanorum Fragmenta*; V. = Vahlen; W. = Warmington.

In addition to these principles, across *Fragmentary Republican Latin* all editors have sometimes had to make individual decisions in response to the particular needs of each writer, literary genre, or the numbering system adopted. In those cases editors outline their supplementary considerations in the introduction to their volumes.

FURTHER READING

Introductions and overviews of Republican literature, including fragmentary works, can be found in all major histories of Roman literature (in English see especially Kenney and Clausen 1982; Conte 1994; von Albrecht 1997). Portraits of the main Roman writers with bibliography are also offered in Cavallo/Fedeli/Giardina 1991. A select, annotated bibliography on Republican poetry can be found in Manuwald 2010. Suerbaum 2002, a handbook dedicated to early Roman literature, provides full information on all early Roman writers and their works, including bibliography and key *testimonia*.

For the relationship of early Roman literature and culture to the Greek world, see Gruen 1990, Gruen 1992, Farrell 2005, Feeney 2016; on the question of when "early Republican literature" emerged as a category, see Goldberg 2005b, and on the label "archaic" see Goldberg 2007a.

In addition to Warmington's Loeb and editions of individual authors (see respective introductions), dramatic fragments from the Republican period are collected in Ribbeck, *Scaenicae Romanorum poesis fragmenta* (1897/1898), fragments of other genres in *Fragmenta Poetarum Latinorum* (*FPL*) (^{4}2011). For general considerations on editing fragments, see Most 1997.

Besides literature on individual authors (see respective introductions), the main literary genres represented in the Republican period have been treated comprehensively. For epic see Goldberg 1995; for tragedy see Boyle 2006 and also Ribbeck 1875 (which accompanies his edition and explains his view of the plot of each tragedy); for comedy see Duckworth 1952 and Wright 1974 (one of the few works to discuss in detail poets whose works have been transmitted in fragments); for *praetexta* see Manuwald 2001 and Kragelund 2002; for drama generally see Beare 1964 and Manuwald 2011.

GESINE MANUWALD
Series Editor

INTRODUCTION TO ENNIUS

LIFE

Quintus Ennius can lay claim to one of the fullest biographies to be found among the literary figures of early Rome, the result of both the autobiographical statements identified in his poetry and the abiding interest of later generations in his life and work. The following facts, likely to be correct in outline, if not always in detail, are well attested in ancient sources.

Ennius was born in 239 BC (T 18, 29, 84, 97 [with wrong date]) and, like all the early Roman poets, was not, strictly speaking, Roman by birth; nor was Latin his native language. He was born in the Calabrian town of Rudiae (T 9, 47, 48, 53, 57, 99) and claimed descent from the legendary king Messapus, eponymous hero of Messapia (T 103). His name, like that of his sister's son Pacuvius, may be Oscan. As a native of Magna Graecia, Ennius would have been well versed in Greek language and culture, along with his native Oscan and the Roman culture into which he moved: thus he was said to have claimed to possess three hearts, Greek, Oscan, and Latin (T 83). He came to Rome in 204 BC, brought from Sardinia in the entourage of Cato, who had passed through the island while quaestor (T 38; cf. 91, 97), and took up independent residence on the Aventine Hill (T 97), where he was among the first teachers to introduce Greek learning to Romans through public readings of Greek and Latin texts (T 69). He died at the age of seventy in 169 BC (T 19, 33, 99). A funerary epigram, which may be his own composition, survives (*Epigr.* F 2).

Though a foreigner living in comparatively modest circumstances (T 33, perhaps 95), Ennius came to be on familiar terms with some of the most distinguished families of the time, including the Sulpicii Galbae (T 27) and the Scipios, both Scipio Nasica (T 14) and the great Africanus (T 42, 90, 113). That association encouraged a later belief that his portrait bust adorned the tomb of the Scipios (T 9, 49, 53, 56, 62) or even that he himself was buried there (T 99). His most important connection, however, was with M. Fulvius Nobilior, who as consul in 189 BC included the poet in his entourage when he embarked on a campaign in Aetolia (T 10, 29, 88, 92, 95). That experience seems to have marked a turning point in Ennius' poetic career, and his eventual Roman citizenship was attributed to Fulvian patronage (T 20). The description in the *Annals* of the so-called Good Companion (8 *Ann.* F 12), a modest, discreet, loyal, and affable retainer, was later identified as a self-portrait (T 82).

While modern scholarship generally accepts and works from these facts of the ancient biography, their assessment has varied significantly. A traditional line of interpretation, centering on Ennius' well-documented association with distinguished Romans and understanding the political life of the middle Republic as dominated by shifting alliances among various aristocratic factions, sees Ennius as essentially a poet for hire, advancing the partisan interests of one or another patron. That is certainly the easiest way to understand the occasional poem, undoubtedly encomiastic whatever its genre, entitled *Scipio* and the *praetexta* play *Ambracia*, which must have celebrated Nobilior's triumph over the Aetolians, and it explains why Cato publicly criticized Nobilior for having included a poet in his entourage (T 29). The case for reading Ennius' career this way was well put by Badian 1972, taken considerably further by Martina 1979, and figures prominently in the commentary on the *Annals* by Skutsch 1985. The first challenge to this view came just a little later by scholars who took the very range of Ennius' aristocratic connections as an indication of more than narrow partisan loyalties: his career as teacher and dramatist provided a significant measure of financial independence, while his efforts to create a new Roman literary identity transcended partisan divides. There would thus be a fundamental truth, as well as the core of an artistic program, in Cicero's assertion that in praising individual Romans Ennius was, ultimately, praising all Romans (T 9). This view, less fixated on factional politics and class distinction and more respectful of Ennius' artistic integrity, was initially advanced by Goldberg 1989; Gruen 1990, 106–22; and Goldberg 1995, 111–34, and has since been developed in different ways by scholars who interpret Ennius' career and his interaction with figures like Fulvius Nobilior as part of a broadly cultural rather than narrowly political agenda. Contemporary investigations treat Ennius as instrumental in bringing about major developments in Roman religion

(Rüpke 1995, 331–68; 2006), social organization (Rüpke 2000, 2001; Gildenhard 2003), and popular culture (Wiseman 2009, 134–37; 2015, 63–70).[8]

WORKS: AN OVERVIEW

Ennius was active in a wide range of literary endeavors and, with the apparent exception of comedy (T 4), found success in all of them.[9] He was a prolific writer of trage-dies, producing plays into the very last year of his long life (T 19): Cicero saw him as the first of the three canonical Roman tragic poets (T 15, 21, 25; cf. 78). The steady se-quence of commissions for the public festivals implies a wide circle of contacts among Roman aristocrats and a considerable degree of popularity, as does Plautus' easy allusion to his *Achilles* (*Ach.* t 1). Later claims that Ennius "taught" Pacuvius (T 3) and shared lodging with the comic dramatist Caecilius Statius (T 98) further indicate his sta-tus in the theatrical community of the time. And his rep-utation lived after him. Cicero frequently cited and ad-mired his tragedies (e.g., T 25, 30), audiences even in the late Republic could recognize an Ennian aria from its opening notes (T 26), and some dramas, like *Medea exul*,

[8] References here are representative, not complete. Suer-baum 2003 provides a full bibliographic survey, complementing the detailed discussion of Ennius' life and work in Suerbaum 2002, 119–42.

[9] Gratwick in Kenney and Clausen 1982 provides an insightful introduction. For Ennius in the context of Roman tragedy, see Boyle 2006, 56–87, and for epic, Goldberg 2005b. Ennius' recep-tion in antiquity is surveyed by Prinzen 1998.

became literary landmarks (T 28). Later generations often paired (and sometimes confused) Ennius with Accius (T 46, 52, 60, 68, 96; cf. 78). Ennius' tragic diction appealed to the archaizing taste of Fronto (T 74) and remained of interest to the grammarians of later antiquity, but by the late Republic his reputation was increasingly dependent on a second great endeavor, the epic *Annals.*

From its earliest days, epic at Rome was mindful of the Greek tradition behind it. The first preserved attempt at epic composition in Latin was a version of the *Odyssey* by Livius Andronicus (ca. 280/70–200 BC), and the slightly later poem by Naevius (ca. 280/60–200 BC) on the First Punic War (*Bellum Punicum*) seems to have drawn on the *Odyssey*'s use of embedded narrative. Ennius embraced Homeric tradition still more fully, and in the process made epic more fully Roman. He abandoned the traditional Saturnian verse form of Livius Andronicus and Naevius for Homer's dactylic hexameter, apparently the first poet in Latin to do so (T 109, 110), and with the new verse form came the opportunity to exploit a wide range of stylistic devices, allusions, echoes, and outright borrowings from Homer. The resulting poem, which told the story of Rome from the arrival of Aeneas down to events of his own time, was nevertheless in subject, organization, and moral compass quintessentially Roman in its display of Roman achievements portrayed with Homeric grandeur, and the experiment endured. Ennius gave Roman epic its canonical shape and pioneered many of its most characteristic features. His *Annals* quickly became a classic. Even so unremarkable a stylist as the anonymous author of *De bello Hispaniensi* quotes it with self-conscious pride (Inc. *Ann.* F 33, 119), and although largely eclipsed a genera-tion later by Virgil's still greater achievement, it remained for centuries a subject of literary reference and commentary (e.g., T 65, 70, 71). In the Flavian period, Silius Italicus cast a fictionalized Ennius as a combatant in his own Punic epic (T 67), and over a century after that an itinerant scholar could still draw crowds by discoursing, albeit with dubious accuracy, on fine points of Ennian diction (T 85).

Ennius also pioneered a number of other literary forms new to Latin. These include the philosophical *Protrepticus*, *Praecepta*, and *Epicharmus* in verse and *Euhemerus* (probably) in prose, collections of epigrams in elegiac couplets (*Epigrams*) and Sotadeans (*Sota*), and a didactic poem on gastronomy (*Hedyphagetica*). In addition to tragedies and comedies, he wrote plays on Roman themes (*praetextae*) and a panegyric work that posterity knew as *Scipio*. Perhaps most important of all, though now consigned to the relative obscurity of *opera minora* (minor works), was a highly innovative collection of occasional poems, moralistic, parodic, and sometimes autobiographical in character, that at some point acquired the title *Satires* (*Saturae*), which may well have influenced Lucilius and certainly informed the satiric persona of Horace.

None of this work is firmly dated, but some general points of chronology can be inferred from the record. Ennius may of course have written poetry before he came to Rome, but all his extant work seems to fall between his arrival there in about 204 and his death in 169 BC. More specifically, the poem in praise of Scipio is unlikely to have been written before Africanus' triumph in 201 BC, and the praetexta *Ambracia* must postdate the capture of that city by Fulvius Nobilior in 189. Since *Hedyphagetica* (F 1) displays some knowledge of Aetolian geography, it was probably composed (or at any rate revised) after Ennius' travel there with Fulvius. The design and composition of the *Annals* remain unclear. A good deal of the work certainly postdates the Aetolian campaign. Other hints are more problematic. If the elder Pliny's report (16 *Ann.* t 1) that Ennius added Book 16, which seems to have recorded events of the early 170s, to an original fifteen-book epic derives from Ennius' own preface to the addition, Gellius' otherwise reasonable claim (T 84) that Ennius wrote Book 12 in his sixty-seventh year (i.e., 173/172 BC) becomes doubtful, since that would entail extraordinary productivity in the last years of his life, when, as we know, he was still also producing tragedy (T 19).[10]

While no work of Ennius survives complete, more survives in fragments than of any of the other "lost" poets of early Rome, a clear indication of his importance to later readers. As heir to Hellenistic as well as classical Greek traditions, he helped stimulate Roman interest in a wide range of intellectual pursuits and played a major role in setting Latin literature on the assimilationist course that was to be its hallmark throughout the Republican period.

RECEPTION

Ennius was widely regarded as the "father" of Roman literature, not just by Republican authors who set him beside Homer (T 2, 36), but also by the Augustans, who saw

---

[10] So Skutsch 1985, 4–5, 674–76, who assumes that Ennius composed his books in chronological sequence.

him as a pioneer (T 44, 50, 102), even while conceding that his versification was by their standards crude and unpolished (e.g., T 51, 52, 54; cf. 56). Later in the first century, Seneca found his vocabulary old-fashioned (T 60), and Quintilian was respectful yet distant (T 66), but Ennius' status rose again with the archaizing tastes of the second century. Fronto (T 73–81) and Gellius (T 61, 82–85) read him with care, there were public recitations of his work, and texts remained in circulation. Direct knowledge of Ennius grew rarer in succeeding centuries as interest in him became increasingly grammatical and morphological, and even the commentators on Virgil, who preserve a considerable body of material, seem to derive their knowledge indirectly. Ennius was little more than a name by late antiquity, but still a potent one, thanks in part to Cicero's praise of him and the body of quotations that could be culled from classical texts by medieval authors.[11]

Ennius' memory was revived by the early humanists. He is a prominent figure in Petrarch's *Africa* (ca. 1338–1374) and is referred to elsewhere in his works (e.g., *Fam.* 4.15, 10.4, 22.2). Ennius is also mentioned in Boccaccio's *Genealogia deorum gentilium* (ca. 1360–1374), in Angelo Poliziano's *Nutricia* (1486), and in Marcus Hieronymus Vida's *De arte poetica* (1527). The fragments of Ennius' work were collected several times before the end of the sixteenth century, and editors worked assiduously to dis-

---

[11] See, for example, Naso (Muadwinus), *Ecloga* 1.71–81; Theodulus, *Egloga* 285–88; Alanus ab Insulis, *Anticlaudianus* 1.165–66; Berengarus, *Apologia pro Petro Abelardo* (*PL* 178 Migne, col. 1865A); John of Salisbury, *Entheticus in Polycraticum* (*PL* 199 Migne, col. 384C).

cover new material, not all of which turned out to be reliable. The introductions to these early editions nevertheless say much for Ennius' reception in this period.[12]

EDITIONS AND COMMENTARIES

The first attempt to gather all the extant fragments of Ennius in a single publication was undertaken in the mid-sixteenth century by the indefatigable printer and classical scholar Robertus Stephanus (Robert Estienne, 1503–1559) and brought to press by his son Henri in 1564 as part of an omnibus edition of all the Roman fragmentary poets. The first edition specifically devoted to Ennius was the work of Hieronymus Columna (Girolamo Colonna, 1534–1586), published in Naples in 1590. Colonna's collection is fuller and more carefully sourced than the Stephanus edition, and he followed his texts with extensive, often shrewd commentary (moved to the bottom of the page in the 1707 reissue).[13] Not much later, M. Antonius Delrius (M. A. del Río, 1551–1608) produced an edition of the tragedies in *Syntagma tragoediæ Latinæ* (Antwerp, 1593) and P. Merula (Paul van Merle, 1558–1607) an edition of the epic (Leiden, 1595). Merula further augmented the collection of epic fragments, but he was less critical of his

12 Goldschmidt 2012. A set of these fragments deemed largely spurious by modern editors appears in Volume II of the present edition as *Quotations Derived from Unknown Sources*.

13 Colonna's work remains valuable. Its 1707 reissue is widely available online, e.g., https://archive.org/details/qenniipoetaevet00vossgoog.

sources than was Colonna, and his claims for Ennian authorship must be used with caution.[14]

Major progress was made in the nineteenth century, beginning with F. H. Bothe's edition of the Roman dramatists, first issued in 1823/24. In 1852 Johannes Vahlen won a competition at the University of Bonn (Germany) with a critical edition of the fragments of the *Annals*, published as *Quaestiones Ennianae criticae*. This prompted him to undertake an edition of all fragments of Ennius, published in 1854 as *Ennianae poesis reliquiae* and eventually followed by a much revised second edition in 1903 (reprinted several times since), which for the first time presented all the evidence for Ennius' life and work in coherent form. This soon became the standard edition and set the modern study of Ennius on a firm footing (cf. Knapp 1911). Another edition of Ennius' fragments, with an often different constitution of the text, was prepared by Lucianus Mueller (1884). At about the same time, Otto Ribbeck embarked on an edition of all Roman dramatic fragments as *Scaenicae Romanorum poesis fragmenta*: the first edition of this two-volume work (tragic and comic fragments) appeared in 1852/55, followed by a considerably revised second edition in 1871/73 and then a slightly modified third edition with reduced apparatus in 1897/98. A kind of revised version of Ribbeck's work, of which only the first volume including the tragic fragments was completed, was

[14] The trenchant observations of Niebuhr 1870, 21, are taken up by Vahlen 1928, cxxxii, whose survey of early editions (cxxxi–cxliv) remains fundamental. For Merula's apparent forgeries (F 15–29 of our *Quotations Derived from Unknown Sources*), see Goldschmidt 2012, 14–16.

produced by Alfred Klotz (1953). An edition devoted to Ennius' so-called minor works was published by Ettore Bolisani in 1935.

The first advance of the twentieth century was a commentary on the *Annals*, the first ever in English, by E. M. Steuart (1925), widely praised on first appearance but soon overshadowed by the Loeb edition of E. H. Warmington, the forerunner to this one, in the first of his four-volume *Remains of Old Latin (ROL)*, published in 1935. This was the first edition of all of Ennius with translation into any modern language together with annotation in the vernacular. Translations in other modern languages have since appeared: French (Ernout [1]1916, [2]1957 [selection]; Heurgon 1960); Italian (Magno 1979; Traglia 1986); German (Engelsing 1983; Petersmann and Petersmann 1991 [selection]; Schönberger 2009 [selection]); Spanish (Segura Morena 1984; Martos 2006).

New scholarly editions and commentaries began appearing with some frequency in the later twentieth century. These include the first full-scale modern editions with detailed commentary, first of the tragic fragments by H. D. Jocelyn (1967), and then of the *Annals* by Otto Skutsch (1985). Text and commentary on the minor works are included in Edward Courtney's two anthologies (1993, 1999) and in a dedicated volume by Alessandro Russo (2007). An extensive commentary on the *Annals* with a new text and facing Italian translation in five volumes, the work of a team led by Enrico Flores at the University of Naples, was published in 2000 to 2009. A fresh edition with extensive apparatus of the tragic fragments by Gesine Manuwald appeared in 2012 as the second volume of *Tragicorum Romanorum Fragmenta (TrRF)*, and an edition of the minor works by Jürgen Blänsdorf in *Fragmenta Poetarum Latinorum (FPL⁴)* in 2011.

THIS EDITION

Interested readers could find books containing works by Ennius until at least the later second century AD (T 75, 85), but no continuous transmission preserved them for later posterity. Thus no works of his survived antiquity intact. We know them only through the work of other authors, who over succeeding centuries quoted, echoed, or otherwise appealed to Ennius and his authority, invariably for their own purposes and not always with direct or accurate knowledge of the object of their attention. Cicero and Varro, for example, quote Ennius with admiration—he was a formative influence on their own literary sensibilities—but the quotations can be so tightly woven into their new contexts that the poet's exact words become difficult to discern, while Lucretius' debts to Ennius, however palpable in his vocabulary and verse structure, are often easier to sense than to quantify. So too in the case of Virgil, whose debts may be even greater but would certainly be still harder to detect had Servius and Macrobius (and the larger scholarly tradition they represent) not pointed them out through a long sequence of comments and quotations.[15] Then there are the grammarians and lexicographers such as Nonius Marcellus, Festus, Priscian, and Diomedes, who quote words and phrases long since

---

[15] The tightness of the bond between quoting author and author quoted inevitably, though not always perceptibly, also affects the reception of both. See, for example, Zetzel 2007 (Cicero and Ennius) and Elliott 2008 (Virgil and Ennius).

plucked from their original contexts to illustrate oddities of grammar and morphology, together with the chronicle of Jerome, and a few other late references. The result is a significant mass of material, all of it important for understanding the magnitude of Ennius' achievement and his seminal place in the history of Roman literature, but much of it difficult to present and to evaluate. Our knowledge of Ennius' works is accordingly somewhat tentative, and the web of presumptions supporting that knowledge is easily disrupted. The present edition divides the ancient evidence into Testimonia and Fragments on the principles set out in the *FRL* Series Introduction. A few additional points specific to the case of Ennius:

TESTIMONIA. A wide variety of sources from the second century BC to the very limits of classical antiquity record, albeit with varying degrees of accuracy and personal knowledge, facts and opinions about Ennius' life and works. This body of material, which includes the main sources of information about his biography, output, and standing through the centuries, is presented here as Testimonia arranged in chronological order by source (T 1–114). A smaller set of extracts referring to the creation, content, or reception of individual works and thus most useful for engaging with their specific challenges, will be found set before the relevant fragments and distinguished by a lower case letter (e.g., 1 *Ann.* t 1). Extracts that fulfill both functions, as some inevitably do, are printed as Testimonia and cross-referenced as appropriate.

FRAGMENTS. Ennius' poetry survives in two main ways, either embedded as explicit quotations in the works of later authors, or by indirect quotation, where Ennius' exact words appear to have been adapted to the quoting source's new context by changes in tense, case, or grammatical structure. We also occasionally find ideas attributed to Ennius where the presentation leaves uncertain whether or to what extent the words used by the source are the poet's own or have been paraphrased or otherwise recast. Editors since Stephanus in the sixteenth century commonly obscure these distinctions by privileging on the page what they took to be the poet's own words over the context that preserved them and relegating their sources to footnotes, marginal references, and brief quotations. H. D. Jocelyn was the first editor to present the fragmentary texts of Ennius fully embedded in the secondary contexts, a practice we follow in this edition. There are two reasons for thus putting nearly as much stress on the process of transmission as on the texts transmitted: first, by directly confronting the difficulty of extracting fragment from source, the reader is in a better position to recognize the fragility of the editorial decisions that define each fragmentary text, and second, because the texts of Ennius, like those of any fragmentary author, come wrapped in the history of their reception. That is in its own right a story that needs to be told. To see what Ennius wrote is not the only reason to consult an edition of his work. How that work was read, what place it occupied in Roman literary and cultural history, how its reception changed over time and compares to the reception of other "lost" works of Roman (and Greek) literature are questions increasingly asked, and this edition strives to make as accessible as possible the evidence needed for answering them. As with all Loeb volumes, this material is presented in two ways:

1. Latin texts. The text of Ennius' tragic fragments presented here derives from the fully documented edition

published in 2012 as the second volume of *Tragicorum Latinorum Fragmenta* (*TrRF*): its text, fragment numbers and organization have been adopted, though with a much reduced critical apparatus. The fragments of each tragedy are thus arranged in chronological order by the source and do not reflect any hypothetical reconstruction of its plot.[16] The principle of presenting fragments in chronological order by source has also been adopted for the *praetextae*, the comedies, and, with due allowance for the book numbers sometimes included with quotations from the *Satires*, for the minor works. The preference throughout is to number sequentially by fragment rather than by individual line; a key to the numbering systems used in previous editions is provided in the concordance. For the *Annals* the provided text is, with few modifications, that of Otto Skutsch (1985), the edition that has done so much to stimulate renewed interest in the poem. It has seemed both prudent and convenient to preserve its order of presentation and its line numbers, including its extensive set of Unplaced Fragments of the *Annals*. Skutsch separated from this set of fragments others sometimes ascribed to the *Annals* but of doubtful authenticity: they are printed here with unnumbered lines as Doubtful Fragments of the *Annals*. We also include two additional categories that overlap, at least in part, with Vahlen's *Incerta* and the *Spuria* and *Vestigia* of Skutsch. These consist first of quotations

16 Since only the fullest source, not necessarily the earliest, is given in full, the chronological sequence established by *TrRF* may occasionally appear to be disrupted. For economy of presentation, the collection of *Dubia* in *TrRF* has been amalgamated with other incerta under *Unidentified Works*.

from and explicit statements about works by Ennius that cannot be further identified (*Unidentified Works*) and then quotations ascribed by one or another source to Ennius but of particularly doubtful authenticity (*Quotations Derived from Unknown Sources*).

A word about metrical notation: the Ennian corpus in all its diversity employs a wide variety of quantitative verse forms, from the iambo-trochaic and lyric meters characteristic of Roman drama to the distinctive Sotadean, to the dactylic hexameter and elegiac couplet, which Ennius himself so momentously introduced to Latin (T 109, 110). The fragmentary nature of the evidence, however, can make the scansion of individual verses difficult to ascertain, the rules of early prosody can be loose, and the record is neither large enough nor coherent enough to define metrical norms with any certainty or to reveal clear patterns of development. Thus we find dactyls that may be anapests (Inc. *Ann.* F 110), trochees that may have been recast as dactyls in the course of transmission (*Scipio* F 6), and numerous phrases of indeterminate shape. The end-stopped hexameters of the *Hedyphagetica*, so distinct from those of the *Annals* in their acceptance of elision, hiatus, and even iambic shortening, more likely stand as evidence of generic difference than of technical evolution. We identify meters wherever possible (a particularly important, if problematic task in cases like tragedy and satire, where the genre does not dictate the meter) and use a traditional vocabulary to do so, but since detailed discussion of metrical complexity is beyond the scope of the Loeb series, these represent suggestions rather than firm declarations. Particularly problematic cases are identified in the notes.

2. Translations. Readers come to Loeb editions for different reasons, some naturally looking more to the right-hand page and some to the left. Those needs tend to converge with editions of fragments, however, since almost everyone needs at least some of the material on both pages, namely, a basic text, access to its challenges, and clues to the editor's intention as well as the author's meaning. Because translation can be especially problematic when fragments are small, grammatical structures ambiguous, and levels of diction uncertain, it is sometimes easier to know what the words say than what the passage means. We therefore cling as closely as possible to the letter of the text, since the spirit is so often elusive and efforts to capture it are more likely to distort than to clarify the evidence and to close off interpretative possibilities rather than open them. That is less true for the Testimonia, which are integral to the understanding of any fragmentary author but are not so intractable. As excerpts rather than fragments, genuine stylistic decisions can be made to distinguish artful texts from purely utilitarian ones. We have sought to make all of them comprehensible on first reading, perhaps no more readable than the originals but certainly no less so. Behind all our editorial decisions lies a commitment to clarity, consistency, and utility in the presentation of this unavoidably heterogeneous body of material, but when necessary, we have not hesitated to sacrifice consistency in the interests of our other two objectives.

This project began with a simple division of labor, SMG responsible for the *Annals*, *Satires*, and *Scipio*, GM for the Testimonia, dramatic fragments, and remaining minor works. Things did not work out quite that way. A long and stimulating series of conversations and exchanges produced in the end a significantly more seamless collaboration for which the two editors are pleased to take joint responsibility.

BIBLIOGRAPHY

Two works by Werner Suerbaum greatly facilitate the modern study of Ennius, that is, an exhaustive review, complete with ancient testimonia and modern scholarship, of his life, works, and reception, and a comprehensive, fully indexed book-length bibliography of twentieth-century scholarship:

Suerbaum, Werner, ed. *Handbuch der lateinischen Literatur der Antike. Erster Band. Die archaische Literatur. Von den Anfängen bis Sullas Tod. Die vorliterarische Periode und die Zeit von 240–78 v. Chr. (HLL 1).* HbdA VIII.1. München, 2002.

————. *Ennius in der Forschung des 20. Jahrhunderts. Eine kommentierte Bibliographie für 1900–1999 mit systematischen Hinweisen nebst einer Kurzdarstellung des Q. Ennius (239–169 v. Chr.).* Bibliographien zur Klassischen Philologie 1. Hildesheim / Zürich / New York, 2003.

The evolution of modern Ennian scholarship is apparent in three important collections of essays:

Skutsch, Otto, ed. *Ennius. Sept exposés suivis de discussions* par O. Skutsch, H. D. Jocelyn, J. H. Waszink, E. Badian, J. Untermann, P. Wülfing-von Martitz, W.

Suerbaum. Entretiens préparés et présidés par Otto Skutsch. Entretiens sur l'antiquité classique, Tome XVII. Vandœuvres-Genève, 1972.

Rossi, Andreola, and Brian W. Breed, eds. *Ennius and the Invention of Roman Epic. Arethusa* 39.3. 2006.

Fitzgerald, William, and Emily Gowers, eds. *Ennius Perennis. The Annals and Beyond.* Cambridge Classical Journal, Proceedings of the Cambridge Philological Society, Suppl. Vol. 31. Oxford, 2007.

The following bibliography lists editions used and works cited in the present edition. It is not intended to provide a complete bibliography of scholarship on Ennius to date.

1. EDITIONS INCLUDING
FRAGMENTS OF ENNIUS

Blänsdorf, Jürgen, ed. [*FPL*[4]]. *Fragmenta poetarum Latinorum epicorum et lyricorum praeter Enni Annales et Ciceronis Germanicique Aratea, post W. Morel et K. Büchner editionem quartam auctam curavit.* Berlin / New York, 2011.

Bolisani, Ettore, ed. *Ennio minore.* Padova, 1935.

Bothe, Fridericus Henricus, ed. *Poetae scenici Latinorum. Collatis codd. Berolinensibus, Florentino, Friburgensi, Gothano, Guelpherbytanis, Helmstadiensibus, Monacensi, Palatino, Parisio, Ultrajectino, aliisque spectatae fidei libris. Volumen quintum: Fragmenta, Pars prior: Fragmenta tragicorum.* Halberstadt, 1823 (reissued Leipzig, 1834).

———. *Poetae scenici Latinorum. Collatis codd. Beroli-*

*nensibus, Florentino, Friburgensi, Gothano, Guelpher-
bytanis, Helmstadiensibus, Monacensi, Palatino, Pari-
sio, Ultrajectino, aliisque spectatae fidei libris. Volumen
quintum: Fragmenta, Pars posterior: Fragmenta comi-
corum.* Halberstadt, 1824 (reissued Leipzig, 1834).

Columna, Hieronymus, ed. *Q. Ennii poetae vetustissimi
fragmenta, quae supersunt, ab Hieron. Columna con-
quisita disposita et explicata ad Joannem Filium.* Edita
Neapoli ex typographia Horatii Salviani CIƆ IƆ XC
[1590]; repr.: *Q. Ennii poetae vetustissimi fragmenta
quae supersunt ab Hieron. Columna conquisita dispo-
sita et explicata ad Joannem Filium. Nunc ad editionem
Neapolitanam CIƆ IƆ XC. recusa accurante Francisco
Hesselio, I.C. & in Ill. Roterod. Athenaeo Hist. & Eloq.
Prof. accedunt. Praeter Eruditorum Virorum emenda-
tiones undique conquisitas; M. A. Delrii opinationes,
nec non G. J. Vossii castigationes & notae in Fragmenta
Tragoediarum Ennii; ut & Index omnium verborum
Ennianorum.* Amsterdam, 1707.

Courtney, Edward, ed. *The Fragmentary Latin Poets.* Ox-
ford, 1993 [corr. repr. 2003].

———. *Archaic Latin Prose.* American Philological As-
sociation, American Classical Studies 42. Atlanta, 1999.

Delrius, Martinus Antonius, ed. *Syntagma tragoediæ La-
tinæ. In tres partes distinctum. Quid in ijsdem continea-
tur, sequens paginae indicabit.* [Part I: Προλεγομένων
libri III, Fragmenta veterum tragicorum (pp. 93–160),
Opinationes in eadem (pp. 161–88)]. Antwerpen, 1593.

Engelsing, Rolf, trans. *Ennius deutsch. Quintus Ennius.
239–169. Dichtungen, Geschichte.* Berlin, 1983.

Ernout, Alfred, ed. *Recueil de textes latins archaïques.
Nouvelle édition.* Paris, ²1957 [¹1916].

Flores, Enrico et al., eds. *Quinto Ennio, Annali.* 5 vols. Forme materiali e ideologie del mondo antico 33 / 34 / 35 / 36 / 38. Napoli, 2000–2009.

Garbarino, Giovanna, ed. *Roma e la filosofia greca dalle origini alla fine del II seccolo a. C. Raccolta di testi con introduzione e commento.* 2 vols. Historica, Politica, Philosophica. Il pensiero antico–Studi e testi 6. Torino / Milano / Genova / Padova / Bologna / Firenze / Pescara / Roma / Napoli / Bari / Palermo, 1973.

Heurgon, Jacques, ed. *Ennius.* 2 vols. Les cours de Sorbonne, Latin. Paris, 1960.

Jocelyn, H. D. [Joc.], ed. *The Tragedies of Ennius. The Fragments Edited with an Introduction and Commentary.* Cambridge Classical Texts and Commentaries 10. Cambridge, 1967 [repr. with corr. 1969].

Klotz, Alfred [Kl.], ed. *Scaenicorum Romanorum fragmenta.* Volumen prius. *Tragicorum fragmenta,* adiuvantibus Ottone Seel et Ludovico Voit. München, 1953.

Magno, Pietro, ed. and trans. *Quinto Ennio.* Fasano di Puglia, 1979.

Manuwald, Gesine, ed. *Tragicorum Romanorum Fragmenta (TrRF). Volumen II. Ennius.* Göttingen, 2012.

Martos, Juan, ed. and trans. *Ennio. Fragmentos. Introducción, Traducción y Notas.* Biblioteca Clásica Gredos 352. Madrid, 2006.

Masiá, Andrés, ed. *Ennio. Tragedias. Alcmeo. El ciclo troyano.* Classical and Byzantine Monographs XLVI. Amsterdam, 2000.

Merula, Paulus, ed. *Q. Enni, poetae cum primis censendi, annalium libb. XIIX. Quae apud varios Auctores superant, Fragmenta: conlecta, composita, inlustrata ab Paullo G. F. P. N. Merula, qui eadem fixit, dicavit, sacra-*

vit S. P. Q. Dordraceno L. M. Ioh. Mauritius. Leiden, 1595.

Mueller, Lucianus, ed. *Q. Enni carminum reliquiae. Accedunt Cn. Naevi Belli Poenici quae supersunt. Emendavit et adnotavit.* St. Petersburg, 1884.

Petersmann, Hubert, and Astrid Petersmann, eds. and trans. *Die römische Literatur in Text und Darstellung. Band 1. Republikanische Zeit I. Poesie.* RUB 8066. Stuttgart, 1991.

Ribbeck, Otto [R.¹/R.²/R.³], ed. *Scaenicae Romanorum poesis fragmenta. Vol. I. Tragicorum Romanorum fragmenta.* Leipzig, ¹1852 / ²1871 / ³1897.

——— [R.¹ / R.² / R.³], ed. *Scaenicae Romanorum poesis fragmenta. Vol. II. Comicorum Romanorum praeter Plautum et Terentium fragmenta.* Leipzig, ¹1855 / ²1873 / ³1898.

Russo, Alessandro, ed. *Quinto Ennio. Le opere minori. Introduzione, edizione critica dei frammenti e commento. Vol. I: Praecepta, Protrepticus, Saturae, Scipio, Sota.* Testi e studi di cultura classica 40. Pisa, 2007.

Schönberger, Otto, ed. and trans. *Quintus Ennius. Fragmente (Auswahl). Lateinisch / Deutsch. Ausgewählt, übersetzt und herausgegeben.* RUB 18566. Stuttgart, 2009.

Segura Morena, Manuel, ed. and trans. *Quinto Ennio. Fragmentos. Texto revisado y traducido.* Colección hispánica de autores griegos y latinos. Madrid, 1984.

Skutsch, Otto [Sk.], ed. *Ennius, Quintus. The Annals.* Edited with introduction and commentary. Oxford, 1985.

Stephanus, Robertus and Henricus, eds. *Fragmenta poetarum veterum Latinorum, quorum opera non extant: Ennii, Pacuvii, Accii, Afranii, Lucilii, Naevii, Laberii,*

Caecilii, aliorumque multorum: Undique à Rob. Ste-phano summa diligentia olim congesta: nunc autem ab Henrico Stephano eius filio digesta, & priscarû quæ in illis sunt vocum expositione illustrata: additis etiâ ali-cubi versibus Graecis quos interpretâtur. Genève, 1564.

Steuart, E. M., ed. *The Annals of Q. Ennius.* Cambridge, 1925.

Traglia, Antonio, ed. *Poeti latini arcaici. Volume primo. Livio Andronico, Nevio, Ennio.* Classici Latini. Torino, 1986.

Traina, Alfonso, ed. *Comoedia. Antologia della palliata. In Appendice: Elogia e tabulae triumphales.* Padova, [1]1960, [2]1966, [3]1969, [4]1997, [5]2000.

Vahlen, Iohannes [V.[1]], ed. *Ennianae poesis reliquiae,* re-censuit. Leipzig, 1854.

——— [V.[2]], ed. *Ennianae poesis reliquiae,* iteratis curis recensuit. Leipzig, 1903 (= Leipzig, [3]1928; Amsterdam, 1963, 1967).

Warmington, E. H. [W.], ed. and trans. *Remains of Old Latin.* 4 vols. Loeb Classical Library 294, 314, 329, 359. London, 1935–1940. Vol. 1, *Ennius and Caecilius.* Lon-don, 1935 [[2]1967, repr. 1988, etc.].

2. EDITIONS OF TRANSMITTING AUTHORS

2.1. Apuleius (Apul.)

Helm, Rudolf, ed. *Apulei Platonici Madaurensis opera quae supersunt. Vol. II, Fasc. 1. Pro se de magia liber (apologia).* Editio stereotypa editionis alterius cum ad-dendis. Leipzig, 1959 [[1]1912, [4]1963, [5]1972, repr.].

Hunink, Vincent, ed. *Apuleius of Madauros, Pro se de magia (Apologia). Edited with a Commentary.* 2 vols. Amsterdam, 1997.

Moreschini, Claudio, ed. *Apulei Platonici Madaurensis opera quae supersunt Vol. III. De philosophia libri.* Stuttgart / Leipzig, 1991.

2.2. Arnobius (Arn.)

Marchesi, Concetto, ed. *Arnobii Adversus nationes libri VIII.* Corpus Scriptorum Latinorum Paravianum. Torino / Milano / Padova / Firenze / Pescara / Bari / Napoli / Catania / Palermo, ²1953.

2.3. Ausonius (Auson.)

Green, R. P. H., ed. *Decimi Magni Ausonii opera. Recognovit brevique adnotatione critica instruxit.* Oxford, 1999.

2.4. Aurelius Augustinus (August.)

Dombart, Bernardus, and Alfonsus Kalb, eds. *Sancti Aurelii Augustini episcopi De civitate dei, libri XXII.* Recognoverunt. Stuttgart, 1981.

Goldbacher, A., ed. *S. Aureli Augustini Hipponiensis Episcopi Epistulae. Recensuit et commentario critico instruxit. Pars IV. Ep. CLXXXV–CCLXX.* CSEL 57. Wien / Leipzig, 1911.

Pinborg, Jan, and B. Darrell Jackson, eds. *Augustine. De dialectica. Translated with Introduction and Notes by B. D. J., from the Text newly Edited by J. P. Dordrecht.*

Synthese Historical Library, Texts and Studies in the History of Philosophy 16. Boston, 1975.

2.5. Censorinus (Censorinus)

Sallmann, Nicolaus, ed. *Censorini De die natali liber ad Q. Caerellium. Accedit anonymi cuiusdam Epitoma disciplinarum (Fragmentum Censorini).* Leipzig, 1983.

2.6. Flavius Sosipater Charisius (Charis.)

Barwick, Karl [B.], ed. *Flavii Sosipatri Charisii artis grammaticae libri V.* Edidit C. B. Addenda et corrigenda collegit et adiecit F. Kühnert. Leipzig, 1964 [repr. Stuttgart / Leipzig, 1997].

Keil, Heinrich [K.], ed. *Grammatici Latini. Vol. I. Flavii Sosipatri Charisii Artis grammaticae libri V, Diomedis Artis grammaticae libri III, ex Charisii arte grammatica excerpta.* Leipzig, 1857 [repr. Hildesheim, 1961].

2.7. M. Tullius Cicero (Cic.)

Clark, Albertus Curtis, ed. *M. Tulli Ciceronis orationes [I]. Pro Sex. Roscio, De imperio Cn. Pompei, Pro Cluentio, In Catilinam, Pro Murena, Pro Caelio. Recognovit brevique adnotatione critica instruxit.* Oxford, 1905.

———. *M. Tulli Ciceronis orationes [IV]. Pro P. Quinctio, Pro Q. Roscio comoedo, Pro A. Caecina, De lege agraria contra Rullum, Pro C. Rabirio perduellionis reo, Pro L. Flacco, In L. Pisonem, Pro C. Rabirio Postumo. Recognovit brevique adnotatione critica instruxit.* Oxford, 1909.

———. *M. Tulli Ciceronis orationes* [VI]. *Pro Tullio, Pro Fonteio, Pro Sulla, Pro Archia, Pro Plancio, Pro Scauro. Recognovit brevique adnotatione critica instruxit.* Oxford, 1911.

Giomini, Remo, ed. *M. Tulli Ciceronis scripta quae manserunt omnia. Fasc. 46. De divinatione, De fato, Timaeus.* Leipzig, 1975.

Giusta, Michelangelus, ed. *M. Tulli Ciceronis Tusculanae disputationes.* Torino, 1984.

Grilli, Albertus, ed. *M. Tulli Ciceronis Hortensius edidit commentario instruxit.* Testi e documenti per lo studio dell'antichità 5. Milano / Varese, 1962.

Kasten, Helmut, ed. *M. Tulli Ciceronis scripta quae manserunt omnia. Fasc. 8. Oratio pro Sexto Roscio Amerino.* Post Alfredum Klotz recognovit. Leipzig, 1968.

Klotz, Alfred, ed. *M. Tulli Ciceronis scripta quae manserunt omnia. Fasc. 23. Orationes in P. Vatinium, pro M. Caelio.* Leipzig, 1915.

———. *M. Tulli Ciceronis scripta quae manserunt omnia. Volumen IV. Orationes pro P. Quinctio, pro Sex. Roscio Amerino, pro Q. Roscio comoedo recognovit A. Klotz, Orationes pro M. Tullio, pro M. Fonteio, pro A. Caecina recognovit F. Schoell.* Leipzig, 1923.

Kumaniecki, Kazimierz F., ed. *M. Tulli Ciceronis scripta quae manserunt omnia. Fasc. 3. De oratore.* Leipzig, 1969.

Maslowski, Tadeusz, ed. *M. Tullius Cicero scripta quae manserunt omnia. Fasc. 22. Oratio Pro P. Sestio.* Leipzig, 1986.

———. *M. Tullius Cicero scripta quae manserunt omnia. Fasc. 24. Oratio de provinciis consularibus, Oratio Pro L. Cornelio Balbo. Edidit T. M. Opus editoris morte interruptum praefatione instruxit M. D. Reeve.* Berlin / New York, 2007.

Moreschini, Claudio, ed. *M. Tullius Cicero. Scripta quae manserunt omnia. Fasc. 43. De finibus bonorum et malorum.* München / Leipzig, 2005.

Nisbet, R. G. M., ed. *M. Tulli Ciceronis in L. Calpurnium Pisonem oratio.* Edited with text, introduction, and commentary. Oxford, 1961.

Peterson, Gulielmus, ed. *M. Tulli Ciceronis Orationes [III]. Divinatio in Q. Caecilium, In C. Verrem. Recognovit brevique adnotatione critica instruxit. Editio altera, recognita et emendata.* Oxford, 1917 [¹1907].

Plasberg, Otto, ed. *M. Tulli Ciceronis scripta quae manserunt omnia. Fasc. 43. Academicorum reliquiae cum Lucullo.* Leipzig, 1922.

———. *M. Tulli Ciceronis scripta quae manserunt omnia. Fasc. 45. De natura deorum. Recognovit O. Plasberg. Iterum edidit appendicem adiecit W. Ax.* Leipzig, 1933 [¹1917].

Powell, J. G. F., ed. *M. Tulli Ciceronis De re publica, De legibus, Cato maior de senectute, Laelius de amicitia. Recognovit brevique adnotatione critica instruxit.* Oxford, 2006.

Reynolds, L. D., ed. *M. Tulli Ciceronis de finibus bonorum et malorum libri quinque. Recognovit brevique adnotatione critica instruxit.* Oxford, 1998.

Shackleton Bailey, D. R., ed. *M. Tulli Ciceronis Epistulae ad Atticum.* 2 vols. Stuttgart, 1987.

———. *M. Tulli Ciceronis Epistulae ad familiares libri I–XVI.* Stuttgart, 1988.

Stroebel, Eduard, ed. *M. Tulli Ciceronis scripta quae manserunt omnia. Fasc. 2. Rhetorici libri duo qui vocantur de inventione.* Leipzig, 1915.

Westman, Rolf, ed. *M. Tulli Ciceronis scripta quae manserunt omnia. Fasc. 5. Orator.* Leipzig, 1980.

Wilkins, A. S., ed. *M. Tulli Ciceronis Rhetorica.* 2 vols. *Recognovit brevique adnotatione critica instruxit.* Oxford, 1902 / 1903.

Winterbottom, Michael, ed. *M. Tulli Ciceronis De officiis. Recognovit brevique adnotatione critica instruxit.* Oxford, 1994.

2.8. Diomedes (Diom.)

Keil, Heinrich [K.], ed. *Grammatici Latini. Vol. I. Flavii Sosipatri Charisii Artis grammaticae libri V, Diomedis Artis grammaticae libri III, ex Charisii arte grammatica excerpta.* Leipzig, 1857 [repr. Hildesheim, 1961].

2.9. Aelius Donatus (Donat.)

Keil, Heinrich [K.], ed. *Grammatici Latini. Vol. IV. Probi Donati Servii qui feruntur de arte grammatica libri ex recensione Henrici Keilii; Notarum Laterculi ex recensione Theodori Mommseni.* Leipzig, 1864 [repr. Hildesheim, 1961].

Wessner, Paulus, ed. *Aeli Donati quod fertur Commentum Terenti, accedunt Eugraphi commentum et Scholia Bembina, Vol. I.* Leipzig, 1902.

2.10. Sex. Pompeius Festus (Fest.)/Paulus (Paul. Fest.)

Lindsay, Wallace M. [L.], ed. *Sexti Pompei Festi De verborum significatu quae supersunt cum Pauli Epitome.* Leipzig, 1913 [repr. Hildesheim / New York, 1965].

2.11. M. Cornelius Fronto (Fronto)

van den Hout, Michael J. P., ed. *M. Cornelii Frontonis epistulae schedis tam editis quam ineditis Edmundi Hauleri usus iterum edidit.* Leipzig, 1988.

2.12. Fabius Planciades Fulgentius (Fulg.)

Pizzani, Ubaldo, ed. *Fabio Planciade Fulgenzio. Definizione di parole antiche. Introduzione, testo, traduzione e note.* Roma, 1968.

Wessner, Paul, ed. "Fabii Planciadis Fulgentii expositio sermonum antiquorum." *Commentationes Philologae Ienenses, ediderunt seminarii philologorum Ienensis professores. Voluminis sexti fasciculus posterior,* 63–144. Leipzig, 1899.

2.13. Aulus Gellius (Gell.)

Marshall, P. K., ed. *A. Gellii Noctes Atticae. Recognovit brevique adnotatione critica instruxit.* 2 vols. Oxford, 1968 [ed. corr. 1990].

2.14. Grammatici incerti (Gramm. inc.)

Keil, Heinrich [K.], ed. *Grammatici Latini. Vol. V. Artium scriptores minores. Cledonius, Pompeius, Iulianus, Excerpta ex commentariis in Donatum, Consentius, Phocas, Eutyches, Augustinus, Palaemon Asper, De nomine et pronomine, De dubiis nominibus, Macrobii excerpta.* Leipzig, 1868 [repr. Hildesheim, 1961].

———. *Grammatici Latini. Vol. VI. Scriptores artes met-*

ricae: Marius Victorinus, Maximus Victorinus, Caesius Bassus, Atilius Fortunatianus, Te-rentianus Maurus, Marius Plotius Sacerdos, Rufinus, Mallius Theodorus, Fragmenta et excerpta metrica. Leipzig, 1874 [repr. Hildesheim, 1961].

2.15. Eusebius Hieronymus (Hieron.)

Hilberg, Isidorus, ed. *Sancti Eusebii Hieronymi Epistulae. Pars I: Epistulae I–LXX.* CSEL LIV: S. Eusebii Hieronymi opera I.I. Wien / Leipzig, 1910 [repr. New York / London, 1961; ed. altera suppl. aucta].

——. *Sancti Eusebii Hieronymi Epistulae. Pars III: Epistulae CXXI–CLIV.* CSEL LV: S. Eusebii Hieronymi opera I.III. Wien / Leipzig, 1918 [repr. New York / London, 1961; ed. altera suppl. aucta, Wien, 1996].

Lardet, Pierre, ed. *S. Hieronymi Presbyteri Opera. Pars III: Opera polemica I. Contra Rufinum.* CCSL LXXIX. Turnhout, 1982.

2.16. Horace (Hor.)

Shackleton Bailey, D. R., ed. *Q. Horati Flacci opera.* Stuttgart, 1985.

2.17. Isidorus (Isid.)

Andrés Sanz, María Adelaida, ed. *Isidori Hispalensis Episcopi liber Differentiarum [II].* Corpus Christianorum, Series Latina CXI A. Turnhout, 2006.

Becker, Gustav, ed. *Isidori Hispalensis De natura rerum liber.* Berlin, 1857 [repr. Amsterdam, 1967].

Codoñer, Carmen, ed. *Isidoro de Sevilla. Diferencias. Libro I. Introducción, Edición crítica, traducción y notas.* Collection Auteurs latin du moyen âge 8. Paris, 1992.

Lindsay, Wallace M., ed. *Isidori Hispalensis Episcopi Etymologiarum sive originum libri XX. Recognovit breuique adnotatione critica instruxit.* 2 vols. Oxford, 1911.

2.18. Iulius Rufinianus (Iul. Ruf.)

Halm, Carolus, ed. *Rhetores Latini minores. Ex codicibus maximam partem primum adhibitis emendabat.* Leipzig, 1863.

2.19. Iulius Victor (Iul. Vict.)

Halm, Carolus, ed. *Rhetores Latini minores. Ex codicibus maximam partem primum adhibitis emendabat.* Leipzig, 1863.

2.20. Lactantius Placidus (Lactant.)

Brandt, Samuel, ed. *L. Caeli Firmiani Lactanti Opera omnia, accedunt carmina eius quae feruntur et L. Caecilii qui inscriptus est de mortibus persecutorum liber, recensuerunt Samuel Brandt et Georgius Laubmann. Pars I: Divinae institutiones et Epitome divinarum institutionum recensuit S. B.* Prag / Wien / Leipzig, 1890.

Sweeney, Robertus Dale, ed. *Lactantii Placidi in Statii Thebaida commentum Volumen I. Anonymi in Statii Achilleida commentum. Fulgentii ut fingitur Planciadis super Thebaiden commentariolum.* Stuttgart / Leipzig, 1997.

2.21. Lucretius (Lucr.)

Bailey, Cyril, ed. *Titi Lucreti Cari de rerum natura libri six. Edited with prolegomena, critical apparatus, translation, and commentary.* Oxford, 1949.

2.22. Ambrosius Theodosius Macrobius (Macrob.)

Kaster, R. A., ed. *Ambrosii Theodosii Macrobii Saturnalia. Recognovit brevique adnotatione critica instruxit.* Oxford, 2011.

2.23. Nonius Marcellus (Non.)

Lindsay, Wallace M. [L.], ed. *Nonii Marcelli De compendiosa doctrina libros XX, Onionsianis copiis usus edidit.* 3 vols. Leipzig, 1903 [repr. Hildesheim, 1964; includes page numbers according to edition of Mercerus (M.)].

2.24. *Origo gentis Romanae (Origo gen. Rom.)*

Pichlmayr, Franciscus, ed. *Sexti Aurelii Victoris Liber de Caesaribus. Praecedunt Origo gentis Romanae et Liber de viris illustribus urbis Romae, subsequitur Epitome de Caesaribus. Recensuit Fr. Pichlmayr. Editio stereotypa correctior editionis primae, addenda et corrigenda iterum collegit et adiecit R. Gruendel.* Leipzig, 1966.

2.25. Orosius (Oros.)

Arnaud-Lindet, Marie-Pierre, ed. *Orose. Histoires (Contre les Païens). Tome I. Livres I–III. Texte établi et traduit.* Paris, 1990.

2.26. Panegyrici Latini (Pan. Lat.)

Mynors, R. A. B., ed. *XII Panegyrici Latini. Recognovit brevique adnotatione critica instruxit*. Oxford, 1964.

2.27. Phaedrus (Phaedr.)

Postgate, Iohannes Percival, ed. *Phaedri Fabulae Aesopiae cum Nicolai Perotti prologo et decem novis fabulis. Recognovit brevique adnotatione critica instruxit*. Oxford, [1920].

2.28. Plinius maior (Plin.)

Mayhoff, Carolus, ed. *C. Plini Secundi Naturalis Historiae libri XXXVII post Ludovici Iani obitum recognovit et scripturae discrepantia adiecta edidit*. 6 vols. Stuttgart, 1892–1909.

2.29. Porphyrio (Porph.)

Meyer, Gulielmus, ed. *Pomponii Porphyrionis commentarii in Q. Horatium Flaccum. Recensuit*. Leipzig, 1874.

2.30. Priscianus (Prisc.)

Hertz, Martin, ed. *Grammatici Latini. Vol. II/III. Prisciani grammatici Caesariensis Institutionum grammaticarum libri XVIII*. Leipzig, 1855/59 [repr. Hildesheim, 1961].
Keil, Heinrich, ed. *Grammatici Latini. Vol. III. Prisciani grammatici Caesariensis De figuris numerorum, De metris Terentii, De praeexercitamentis rhetoricis libri, Institutio de nomine et pronomine et verbo, Partitiones*

duodecim versuum Aeneidos principalium. Accedit Prisciani qui dicitur liber de accentibus. Leipzig, 1859 [repr. Hildesheim, 1961].

2.31. Propertius (Prop.)

Heyworth, Stephen, ed. *Sexti Properti elegos critico apparatu instructos edidit.* Oxford, 2007.

2.32. M. Fabius Quintilianus (Quint.)

Winterbottom, Michael, ed. *M. Fabi Quintiliani Institutionis oratoriae libri duodecim. Recognovit brevique adnotatione critica instruxit.* 2 vols. Oxford, 1970.

2.33. *Rhetorica ad Herennium (Rhet. Her.)*

Marx, Fridericus [Friedrich], ed. *M. Tulli Ciceronis scripta quae manserunt omnia. Fasc. 1. Incerti auctoris de ratione dicendi ad C. Herennium lib. IV. Iterum recensuit Fridericus Marx. Editionem stereotypam correctiorem cum addendis curavit Winfried Trillitzsch.* Leipzig, 1964.

2.34. Rufinus Lupus (Rufin.)

Halm, Carolus, ed. *Rhetores Latini minores. Ex codicibus maximam partem primum adhibitis emendabat.* Leipzig, 1863.

Keil, Heinrich [K.], ed. *Grammatici Latini. Vol. VI. Scriptores artes metricae: Marius Victorinus, Maximus Victorinus, Caesius Bassus, Atilius Fortunatianus, Terenti-*

anus Maurus, Marius Plotius Sacerdos, Rufinus, Mallius Theodorus, Fragmenta et excerpta metrica. Leipzig, 1874 [repr. Hildesheim, 1961].

2.35. Rutilius Lupus (Rut. Lup.)

Halm, Carolus, ed. *Rhetores Latini minores. Ex codicibus maximam partem primum adhibitis emendabat.* Leipzig, 1863.

2.36. Scholia (Pseudacronis) in Horatium (Schol. ad Hor.)

Keller, Otto, ed. *Pseudacronis Scholia in Horatium vetustiora.* 2 vols. Leipzig, 1902/4.

2.37. Scholia in Lucanum (Schol. ad Luc.)

Endt, Ioannes, ed. *Adnotationes super Lucanum primum ad vetustissimorum codicum fidem edidit.* Leipzig, 1909.

2.38. Scholia in Petronium (Schol. ad Petron.)

Titi Petronii Arbitri Satyricôn quae supersunt. Cum integris Doctorum Virorum Commentariis; & Notis Nicolai Heinsii & Guilielmi Goesii antea ineditis; Quibus additae DVPEYRATII & auctiores BOVRDELOTII ac REINESII notae. Adjiciuntur Jani Dousae Praecidanea, D. Jos. Ant. Gonsali de Salas Commenta, Variae Dissertationes & Praefationes, quarum Index post praefationem exhibetur. Curante Petro Burmanno. Cujus accedunt curae secundae. Editio altera. Tomus primus. Amstelaedami, CIƆ IƆ CCXXXXIII.

2.39. Scholiastae Ciceronis (Schol. ad Cic.)

Stangl, Thomas, ed. *Ciceronis Orationum Scholiastae. Asconius. Scholia Bobiensia. Scholia Pseudasconii Sangallensia. Scholia Cluniacensia et recentiora Ambrosiana ac Vaticana. Scholia Lugdunensia sive Gronoviana et eorum excerpta Lugdunensia. Volumen II: Commentarios continens.* Wien / Leipzig, 1912.

2.40. Scholiastae Vergili (Schol. ad Verg. et Glossae)

Baschera, Claudio, ed. *Gli scholii veronesi a Virgilio. Introduzione, edizione critica e indici.* Verona, 1999.

Hagen, Hermannus, ed. *Appendix Serviana. Ceteros praeter Servium et Scholia Bernensia Vergilii commentatores continens. Recensuit.* Leipzig, 1902 (vol. III, fasc. II) [repr. Leipzig, 1927].

Keil, Heinrich [K.], ed. *M. Valerii Probi in Vergilii Bucolica et Georgica commentarius. Accedunt Scholiorum Veronensium et Aspri quaestionum Vergilianarum fragmenta.* Halle, 1848.

2.41. Scriptores Historiae Augustae (SHA)

Hohl, Ernst, Wolfgang Seyfarth, and Christa Samberger, eds. *Scriptores Historiae Augustae.* 2 vols. Leipzig, 1927 [repr. [4/2]1965].

2.42. Seneca minor (Sen.)

Roncali, Renata, ed. *L. Annaei Senecae Ἀποκολοκύντωσις.* Leipzig, 1990.

Reynolds, L.D., ed. *L. Annaei Senecae Ad Lucilium epistulae morales. Recognovit et adnotatione critica instruxit.* Oxford, 1965.

2.43. Servius (Serv. et Serv. Dan.)

Thilo, Georgius, ed. *Servii grammatici qui feruntur in Vergilii carmina commentarii. Vol. I. Aeneidos librorum I–V commentarii.* Leipzig / Berlin, 1881 [repr. Leipzig / Berlin, 1923].

———. *Servii grammatici qui feruntur in Vergilii carmina commentarii. Vol. II. Aeneidos librorum VI–XII commentarii.* Leipzig / Berlin, 1884 [repr. Leipzig / Berlin, 1923].

———. *Servii Grammatici qui feruntur in Vergilii carmina commentarii. Vol. III, Fasc. 1. In Bucolica et Georgica commentarii.* Leipzig, 1887 [repr. Leipzig, 1927, Hildesheim, 1961].

2.44. P. Terentius Afer (Ter.)

Kauer, Robert, and Wallace M. Lindsay, eds. *P. Terenti Afri Comoediae. Recognoverunt brevique adnotatione critica instruxerunt Robert Kauer / Wallace M. Lindsay. Supplementa apparatus curavit Otto Skutsch.* Oxford, 1958.

2.45. Tertullianus (Tert.)

Fredouille, Jean-Claude, ed. and trans. *Tertullien. Contre les Valentiniens, Tome I. Introduction, texte critique, traduction.* Sources Chrétiennes 280. Paris, 1980.

2.46. M. Terentius Varro (Varro)

Flach, Dieter, ed. and trans. *Marcus Terentius Varro. Gespräche über die Landwirtschaft. Herausgegeben, übersetzt und erläutert.* 3 vols. Texte zur Forschung 65–67. Darmstadt, 1996–2002.

Goetz, Georgius, and Fridericus Schoell, eds. *M. Terenti Varronis De Lingua Latina quae supersunt. Accedunt grammaticorum Varronis librorum fragmenta.* Leipzig, 1910.

3. SECONDARY LITERATURE: WORKS CITED

Aberson, Michel. *Temples votifs et butin de guerre dans la Rome republicaine.* Rome, 1994.

Aicher, P. J. "Ennian Artistry: *Annals* 175–179 and 78–83 (Sk.)." *CJ* 85 (1989/90): 218–24.

von Albrecht, Michael. "Ein Pferdegleichnis bei Ennius." *Hermes* 97 (1969): 333–45; revised and reprinted as "Ennius: A Clash of Two Cultures." In *Roman Epic. An Interpretive Introduction,* 63–73. Leiden, 1999.

———. "Zur 'Tarentilla' des Naevius." *MH* 32 (1975): 230–39.

———. "Ennius' *Annales.*" In *Das römische Epos,* edited by Erich Burck, 33–44. Grundriß der Literaturgeschichten nach Gattungen. Darmstadt, 1979.

———. *A History of Roman Literature. From Livius Andronicus to Boethius. With Special Regard to Its Influence on World Literature.* Revised by Gareth Schmeling and by the author. 2 vols. Vol. 1 translated with the assistance of F. and K. Newman; Vol. 2 translated with the assistance of R. R. Caston and F. R. Schwartz. Mne-mosyne Suppl. 165. Leiden / New York / Köln, 1997 [German original: 1994].

Arcellaschi, André. "Essai de datation de la Médée d'Ennius." *Caesarodunum* 10bis (1976): 65–70.

——. *Médée dans le théâtre latin d'Ennius à Sénèque.* Collection de l'École française de Rome 132. Roma, 1990; chapter on Ennius' *Medea* repr. as: "La Médée d'Ennius." In *Medeas. Versiones de un mito desde Grecia hasta hoy*, 2 vols., edited by Aurora López and Andrés Pociña, 367–87. Granada, 2002.

Aretz, Susanne. *Die Opferung der Iphigeneia in Aulis. Die Rezeption des Mythos in antiken und modernen Dramen.* BzA 131. Stuttgart / Leipzig, 1999.

Aricò, Giuseppe. "La tragedia romana arcaica." *Lexis* 15 (1997): 59–78.

Arkins, B. "Tradition Reshaped: Language and Style in Euripides' Medea 1–19, Ennius' Medea exul 1–9 and Catullus 64.1–30." *Ramus* 11 (1982): 116–33.

Auhagen, Ulrike. [2000a] "Ennius' *Andromacha* im politischen Kontext der Zeit." In Manuwald 2000, 199–210.

——. [2000b] "Monologe bei Ennius und Catull." In *Dramatische Wäldchen. Festschrift für Eckard Lefèvre zum 65. Geburtstag*, edited by Ekkehard Stärk and Gregor Vogt-Spira, 173–87. Spudasmata 80. Hildesheim / Zürich / New York, 2000.

Badian, Ernest. "Ennius and His Friends." In O. Skutsch 1972, 149–208.

Baker, R. J. "'Well Begun, Half Done': *otium* at Catullus 51 and Ennius, *Iphigenia*." *Mnemosyne* 42 (1989): 492–97.

Baldwin, Barry. "Fulgentius and His Sources." *Traditio* 44 (1988): 37–57.

Barbantani, Silvia. *FATIS NIKHFOROS. Frammenti di elegia encomiastica nell' età delle Guerre Galatiche: Supplementum Hellenisticum 958 e 969.* Biblioteca di Aevum Antiquum: Instituto di Filologia Classica e di Papirologia. Milan, 2001.

Barchiesi, Alessandro. "Figure dell' intertestualità nell' epica romana." *Lexis* 13 (1995): 49–67.

Barchiesi, Marino. *Nevio epico. Storia, interpretazione, edizione critica dei frammenti del primo epos latino.* Padova, 1962.

Beare, W. *The Roman Stage. A Short History of Latin Drama in the Time of the Republic.* 3rd ed. London, 1964.

Beck, Hans, and Uwe Walter. *Die frühen römischen Historiker I, von Fabius Pictor bis Cn. Gellius.* Stuttgart, 2001.

Bergk, Theodor. "Quaestionum Ennianarum specimen." In *Indices lectionum et publicarum et privatarum quae in academia Marburgensi per semestre aestivum a. MDCCCXLIV . . . habendae proponuntur,* III–XVII; repr. in: Bergk 1884, 211–35.

———. "Kritische Studien zu Ennius." *Jahrbücher für classische Philologie,* VII. Jg., 83. Bd. (1861): 316–34, 495–508, 617–38; repr. in: Bergk 1884, 246–311.

———. *Kleine philologische Schriften von Theodor Bergk. Herausgegeben von Rudolf Peppmüller. I. Band. Zur römischen Literatur.* Halle a. S., 1884.

Bettini, Maurizio. *Studi e note su Ennio.* Pisa, 1979.

———. "A proposito dei versi sotadei, greci e romani: con

alcuni capitoli di 'analisi metrica lineare.'" *MD* 9 (1982): 59–105.

Biliński, Bronisław. "Rôle idéologique de la tragédie romaine sous la république. I. L'Alexandre d'Ennius et les premières révoltes d'esclaves." In *Tragica II*, 7–54. Prace Wrocławskiego towarzystwa naukowego / Travaux de la Société des Sciences et des Lettres de Wrocław, Ser. A. 54. Wrocław, 1954.

Blok, P. I. "De fragmentis Ennianis a Paullo Merula editis." *Mnemosyne* 28 (1900): 1–12.

Bo, Domenico. "Sugli Hedyphagetica di Ennio." *RIL* 89/90 (1956): 107–20.

Boyle, Anthony J., ed. *Roman Epic*. London / New York, 1993.

———. *An Introduction to Roman Tragedy*. London / New York, 2006.

Brandt, Paulus, ed. *Corpusculum poesis epicae Graecae ludibundae. Fasciculus prior continens parodiae epicae Graecae et Archestrati reliquiae*. Leipzig, 1888.

Brink, Charles O. "Ennius and the Hellenistic Worship of Homer." *AJPh* 93 (1972): 547–67.

Broccia, Giuseppe. "Di alcune traduzioni tragiche di Ennio (sc. 203–204, 206 Vahl.²)." *AFLM* 33 (2000): 127–35.

Brooks, R. A. *Ennius and Roman Tragedy*. PhD diss., Harvard University, 1949 [repr. New York, 1981, ed. K. J. Reckford (Monographs in Classical Studies)].

Bruno, Massimo. "Ennio, Scen. 260–61 V² (219–20 Jocelyn)." *Maia* 32 (1980): 43–51.

Brunt, Peter A. "On Historical Fragments and Epitomes." *CQ* 30 (1980): 477–94.

Bryce, Jackson. *The Library of Lactantius*. New York / London, 1990.

Büchner, Karl. "Der Soldatenchor in Ennius' Iphigenie." *GB* 1 (1973): 51–67; repr. in: *Studien zur römischen Literatur, Bd. 10,* 1–15. Wiesbaden, 1979.

Caldini Montanari, Roberta. "A che punto è la notte? Le stelle dell'Orsa Maggiore come orologio notturno nella poesia latina a partire da Ennio (con una premessa su Eur., IA 6–8)." *Mene* 7 (2007): 5–91.

Cameron, Alan. *Callimachus and His Critics.* Princeton, 1995.

Casali, Sergio. "The Poet at War: Ennius on the Field in Silius's *Punica.*" In Rossi and Breed 2006, 569–93.

Castagna, Luigi. *Quinti Ennii et Marci Pacuvii Lexicon Sermonis Scaenici.* Alpha–Omega, Reihe A, Lexika, Indizes, Konkordanzen zur klassischen Philologie, CLXII. Hildesheim / Zürich / New York, 1996.

Catone, Nicola. *Grammatica Enniana.* Collezione filologica, Testi e manuali. Firenze, 1964.

Cavallo, Guglielmo, Paolo Fedeli, and Andrea Giardina, eds. *Lo spazio letterario di Roma antica. Volume V. Cronologia e bibliografia della letteratura Latina.* Roma, 1991.

Caviglia, Franco. "Il Telamo di Ennio." *ASNP* Ser. 2, 39 (1970): 469–88.

Cazzaniga, Ignazio. "Ad Ennio, Andromeda fr. III v. 98 Kl." *RFIC* 95 (1967): 258–59.

———. "In Ennii Andromedam adnotationes tres." In *Studi di storiografia antica in memoria di Leonardo Ferrero,* 49–52. Torino, 1971.

Charlet, Jean-Louis. "Un humaniste trop peu connu, Niccolò Perotti: prolégomènes à une nouvelle édition du *Cornu copiae.*" *REL* 65 (1987): 210–27.

Citti, Vittorio. "Enn. trag. 348 V.² = 300 Joc." *QCTC* 4–5

(1986–1987 [1990]) = Giuseppe Aricò, ed. *Atti del I seminario di studi sulla tragedia romana (Palermo 26–28 ottobre 1987)*, 93–97.

Classen, Carl Joachim. "Ennius: ein Fremder in Rom." *Gymnasium* 99 (1992): 121–45; repr. in: *Die Welt der Römer. Studien zu ihrer Literatur, Geschichte und Religion.* Unter Mitwirkung v. Hans Bernsdorff hg. v. Meinolf Vielberg, 62–83. UaLG 41. Berlin / New York, 1993.

Clivaz, Claire, Jérôme Meizoz, François Vallotton, and Joseph Verheyden, avec la collaboration de Benjamin Bertho, eds. *Lire Demain. Des manuscrits antiques à l'ère digitale.* Lausanne, 2012.

Coffey, Michael. *Roman Satire.* 2nd ed. Bristol, 1989.

Connors, Catherine. "Ennius, Ovid and Representations of Ilia." *MD* 32 (1994): 99–112.

———. "Epic Allusion in Roman Satire." In *The Cambridge Companion to Roman Satire,* edited by Kirk Freudenburg, 123–45. Cambridge, 2005.

Conte, Gian Biagio. *Latin Literature. A History.* Translated by Joseph B. Solodow. Revised by Don Fowler and Glenn W. Most. Baltimore / London, 1994 [Italian original: 1987].

———. *The Poetry of Pathos: Studies in Virgilian Epic.* Edited by S. J. Harrison. Translated by Elaine Fantham and Glenn W. Most. Oxford, 2007.

Contin Cassata, Adriana. "Nota Enniana (Medea fr. I, SC. 246 ss. Vahl.²)." In *Studi sulla lingua poetica latina,* 11–18. Pref. di Alfonso Traina. Ricerche di storia della lingua latina 1. Roma, 1967 .

Cornell, T. J. et al., eds. *The Fragments of the Roman Historians.* 3 vols. Oxford, 2013.

Courcelle, Pierre. "Le retentissement profane et chrétien d'un vers d'Ennius." *REL* 48 (1970): 107–12.

Crawford, Michael. *Roman Republican Coinage.* 2 vols. Cambridge, 1974.

Damon, Cynthia. *The Mask of the Parasite. A Pathology of Roman Patronage.* Ann Arbor, 1997.

Dangel, Jacqueline. "Au-delà du réel et poétique de l'indicible: Le songe d'Ilia." In *Moussyllanea. Mélanges de linguistique et de littérature ancienne offerts à C. Moussy,* edited by B. Bureau and C. Nicolas, 281–93. Louvain / Paris, 1998.

D'Anna, Giovanni. "La 'fortuna' di Ennio. I—Dal sec. II a. C. all'età di Cesare." *C&S* 22, no. 86 (1983a): 58–63.

———. "La 'fortuna' di Ennio. II—L'età augustea." *C&S* 22, no. 88 (1983b): 29–36.

D'Antò, Vincenzo. "L'Athamas di Ennio e di Accio." *BStudLat* 1 (1971): 371–78.

Della Casa, Adriana. "Ennio di fronte all' 'Ecuba di Euripide." *Dioniso* 36 (1962): 63–76; repr. in: *Grammatica e letteratura. Scritti scelti di Adriana Della Casa,* 25–37. Genova, 1994.

Dominik, William J. "From Greece to Rome: Ennius' *Annales.*" In Boyle 1993, 37–58.

Dondoni, Lucia. "La tragedia di Medea. Euripide e i poeti arcaici latini." *RIL* 92 (1958): 84–104.

Drabkin, Norma Löwenstein. *The Medea exul of Ennius.* PhD diss., Columbia University, New York, 1937.

Duckett, Eleanor Shipley. *Studies in Ennius.* Bryn Mawr College Monographs XVIII. PhD diss., Bryn Mawr, 1915.

Duckworth, George E. *The Nature of Roman Comedy. A Study in Popular Entertainment.* Princeton, 1952; *Sec-*

ond Edition. With a Foreword and Bibliographical Appendix by Richard Hunter. Norman / Bristol, 1994.

Elliott, Jackie. "The Voices of Ennius' *Annals.*" In Fitzgerald and Gowers 2007, 38–54.

———. "Ennian Epic and Ennian Tragedy in the Language of the *Aeneid.* Aeneas' Generic Wandering and the Construction of the Latin Literary Past." *HSCPh* 104 (2008): 241–72.

———. *Ennius and the Architecture of the Annales.* Cambridge, 2013.

Enk, P. J. "Roman Tragedy." *NPh* 41 (1957): 282–307.

Erasmo, Mario. *Roman Tragedy. Theater to Theatricality.* Austin, 2004.

Fabrizi, Virginia. "Ennio e *l'Aedes Herculis Musarum.*" *Athenaeum* 96 (2008): 193–219.

———. *Mores veteresque novosque: rappresentazioni del passato e del presente di Roma negli Annales di Ennio.* Pisa, 2012.

Faller, Stefan. "Romanisierungstendenzen in der *Iphigenia* des Ennius." In Manuwald 2000, 211–29.

Fantham, Elaine. "'Dic si quid potes de Sexto Annali': The Literary Legacy of Ennius' Pyrrhic War." In Rossi and Breed 2006, 549–68.

Fantuzzi, Marco. "La censura delle Simplegadi: Ennio, Medea, fr. 1 Jocelyn." *QUCC* n.s. 31.1 (1989): 119–29.

Faoro, Andrea. "Nota sulla Nemea di Ennio." *A&R* 34 (1989): 104–6.

Farrell, Joseph. "The Origins and Essence of Roman Epic." In *A Companion to Ancient Epic,* edited by John Miles Foley, 417–28. Malden, MA / Oxford, 2005.

Feeney, Denis C. *The Gods in Epic. Poets and Critics of the Classical Tradition.* Oxford, 1991.

———. *Caesar's Calendar. Ancient Time and the Beginning of History.* Berkeley, 2007.

———. *Beyond Greek. The Beginnings of Latin Literature.* Cambridge, MA, 2016.

Fitzgerald, William, and Emily Gowers, eds. *Ennius Perennis. The Annals and Beyond.* Cambridge Classical Journal, Proceedings of the Cambridge Philological Society, Suppl. Vol. 31. Oxford, 2007.

Fleckenstein, Helmuth. *Enniusstudien.* PhD diss., Frankfurt am Main, 1953.

Flower, Harriet. "*Fabulae praetextae* in Context: When Were Plays on Contemporary Themes Performed in Republican Rome?" *CQ* 45 (1995): 170–90.

Fraenkel, Eduard. "Zur Medea des Ennius." *Hermes* 67 (1932): 355–56.

———. "Additional Note on the Prose of Ennius." *Eranos* 49 (1951): 50–56.

Frassinetti, Paolo. "Sul 'Cresfonte' di Ennio." *CCC* 2 (1981): 15–23.

Fucarino, Carmelo. "Ennio buongustaio. L'arte culinaria come metafora del mutamento civile." *ALGP* 28–30 (1991/93): 189–203.

Galasso, Luigi, and Fausto Montana, eds. *Euripide. Medea. Con una premessa di Franco Montanari.* I classici. Milano, 2004.

Garelli-François, Marie-Hélène. "À propos du Thyeste d'Ennius: tragédie et histoire." *Rome et le tragique. Colloque international 26, 27, 28 mars 1998 CRATA, Pallas* 49 (1998): 159–71 (summary: 397–98).

Geel, Iacobus. *De Telepho Euripidis commentatio.* Commentationes Latinae tertiae classis Instituti Regii Belgici 4. Amsterdam, [1830].

Gildenhard, Ingo. "The 'Annalist' Before the Annalists. Ennius and His *Annales.*" In *Formen römischer Geschichtsschreibung von den Anfängen bis Livius,* edited by Ulrich Eigler et al., 93–114. Darmstadt, 2003.

———. "Virgil vs. Ennius, or: The Undoing of the Annalist." In Fitzgerald and Gowers 2007, 73–102.

———. "Buskins & SPQR: Roman Receptions of Greek Tragedy." In *Beyond the Fifth Century: Interactions with Greek Tragedy from the Fourth Century BCE to the Middle Ages,* edited by Ingo Gildenhard and Martin Revermann, 153–85. Berlin / New York, 2010.

Gold, Barbara K. *Literary Patronage in Greece and Rome.* Chapel Hill / London, 1987.

Goldberg, Sander M. "Poetry, Politics, and Ennius." *TAPhA* 119 (1989): 247–61.

———. *Epic in Republican Rome.* New York / Oxford, 1995.

———. *Constructing Literature in the Roman Republic. Poetry and Its Reception.* Cambridge, 2005a.

———. "Early Republican Epic." In *A Companion to Ancient Epic,* edited by John Miles Foley, 429–39. Malden, MA / Oxford, 2005b.

———. "Ennius after the Banquet." In Rossi and Breed 2006, 427–47.

———. "Antiquity's Antiquity." In *Latinitas Perennis. Volume I. The Continuity of Latin Literature,* edited by Wim Verbaal, Yanick Maes, and Jan Papy, 17–29. Brill's Studies in Intellectual History 144. Leiden / Boston, 2007a.

———. "Research Report: Reading Roman Tragedy." *IJCT* 13 (2007b): 571–84.

———. Rev. of Enrico Flores et al., *Gli Annales di Ennio.* 4 vols. (Napoli, 2007–8). *Paideia* 64 (2009): 637–55.

———. "Lucilius and the *poetae seniores.*" In *Lucilius and Satire in Second Century B.C. Rome,* edited by Brian Breed, Elizabeth E. Keitel, and Rex Wallace. Cambridge, 2018.

Goldschmidt, Nora. "Absent Presence: *pater* Ennius in Renaissance Europe." *CRJ* 4 (2012): 1–19.

———. *Shaggy Crowns. Ennius' Annales and Virgil's Aeneid.* Oxford, 2013.

Gowers, Emily. "The *Cor* of Ennius." In Fitzgerald and Gowers 2007, 17–37.

Gratwick, A. S. "Ennius' *Annales*" and "The Satires of Ennius and Lucilius." In Kenney and Clausen 1982, 60–76, 156–62.

Grilli, A. *Studi enniani.* Pubblicazioni del Sodalizio Glottologico Milanese 3. Brescia, [1965].

———. "Superstitiosi vates (Enn. sc. 321 V.²)." In *Studi in onore di Albino Garzetti,* edited by Clara Stella and Alfredo Valvo, 227–30. Brescia, 1996.

Gruen, Erich S. *Studies in Greek Culture and Roman Policy.* Cincinnati Classical Studies. New Series. Vol. VII. Leiden / New York / Copenhagen / Köln, 1990 (paperback ed.: Berkeley / London, 1996).

———. *Culture and National Identity in Republican Rome.* Cornell Studies in Classical Philology LII. Ithaca, 1992.

Habinek, Thomas. "The Wisdom of Ennius." In Rossi and Breed 2006, 471–88.

Handley, Eric W., and John Rea. *The Telephus of Euripides.* BICS Suppl. 5. London, 1957.

Hardie, Philip. *Virgil's Aeneid: Cosmos and Imperium.* Oxford, 1986.

————. "Poets, Patrons, Rulers: The Ennian Traditions." In Fitzgerald and Gowers 2007, 129–44.

Hartung, I. A. *Euripides restitutus sive scriptorum Euripidis ingeniique censura, quam faciens fabulas quae exstant explanavit examinavitque, earum quae interierunt reliquias composuit atque interpretatus est, omnes quo quaeque ordine natae esse videntur disposuit et vitam scriptoris enarravit.* 2 vols. Hamburg, 1843/44.

Hermann, Gottfried. "De Aeschyli tragoediis fata Aiacis et Teucri complexis." (1838): 3–21. In Gottfried Hermann. *Opuscula. Vol. VII*, 362–87. Leipzig, 1839 [repr. Hildesheim / New York, 1970].

Herrmann, Léon. "Un nouveau vers de l'Epicharme d'Ennius." *RBPh* 7 (1928): 131–38.

Herzog-Hauser, Gertrud. "Ennius imitateur d'Euripide." *Latomus* 2 (1938): 225–32.

Heslin, Peter. *The Museum of Augustus. The Temple of Apollo in Pompeii, the Portico of Philippus in Rome, and Latin Poetry.* Los Angeles, 2015.

Hinds, Stephen. *Allusion and Intertext. Dynamics of Appropriation in Roman Poetry.* Cambridge, 1998.

Hose, Martin. "Anmerkungen zur Verwendung des Chores in der römischen Tragödie der Republik." In *Der Chor im antiken und modernen Drama,* edited by Peter Riemer and Bernhard Zimmermann, 113–38. Drama 7. Stuttgart, 1999.

Housman, A. E. "Ennius in Pers. VI 9." *CR* 48 (1934): 50–51.

van den Hout, Michael P. J. *A Commentary on the Letters*

of M. Cornelius Fronto. Mnemosyne Suppl. 190. Leiden / Boston / Köln, 1999.

Jaeger, Mary. *Archimedes and the Roman Imagination.* Ann Arbor, 2011.

Jahn, Otto. *Telephus und Troilus. Ein Brief an Herrn Professor F. G. Welcker in Bonn.* Kiel, 1841.

Jiráni, O. "Achilles či Achilles Aristarchi? Příspěvek k tragoediím Enniovým." *LT* 32 (1905): 194–99.

Jocelyn, Henry David. [1969a] *"Imperator histricus."* *YCS* 21 (1969): 97–123.

———. [1969b] "The Fragments of Ennius' Scenic Scripts." *AC* 38 (1969): 181–217.

———. [1972a] "Ennius as a Dramatic Poet." In Skutsch 1972, 39–88 (discussion: 89–95).

———. [1972b] "The Poems of Quintus Ennius." *ANRW* I 2 (1972): 987–1026.

———. "The Sources of the *Cornu Copiae* of Niccolò Perotti and Their Integrity: Some Methodological Remarks." In *Memores tui. Studi di Letteratura classica ed umanistica in onore di Marcello Vitaletti,* edited by Sesto Prete, 99–111. Sassoferrato, 1990.

———. "Les Géorgiques de Virgile et le tragique (Virgile, Géorg., III, 139–142 et Ennius, Sc., 76–77 Vahlen)." In Marie-Hélène Garelli-François, ed. *Rome et le tragique. Colloque international 26, 27, 28 mars 1998 CRATA, Pallas* 49 (1998): 297–321 (summary: 406).

Kaster, Robert A. *Guardians of Language. The Grammarian and Society in Late Antiquity.* The Transformation of the Classical Heritage 11. Berkeley / London, 1988.

———, ed. *Suetonius. De grammaticis et rhetoribus.* Oxford, 1995.

Keith, Alison M. *Engendering Rome. Women in Latin Epic.* Cambridge, 2000.

Kenney, E. J., and W. V. Clausen, eds. *The Cambridge History of Classical Liteature II: Latin Literature.* Cambridge, 1982.

Kerényi, Karl. *Pythagoras und Orpheus. Präludien zu einer zukünftigen Geschichte der Orphik und des Pythagoreismus.* Dritte, erweiterte Ausgabe. Albae Virgiliae IX. Zürich, 1950.

Kerkhecker, Arnd. "Zur internen Gattungsgeschichte der römischen Epik: das Beispiel Ennius." In *L'histoire littéraire immanente dans la poésie latine,* edited by E. A. Schmidt et al., 1–38. Entretiens sur l'antiquité classique, Tome XLVII. Vandœuvres-Genève, 2001.

Kerkhof, Rainer. *Dorische Posse, Epicharm und Attische Komödie.* BzA 147. München / Leipzig, 2001.

Kessissoglu, Alexander. "Enniana." *RhM* 133 (1990): 70–80.

Kissel, Walter, ed. *Aules Persius Flaccus: Satiren, herausgegeben, übersetzt und kommentiert.* Heidelberg, 1990.

Kleve, Knut. "Ennius in Herculaneum." *BCPE / CronErc* 20 (1990): 5–16.

———. "Phoenix from the Ashes: Lucretius and Ennius in Herculaneum." In *The Norwegian Institute at Athens. The First Five Lectures,* edited by Øivind Andersen and Helène Whittaker, 57–64. Papers from the Norwegian Institute at Athens 1. Athenai, 1991.

Klimek-Winter, Rainer. *Andromedatragödien. Sophokles, Euripides, Livius Andronikos, Ennius, Accius. Text, Einleitung und Kommentar.* BzA 21. Stuttgart, 1993.

Klussmann, E. "Der Achilles des Ennius." *Neue Jahr-*

bücher für Philologie und Pädagogik 15 / *Jahn. et Klotz. Annal. Suppl.* (1845): 325–28.

Knapp, Charles. "Vahlen's Ennius." *AJP* 32 (1911): 1–35.

Koster, Severin. "Eurypylus, der Schmerzverächter." In Manuwald 2000, 231–39.

Kragelund, Patrick. "SO Debate: Historical Drama in Ancient Rome: Republican Flourishing and Imperial Decline?" *SO* 77 (2002): 5–105.

Krevans, Nita. "Ilia's Dream: Ennius, Virgil, and the Mythology of Seduction." *HSCP* 95 (1993): 257–71.

Krug, H. "Zum Text von Ennius' Euhemerus." *Forschungen und Fortschritte* 24 (1948): 57–59.

Kruschwitz, Peter. "Überlegungen zum Text der Hedyphagetica des Ennius." *Philologus* 142 (1998): 261–74.

Kutáková, Eva. "Cruenta maenas." *LT* 92 (1969): 250–56 (German summary: 256).

Ladewig, Theodor. "Analecta scenica." *Schulprogramm Neustrelitz* (1848): 1–40; repr. in: *Schriften zum römischen Drama republikanischer Zeit,* edited by Ursula Gärtner and Ekkehard Stärk, 199–248. BzA 61. München / Leipzig, 2001.

Laughton, E. "The Prose of Ennius." *Eranos* 49 (1951): 35–49.

Lausberg, Marion. *Das Einzeldistichon. Studien zum antiken Epigramm.* Studia et testimonia antiqua XIX. München, 1984.

Lefèvre, Eckard. "Ennius' Medea im römisch-politischen Kontext." In *Studien zu antiken Identitäten,* edited by Stefan Faller, 39–51. Identitäten und Alteritäten, Bd. 9, Altertumswiss. Reihe, Bd. 2. Würzburg, 2001.

Lenchantin de Gubernatis, Massimo. "Appunti sull'ellenismo nella poesia arcaica latina." *AAT* 63 (1913): 389/91–456/68.

———. *Ennio. Saggio critico.* Torino, 1915 [repr. Roma, 1978 (Philologica 7)].

Lennartz, Klaus. *Non verba sed vim. Kritisch-exegetische Untersuchungen zu den Fragmenten archaischer römischer Tragiker.* BzA 54. Stuttgart / Leipzig, 1994.

———. "Ennius und die verbannten Kinder (Enn. 224f. Klotz, S. 349 Jocelyn)." *Hermes* 129 (2001): 131–33.

Lentano, Mario. "Plauto e le Sabine. Modelli narrativi e valenze antropologiche." *Aufidus* 9 (1989): 7–27.

Liuzzi, Dora. "Ennio ed il pitagorismo." *Annali, Facoltà di Magistero, Lecce* 3 (1973–74): 281–99.

Lloyd-Jones, Hugh, and Peter Parsons, eds. *Supplementum Hellenisticum.* Texte und Kommentare 11. Berlin / New York, 1983.

Lo-Cascio, Santi. "L'influenza ellenica nell'origine della poesia latina." *RFIC* 20 (1892): 41–124.

Lyne, R. O. A. M. "The Neoteric Poets." *CQ* 28 (1978): 167–87.

Maas, Paul. "ΤΡΩΓΑΛΙΑ." *Hermes* 67 (1932): 243–44.

MacKay, L. A. "In Defence of Ennius." *CR* 13 (1963): 264–65.

Mactoux, Marie-Madeleine, and Vittorio Citti. "L'esclavage dans les tragédies d'Ennius." *QCTC* 6–7 (1988–89 [1991]) = Giuseppe Aricò, ed. *Atti del II seminario di studi sulla tragedia romana (Palermo 8–11 novembre 1988),* 9–36 (discussion: 36–39).

Manuwald, Gesine, ed. *Identität und Alterität in der frührömischen Tragödie.* Identitäten und Alteritäten, Bd. 3, Altertumswiss. Reihe, Bd. 1. Würzburg, 2000.

————. *Fabulae praetextae. Spuren einer literarischen Gattung der Römer.* Zetemata 108. München, 2001.

————. "Römische Tragödien und Praetexten republikanischer Zeit: 1964–2002." *Lustrum* 43 (2001 [2004]): 11–237.

————. "Epic Poets as Characters: On Poetics and Multiple Intertextuality in Silius Italicus' *Punica.*" *RFIC* 135 (2007 [2008]): 71–90.

————. "Poetry, Latin: Overview: Archaic through Republic." *Oxford Bibliographies Online Classics* 2010 (http://www.oxfordbibliographiesonline.com/display/id /obo-9780195389661–).

————. *Roman Republican Theatre.* Cambridge, 2011.

————. "Editing Roman (Republican) Tragedy: Challenges and Possible Solutions." In *Brill's Companion to Roman Tragedy,* edited by George W. M. Harrison, 3–23. Leiden / Boston, 2015.

Marabini Moevs, M. T. "Le Muse di Ambracia." *BdA* 12 (1981): 1–58.

Mariotti, Scevola. "Falsi Enniani di Girolamo Colonna?" In *Studi filologici e storici in onore di Vittorio de Falco.* Napoli, 1971, 267–83; repr. in: *Lezioni su Ennio, seconda edizione accresciuta,* 131–46. Ludus philologiae 4. Urbino, 1991.

————. "Nota di metrica enniana." In *Studi di poesia latina in onore di Antonio Traglia,* I, 55–61. Storia e letteratura. Raccolta di studi e testi 146. Roma, 1979; repr. in: *Lezioni su Ennio, seconda edizione accresciuta,* 119–25. Ludus philologiae 4. Urbino, 1991.

————. *Lezioni su Ennio, seconda edizione accresciuta.* Ludus philologiae 4. Urbino, 1991. [first ed.: *Lezioni su*

Ennio. Pesaro, 1951; corr. repr. (Studi e contributi, Serie letteraria, vol. I)].

Martina, M. "Ennio, *poeta cliens.*" *QFC* 2 (1979): 13–74.

———. "Aedes Herculis Musarum." *DArch* 3 (1981): 49–68.

Masiá González, Andrés. "Sobre Salmacida spolia, v. 18 Vahlen del Aiax de Ennio." *Emerita* 60 (1992): 51–55.

———. "Revisión de los fragmentos I y VIII del Telephus de Ennio." In *Homenatge a Miquel Dolç. Actes del XII Simposi de la Secció Catalana i I de la Secció Balear de la SEEC, Palma, 1 al 4 de febrer de 1996,* edited by M. del C. Bosch and M. A. Fornés, 351–57. Palma de Mallorca, 1997.

———. "Acerca de los fragmentos VI y XIV Vahlen de la Hecuba de Ennio." *QUCC* 62 (1999): 99–105.

Mette, Hans Joachim. "Die römische Tragödie und die Neufunde zur griechischen Tragödie (insbesondere für die Jahre 1945–1964)." *Lustrum* 9 (1964): 5–211.

Meunier, Nicolas L. J. "Ennius, les astres et les théories anciennes de la vision. À propos de *sol albus* et *radiis icta lux* (v. 84–85 Sk.)." *RPh* 86 (2012): 101–21.

Mommsen, Theodor. "Festi codicis quaternium decimum sextum denuo edidit Th. Mommsen." In *Philologische und historische Abhandlungen der Kgl. Akad. d. Wiss. zu Berlin,* 57–86. Berlin, 1865; repr. in: *Gesammelte Schriften von Theodor Mommsen. Siebenter Band. Philologische Schriften von Theodor Mommsen,* 269–79 (prolegomena). Berlin, 1909 [repr. Berlin / Zürich, 1965].

Monaco, Giusto. "Sul prologo della "Medea" di Ennio." *SIFC* 24 (1950): 249–53; repr. in: *Pan* 11–12. *Scritti minori di G. Monaco* (1987–88): 55–58.

Montanari, Ornella, ed. *Archestrato di Gela. I. Testimonianze e frammenti.* Università degli studi di Bologna, Dipartimento di Filologia classica e medioevale, Studi di filologia greca. Bologna, 1983.

Morel, Willy. "Andromacha Aechmalotis." *PhW* no. 19/20 (May 15, 1937): 558–60.

Morelli, Alfredo Mario. "Lo *Scipio* e la poesia celebrativa enniana per Scipione." In *Si verba tenerem. Studi sulla poesia latina in frammenti,* edited by Bruna Pieri and Daniele Pellacani, 53–77. Berlin, 2016.

Morelli, G. "Per la ricostruzione dell'Achilles di Ennio." *QCTC* 10 (1992 [1993]) = Giuseppe Aricò, ed. *Atti del IV seminario di studi sulla tragedia romana (Palermo 23–26 marzo 1992),* 43–62.

Morgan, Llewelyn. "A Metrical Scandal in Ennius." *CQ* 64 (2014): 152-59.

Most, Glenn W., ed. *Collecting Fragments—Fragmente sammeln.* Aporemata 1. Göttingen, 1997.

Muecke, Frances. "Rome's First 'Satirists': Themes and Genre in Ennius and Lucilius." In *The Cambridge Companion to Roman Satire,* edited by Kirk Freudenburg, 33–47. Cambridge, 2005 .

Mueller, Lucian. *Quintus Ennius. Eine Einleitung in das Studium der römischen Poesie.* St. Petersburg, 1884.

Neblung, Dagmar. *Die Gestalt der Kassandra in der antiken Literatur.* BzA 97. Stuttgart / Leipzig, 1997.

Newlands, Carole E. *Playing with Time: Ovid and the Fasti.* Ithaca, 1995.

Niebuhr, Barthold Georg. *Lectures on the History of Rome, from the Earliest Times to the Fall of the Western Empire.* Edited by Leonhard Schmitz. London, 1870.

de Nonno, Mario, Paolo de Paolis, and Carlo di Giovine. "Bibliografia della letteratura Latina." In *Lo Spazio letterario di Roma antica. Volume V. Cronologia e bibliografia della letteratura latina,* edited by Guglielmo Cavallo, Paolo Fedeli, and Andrea Giardina, 147–583. Roma, 1991.

Norden, Eduard. *Ennius und Vergilius. Kriegsbilder aus Roms großer Zeit.* Leipzig / Berlin, 1915 [repr. 1966].

Nosarti, Lorenzo. "Divagazioni sul mito di Medea nel teatro latino arcaico." In Lorenzo Nosarti. *Filologia in frammenti. Contributi esegetici e testuali ai frammenti dei poeti latini,* 53–78. Bologna, 1999.

Nouilhan, Michèle. "Adjectifs et adverbes dans les Tragédies d'Ennius." *Pallas* 16 (1969): 25–78.

Oliver, Revilo P. "'New Fragments' of Latin Authors in Perotti's *Cornucopiae.*" *TAPhA* 78 (1947): 376–424.

Olson, S. Douglas, and Alexander Sens, eds. and trans. *Archestratos of Gela. Greek Culture and Cuisine in the Fourth Century BCE. Text, Translation, and Commentary.* Oxford, 2000.

Osannus [Osann], Fridericus. *Analecta critica poesis Romanorum scaenicae reliquias illustrantia, scripsit F. O. Vimariensis. Insunt Plauti fragmenta ab Angelo Maio in codice Ambrosiano nuper reperta.* Berlin, 1816.

Otis, Brooks. *Virgil. A Study in Civilized Poetry.* Oxford, 1963.

Paduano, Guido. *Il mondo religioso della tragedia romana.* Firenze, 1974.

———. "La conoscenza come fonte di emarginazione sociale: Cassandra e Medea in Ennio." In Manuwald 2000, 255–64.

Pascal, Carlo. "Ennio nel medio evo." *Athenaeum* 1

(1913): 373–81; repr. in: *Scritti varii di letteratura latina*, 57–65. Torino / Milano / Firenze / Roma / Napoli / Palermo, 1920.

―――. "Lo *Scipio* di Ennio." *Athenaeum* 3 (1915): 369–95; repr. in: *Scritti varii di letteratura latina*, 3–26. Torino / Milano / Firenze / Roma / Napoli / Palermo, 1920.

―――. "Le opere spurie di Epicarmo e l'*Epicharmus* di Ennio." *Rivista di Filologia* 47 (1919): 54–75; repr. in: *Scritti varii di letteratura latina*, 27–47. Torino / Milano / Firenze / Roma / Napoli / Palermo, 1920.

Pelosi, Teresa. "Il fr. inc. inc. fab. 210 Ribb.[2] e l'Ifigenia di Ennio." *A&R* 33 (1988): 147–57.

Petaccia, Raffaella. "Der griechische Mythos in der republikanischen Tragödie Roms. Aitiologische Tendenzen in Ennius' *Telephus*." In *Rezeption und Identität. Die kulturelle Auseinandersetzung Roms mit Griechenland als europäisches Paradigma*, edited by Gregor Vogt-Spira and Bettina Rommel (unter Mitwirkung von Immanuel Musäus), 155–68. Stuttgart, 1999.

Pinto, Joaquín Balcells. *Ennio. Estudio sobre la poesía latina arcaica.* Colección "Estudio." Barcelona, 1914.

Powell, Ioannes U., ed. *Collectanea Alexandrina. Requiae minores poetarum Graecorum aetatis Ptolemaicae, 323–146 A. C., epicorum, elegiacorum, lyricorum, ethicorum. Cum epimetris et indice nominum*, Oxford, 1925 [repr. 1970].

Prinzen, Herbert. *Ennius im Urteil der Antike.* Drama 8. Stuttgart / Weimar, 1998.

Przychocki, Gust. "Ad Euripidis Hypsipylam adnotationes." *WS* 31 (1909): 300–305.

Ramsey, John T. "The Recovery of More Ennius from

a Misinformed Ciceronian Scholiast." *CQ* 64 (2014): 160–65.

Reggiani, Renato. "Rileggendo alcuni frammenti tragici di Ennio, Pacuvio e Accio." *QCTC* 4–5 (1986–87 [1990]) = Giuseppe Aricò, ed. *Atti del I seminario di studi sulla tragedia romana (Palermo 26–28 ottobre 1987)*, 31–88 (discussion: 89–92).

Resta Barrile, A. *Ennio e il mito di Andromeda*. Bologna, 1998.

Ribbeck, Otto. *In tragicos Romanorum poetas coniectanea. Specimen I. Dissertatio inauguralis quam consensu et auctoritate amplissimi philosophorum ordinis in Alma Litterarum Universitate Friderica Guilelma ad summos in philosophia honores rite capessendos die XXV. M. Maji A. MDCCCXLIX H. L. Q. S. publice defendet auctor Otto Ribbeck*. Berlin, 1849.

———. *Die römische Tragödie im Zeitalter der Republik*. Leipzig, 1875 [repr. with introduction by W.-H. Friedrich, Hildesheim, 1968].

Riposati, Benedetto. "A proposito di un frammento dell' 'Hectoris lytra' di Ennio." In *Studi in onore di Luigi Castiglioni. I*, 789–800. Firenze, 1960.

Risicato, Antonino. *Lingua parlata e lingua d'arte in Ennio*. Messina, 1966 [¹1950].

Romano, Elisa. "Oraculi divini e response di giuristi. Note sulla *interpretatio* enniana nell'*Euhemerus*." In *Amicitiae templa serena. Studi in onore di Giuseppe Aricò. Vol. II*, edited by Luigi Castagna and Chiara Riboldi, 1433–48. Milano, 2008.

van Rooy, C. A. *Studies in Classical Satire and Related Literary Theory*. Leiden, 1965.

De Rosalia, Antonino. "Funzione comunicativa e funzione

emotiva nel linguaggio dei tragici latini arcaici." *Dioniso* 54 (1983): 43–57.

———. "Rassegna degli studi sulla tragedia latina arcaica (1965–1986)." *BStudLat* 19 (1989): 76–144.

———. "La fruizione ciceroniana dei testi tragici di Ennio." *Paideia* 45 (1990): 139–74.

———. "Rilettura di Enn. trag. 314–325 R.³ in Cic. Tusc. 2, 38–39." *QCTC* 10 (1992 [1993]) = Giuseppe Aricò, ed. *Atti del IV seminario di studi sulla tragedia romana (Palermo 23–26 marzo 1992)*, 25–39 (discussion: 40–41).

Rosato, Claudio. [2003a] "Noterella enniana." In *Ricerche euripidee,* edited by Onofrio Vox, 161–66. Satura 1. Lecce, 2003a.

———. [2003b] "Euripide sulla scene latina arcaica. Una bibliografia." In *Ricerche euripidee,* edited by Onofrio Vox, 169–96. Satura 1. Lecce, 2003b.

———. *Euripide sulla scena latina arcaica. La "Medea" di Ennio e le "Baccanti" di Accio.* Satura 3. Lecce, 2005.

Rosén, Haiim B. "Die Grammatik des Unbelegten. Dargestellt an den Nominalkomposita bei Ennius." *Lingua* 21 (1968): 359–81.

Röser, Wolfgang. *Ennius, Euripides und Homer.* PhD diss., Freiburg i. Br., Würzburg, 1939.

Rosner, Hedwig. *Die Stoffwahl in der römischen Tragödie.* PhD diss., Innsbruck, 1970.

Rossi, Andreola, and Brian W. Breed, eds. *Ennius and the Invention of Roman Epic. Arethusa* 39.3 (2006).

Rüpke, Jörg. *Kalender und Öffentlichkeit.* Berlin, 1995.

———. "Räume literarischer Kommunikation in der Formierungsphase römischer Literatur." In *Moribus antiquis res stat Romana. Römische Werte und römische*

Literatur im 3. und 2. Jh. v. Chr., edited by Maximilian Braun et al., 31–52. BzA134. Leipzig, 2000.

———. "Kulturtransfer als Rekodierung: Zum literaturgeschichtlichen und sozialen Ort der frühen römischen Epik." In *Von Göttern und Menschen erzählen. Formkonstanzen und Funktionswandel vormoderner Epik*, edited by J. Rüpke, 42–64. PAB 4. Stuttgart, 2001.

———. "Ennius' Fasti in Fulvius' Temple: Greek Rationality and Roman Tradition." In Rossi and Breed 2006, 489–512.

Russo, Alessandro. "Un verso dagli *Hedyphagetica* di Ennio?" In *L'Officina Ellenistica. Poesia dotta e popolare in Grecia e a Roma,* edited by Luigi Belloni, Lia de Finis, and Gabriella Moretti, 91–116. Labirinti 69. Trento, 2003.

Rychlewska, Ludovica. "De Ennii Iphigenia." *Eos* 49.1 (1957/58): 71–81.

de Saint-Denis, Eugène. *Le vocabulaire des animaux marins en latin classique.* Études et commentaires II. Paris, 1947.

Salem, M. S. "Ennius and the 'Isiaci coniectores.'" *JRS* 28 (1938): 56–59.

Scafoglio, Giampiero. "Alcune osservazioni sull'Hecuba di Ennio." *Maia* 59 (2007): 278–82.

Schade, Gerson. "Ennius und Archestratos." *Philologus* 142 (1998): 275–78.

Schierl, Petra, ed. and trans. *Die Tragödien des Pacuvius. Ein Kommentar zu den Fragmenten mit Einleitung, Text und Übersetzung.* TuK 28. Berlin / New York, 2006.

Schöll, Adolf. *Beiträge zur Geschichte der griechischen Poesie. Erster Theil. Zur Kenntniß der tragischen Poesie der Griechen. Erster Band. Die Tetralogien der at-tischen Tragiker.* Berlin, 1839.

Scholz, Udo W. "Der 'Scipio' des Ennius." *Hermes* 112 (1984): 183–99.

Schönberger, Otto. "Zum Klagelied der Andromache." *Hermes* 84 (1956): 255–56.

Sciarrino, Enrica. "A Temple for the Professional Muse: The *Aedes Herculis Musarum* and Cultural Shifts in Second-Century B.C. Rome." In *Rituals in Ink,* edited by Alessandro Barchiesi, Jörg Rüpke, and Susan Stephens, 45–56. München, 2004.

Selem, Antonio. "Note all'Iphigenia di Ennio (Scen. 213–221 V²; 357 a Kl.)." *Atti dell'Accademia di scienze, lettere e arti di Udine,* Triennio 1963–66, Serie VII, Volume V (1° del Triennio), 263–303. Udine, 1967.

Skutsch, Franz. "Ennius (3)." *RE* V 2 (1905): 2589–628.

———. "Zu Ennius' Iphigenia." *RhM* 61 (1906): 605–19; repr. in: *Kleine Schriften von Franz Skutsch,* 296–309. Herausgegeben von Wilhelm Kroll. Mit einem Bildnis Franz Skutschs. Leipzig / Berlin, 1914.

Skutsch, Otto. "Enniana II." *CQ* 42 (1948): 94–101; repr. in: O. Skutsch 1968, 30–45.

———. "Der ennianische Soldatenchor." *RhM* 96 (1953): 193–201; repr. in: O. Skutsch 1968, 157–65.

———. "Notes on Ennian Tragedy." *HSPh* 71 (1967): 125–142; repr. in: O. Skutsch 1968, 174–93.

———. *Studia Enniana.* London, 1968.

———, ed. *Ennius. Sept exposes suivis de discussions* par O. Skutsch, H. D. Jocelyn, J. H. Waszink, E. Badian, J. Untermann, P. Wulfing-von Martitz, W. Suerbaum. Entretiens préparés et présidés par Otto Skutsch.

Entretiens sur l'antiquité classique, Tome XVII. Vandœuvres-Genève, 1972.

———. "Shepherds in Epirus (Varro *RR* 2.2.1)." *LCM* 3 (1978): 261–62.

———. "On the Epigrams of Ennius." *LCM* 10 (1985): 146–48.

———. "Ennius Andromacha 81–2 Joc. (86–7 Vah.) and 101–2 (111)." *LCM* 12 (1987): 38–39.

Snell, Bruno. *Euripides Alexandros und andere Strassburger Papyri mit Fragmenten griechischer Dichter.* Hermes Einzelschriften 5. Berlin, 1937.

Sommerstein, Alan H. "*Sherlockismus* and the study of fragmentary tragedies." In Alan H. Sommerstein. *The Tangled Ways of Zeus and Other Studies in and Around Greek Tragedy,* 61–81. Oxford, 2010.

Soubiran, Jean. "Les débuts du trimètre tragique à Rome: I. Le fragment de l'Athamas d'Ennius." *Pallas* 31 (1984): 83–96, 191.

Stabryła, Stanisław. *Latin Tragedy in Virgil's Poetry.* Translated by Marianna Abrahamowicz and Maria Wielopolska. Polska Akademia Nauk—Oddzia w Krakowie, Prace komisji filologii klasycznej, Nr 10. Wrocław / Warszawa / Kraków, 1970.

Starr, Raymond J. "The Ennianist at Puteoli: Gellius 18.5." *RhM* 132 (1989): 411–12.

Stockert, Walter. "Zum Lebensopfer in der römischen Tragödie." In *Ad fontes! Festschrift für Gerhard Dobesch zum fünfundsechzigsten Geburtstag am 15. September 2004 dargebracht von Kollegen, Schülern und Freunden. Unter der Ägide der Wiener Humanistischen Gesellschaft herausgegeben von Herbert Heftner und Kurt Tomaschitz,* 273–79. Wien, 2004.

Suerbaum, Werner. *Untersuchungen zur Selbstdarstellung älterer römischer Dichter. Livius Andronicus, Naevius, Ennius.* Spudasmata 19. Hildesheim, 1968.

———. "Ennius bei Petrarca. Betrachtungen zu literarischen Ennius-Bildern." In Skutsch 1972, 291–347 (discussion: 348–52).

———. "Ennius als Dramatiker." In *Orchestra. Drama—Mythos—Bühne. Festschrift für Hellmut Flashar anläßlich seines 65. Geburtstages,* edited by Anton Bierl and Peter von Möllendorff (unter Mitwirkung von Sabine Vogt), 346–62. Stuttgart / Leipzig, 1994.

———. "Der Pyrrhos-Krieg in Ennius' *Annales* VI im Lichte der ersten Ennius-Papyri aus Herculaneum." *ZPE* 106 (1995): 31–52.

Thompson, D'Arcy Wentworth. *A Glossary of Greek Fishes.* St. Andrews University Publications XLV. London, 1947.

Timpanaro, Sebastiano. "Per una nuova edizione critica di Ennio. 6.—Frammenti di dubbia autenticità." *SIFC* 22 (1947): 179–207.

———. "Note a Livio Andronico, Ennio, Varrone, Virgilio." *Annali della Scuola Normale Superiore di Pisa* 18 (1949): 186–204.

———. "Dall'Alexandros di Euripide all'Alexander di Ennio." *RFIC* 124 (1996): 5–70; repr. in: *Contributi di filologia greca e latina,* a cura di Emanuele Narducci, con la collaborazione di Paolo Carrara, Giuseppe Ramires, Alessandro Russo, 91–153 (cum Appendice: *Le postille autografe di S. T. all'articolo "Dall'*Aléxandros *di Euripide all'*Alexander *di Ennio"* [a cura di Alessandro Russo]). Studi e Testi 25. Firenze, 2005.

Traina, Alfonso. *Vortit barbare. Le traduzioni poetiche da*

Livio Andronico a Cicerone. Seconda edizione riveduta e aggiornata. Roma, 1974 [¹1970]; includes (pp. 113–65): "Pathos ed ethos nelle traduzioni tragiche di Ennio." *Maia* 16 (1964): 112–42 (= Studi in onore di G. Perrotta, Bologna, 1964, 630–60), 276–77.

Vahlen, Iohannes. "Zu Ennius." *RhM* 16 (1861): 571–85; repr. in: Vahlen 1911, 409–23.

———. "De Ennii Medea." *Index lectionum aestivarum* (1877): 3–9; repr. in: Vahlen 1907, 34–41.

———. "De Ennii Iphigenia." *Index lectionum aestivarum* (1878): 3–10; repr. in: Vahlen 1907, 52–61.

———. "De Ennii Alcmaeone." *Index lectionum hibernarum* (1887/88): 3–8; repr. in: Vahlen 1907, 379–85.

———. *Iohannis Vahleni Professoris Berolinensis Opuscula Academica. Pars Prior. Prooemia indicibus lectionum praemissa I–XXXIII ab a. MDCCCLXXV ad a. MDCCCLXXXI.* Leipzig, 1907.

———. *Gesammelte Philologische Schriften. Erster Teil. Schriften der Wiener Zeit. 1858–1874.* Leipzig / Berlin, 1911 [repr. Hildesheim / New York, 1970].

Vogt-Spira, Gregor. "Ennius, Medea: Eine Fremde in Rom." In Manuwald 2000, 265–75.

Walbank, F. W. "The Scipionic Legend." *PCPhS* 13 (1967): 54–69.

Waszink, J. H. "Problems Concerning the *Satura* of Ennius." In Skutsch 1972, 209–51.

Webster, T. B. L. "The Andromeda of Euripides." *BICS* 12 (1965): 29–33.

Wecklein, N. "Ueber den Kresphontes des Euripides." In *Festschrift für Ludwig Urlichs zur Feier seines fünfundzwanzigjährigen Wirkens an der Universität Würzburg dargebracht von seinen Schülern,* 1–23. Würzburg, 1880.

Welcker, Friedrich Gottlieb. *Die Griechischen Tragödien mit Rücksicht auf den epischen Cyclus.* 3 vols. RhM Suppl. 2.1–3. Bonn, 1839–1841.

Welsh, Jarrett T. "Accius, Porcius Licinus, and the Beginning of Latin Literature." *JRS* 101 (2011): 31–50.

———. "The Text of Ennius' Portrait of a Parasite." *Phoenix* 67 (2013): 107–34.

Wigodsky, Michael. *Vergil and Early Latin Poetry.* Hermes Einzelschriften 24. Wiesbaden, 1972.

Williams, Gordon. *Tradition and Originality in Roman Literature.* Oxford, 1968 [reissued with corr. 1985].

Winiarczyk, Marcus. *Euhemeri Messenii reliquiae.* Stuttgart / Leipzig, 1991.

———. "Ennius' Euhemerus sive Sacra historia.'" *RhM* 137 (1994): 274–91.

Wiseman, T. P. "Fauns, Prophets, and Ennius' *Annales.*" In Rossi and Breed 2006, 513–29.

———. *Remembering the Roman People, Essays on Late Republican Politics and Literature.* Oxford, 2009.

———. [2015a] *The Roman Audience. Classical Literature as Social History.* Oxford, 2015a.

———. [2015b] "Rome on the Balance: Varro and the Foundation Legend." In *Varro Varius. The Polymath of the Roman World,* edited by D. J. Butterfield, 93–122. Cambridge Classical Journal Supplement 39. Cambridge, 2015b.

Wright, John. *Dancing in Chains. The Stylistic Unity of the Comoedia Palliata.* Papers and Monographs of the American Academy in Rome XXV. Roma, 1974.

Zetzel, J. E. G. "Ennian Experiments." *AJPh* 95 (1974): 137–40.

———. "The Influence of Cicero on Ennius." In Fitzgerald and Gowers 2007, 1–16.

Ziegler, Konrat. "Zur Iphigenia des Ennius." *Hermes* 85 (1957): 495–501.

———. *Das hellenistiche Epos: ein vergessenes Kapitel griechischer Dichtung.* 2nd ed. Leipzig, 1966.

Zilliacus, Henrik. "Euripides Medeia 214–221 und Ennius." *Arctos* 12 (1978): 167–71.

Zimmermann, Bernhard. *"Laudes Atheniensium* in der römischen Tragödie der republikanischen Zeit? Überlegungen zu Ennius, *Erechtheus* und *Eumenides.*" In Manuwald 2000, 277–84.

Zwierlein, Otto. "Der Ruhm der Dichtung bei Ennius und seinen Nachfolgern." *Hermes* 110 (1982): 85–102.

TESTIMONIA

TESTIMONIA (T 1–114)

T 1 Ter. *An.* 18–21

> qui quom hunc accusant, Naevium Plautum Ennium
> accusant quos hic noster auctores habet,
> 20   quorum aemulari exoptat neglegentiam
> potius quam istorum obscuram diligentiam.

T 2 (cf. T 41) Lucil. 341–47 M. = 404–10 W.

> epistula item quaevis non magna poema est.
> illa poesis opus totum (tota{que} Ilias una
> est, una ut θέσις Annales Enni) atque opus unum
> est, maius multo est quam quod dixi ante poema.
> 345   qua propter dico: nemo qui culpat Homerum,
> perpetuo culpat, neque quod dixi ante poesin:
> versum unum culpat, verbum, entymema, locum
>   ⟨unum⟩.

T 3 Pompilius, *Epigr.* (Non., p. 88.5–7 M. = 125 L.; Varro, *Sat. Men.* 356 B.), p. 89 *FPL*[4]

> Pacui discipulus dicor. porro is fuit ⟨Enni⟩,
> Ennius Musarum. Pompilius clueor.

TESTIMONIA (T 1–114)

T 1 Terence, *The Woman of Andros*

When they [Terence's critics] accuse him, they accuse
Naevius, Plautus, Ennius, whom our man here regards as
authorities, whose carelessness he would prefer to emu-
late than the obscure pedantry of those people.

T 2 (cf. T 41) Lucilius

Similarly, any epistle [in verse] that is not long is a *poema*
[poem], but the above mentioned *poesis* [poetry] is a com-
plete work (just as the complete *Iliad* is a single work and
Ennius' *Annals* makes one theme) and a single piece; it is
a thing much bigger than what I earlier called *poema*.
Therefore I say: nobody who criticizes Homer criticizes
him in everything, nor that which I earlier called *poesis*:
he criticizes a single verse, a word, a thought, a single pas-
sage.[1]

  [1] The Latin text is that of Marx.

T 3 Pompilius

I am called a pupil of Pacuvius. He in turn was a pupil of
Ennius, Ennius of the Muses. I am called Pompilius.[1]

  [1] As a pupil of Pacuvius, he was presumably a Roman trage-
dian. On the epigram see Lausberg 1984, 277–78.

T 4 Volcacius, *Carm.* F 1 *FPL*[4] (p. 113) ap. Gell. *NA* 15.24

Sedigitus in libro, quem scripsit de poetis, quid de his sentiat, qui comoedias fecerunt, et quem ex omnibus praestare ceteris putet ac deinceps, quo quemque in loco et honore ponat, his versibus suis demonstrat:

> multos incertos certare hanc rem vidimus,
> palmam poetae comico cui deferant.
> eum meo iudicio errorem dissolvam tibi,
> ut, contra si quis sentiat, nihil sentiat.
> Caecilio palmam Statio do comico.[1]
> Plautus secundus facile exuperat ceteros.
> dein Naevius, qui fervet, pretio in tertiost.
> si erit, quod quarto detur, dabitur Licinio.
> post insequi Licinium facio Atilium.
> in sexto consequetur hos Terentius.
> Turpilius septimum, Trabea octavum optinet,
> nono loco esse facile facio Luscium.
> decimum addo causa antiquitatis Ennium.

[1] do comico *vel* do cominico *vel* dominico *codd.*: do mimico *ed. Juntina, Gronovius*

T 5 (cf. T 12) *Rhet. Her.* 4.2

etenim cum possimus ab Ennio sumere aut a Gracco ponere exemplum, videtur esse adrogantia illa relinquere et ad sua devenire.

T 4 Volcacius Sedigitus in Gellius, *Attic Nights*

In the book he wrote about poets, Sedigitus[1] demonstrates in the following verses what he thinks of those who wrote comedies and whom he believes to surpass all others, and finally to which position of honor he assigns each individual: "we see that many debate this matter, being uncertain to which comic poet they should assign the victory palm. By my judgment, I will resolve this uncertainty for you, so that, if anyone thinks otherwise, that opinion has no value. I give the victory palm to the comic poet Caecilius Statius. Plautus, in second place, easily surpasses the others. Then Naevius, who is passionate, is in third position. If there is something to give to the one in fourth place, it will be given to Licinius. I have Atilius following Licinius. In sixth place Terence will follow them, Turpilius holds seventh, Trabea eighth position. I easily put Luscius [Lanuvinus] in ninth place. As the tenth poet I add Ennius by virtue of his antiquity."

[1] Volcacius Sedigitus, an early Roman scholar, ca. 100 BC.

T 5 (cf. T 12) *Rhetorica ad Herennium*

For when we can take an example from Ennius or offer one from Gracchus,[1] it seems presumptuous to neglect these and have recourse to our own.

[1] C. Sempronius Gracchus (153–121 BC, trib. pl. 123/2 BC).

T 6 *Rhet. Her.* 4.7

ita ut si de tragoediis Ennii velis sententias eligere aut de
Pacuvianis periodos,[1] sed si, quia plane rudis id facere
nemo poterit, cum feceris, te litteratissimum putes, inep-
tus sis, propterea quod id facile faciat quivis mediocriter
litteratus, . . .

    [1] periodos *vel* nuntios *codd.*

T 7 (= 8 *Ann.* F 1) Cic. *Mur.* 30

omnia ista nobis studia de manibus excutiuntur simulat-
que aliqui motus novus bellicum canere coepit. etenim, ut
ait ingeniosus poeta et auctor valde bonus . . .

T 8 (= *Inc.* F 2) Cic. *Arch.* 18

atque sic a summis hominibus eruditissimisque accepimus
ceterarum rerum studia et doctrina et praeceptis et arte
constare, poetam natura ipsa valere et mentis viribus exci-
tari et quasi divino quodam spiritu inflari. quare suo iure
noster ille Ennius sanctos appellat poetas, quod quasi deo-
rum aliquo dono atque munere commendati nobis esse
videantur.

T 9

a Cic. *Arch.* 22

carus fuit Africano superiori noster Ennius, itaque etiam
in sepulcro Scipionum putatur is esse constitutus ex mar-
more. at eis laudibus certe non solum ipse qui laudatur sed
etiam populi Romani nomen ornatur. in caelum huius

---

    [1] P. Cornelius Scipio Africanus (ca. 236–183 BC, cos. 205 BC).

T 6 *Rhetorica ad Herennium*

It is as if you wanted to choose maxims from the tragedies of Ennius or periods from those of Pacuvius, but if, because nobody completely unschooled can do this, you thought when you had done it that you are very cultivated: you would be foolish because anyone moderately well-read could do this easily, . . .

T 7 (= 8 *Ann.* F 1) Cicero, *Pro Murena*

All these studies of ours are shaken from our hands as soon as some new disturbance begins to blow the war trumpet. In fact, as a talented poet and very fine author [Ennius] says, . . .

T 8 (= *Inc.* F 2) Cicero, *Pro Archia*

And thus we have gathered from the greatest and most learned men that the study of other things is based upon learning, rules, and art, but that a poet is proficient by nature itself and aroused by the powers of the mind and inspired as if by some kind of divine spirit. For that reason, our famous Ennius with full justification calls poets "sacred," since they seem to be entrusted to us as if by some gift and present from the gods.

T 9

a Cicero, *Pro Archia*

Our Ennius was dear to the elder Africanus,[1] and so his image in marble is even thought to have been placed in the tomb of the Scipios. But surely not only is he who is praised adorned by this praise, but so too the name of the Roman people. Cato, the great-grandfather of this Cato

7

proavus Cato tollitur; magnus honos populi Romani rebus
adiungitur. omnes denique illi Maximi, Marcelli, Fulvii
non sine communi omnium nostrum laude decorantur.
ergo illum qui haec fecerat, Rudinum hominem, maiores
nostri in civitatem receperunt; nos hunc Heracliensem
multis civitatibus expetitum, in hac autem legibus consti-
tutum de nostra civitate eiciamus?

b Schol. Bob. ad Cic. *Arch.* 22

ergo illum qui haec fecerat, Rudinum hominem: natione
Rudinus fuit Q. Ennius, quem superior Africanus dilec-
tum familiarissime etiam communicato sepulchri honore
dicitur in maiorum suorum numerum redegisse. sepul-
chrum fuisse traditum extra portam Capenam mille ferme
passibus ab urbe seiunctum.

T 10 Cic. *Arch.* 27

iam vero ille qui cum Aetolis Ennio comite bellavit Fulvius
non dubitavit Martis manubias Musis consecrare. quare in
qua urbe imperatores prope armati poetarum nomen et
Musarum delubra coluerunt, in ea non debent togati iu-
dices a Musarum honore et a poetarum salute abhorrere.

---

[1] M. Fulvius Nobilior (cos. 189, cens. 179 BC); cf. T 20, 29,
92, 95, 96. As consul, he campaigned in Aetolia, besieging and
capturing the city of Ambracia. Spoils from Ambracia were even-
tually dedicated in a temple to Hercules of the Muses. See *Annals*
Introduction.

here,[2] is exalted to the sky: a great honor is added to the history of the Roman people. In the end, all those Maximi, Marcelli, and Fulvii are not glorified without communal praise for all of us. For that reason our ancestors received into the community the man who had done these things, a man from Rudiae. Shall we thrust out from our community this man from Heraclea,[3] desired by many communities, though legally established in this one?

[2] M. Porcius Cato Uticensis (95–46 BC), and his great-grandfather, M. Porcius Cato Censorius (234–149 BC).

[3] The Greek poet Archias, defended by Cicero.

b Scholia Bobiensia to Cicero, *Pro Archia*

"for that reason, the man who had done these things, a man from Rudiae": by nationality, Ennius was a man from Rudiae; the elder Africanus is said to have liked him most dearly and, having even shared the honor of his tomb, to have brought him among the number of his ancestors. The tomb is reported to have been outside the Capenan Gate, separated by about a thousand feet from the city [of Rome].

T 10 Cicero, *Pro Archia*

And furthermore, he who fought against the Aetolians with Ennius as his companion, that famous Fulvius,[1] did not hesitate to dedicate the spoils of Mars to the Muses. For that reason, in a city where commanders practically under arms cultivated the name of poets and the shrines of the Muses, judges in civilian garb should not shrink from honoring the Muses and looking after poets.

T 11 (= 7 *Ann.* F 20) Cic. *Balb.* 51

neque enim ille summus poeta noster Hannibalis illam magis cohortationem quam communem imperatoriam voluit esse: . . .

T 12 Cic. *De or.* 1.154

in cotidianis autem commentationibus equidem mihi adulescentulus proponere solebam illam exercitationem maxime, qua C. Carbonem nostrum illum inimicum solitum esse uti sciebam, ut aut versibus propositis quam maxime gravibus aut oratione aliqua lecta ad eum finem quem memoria possem comprehendere, eam rem ipsam quam legissem verbis aliis quam maxime possem lectis pronuntiarem. sed post animadverti hoc esse in hoc vitii, quod ea verba, quae maxime cuiusque rei propria quaeque essent ornatissima atque optima occupasset aut Ennius, si ad eius versus me exercerem, aut Gracchus si eius orationem mihi forte posuissem: ita, si isdem verbis uterer nihil prodesse, si aliis etiam obesse, cum minus idoneis uti consuescerem.

T 13 (= 10 *Ann.* F 5) Cic. *De or.* 1.198

. . . amplissimus quisque et clarissimus vir, ut ille, qui propter hanc iuris civilis scientiam sic appellatus a summo poeta est: egregie cordatus homo, catus Aelius Sextus . . .

---

[1] Sex. Aelius Paetus Catus (cos. 198, cens. 194 BC).

T 11 (= 7 *Ann.* F 20) Cicero, *Pro Balbo*

For our greatest poet [Ennius] did not want this to be so much an exhortation for Hannibal as for commanders in general: . . .

T 12 Cicero, *On the Orator*

In my daily studies as a very young man, I [the speaker Crassus] used to set for myself that exercise in particular which I knew Carbo,[1] that old enemy of ours, used to employ: I would take verses that were as weighty as possible or read as much of an oration as I could retain in memory. Then I would express the very matter I had read, choosing words as different as I possibly could. But I later noticed the following flaw in this procedure, namely that those words most suited to each matter and most elaborate and best had been used by either Ennius, if I was practicing with his verses, or by Gracchus,[2] if I had happened to set an oration of his as my model: so, if I used the same words, the exercise was useless, if I used others, it was even an obstacle, since I was growing accustomed to using less appropriate ones.

[1] C. Papirius Carbo (d. 119 BC, cos. 120 BC).　　[2] C. Sempronius Gracchus (153–121 BC, trib. pl. 123/2 BC); cf. T 6.

T 13 (= 10 *Ann.* F 5) Cicero, *On the Orator*

. . . each most respected and famous man, like the one who, because of this knowledge of civil law, was thus described by the greatest poet [Ennius]: "an extremely sensible man, the shrewd Aelius Sextus"[1] . . .

T 14 Cic. *De or.* 2.276

ut illud Nasicae, qui cum ad poetam Ennium venisset
eique ab ostio quaerenti Ennium ancilla dixisset domi non
esse, Nasica sensit illam domini iussu dixisse et illum intus
esse. paucis post diebus cum ad Nasicam venisset Ennius
et eum ad ianuam quaereret, exclamat Nasica se domi non
esse. tum Ennius quid? ego non cognosco vocem inquit
tuam? hic Nasica: homo es impudens: ego cum te quae-
rerem, ancillae tuae credidi te domi non esse, tu mihi non
credis ipsi?

T 15 Cic. *De or.* 3.27

atque id primum in poetis cerni licet, quibus est proxima
cognatio cum oratoribus, quam sint inter sese Ennius, Pa-
cuvius Acciusque dissimiles, quam apud Graecos Aeschy-
lus, Sophocles, Euripides, quamquam omnibus par paene
laus in dissimili scribendi genere tribuatur.

T 16 Cic. *Att.* 4.15.6

deinde Antiphonti operam. is erat ante manu missus quam
productus. ne diutius pendeas, palmam tulit. sed nihil tam
pusillum, nihil tam sine voce, nihil tam—verum haec tu
tecum habeto. in Andromacha tamen maior fuit quam
Astyanax, in ceteris parem habuit neminem.

---

[1] An actor, otherwise unknown.   [2] I.e., in size: Cicero
puns on *maior*, "taller" here, not "better." The playwright is un-
named, but the only Republican *Andromacha* known is by En-
nius.

T 14 Cicero, *On the Orator*

Like that story about Nasica:[1] when he went to visit the
poet Ennius and asked for him at the door, the maid said
that Ennius was not at home, but Nasica suspected she
had said this on her master's order and that he was inside.
A few days later, when Ennius went to visit Nasica and
asked for him at the door, Nasica called out that he was
not at home. Then Ennius said: "What's that? Don't I rec-
ognize your voice?" Thereupon Nasica said: "You are
shameless! When I asked for you, I believed your maid
that you were not at home. Will you not believe me my-
self?"

[1] P. Cornelius Scipio Nasica (cos. 191 BC), or possibly his son,
P. Cornelius Scipio Nasica Corculum (cos. 162 BC).

T 15 Cicero, *On the Orator*

And above all it may be observed in the case of poets, who
have a very close affinity to orators, how different Ennius,
Pacuvius, and Accius are from each other, as among the
Greeks are Aeschylus, Sophocles, and Euripides, although
all of them are granted almost the same praise for their
different styles of writing.

T 16 Cicero, *Letters to Atticus*

Then [i.e., at the theater] I turned my attention to Anti-
phon.[1] He had been freed before being brought on stage.
So as not to keep you dangling too long, he took the palm.
But nothing so puny, nothing so without voice, nothing
so—but keep this to yourself. In *Andromacha* at least he
was taller than Astyanax, in the others he did not have
anyone as his equal.[2]

13

T 17 (cf. 9 *Ann.* F 6) Cic. *Brut.* 57

quem vero exstet et de quo sit memoriae proditum elo-
quentem fuisse et ita esse habitum, primus est M. Corne-
lius Cethegus, cuius eloquentiae est auctor et idoneus
quidem mea sententia Q. Ennius, praesertim cum et ipse
eum audiverit et scribat de mortuo; ex quo nulla suspicio
est amicitiae causa esse mentitum.

T 18 (= 7 *Ann.* F 1) Cic. *Brut.* 71–76

quid, nostri veteres versus ubi sunt? quos olim Fauni va-
tesque canebant, cum neque Musarum scopulos * * * nec
dicti studiosus quisquam erat ante hunc ait ipse de se nec
mentitur in gloriando: sic enim sese res habet. nam et
Odyssia Latina est sic {in} tamquam opus aliquod Daedali
et Livianae fabulae non satis dignae quae iterum legantur.
[72] atqui hic Livius {qui} primus fabulam C. Claudio
Caeci filio et M. Tuditano consulibus docuit anno ipso ante
quam natus est Ennius, post Romam conditam autem
quarto decumo et quingentensimo, ut hic ait, quem nos
sequimur. . . . [73] . . . in quo tantus error Acci fuit, ut his
consulibus XL annos natus Ennius fuerit; quoi si aequalis
fuerit Livius, minor fuit aliquanto is, qui primus fabulam
dedit, quam ei, qui multas docuerant ante hos consules, et
Plautus et Naevius. [74] . . . [75] . . . tamen illius, quem in
vatibus et Faunis adnumerat Ennius, bellum Punicum
quasi Myronis opus delectat. [76] sit Ennius sane, ut est

---

[1] I.e., Cicero's friend Atticus, whose antiquarian research es-
tablished the year 240 for this milestone. The poet Accius had
advocated a significantly later chronology, which Cicero proceeds
to refute. See Gruen 1990, 80–82; Welsh 2011.

T 17 (cf. 9 *Ann.* F 6) Cicero, *Brutus*

Of those, however, who are certainly on record and known to have been eloquent and recognized as such, the first is Cornelius Cethegus [cos. 204 BC], of whose eloquence Ennius is a witness and indeed, in my view, a suitable one, especially since he had heard him himself and writes about him after his death; there is thus no suspicion that he lied for the sake of friendship.

T 18 (= 7 *Ann.* F 1) Cicero, *Brutus*

Well, where are our [Roman] ancient verses "which Fauns and bards once sang, when neither ⟨anybody had scaled⟩ the rocks of the Muses nor was there anybody learned before this man"? So he [Ennius] says about himself, and he does not lie in glorifying himself: for the matter is like this. The Latin *Odyssey* [Livius Andronicus' epic] is, as it were, like some work of Daedalus, and the dramas of Livius [Andronicus] are not worth a second reading. [72] Yet this Livius was the first to bring a play on stage, in the consulship of Gaius Claudius, Caecus' son, and Marcus Tuditanus [240 BC], in the very year before Ennius was born, in the 514th year after the founding of Rome, as he says, whom we follow.[1] . . . [73] . . . In this Accius' error was so great that under these consuls [Gaius Cornelius Cethegus and Quintus Minucius Rufus in 197 BC] Ennius was 40 years old; if Livius were a contemporary of his, he who was the first to produce a play [Livius] would be considerably younger than those who produced many before these consuls, both Plautus and Naevius. [74] . . . [75] . . . The *Bellum Punicum* of that poet whom Ennius counts among the soothsayers and Fauns [Naevius] nevertheless gives pleasure as a work of Myron does. [76] Granted that

15

certe, perfectior: qui si illum, ut simulat, contemneret, non omnia bella persequens primum illud Punicum acerrimum bellum reliquisset. sed ipse dicit cur id faciat. scripsere inquit alii rem vorsibus; et luculente quidem scripserunt, etiam si minus quam tu polite. nec vero tibi aliter videri debet, qui a Naevio vel sumpsisti multa, si fateris, vel, si negas, surripuisti.

T 19 Cic. *Brut.* 78

nam hoc praetore ludos Apollini faciente cum Thyesten fabulam docuisset, Q. Marcio Cn. Servilio consulibus mortem obiit Ennius.

T 20 Cic. *Brut.* 79

Q. Nobiliorem M. f. iam patrio instituto deditum studio litterarum—qui etiam Q. Ennium, qui cum patre eius in Aetolia militaverat, civitate donavit, cum triumvir coloniam deduxisset—et T. Annium Luscum huius Q. Fulvi conlegam non indisertum dicunt fuisse; . . .

Ennius is more polished, as he surely is: if, as he pretends, he faulted him, he would not in recounting all our wars have left that first, most bitter Punic war alone. But he himself says why he does so. "Others," he says, "have written about this subject in verses": and, they wrote about it splendidly, even if not in as polished a way as you did. Nor in fact should it seem any different to you, who either appropriated, if you confess it, or, if you deny it, stole much from Naevius.

T 19 Cicero, *Brutus*

In the consulship of Quintus Marcius and Gnaeus Servilius [169 BC], the year this man[1] as praetor organized the games in honor of Apollo, Ennius, when he had produced the play *Thyestes*, met his death.

[1] C. Sulpicius Gallus (cos. 166 BC).

T 20 Cicero, *Brutus*

They say that Quintus Nobilior,[1] Marcus' son, already inclined to the study of literature by his father's example—Quintus, who also bestowed citizenship on Ennius, who had campaigned with his father in Aetolia, when as a triumvir he had founded a colony[2]—and that Titus Annius Luscus [cos. 153 BC], the colleague of this Quintus Fulvius, were not without eloquence . . .

[1] Q. Fulvius Nobilior (cos. 153 BC).   [2] In 184 BC (cf. Liv. 39.44.10). The tradition is suspect: Q. Fulvius Nobilior would have been young for a triumvir.

T 21 Cic. *Orat.* 36

sed in omni re difficillimum est formam, qui χαρακτήρ
Graece dicitur, exponere optimi, quod aliud aliis videtur
optimum. Ennio delector, ait quispiam, quod non discedit
a communi more verborum. Pacuvio, inquit alius: omnes
apud hunc ornati elaboratique sunt versus, multa apud
alterum negligentius. fac alium Accio; varia enim sunt
iudicia, ut in Graecis, nec facilis explicatio quae forma
maxime excellat.

T 22 Cic. *Orat.* 109

an ego Homero Ennio reliquis poetis et maxime tragicis
concederem ut ne omnibus locis eadem contentione ute-
rentur crebroque mutarent, nonnumquam etiam ad coti-
dianum genus sermonis accederent, ipse numquam ab illa
acerrima contentione discederem?

T 23 Cic. *Opt. gen.* 2

itaque licet dicere et Ennium summum epicum poetam,
si cui ita videtur, et Pacuvium tragicum et Caecilium for-
tasse comicum.

T 24 Cic. *Opt. gen.* 18

huic labori nostro duo genera reprehensionum opponun-
tur. unum hoc: verum melius Graeci. a quo quaeratur
ecquid possint illi melius Latine. alterum: quid istas potius

---

[1] The translation of Greek orations into Latin.

T 21 Cicero, *Orator*

But in every matter it is very difficult to articulate the form, which in Greek is called "character," of the best, since what is best seems different to different people. "I like Ennius," says one, "since he does not depart from the common use of words." "I like Pacuvius," says another. "All his verses are ornate and elaborate; in the former a lot is rather careless." Suppose another likes Accius. Assessments vary, as among the Greeks, and an account of which form most stands out is not easy.

T 22 Cicero, *Orator*

Should I concede to Homer, Ennius, and the other poets, and especially to tragic poets, that they do not use the same impassioned style everywhere but change the style frequently, sometimes even approaching an everyday type of speech, while I myself should never depart from that most vehement, impassioned style?

T 23 Cicero, *The Best Kind of Orator*

Therefore one may say that Ennius is the greatest epic poet, if he seems so to anyone, and Pacuvius the greatest tragic poet, and Caecilius [Statius] perhaps the greatest comic poet.

T 24 Cicero, *The Best Kind of Orator*

Against this project of ours[1] two kinds of objection are raised. One is this: "The Greeks are better." Such a person should be asked whether they could produce anything better in Latin. The other is: "Why should I read those

legam quam Graecas? idem Andriam et Synephobos nec
minus {Terentium et Caecilium quam Menandrum le-
gunt, nec} Andromacham aut Antiopam aut Epigonos
Latinos recipiunt{; sed tamen Ennium et Pacuvium et
Accium potius quam Euripidem et Sophoclem legunt}.
quod igitur est eorum in orationibus e Graeco conversis
fastidium, nullum cum sit in versibus?

T 25 Cic. *Acad.* 1.10

quid enim causae est cur poetas Latinos Graecis litteris
eruditi legant, philosophos non legant? an quia delectat
Ennius Pacuvius Accius multi alii, qui non verba sed
vim Graecorum expresserunt poetarum—quanto magis
philosophi delectabunt, si ut illi Aeschylum Sophoclem
Euripidem sic hi Platonem imitentur Aristotelem Theo-
phrastum? oratores quidem laudari video si qui e nostris
Hyperidem sint aut Demosthenem imitati.

T 26 Cic. *Acad.* 2.20

. . . ; quam multa quae nos fugiunt in cantu exaudiunt in
eo genere exercitati, qui primo inflatu tibicinis Antiopam
esse aiunt aut Andromacham, cum id nos ne suspicemur
quidem.

[orations in translation] rather than in the original Greek?" The same people accept *Andria* and *Synephebi* and equally *Andromacha* or *Antiopa* or *Epigoni* in Latin.[2] Why then do they have an aversion to orations translated from Greek, when there is none with respect to poetry?

[2] Plays by Terence, Caecilius Statius, Ennius (cf. *Trag.* F 23–33), Pacuvius, and Accius, respectively.

T 25 Cicero, *Posterior Academics*

For what is the reason that people educated in Greek literature read Latin poets but do not read [Latin] philosophers? Is it because Ennius, Pacuvius, Accius, and many others who have rendered not the words, but the sense of Greek poets provide pleasure? How much more pleasure will philosophers provide if they imitate Plato, Aristotle, and Theophrastus, as those [poets] imitated Aeschylus, Sophocles, and Euripides? I see that our orators at any rate are praised if any of them has imitated Hyperides or Demosthenes.

T 26 Cicero, *Prior Academics*

. . . how much of what escapes us in singing do those hear who are trained in that genre, who at the first notes of the piper say that this is "Antiopa" or "Andromacha,"[1] while we have not even an idea of this.

[1] Tragedies by Pacuvius and Ennius (cf. *Trag.* F 23–33). The reference is either to the overtures to entire plays or to the opening notes of individual arias.

T 27 (= 1 *Ann.* F 3 = *Epi.* F 1) Cic. *Acad.* 2.51

eadem ratio est somniorum. num censes Ennium, cum in
hortis cum Ser. Galba vicino suo ambulavisset, dixisse vi-
sus sum mihi cum Galba ambulare? at cum somniavit ita
narravit visus Homerus adesse poeta, idemque in Epi-
charmo: nam videbar somniare me{e}d ego esse mortuum.

T 28 Cic. *Fin.* 1.4–7

iis igitur est difficilius satisfacere qui se Latina scripta di-
cunt contemnere. in quibus hoc primum est in quo ad-
mirer, cur in gravissimis rebus non delectet eos sermo
patrius, cum idem fabellas Latinas ad verbum e Graecis
expressas non inviti legant. quis enim tam inimicus paene
nomini Romano est qui Enni Medeam aut Antiopam Pa-
cuvi spernat aut reiciat, quod se isdem Euripidis fabulis
delectari dicat, Latinas litteras oderit? Synephebos ego,
inquit, potius Caecili aut Andriam Terenti quam utramque
Menandri legam? [5] a quibus tantum dissentio ut, . . .
mihi quidem nulli satis eruditi videntur quibus nostra
ignota sunt. an utinam ne in nemore—[*Trag.* F 89.1] nihilo
minus legimus quam hoc idem Graecum, quae autem de
bene beateque vivendo a Platone disputata sunt, haec
explicari non placebit Latine? [6] . . . [7] quamquam si
plane sic verterem Platonem aut Aristotelem ut verterunt

T 27 (= 1 *Ann.* F 3 = *Epi.* F 1) Cicero, *Prior Academics*

The same principle applies to dreams. Do you suppose that Ennius, when he had gone for a walk in the garden with his neighbor Servius Galba[1] said, "I seemed to go for a walk with Galba"? But when he dreamed, he reported thus: "the poet Homer seemed to be present," and the same poet says in *Epicharmus*: "for I seemed to dream that I was dead."

[1] Ser. Sulpicius Galba (aedile 189, praetor 187 BC).

T 28 Cicero, *On Ends*

It is therefore more difficult to satisfy those who say they scorn writing in Latin. As for them, the first thing that amazes me is this: why does their native language not please them in very serious matters, when the same people are not unwilling to read Latin plays translated word for word from Greek ones? Who is so hostile to practically the very name "Roman" that he despises and rejects Ennius' *Medea* or Pacuvius' *Antiopa* because he says he finds pleasure in the corresponding plays of Euripides but hates Latin literature? "Shall I," he says, "read Caecilius' *Synephebi* or Terentius' *Andria* in preference to either of these comedies by Menander?" [5] I disagree with these people to such an extent that . . . To me, at any rate, no one to whom our writings are unknown seems sufficiently educated. Indeed, do we read "if only in the grove—" [*Trag.* F 89.1] no less than the very same passage in the Greek, but what has been argued about living well and happily by Plato will not please when it is set out in Latin? [6] . . . [7] However, if I translated Plato or Aristotle exactly

nostri poetae fabulas, male, credo, mererer de meis civi-
bus si ad eorum cognitionem divina illa ingenia transfer-
rem! sed id neque feci adhuc nec mihi tamen ne faciam
interdictum puto. locos quidem quosdam, si videbitur,
transferam, et maxime ab eis quos modo nominavi, cum
inciderit ut id apte fieri possit, ut ab Homero Ennius,
Afranius a Menandro solet.

T 29 (cf. T 10, 18) Cic. *Tusc.* 1.3

doctrina Graecia nos et omni litterarum genere superabat;
in quo erat facile vincere non repugnantes. nam cum apud
Graecos antiquissimum e doctis genus sit poetarum, si
quidem Homerus fuit et Hesiodus ante Romam conditam,
Archilochus regnante Romulo, serius poeticam nos acce-
pimus. annis fere CCCCCX post Romam conditam Livius
fabulam dedit C. Claudio, Caeci filio, M. Tuditano con-
sulibus, anno ante natum Ennium, qui fuit maior natu
quam Plautus et Naevius. sero igitur a nostris poetae vel
cogniti vel recepti. quamquam est in Originibus solitos
esse in epulis canere convivas ad tibicinem de clarorum
hominum virtutibus, honorem tamen huic generi non
fuisse declarat oratio Catonis, in qua obiecit ut probrum
M. Nobiliori, quod is in provinciam poetas duxisset. duxe-
rat autem consul ille in Aetoliam, ut scimus, Ennium.

as our poets have translated plays, I would do poor service, I believe, to my countrymen if I brought these divine intellects over for them to get to know! I have not done this so far, yet neither do I believe I am forbidden to do so. Still, I will only translate certain passages, if it seems right, and particularly from those I have just mentioned, when the appropriate occasion for doing so arises, just as Ennius is accustomed to do with regard to Homer, and Afranius to Menander.

T 29 (cf. T 10, 18) Cicero, *Tusculan Disputations*

In learning and in every kind of literature Greece surpassed us: it was easy to prevail over those who did not offer resistance. For while among the Greeks the class of poets is the oldest of the learned ones, if, at any rate, Homer and Hesiod lived before the founding of Rome and Archilochus in the reign of Romulus, we admitted poetry rather later. About 510 years after the founding of Rome, Livius [Andronicus] produced a play in the consulship of Gaius Claudius, Caecus' son, and Marcus Tuditanus [240 BC], in the year before the birth of Ennius. He [Andronicus] was older than Plautus and Naevius. Poets were thus recognized and welcomed late by our people. While it is said in *Origins* [a historical work by Cato] that guests at dinner parties were accustomed to sing to the accompaniment of a piper about the accomplishments of famous men, Cato's speech in which he put forward as a criticism of Marcus Nobilior that he had taken poets to his province, nonetheless demonstrates that there was no honor for this class. That man [Nobilior], as consul, had in fact, as we know, taken Ennius to Aetolia.

T 30 (= *Trag.* F 23) Cic. *Tusc.* 3.45–46

o poetam egregium, quamquam ab his cantoribus Eupho-
rionis contemnitur! sentit omnia repentina et necopinata
esse graviora. . . . [46] praeclarum carmen! est enim et
rebus et verbis et modis lugubre.

T 31 Cic. *Nat. D.* 1.119

quid qui aut fortis aut claros aut potentis viros tradunt post
mortem ad deos pervenisse, eosque esse ipsos quos nos
colere precari venerarique soleamus, nonne expertes sunt
religionum omnium? quae ratio maxime tractata ab Euhe-
mero est, quem noster et interpretatus est et secutus prae-
ter ceteros Ennius . . .

T 32 Cic. *Nat. D.* 2.93

hoc qui existimat fieri potuisse, non intellego, cur non
idem putet, si innumerabiles unius et viginti formae litte-
rarum, vel aureae vel qualeslibet, aliquo coiciantur, posse
ex iis in terram excussis Annales Enni ut deinceps legi
possint effici; quod nescio an ne in uno quidem versu pos-
sit tantum valere fortuna.

T 30 (= *Trag.* F 23) Cicero, *Tusculan Disputations*

Oh, excellent poet [Ennius], however much he is scorned by these flatterers of Euphorion![1] He recognizes that everything sudden and unexpected is more grievous to bear. . . . [46] A wonderful song! For it is mournful in content, language, and rhythm.

[1] Euphorion of Chalcis, a Greek poet of the third century BC, taken as the model for a "new" style of writing in Latin poetry. See Lyne 1978.

T 31 Cicero, *On the Nature of the Gods*

Now, those who pass on the idea that brave or famous or powerful men have reached the position of gods after death, and that these are the very ones we are accustomed to worship, implore, and revere—do they not lack all religious awe? This theory was developed by Euhemerus in particular, whom our Ennius especially translated and imitated . . .

T 32 Cicero, *On the Nature of the Gods*

As for anyone who believes this[1] could have happened, I do not understand why the same person does not believe that, if countless shapes of the twenty-one letters of the alphabet, of gold or whatever, were thrown together in some container, Ennius' *Annals* could be constructed and then read from those scattered on the ground. I doubt that chance could have that ability for even a single verse.

[1] That the world was created by a random conglomeration of atoms.

T 33 Cic. *Sen.* 14

equi fortis et victoris senectuti comparat suam [Inc. *Ann.*
F 67]. quem quidem probe meminisse potestis; anno enim
undevicesimo post eius mortem hi consules, T. Flaminius
et M'. Acilius, facti sunt; ille autem Caepione et Philippo
iterum consulibus mortuus est, cum ego quinque et sexa-
ginta annos natus legem Voconiam magna voce et bonis
lateribus suasi [Cato, fr. 156–60 *ORF*⁴]. sed annos septua-
ginta natus, tot enim vixit Ennius, ita ferebat duo quae
maxima putantur onera, paupertatem et senectutem, ut
eis paene delectari videretur.

T 34 Cic. *Div.* 1.23

sus rostro si humi A litteram impresserit, num propterea
suspicari poteris Andromacham Enni ab ea posse de-
scribi?

T 35 Cic. *Off.* 1.114

suum quisque igitur noscat ingenium, acremque se et
bonorum et vitiorum suorum iudicem praebeat, ne scae-
nici plus quam nos videantur habere prudentiae. illi enim
non optimas sed sibi accommodatissimas fabulas eligunt:
qui voce freti sunt, Epigonos Medumque, qui gestu Mela-
nippam Clytaemestram, semper Rupilius, quem ego me-

T 33 Cicero, *On Old Age*

He [Ennius] compares his old age to that of a strong and
victorious horse. Surely you can remember him well, for
in the nineteenth year after his death, Titus Flaminius and
Manius Acilius were elected consuls [150 BC]; he died
when Caepio and Philippus (for a second time) were con-
suls [169 BC], when I [the speaker, Cato], at the age of 65,
argued for the *Lex Voconia*[1] with a loud voice and great
lung power. But at the age of 70, for so long did Ennius
live [239–169 BC], he was accustomed to bear the two
things considered the greatest burdens, poverty and old
age, so well that he seemed almost to be delighted with
them.

[1] A bill on inheritance rules, proposed by the tribune of the
plebs Q. Voconius Saxa.

T 34 Cicero, *On Divination*

Should a sow trace the letter A on the ground with her
snout, surely you could not therefore suspect that Ennius'
Andromacha could be written out by her?

T 35 Cicero, *On Duties*

All should be conscious of their own abilities and present
themselves as keen judges of both their good qualities and
their defects, so that dramatic actors do not seem to have
more practical wisdom than we have. For they do not
choose the best plays, but those most suited to their tal-
ents: those who trust their voice choose *Epigoni* and *Me-
dus*, those who trust their movement choose *Melanippa*
and *Clytaemestra*. Rupilius, whom I remember, always

mini, Antiopam, non saepe Aesopus Aiacem. ergo histrio
hoc videbit in scaena, non videbit sapiens vir in vita?

T 36 (cf. T 2) Varro, *Sat. Men.* 398 B.

poema est lexis enrythmos, id est, verba plura modice in
quandam coniecta formam; itaque etiam distichon epi-
grammation vocant poema. poesis est perpetuum argu-
mentum ex rhythmis, ut Ilias Homeri et Annalis Enni.
poetice est ars earum rerum.

T 37 Varro, *Rust.* 1.1.4

et quoniam, ut aiunt, dei facientes adiuvant, prius in-
vocabo eos, nec, ut Homerus et Ennius, Musas, sed duo-
decim deos consentis . . .

T 38 (cf. T 91, 97) Nep. *Cato* 1.4

praetor provinciam obtinuit Sardiniam, ex qua quaestor
superiore tempore ex Africa decedens Q. Ennium poetam
deduxerat, quod non minoris aestimamus quam quem-
libet amplissimum Sardiniensem triumphum.

chose *Antiopa*, Aesopus not often *Aiax*.[1] The actor will see this on the stage. Will not the wise man then see it in life?

[1] Tragedies by Accius, Pacuvius, Ennius, respectively (cf. *Aiax*: *Trag.* F 9–12; *Melanippa*: *Trag.* F 101–6).

T 36 (cf. T 2) Varro, *Menippean Satires*

A *poema* [poem] is a piece in rhythmic language, that is, a considerable number of words brought into some form according to rules; therefore they call even an epigrammatic distich a *poema* [poem]. *poesis* [poetry] is a continuous narrative in meter, such as Homer's *Iliad* and Ennius' *Annals*. *poeticē* [i.e., *technē*; poetics] is the art of these things.

T 37 Varro, *On Agriculture*

And since, as they say, the gods help those who take action, I will invoke them first, not, like Homer and Ennius, the Muses, but the Dei Consentes[1] . . .

[1] A Roman name for a group of twelve deities, six male and six female (cf. 7 *Ann.* F 24).

T 38 (cf. T 91, 97) Cornelius Nepos, *Cato*

As praetor [in 198 BC], he[1] governed the province of Sardinia, from which, when returning from Africa as quaestor [in 204 BC], he had previously brought back the poet Ennius, which deed we value no less than any grand Sardinian triumph.

[1] M. Porcius Cato (234–149 BC, cos. 195 BC).

T 39 Vitr. *De arch.* 9, Praef. 16

itaque qui litterarum iucunditatibus instinctas habent mentes non possunt non in suis pectoribus dedicatum habere, sicuti deorum, sic Ennii poetae simulacrum.

T 40

a Hor. *Sat.* 1.10.46–49

hoc erat experto frustra Varrone Atacino
atque quibusdam aliis melius quod scribere possem,
inventore minor; neque ego illi detrahere ausim
haerentem capiti cum multa laude coronam.

b Porph. ad Hor. *Sat.* 1.10.46

hoc erat experto frustra et reliqua: quum alii alia carminum genera consummate scriberent, quorum mentionem habuit, sermonum autem frustra temptasset Terentius Varro Narbonensis, qui Atacinus ab Atace fluvio dictus est, item Ennius, qui quattuor libros saturarum reliquit, et Pacuvius huic generi versificationis non suffecissent, se id scribere ait ita, ut aliis maior sit, Lucilio minor. quem inventorem huius operis merito dixit, quia primus Lucilius huius modi carmina scripsit.

T 41 Hor. *Sat.* 1.10.51–55

                                       age, quaeso,
tu nihil in magno doctus reprehendis Homero?
nil comis tragici mutat Lucilius Acci?

T 39 Vitruvius, *On Architecture*

Therefore those who have minds fired by the pleasantness of literature cannot but have in their hearts a consecrated image, as of the gods, of the poet Ennius.

T 40

a Horace, *Satires*

This genre, attempted in vain by Varro Atacinus [a late-Republican poet] and some others, was there for me to be able to improve upon, though a lesser poet than its inventor [Lucilius]; nor would I dare drag from him the crown clinging with great acclaim to his head.

b Porphyrio, *Commentary on Horace*

"this genre, attempted in vain" and so on: while others whom he has mentioned were writing other genres of poetry very well, Terentius Varro Narbonensis, by contrast, who was called Atacinus from the river Atax, had attempted the genre of satire in vain, so too Ennius, who left four books of satires, and Pacuvius did not manage this genre of versification successfully. He [Horace] says that he writes this in a way to be better than the others but less good than Lucilius, whom he rightly called the inventor of this genre, since Lucilius was the first to write poems of this kind.

T 41 Horace, *Satires*

Come on, please, you learned one, do you fault nothing in great Homer? Does cultured Lucilius try to change

non ridet versus Enni gravitate minores,
55   cum de se loquitur non ut maiore reprensis?

T 42

a Hor. *Sat.* 2.1.16–17

attamen et iustum poteras et scribere fortem,
Scipiadam ut sapiens Lucilius.

b Porph. ad Hor. *Sat.* 2.1.16

attamen et iustum poteras et scribere fortem Scipiadam:
si non potes res gestas Caesaris scribere, at potes iustitiam
et fortitudinem, ut Lucilius Scipioni fecit, qui vitam illius
privatam descripsit, Ennius vero bella.

T 43

a Hor. *Epist.* 1.3.1–2

Iuli Flore, quibus terrarum militet oris
Claudius Augusti privignus, scire laboro.

b Porph. ad Hor. *Epist.* 1.3.1

ad Iulium hanc Florum scribit, qui saturam scripsit: Iuli
Flore, quibus terrarum militet oris. hic Florus scriba fuit
saturarum scriptor, cuius sunt electae ex Ennio Lucilio
Varrone saturae.

nothing of tragic Accius? Does he not ridicule Ennius' verses as lacking in dignity, [55] while he speaks of himself as no greater than those criticized?

T 42

a Horace, *Satires*

Yet, you could write about him as both just and courageous, as the wise Lucilius did about Scipio.

b Porphyrio, *Commentary on Horace*

"yet, you could write about him as both just and courageous, as . . . about Scipio": if you cannot write about the achievements of Caesar [Augustus], you can still write about justice and courage, as Lucilius did for Scipio, as he described his private life, and Ennius, ‹as he described› his campaigns.

T 43

a Horace, *Epistles*

Iulius Florus, I long to know in which regions of the earth Claudius [the future emperor Tiberius], the stepson of Augustus, is campaigning.

b Porphyrio, *Commentary on Horace*

He writes this to Iulius Florus, who wrote satire: "Iulius Florus, in which regions of the earth he is campaigning." This Florus, a secretary, was a writer of satires, whose satires were distinguished among [those of] Ennius, Lucilius, and Varro.

T 44

a Hor. *Epist.* 1.19.6–8

laudibus arguitur vini vinosus Homerus.
Ennius ipse pater numquam nisi potus ad arma
prosiluit dicenda.

b Porph. ad Hor. *Epist.* 1.19.7

pater autem Ennius ideo, quod ipse primus Latinorum ad
heroici versus imitationem adspiraverit. ad arma: ad libros
Annalium, quos Ennius scripsit.

T 45 Hor. *Ars P.* 55–58

ego cur, acquirere pauca
si possum, invideor, cum lingua Catonis et Enni
sermonem patrium ditaverit et nova rerum
nomina protulerit?

T 46

a Hor. *Ars P.* 258–62

hic et in Acci
nobilibus trimetris apparet rarus et Enni
260   in scaenam missos cum magno pondere versus
aut operae celeris nimium curaque carentis
aut ignoratae premit artis crimine turpi.

T 44

a Horace, *Epistles*

By his praise of wine Homer is shown to be a drinker.
Father Ennius himself never leaped up to speak of arms
unless drunk.

b Porphyrio, *Commentary on Horace*

"father Ennius" because he was the first of the Latins to
aspire to the imitation of heroic verse. "to . . . arms": refer-
ring to the books of the *Annals*, which Ennius wrote.

T 45 Horace, *The Art of Poetry*

Why am I regarded with ill will if I can add a little, when
the language of Cato and Ennius has enriched the speech
of our fathers and produced new names for things?

T 46

a Horace, *The Art of Poetry*

It [the pure iambic foot] appears rarely in the noble tri-
meters of Accius, and hurls against Ennius' verses, [260]
sent so ponderously on the stage, the shameful reproach
of either hasty work and excessive lack of care or ignorance
of art.

b Schol. ad Hor. *Ars P.* 258–59

Accius et Ennius legem metri in fabulis minime servave-
runt: nam quosdam versus longiores habent.

T 47

a Hor. *Carm.* 4.8.13–24

    non incisa notis marmora publicis,
    per quae spiritus et vita redit bonis
15   post mortem ducibus, {non celeres fugae
    reiectaeque retrorsum Hannibalis minae,
    non incendia Karthaginis impiae
    eius qui domita nomen ab Africa
    lucratus rediit} clarius indicant
20   laudes quam Calabrae Pierides; neque
    si chartae sileant quod bene feceris,
    mercedem tuleris. quid foret Iliae
    Mavortisque puer, si taciturnitas
    obstaret meritis invida Romuli?

b Schol. ad Hor. *Carm.* 4.8.20

quam Calabr⟨a⟩e Pierides: facta, inquit, clarorum viro-
rum nisi carminibus inlustrentur, aetatis suae memoriam
non excedunt. et significat Ennium, qui facta Africani de-
scripsit, oriundo de Rodino oppido Calabriae; ideo Cala-
brae Musae.

b Scholia to Horace, *The Art of Poetry*

Accius and Ennius barely maintained the law of meter in their plays, for they have some verses too long.[1]

[1] Horace claims that the pure iambic foot is rare in Accius' iambic senarii and poorly employed in those of Ennius (unlike the Greek iambic trimeter, which allowed substitutions only in specific positions). The scholion seems instead to refer the comment to hypermetric verses.

T 47

a Horace, *Odes*

Marble inscribed with public notices, through which spirit and life return to good [15] leaders after death, . . . does not make praise more gloriously known [20] than the Muses of Calabria; nor, if papyrus pages were silent about what you did well, would you carry off any reward. What would the son of Ilia and Mars be if envious silence stood in the way of Romulus' merits?

b Scholia to Horace, *Odes*

"than the Muses of Calabria": the deeds of famous men, he says, if they are not rendered famous by poetry, do not extend beyond the memory of their own age. Further, he refers to Ennius, who described the deeds of Africanus, by his origin in Rudiae, a town in Calabria; therefore Muses of Calabria.

T 48 Strab. 6.3.5, p. 281 C.

..., ἐντεῦθεν δὲ τηρήσαντες φορὸν πνεῦμα προσέχουσι τοῖς μὲν Βρεντεσίνων λιμέσιν, ἐκβάντες δὲ πεζεύουσι συντομώτερον ἐπὶ Ῥοδιῶν (πόλεως Ἑλληνίδος, ἐξ ἧς ἦν ὁ ποιητὴς Ἔννιος).

T 49 Liv. 38.56.4

..., et Romae extra portam Capenam in Scipionum monumento tres statuae sunt, quarum duae P. et L. Scipionum dicuntur esse, tertia poetae Q. Enni.

T 50 Prop. 3.3.1–16

visus eram molli recubans Heliconis in umbra,
    Bellerophontei qua fluit umor equi,
reges, Alba, tuos et regum facta tuorum,
    tantum operis, nervis hiscere posse meis;
5 parvaque tam magnis admoram fontibus ora
    unde pater sitiens Ennius ante bibit
et cecinit Curios fratres et Horatia pila

---

[1] The Corinthian hero Bellerophon was associated with the divine horse Pegasus; the spring Hippocrene on Helicon was said to have been created by the beating of his hooves.

T 48 Strabo, *Geography*

. . . and from there,[1] watching out for a favorable wind, they turn toward the harbors of the Brentesini,[2] but, disembarking, they travel on foot along a shorter route toward Rudiae (a Greek city, from which the poet Ennius came).[3]

[1] The town of Hydrous (mod. Otranto).   [2] Inhabitants of Brundisium in southern Italy.   [3] The phrasing of this passage is odd; the text has been suspected of being corrupt.

T 49 Livy, *History of Rome*

. . . and at Rome outside the Capenan Gate in the tomb of the Scipios there are three statues, of which two are said to be of Publius and Lucius Scipio,[1] the third of the poet Ennius.

[1] P. Cornelius Scipio Africanus (ca. 236–183 BC, cos. 205 BC) and L. Cornelius Scipio Asiagenus (cos. 190 BC).

T 50 Propertius, *Elegies*

I had seemed to lie in the soft shade of Helicon, where the water of Bellerophon's horse flows,[1] and to be able to speak of your kings, Alba, and the deeds of your kings, so great a task, on my strings; [5] and I had moved my meager mouth to the great fountain from which father Ennius, being thirsty, once drank and sang of the brothers Curii and Horatius' missiles[2] and the regal trophies carried on

[2] According to legend, the fight between the Roman Horatii triplets and the Alban Curiatii triplets decided the conflict between Rome and Alba Longa during the regal period (e.g., Liv. 1.24–26).

regiaque Aemilia vecta tropaea rate,
victricesque moras Fabii pugnamque sinistram
10   Cannensem et versos ad pia vota deos,
Hannibalemque Lares Romana sede fugantes,
      anseris et tutum voce fuisse Iovem;
cum me Castalia speculans ex arbore Phoebus
      sic ait aurata nixus ad antra lyra:
15   quid tibi cum tali, demens, est flumine? quis te
      carminis heroi tangere iussit opus?

. . .

T 51 Prop. 4.1.57–64

moenia namque pio conor disponere versu:
      ei mihi, quod nostro est parvus in ore sonus!
sed tamen exiguo quodcumque e pectore rivi
60   fluxerit, hoc patriae serviet omne meae.
Ennius hirsuta cingat sua dicta corona:
      mi folia ex hedera porrige, Bacche, tua,
ut nostris tumefacta superbiat Umbria libris,
      Umbria Romani patria Callimachi!

the ship of Aemilius[3] and Fabius' victorious delays[4] and the unlucky battle [10] of Cannae and the gods attentive to pious vows and the Lares driving Hannibal to flight from their Roman seat and Jupiter made safe by the voice of a goose [presumably all topics of Ennius' *Annals*]; then Phoebus, spotting me from a Castalian[5] tree, spoke thus, leaning on his golden lyre by the cave: [15] "What business do you have with such a river, madman? Who told you to touch the task of heroic song? . . ."

[3] The victory of L. Aemilius Paulus (ca. 228–160 BC, cos. 182, 168 BC) over the Macedonian king Perseus at Pydna (168 BC) postdates the *Annals*. The likely reference here—if Propertius accurately recalls the content of Ennius' poem—is the victory of the praetor L. Aemilius Regillus over Antiochus' fleet at Myonnesus in 190 BC.   [4] Q. Fabius Maximus "Cunctator" (cos. 213 BC), famous for his delaying tactics in the Second Punic War.   [5] Castalia is a fountain on Parnassus, associated with Apollo and the Muses.

T 51 Propertius, *Elegies*

For I try to lay out the walls [of Rome] in pious verse: alas, what a weak sound is in my mouth! But still, whatever stream flows from my feeble breast, [60] all this will serve my country. Let Ennius wreathe his words with a shaggy crown: offer me, Bacchus, leaves from your ivy, so that Umbria, swelling up, shows pride in our books, Umbria, the native country of the Roman Callimachus![1]

[1] Propertius, who here compares himself with the Greek Hellenistic poet Callimachus, came from the Italian region of Umbria.

T 52 Ov. *Am.* 1.15.19–20

Ennius arte carens animosique Accius oris
20   casurum nullo tempore nomen habent
    . . .

T 53 Ov. *Tr.* 3.409–10

Ennius emeruit, Calabris in montibus ortus,
410   contiguus poni, Scipio magne, tibi.

T 54 Ov. *Tr.* 2.259–60

sumpserit Annales—nihil est hirsutius illis—
260   facta sit unde parens Ilia, nempe leget.

T 55 Ov. *Tr.* 2.423–24

utque suo Martem cecinit gravis Ennius ore,
    Ennius ingenio maximus, arte rudis,
    . . .

T 56 Val. Max. 8.14.1

superior Africanus Enni poetae effigiem in monumentis
Corneliae gentis conlocari voluit, quod ingenio eius opera
sua inlustrata iudicaret, non quidem ignarus quam diu
Romanum imperium floreret, et Africa Italiae pedibus es-
set subiecta, totiusque terrarum orbis summum columen
arx Capitolina possideret, eorum exstingui memoriam non
posse, si tamen litterarum quoque illis lumen accessisset,
magni aestimans, vir Homerico quam rudi atque impolito
praeconio dignior.

---

[1] P. Cornelius Scipio Africanus (ca. 236–183 BC, cos. 205 BC).

T 52 Ovid, *The Art of Love*

Ennius, though lacking in art, and Accius of animated speech have names that will at no point fade . . .

T 53 Ovid, *Tristia*

Ennius, born in the Calabrian mountains, earned a place close to you, great Scipio.

T 54 Ovid, *Tristia*

Should she [a matron] take up the *Annals*—nothing is rougher than that—, she will no doubt read how Ilia[1] became a mother.

---

[1] Rhea Silvia, mother of Romulus and Remus. Cf. 1 *Ann.* F 28.

T 55 Ovid, *Tristia*

And as solemn Ennius poured songs about Mars from his mouth, Ennius, in talent outstanding, in art crude, . . .

T 56 Valerius Maximus, *Memorable Doings and Sayings*

The elder Africanus[1] wanted a statue of the poet Ennius placed in the tomb of the Cornelian family, since he regarded his own deeds as glorified by his [Ennius'] talent, certainly not unaware that, as long as the Roman empire flourished and Africa lay supine under Italy's feet and the Capitoline citadel occupied the highest peak of the entire world, their memory could not be extinguished, but nevertheless rating it highly if the light of literature had also come to them, a man more worthy of a Homeric herald than a crude and unpolished one.

T 57 Mela 2.66

sinus est continuo Apulo litore incinctus nomine Urias,
modicus spatio pleraque asper accessu, . . . , post Barium
et Gnatia et Ennio cive nobiles Rudiae, et iam in Calabria
Brundisium . . .

T 58 (= *Sat.* F 19) Pers. 6.9–11

    Lunai portum, est operae, cognoscite, cives:
10   cor iubet hoc Enni, postquam destertuit esse
    Maeonides Quintus pavone ex Pythagoreo.

T 59 Sen. *Dial.* 5.37.5

non aequis quendam oculis vidisti, quia de ingenio tuo
male locutus est: recipis hanc legem? ergo te Ennius, quo
non delectaris, odisset et Hortensius simultates tibi indi-
ceret et Cicero, si derideres carmina eius, inimicus esset.

T 57 Pomponius Mela

There is a bay surrounded continuously by the Apulian shore called Urias [Lago di Varano], moderate in size and mostly difficult of access, . . . then Barium [Bari] and Gnatia [Canosa di Puglia] and Rudiae [Rugge], renowned for its citizen Ennius,[1] and, already in Calabria, Brundisium [Brindisi] . . .

[1] Mela apparently confuses Rudiae in Calabria, the birthplace of Ennius, and Rudiae in Apulia.

T 58 (= *Sat.* F 19) Persius, *Satires*

"Get to know the port of Luna,[1] citizens. It's worth it!" [10] So urged Ennius' soul, after he snored off being Quintus Maeonides [Homer, cf. T. 63] via a Pythagorean peacock.[2]

[1] A harbor town in Italy, later a Roman colony.   [2] A scholiast (1 *Ann.* t 4) reads into this a reference to five transformations (*quintus* = "the fifth"). The phrasing is now more commonly understood as an allusion to Ennius' *praenomen* and the passage thus as an ironic reference to the dream vision at the beginning of the *Annals*.

T 59 Seneca, *Dialogues. De Ira*

You did not look at a certain man with dispassionate eyes, since he spoke badly of your talent: do you take this as a law? Then Ennius, whom you dislike, would hate you, and Hortensius[1] would declare enmity to you, and Cicero, if you ridiculed his poetry, would be an enemy.

[1] Q. Hortensius Hortalus, the famous orator (114–50 BC, cos. 69 BC).

T 60 Sen. *Ep.* 58.5

non id ago nunc hac diligentia ut ostendam quantum tem-
pus apud grammaticum perdiderim, sed ut ex hoc intelle-
gas quantum apud Ennium et Accium verborum situs
occupaverit, cum apud hunc quoque, qui cotidie excutitur,
aliqua nobis subducta sint.

T 61 (= 9 *Ann.* F 6) Sen. *Ep.* ap. Gell. *NA* 12.2.2–11

mihi de omni eius ingenio deque omni scripto iudicium
censuramque facere non necessum est; sed quod de M.
Cicerone et Q. Ennio et P. Vergilio iudicavit, ea res cui-
modi sit, ad considerandum ponemus. [3] in libro enim
vicesimo secundo epistularum moralium, quas ad Luci-
lium conposuit, derídiculos versus Q. Ennii de Cetego
antiquo viro fecisse hos dicit [9 *Ann.* F 6]: . . . [4] ac deinde
scribit de isdem versibus verba haec: admiror eloquentis-
simos viros et deditos Ennio pro optimis ridicula laudasse.
Cicero certe inter bonos eius versus et hos refert [Cic.
Brut. 57–59]. [5] atque id etiam de Cicerone dicit:
   non miror inquit fuisse, qui hos versus scriberet, cum
fuerit, qui laudaret; nisi forte Cicero summus orator age-
bat causam suam et volebat suos versus videri bonos. [6]
postea hoc etiam addidit insulsissime: aput ipsum quoque
inquit Ciceronem invenies etiam in prosa oratione quae-
dam, ex quibus intellegas illum non perdidisse operam,

---

[1] A book of Seneca's *Epistles* (also called *Moral Epistles*, as by
Gellius here) not otherwise extant.

[2] M. Cornelius Cethegus (cos. 204 BC).

T 60 Seneca, *Epistles*

I am not doing this [citing examples of obsolete words] now so diligently to show how much time I have wasted with a grammarian, but for you to understand from this how many words in Ennius and Accius have fallen into disuse, while in him [Virgil] too, who is studied daily, are some words that have been taken away from us.

T 61 (= 9 *Ann.* F 6) Seneca, *Epistles* in Gellius, *Attic Nights*

It is not necessary for me to offer an opinion and assessment of his [Seneca's] talent in general and of his writing in general; but we will put forward for consideration the nature of the opinions he has expressed about Cicero and Ennius and Virgil. [3] For in the twenty-second book of the *Moral Epistles*, which he addressed to Lucilius,[1] he says that Ennius wrote utterly ridiculous verses about Cethegus,[2] a man of an earlier age, as follows: [9 *Ann.* F 6] ". . ." [4] And he then writes the following words about these same lines: "I am amazed that very eloquent men devoted to Ennius have praised this ridiculous stuff as his best. Cicero without doubt counts even these among his [Ennius'] good verses [Cic. *Brut.* 57–59]." [5] And he also says this about Cicero:

"I am not surprised," he says, "that there was a man who could write those lines when there was a man who could praise them; unless perhaps Cicero, the greatest orator, was pleading his own case and wanted his own verses to appear good." [6] Later he very stupidly added this remark: "In Cicero himself, too," he says, "even in prose writings, you will find some passages from which you

49

quod Ennium legit. [7] ponit deinde, quae apud Cicero-
nem reprehendat quasi Enniana, quod ita scripserit in li-
bris de re publica [Cic. *Rep.* 5.11]: ut Menelao Laconi
quaedam fuit suaviloquens iucunditas, et quod alio in loco
dixerit: breviloquentiam in dicendo colat. [8] atque ibi
homo nugator Ciceronis errores deprecatur et non fuit
inquit Ciceronis hoc vitium, sed temporis; necesse erat
haec dici, cum illa legerentur. [9] deinde adscribit Cicero-
nem haec ipsa interposuisse ad effugiendam infamiam
nimis lascivae orationis et nitidae. [10] de Vergilio quoque
eodem in loco verba haec ponit: Vergilius quoque noster
non ex alia causa duros quosdam versus et enormes et
aliquid supra mensuram trahentis interposuit, quam ut
Ennianus populus adgnosceret in novo carmine aliquid
antiquitatis. [11] sed iam verborum Senecae piget; haec
tamen inepti et insubidi hominis ioca non praeteribo: qui-
dam sunt inquit tam magni sensus Q. Ennii, ut, licet scripti
sint inter hircosos, possint tamen inter unguentatos pla-
cere; et, cum reprehendisset versus, quos supra de Cetego
posuimus: qui huiuscemodi inquit versus amant, liqueat
tibi eosdem admirari et Soterici lectos.

may gather that he did not waste his effort in reading Ennius." [7] He then puts forth what he faults in Cicero as if reminiscent of Ennius, because he wrote thus in the books *On the Republic* [Cic. *Rep.* 5.11]: "as the Spartan Menelaus had a certain sweet-speaking charm," and because he said in another passage: "let him cultivate brevity in speaking." [8] And then this vapid critic begs pardon for Cicero's errors and says: "This was not the fault of Cicero, but of the times; it was necessary for such things to be said when such things were read." [9] Then he adds that Cicero inserted these very things to avoid a bad reputation for too extravagant and ornamental a style. [10] Concerning Virgil, too, he offers the following words in the same passage: "Our Virgil too inserted some verses harsh and irregular and extending somewhat beyond the proper length for no other reason than that the crowd used to Ennius might find a touch of antiquity in the new poem." [11] I am already weary of Seneca's words, yet I will not pass by these jokes of that foolish and tasteless man: "There are," he says, "some thoughts in Ennius of such lofty sentiment that, even though written among the unwashed [lit. 'smelling like goats'], they can still give pleasure among the perfumed"; and, after he had criticized the lines we have quoted above about Cethegus: "You may observe," he says, "that those who love verses of this kind are the same people who admire even Sotericus' couches."[3]

[3] Apparently a notoriously unskilled or old-fashioned maker of furniture, not otherwise known.

T 62 Plin. *HN* 7.114

prior Africanus Q. Ennii statuam sepulcro suo inponi ius-
sit clarumque illud nomen, immo vero spolium ex tertia
orbis parte raptum, in cinere supremo cum poetae titulo
legi.

T 63 Mart. 5.10.7–8

> Ennius est lectus salvo tibi, Roma, Marone,
>   et sua riserunt saecula Maeoniden. . .

T 64 Stat. *Silv.* 2.7.73–80

> haec primo iuvenis canes sub aevo,
> ante annos Culicis Maroniani.
> cedet Musa rudis ferocis Enni
> et docti furor arduus Lucreti
> et qui per freta duxit Argonautas
> et qui corpora prima transfigurat.
> quid? maius loquar: ipsa te Latinis
> Aeneis venerabitur canentem.

75

80

T 62 Pliny the Elder, *Natural History*

The elder Africanus[1] ordered a statue of Ennius to be placed on his tomb and that famous name [Africanus] or rather, that trophy snatched from a third part of the world, to be read above his ashes together with the epitaph of a poet.

[1] P. Cornelius Scipio Africanus (ca. 236–183 BC, cos. 205 BC). The honorific *cognomen* "Africanus" celebrated his victories against Hannibal in Africa, culminating in the battle of Zama in 202 BC (cf. Liv. 30.45.6–7).

T 63 Martial, *Epigrams*

Ennius was read by you, Rome, while Maro [Virgil] lived, and his own age scoffed at Maeonides [Homer] . . .

T 64 Statius, *Silvae*

These things [the topics just listed] you [the epic poet Lucan] will sing as a young man at an early age before attaining Maro's years, when he wrote *Culex*.[1] [75] The crude Muse of warlike Ennius will give way and the lofty fury of learned Lucretius and he who led the Argonauts through the straits[2] and he who changes bodies from their original shapes.[3] What more? I shall say something greater: [80] the *Aeneid* itself[4] will honor your singing to the Latins.

[1] The epyllion transmitted under Virgil's name, allegedly written in his youth. [2] The late-Republican poet Varro Atacinus, author of an epic on the Argonauts. [3] Ovid, represented by his *Metamorphoses*. [4] Virgil's poem as the Latin epic par excellence.

T 65 Quint. *Inst.* 1.8.11

nam praecipue quidem apud Ciceronem, frequenter tamen apud Asinium etiam et ceteros qui sunt proximi, videmus Enni Acci Pacuvi Lucili Terenti Caecili et aliorum inseri versus, summa non eruditionis modo gratia sed etiam iucunditatis, cum poeticis voluptatibus aures a forensi asperitate respirant.

T 66 Quint. *Inst.* 10.1.88

Ennium sicut sacros vetustate lucos adoremus, in quibus grandia et antiqua robora iam non tantam habent speciem quantam religionem.

T 67 Sil. 12.390–414

sed vos, Calliope, nostro donate labori,
nota parum magni longo tradantur ut aevo
facta viri, et meritum vati sacremus honorem.
Ennius, antiqua Messapi ab origine regis,
miscebat primas acies, Latiaeque superbum
395   vitis adornabat dextram decus. hispida tellus
miserunt Calabri, Rudiae genuere vetustae,
nunc Rudiae solo memorabile nomen alumno.
is prima in pugna, vates ut Thracius olim,
infestam bello quateret cum Cyzicus Argo,
400   spicula deposito Rhodopeia pectine torsit,

---

[1] The region also known as Calabria was named Messapia after him.   [2] A staff of vine wood was carried by Roman centurions. Ennius' service in this capacity is otherwise unattested. (On this passage see Casali 2006; Manuwald 2007).

T 65 Quintilian, *The Orator's Education*

Particularly in Cicero, but frequently also in Asinius[1] and others nearest to their times, we find inserted lines from Ennius, Accius, Pacuvius, Lucilius, Terence, Caecilius and others for the sake not only of the learning shown but also of the pleasure given by allowing the audience to relax from the asperities of the courtroom in the delights of poetry.[2]

[1] C. Asinius Pollio, 76 BC– AD 4 (cos. 40 BC). On his oratory cf. Quint. *Inst.* 10.1.113; on his attitude to tragedy cf. Tac. *Dial.* 21.7.   [2] Russell's translation, adapted. The construction of *summa* is difficult and controversial.

T 66 Quintilian, *The Orator's Education*

Let us honor Ennius as we do groves made sacred by age, in which huge and ancient trees no longer have so much beauty as sanctity.

T 67 Silius Italicus, *Punica*

But you, Calliope, grant this to my labor that the deeds, too little known, of a great man are passed on to long ages and we enshrine a poet's well-deserved honor. Ennius, from the ancient race of king Messapus,[1] was fighting in the front line, and [395] the proud insignia of the Latin vine adorned his right hand.[2] The rugged land of Calabria sent him, ancient Rudiae gave him birth, Rudiae now a memorable name only because of its son. In the front line, just as the Thracian bard [Orpheus] long ago, when Cyzicus threw the Argo into turmoil through war, [400] put down the lyre and hurled Rhodopeian missiles, he [En-

spectandum sese non parva strage virorum
fecerat, et dextrae gliscebat caedibus ardor.
advolat aeternum sperans fore pelleret Hostus
si tantam labem, ac perlibrat viribus hastam.
405 risit nube sedens vani conamina coepti
et telum procul in ventos dimisit Apollo
ac super his: nimium, iuvenis, nimiumque † superbi
sperata hausisti †. sacer hic ac magna sororum
Aonidum cura est et dignus Apolline vates.
410 hic canet illustri primus bella Itala versu
attolletque duces caelo, resonare docebit
hic Latiis Helicona modis nec cedet honore
Ascraeo famave seni. sic Phoebus, et Hosto
ultrix per geminum transcurrit tempus harundo.

T 68 Plin. *Ep.* 5.3.2–6

quibus ego, ut augeam meam culpam, ita respondeo: facio
non numquam versiculos severos parum, facio; nam et
comoedias audio et specto mimos et lyricos lego et Sota-
dicos intellego; . . . [5] . . . , sed ego verear ne me non
satis deceat, quod decuit M. Tullium . . . ? [6] Neronem
enim transeo, quamvis sciam non corrumpi in deterius
quae aliquando etiam a malis, sed honesta manere quae
saepius a bonis fiunt. inter quos vel praecipue numerandus
est P. Vergilius, Cornelius Nepos et prius Accius Ennius-
que. non quidem hi senatores, sed sanctitas morum non
distat ordinibus.

---

[1] In a list of writers of unserious verse.

nius] had made himself conspicuous by no small destruction of men, and the ardor of his right hand was glowing with the slaughter. Hostus runs near, hoping for eternal fame, if he repels so great a bane, and hurls his lance with force. [405] Sitting on a cloud, Apollo laughed at the attempt of this vain action and sent the missile wide into the wind, and in addition spoke thus: "Too much, young man, too much you have hoped (?). This man is sacred and of great concern to the Aonian sisters and a bard worthy of Apollo. [410] He will be the first to sing of Italic wars in illustrious verse and exalt its leaders to the sky, and he will teach Helicon to resonate with Latin meters and not yield honor or fame to the old man of Ascra [Hesiod]." Thus Phoebus, and an avenging arrow runs through both temples of Hostus.

T 68 Pliny the Younger, *Letters*

To augment my misdeeds, I answer these men [the critics] in this way: I do sometimes compose verses not sufficiently serious, I do; for I listen to comedies and watch mimes and read lyrics and appreciate Sotadic lines [cf. Quint. *Inst.* 1.8.6] . . . [5] . . . But should I fear that it would be unbecoming for me to do what well became M. Tullius [Cicero] . . . ? [6] I pass by Nero,[1] though I know that a practice also sometimes carried out by men of bad character is not changed into something worse, but what is often done by men of good character remains respectable. Among those, particular mention should be made of Virgil, Cornelius Nepos and, earlier, Accius and Ennius. True, these were not senators, but purity of character does not vary with rank.

T 69 Suet. *Gram. et rhet.* 1.2–3

initium quoque eius mediocre extitit, siquidem antiquis-
simi doctorum, qui idem et poetae et semigraeci erant—
Livium et Ennium dico, quos utraque lingua domi forisque
docuisse adnotatum est—nihil amplius quam Graecos
interpretabantur aut si quid ipsi Latine composuissent
praelegebant. [3] nam quod nonnulli tradunt duos libros—
de litteris syllabisque, item de metris—ab eodem Ennio
editos, iure arguit L. Cotta non poetae sed posterioris
Enni esse, cuius etiam de augurali disciplina volumina
ferantur.

T 70 Suet. *Gram. et rhet.* 2.2

hactenus tamen imitati, ut carmina parum adhuc divulgata
vel defunctorum amicorum vel si quorum aliorum pro-
bassent diligentius retractarent ac legendo commentan-
doque etiam ceteris nota facerent: ut C. Octavius Lampa-
dio Naevi Punicum bellum, . . . ; ut postea Q. Vargunteius
Annales Enni, quos certis diebus in magna frequentia
pronuntiabat . . .

T 69 Suetonius, *Lives of Illustrious Men. Grammarians and Rhetoricians*

Its [the study of grammar] beginning, too, was undistinguished, inasmuch as the earliest teachers, who were at the same time poets and half-Greek—I mean Livius [Andronicus] and Ennius, who are on record as having taught both languages in private and in public—, merely clarified the meaning of Greek authors or gave demonstrations by reading from their own Latin compositions. [3] As for what some report, that two books—one on letters and syllables, another on meters—were published by this same Ennius, Lucius Cotta rightly argues that they are not by the poet, but by a later Ennius,[1] whose books on augural lore are also in circulation.

[1] The so-called grammarian Ennius, clearly attested only here, was probably active in the first half of the first century BC.

T 70 Suetonius, *Lives of Illustrious Men. Grammarians and Rhetoricians*

Still, they [the earliest Roman scholars] imitated him [Crates of Mallos] only to the extent that they carefully reviewed poems not yet widely circulated, the works of dead friends or of any others they approved, and made them known to others as well by reading and commenting on them. So C. Octavius Lampadio[1] did for Naevius' *Punic War*, . . . ; as Q. Vargunteius[2] later did for Ennius' *Annals*, which he used to recite on specific days before a large audience . . .

[1] A grammarian at Rome in the second century BC.
[2] Otherwise unknown.

T 71 Suet. *Gram. et rhet.* 8

M. Pompilius Andronicus, natione Syrus, studio Epicureae sectae desidiosior in professione grammatica habebatur minusque idoneus ad tuendam scholam. [2] itaque cum se in urbe non solum Antonio Gniphoni sed ceteris etiam deterioribus postponi videret, Cumas transiit ibique in otio vixit et multa composuit—[3] verum adeo inops atque egens ut coactus sit praecipuum illud opusculum suum Annalium Enni elenchorum sedecim milibus nummum cuidam vendere, quos libros Orbilius suppressos redemisse se dicit vulgandosque curasse nomine auctoris.

T 72 (cf. T 107) Suet. *Vita Verg.* (Suet. *reliq.*, p. 67 Reifferscheid) = Don. auct. *Vita Verg.* 71 (p. 113 Brugnoli/Stok)

cum is aliquando Ennium in manu haberet rogareturque quidnam faceret, respondit se aurum colligere de stercore Ennii. habet enim poeta ille egregias sententias sub verbis non multum ornatis.

T 73 Fronto, Ad M. Caesarem et invicem libri, *Ep.* 1.7.3–4 (p. 15.10–17 van den Hout)

quot litterae istic sunt, totidem consulatus mihi, totidem laureas, triumphos, togas pictas arbitror contigisse.

---

[1] The letters are those in a copy of one of Fronto's speeches that Marcus Aurelius has written out in his own hand.

T 71 Suetonius, *Lives of Illustrious Men. Grammarians and Rhetoricians*

M. Pompilius Andronicus,[1] a Syrian by birth, was considered too lazy in his teaching of grammar and less suitable for running a school because of his devotion to Epicurean philosophy. [2] When, therefore, he saw that he was regarded in the city [of Rome] as inferior not only to Antonius Gnipho,[2] but also to other, lesser teachers, he moved to Cumae, lived there at leisure and composed many works—[3] but so destitute and needy that he was forced to sell that remarkable little masterpiece of his, an examination of Ennius' *Annals*, to someone for 16,000 sesterces: Orbilius[3] says that he recovered these books, which had been kept out of circulation, and saw that they were made available under their author's name.

[1] A grammarian in the first half of the first century BC.

[2] A teacher of grammar and rhetoric at Rome in the first half of the first century BC (cf. T 111).

[3] L. Orbilius Pupillus, a grammarian and teacher at Rome in the first century BC (cf. Hor. *Epist.* 2.1.69–71).

T 72 (cf. T 107) Suetonius, *Lives of Illustrious Men. Virgil*

Once when he [Virgil] held Ennius in his hand and was asked what he was doing, he replied that he was gathering gold from Ennius' muck, for this poet has outstanding ideas buried under not very polished words.

T 73 Fronto, *Correspondence*

As many letters as there are,[1] so many consulships, so many laurels, triumphs, ceremonial robes, I believe, have

[4] quid tale M. Porcio aut Quinto Ennio, C. Graccho aut Titio poetae, quid Scipioni aut Numidico, quid M. Tullio tale usuvenit? quorum libri pretiosiores habentur et summam gloriam retinent, si sunt Lampadionis aut Staberii, Plautii aut D. Aurelii, Autriconis aut Aelii manu scripta e‹xem›pla aut a Tirone emendata aut a Domitio Balbo descripta aut ab Attico aut Nepote.

T 74 Fronto, Ad M. Caesarem et invicem libri, *Ep.* 3.17.3 (p. 49.18–23 van den Hout)

meministi autem tu plurimas lectiones, quibus usque adhuc versatus es, comoedias, Atellan‹a›s, oratores veteres, quorum aut pauci aut praeter Catonem et Gracchum nemo tubam inflat; omnes autem mugiunt vel stridunt potius. quid igitur Ennius egit, quem legisti? quid tragoediae ad versum sublimiter faciundum te iuverunt? plerumque enim ad orationem faciendam versus, ad versificandum oratio magis adiuvat.

T 75 Fronto, Ad M. Caesarem et invicem libri, *Ep.* 4.2.6 (p. 56.1–2 van den Hout)

Sota Ennianus remissus a te et in charta puriore et volumine gratiore et littera festiviore quam antea fuerat videtur.

been granted to me. [4] What fortune of this kind happened to Marcus Porcius [Cato] or Quintus Ennius, Gaius Gracchus or the poet Titius, what to Scipio[2] or Numidicus,[3] what to Marcus Tullius [Cicero]? Their books are regarded as more precious and retain the greatest distinction if copies are written by the hand of Lampadio or Staberius, Plautius or Decius Aurelius, Autrico or Aelius or corrected by Tiro or transcribed by Domitius Balbus or by Atticus or Nepos.[4]

[2] P. Cornelius Scipio Aemilianus Africanus (Numantinus) (185/4–129 BC, cos. 147 BC).   [3] Q. Caecilius Metellus Numidicus (cos. 109, cens. 102 BC).   [4] Scholars who edited or corrected works of the famous writers of prose and poetry just listed. For Lampadio as editor of Ennius, cf. Gell. *NA* 18.5.11 (T 85).

T 74 Fronto, *Correspondence*

You remember the very many readings with which you have been engaged so far: comedies, Atellan plays, old orators, of whom either few or nobody except Cato and Gracchus blow the trumpet, but they all rather bellow or shriek. So what did Ennius, whom you have read, achieve? How have the tragedies helped you make verse in a more elevated tone? For verse frequently aids the creation of oratory, but oratory aids the making of verse even more.

T 75 Fronto, *Correspondence* [Marcus Aurelius to Fronto]

Ennius' *Sota* as sent back by you seems to be on finer sheets and a more attractive volume and in better writing than it had been before.

T 76 Fronto, Ad M. Caesarem et invicem libri, *Ep.* 4.3.2
(pp. 56.18–57.1 van den Hout)

quamobrem rari admodum veterum scriptorum in eum
laborem studiumque et periculum verba industriosius
quaerendi sese commisere, oratorum post homines natos
unus omnium M. Porcius eiusque frequens sectator C.
Sallustius, poetarum maxime Plautus, multo maxime En-
nius eumque studiose aemulatus L. Coelius nec non Nae-
vius, Lucretius, Accius etiam, Caecilius, Laberius quoque.

T 77 Fronto, Ad Antoninum imp. et invicem libri, *Ep.* 4.1
(p. 105.13–18 van den Hout)

mitte mihi aliquid, quod tibi disertissimum videatur, quod
legam, vel tuum aut Catonis aut Ciceronis aut Sallustii aut
Gracchi aut poetae alicuius; χρήζω γὰρ ἀναπαύλης, et
maxime hoc genus, quae me lectio extollat et diffundat ἐκ
τῶν κατειληφυιῶν φροντίδων; etiam si qua Lucretii aut
Enni excerpta habes εὐφωνότατα, ἁδρά et sicubi ἤθους
ἐμφάσεις.

T 78 Fronto, Ad M. Antoninum de eloquentia, *Ep.* 1.2
(pp. 133.11–34.1 van den Hout)

in poetis ⟨aut⟩em quis ignorat, ut gracilis sit Lucilius,
Albucius aridus, sublimis Lucretius, mediocris Pacuvius,
inaequalis Accius, Ennius multiformis?

T 76 Fronto, *Correspondence*

For that reason only a few of the old writers devoted themselves to the toil, study, and risk of seeking out words more industriously: of orators from the beginnings of mankind, uniquely Marcus Porcius [Cato] and his frequent follower Sallust, of poets especially Plautus, most especially Ennius, and Lucius Coelius,[1] who zealously emulated him, and also Naevius, Lucretius, Accius as well, Caecilius[2] and also Laberius.[3]

[1] The historian L. Coelius Antipater (2nd c. BC).
[2] The comic poet Caecilius Statius (ca. 230/20–168/7 BC).
[3] The writer of mimes Decimus Laberius (ca. 106–43 BC).

T 77 Fronto, *Correspondence* [Antoninus Pius to Fronto]

Send me something to read that seems particularly eloquent to you, either of yours or by Cato or Cicero or Sallust or Gracchus or some poet; for I need relaxation, and particularly of such a kind that reading it lifts me up and frees me from the *douleurs* enveloping me; also, if you have any very euphonious excerpts of Lucretius or Ennius, in grand style and anything expressive of character.

T 78 Fronto, *Correspondence*

But as regards the poets, who does not know how plain is Lucilius, how austere Albucius,[1] how elevated Lucretius, how middling Pacuvius, how uneven Accius, how many-sided Ennius?

[1] Apparently a poet.

T 79 Fronto, Ad M. Antoninum de eloquentia, *Ep.* 2.12
(p. 141.5–9 van den Hout)

nam vinea in unius tutela dei sita, eloquentiam vero multi
in caelo diligunt: Minerva orationis magistra, Mercurius
nuntiis praeditus, Apollo paeanum auctor, Liber dithy-
ramborum cognitor, Fauni vaticinantium incitatores, ma-
gistra Homeri Calliopa, magister Enni Homerus et Som-
nus.

T 80 Fronto, Ad M. Antoninum de eloquentia, *Ep.* 4.4
(p. 148.10–11 van den Hout)

Ennium deinde et Accium et Lucretium ampliore iam
mugitu personantis tamen tolerant.

T 81 Fronto, De feriis Alsiensibus, *Ep.* 3.1 (p. 227.8–12
van den Hout)

nec dubito quin te ad ferias in secessu maritimo fruendas
ita compararis: in sole meridiano ut somno oboedires cu-
bans, deinde Nigrum vocares, libros introferre iuberes;
mox ut te studium legendi incessisset, ut te Plauto expo-
lires aut Accio expleres aut Lucretio delenires aut Ennio
incenderes, in horam istam Musarum propriam quintam
. . .

T 82 (= 8 *Ann.* F 12) Gell. *NA* 12.4

descriptum definitumque est a Q. Ennio in Annali septimo
graphice admodum sciteque sub historia Gemini Servili,

T 79 Fronto, *Correspondence*

For the vine is placed in the tutelage of a single god, but many in heaven care for eloquence: Minerva mistress of oratory, Mercury presiding over messages, Apollo the author of paeans, Liber the patron of dithyrambs, the Fauns inspirers of seers, Calliope the tutor of Homer, Homer and Sleep [bringing dreams] the tutors of Ennius.

T 80 Fronto, *Correspondence*

[On the development of poetry and its assessment] Then they nevertheless tolerate Ennius and Accius and Lucretius, already echoing with a deeper roar.

T 81 Fronto, *Correspondence*

I have no doubt that you [Marcus Aurelius] are prepared to enjoy the holiday at your seaside resort [Alsium] in this way: lying down in the midday sun you may yield to the demands of sleep, then call Niger [presumably a secretary or librarian], order him to bring books; then as soon as an eagerness to read has assailed you, you may polish yourself with Plautus or saturate yourself with Accius or soothe yourself with Lucretius or inflame yourself with Ennius, until the fifth hour, belonging to the Muses[1] . . .

[1] The meaning of this final phrase is "enigmatic" (van den Hout, commentary, p. 511). Some suspect a pun on *Quintus* Ennius.

T 82 (= 8 *Ann.* F 12) Gellius, *Attic Nights*

In the seventh book of the *Annals* Ennius describes and defines very vividly and skillfully in the story of Servilius

viri nobilis, quo ingenio, qua comitate, qua modestia, qua fide, qua linguae parsimonia, qua loquendi opportunitate, quanta rerum antiquarum morumque veterum ac novorum scientia quantaque servandi tuendique secreti religione, qualibus denique ad minuendas vitae molestias fomentis, levamentis, solaciis amicum esse conveniat hominis genere et fortuna superioris. [2] eos ego versus non minus frequenti adsiduoque memoratu dignos puto quam philosophorum de officiis decreta. [3] ad hoc color quidam vetustatis in his versibus tam reverendus est, suavitas tam inpromisca tamque a fuco omni remota est, ut mea quidem sententia pro antiquis sacratisque amicitiae legibus observandi, tenendi colendique sint. [4] quapropter adscribendos eos existimavi, si quis iam statim desideraret: . . . [5] L. Aelium Stilonem dicere solitum ferunt Q. Ennium de semet ipso haec scripsisse picturamque istam morum et ingenii ipsius Q. Ennii factam esse.

T 83 (= *Inc.* F 16) Gell. *NA* 17.17.1

Quintus Ennius tria corda habere sese dicebat, quod loqui Graece et Osce et Latine sciret.

T 84 Gell. *NA* 17.21.43–49

Claudium et Tuditanum consules secuntur Q. Valerius et C. Mamilius, quibus natum esse Q. Ennium poetam M. Varro in primo de poetis libro scripsit eumque, cum

---

[1] C. Claudius Centho and M. Sempronius Tuditanus were consuls in 240 BC, Q. Valerius Falto and C. Mamilius Turrinus in 239 BC.

Geminus,[1] a man of distinction, what natural disposition, what courtesy, what modesty, what fidelity, what restraint in speech, what propriety in speaking, what knowledge of ancient matters and customs old and new, what scrupulousness in keeping and guarding a confidence, in short, what remedies, forms of relief and solace for abating the annoyances of life the friend of a man superior in social class and fortune ought to have. [2] These verses I think no less worthy of frequent and assiduous recollection than the philosophers' rules about duties. [3] There is besides such a venerable aura of antiquity in these verses, such a sweetness unmixed and removed from all affectation that, in my opinion at least, they ought to be observed, remembered and nurtured like old and sacred laws of friendship. [4] I therefore thought them worth quoting, in case anyone desired to see them immediately: ". . ." [5] They say that Lucius Aelius Stilo[2] was accustomed to say that Ennius wrote this about himself and that this was a description made of Ennius' own character and disposition.

---

[1] Cn. Servilius Geminus (cos. 217 BC).   [2] L. Aelius Stilo Praeconinus (ca. 154–90 BC), an early Roman grammarian and teacher of Varro.

T 83 (= *Inc.* F 16) Gellius, *Attic Nights*

Quintus Ennius used to say that he had three hearts, because he knew how to speak Greek, Oscan, and Latin.

T 84 Gellius, *Attic Nights*

Claudius and Tuditanus were followed by the consuls Quintus Valerius and Gaius Mamilius,[1] in which year the poet Ennius was born, as Varro wrote in the first book of

septimum et sexagesimum annum ageret, duodecimum Annalem scripsisse idque ipsum Ennium in eodem libro dicere. [44] . . . [49] neque magno intervallo postea Q. Ennius et iuxta Caecilius et Terentius et subinde et Pacuvius et Pacuvio iam sene Accius clariorque tunc in poematis eorum obtrectandis Lucilius fuit.

T 85 (= 7 *Ann.* F 21) Gell. *NA* 18.5

cum Antonio Iuliano rhetore, viro hercle bono et facundiae florentis, complures adulescentuli familiares eius Puteolis aestivarum feriarum ludum et iocum in litteris amoenioribus et in voluptatibus pudicis honestisque agitabamus. [2] atque ibi tunc Iuliano nuntiatur ἀναγνώστην quendam, non indoctum hominem, voce admodum scita et canora Enii Annales legere ad populum in theatro. [3] eamus inquit auditum nescio quem istum Ennianistam: hoc enim se ille nomine appellari volebat. [4] quem cum iam inter ingentes clamores legentem invenissemus—legebat autem librum ex Annalibus Ennii septimum—, hos eum primum versus perperam pronuntiantem audivimus: denique vi magna quadrupes ecus atque elephanti / proiciunt sese, neque multis postea versibus additis celebrantibus eum laudantibusque omnibus discessit. [5] tum Iulianus egrediens e theatro quid vobis inquit de hoc anagnosta et de quadrupede eco videtur? sic enim profecto legit: denique vi magna quadrupes ecus atque ele-

---

[1] A rhetor from Spain, an older contemporary, teacher and friend of Gellius.   [2] The term recalls the itinerant performers of Homer called "Homeristai." See Starr 1989.

On poets, and he adds that he [Ennius], when in his sixty-seventh year, wrote the twelfth book of the *Annals* and that Ennius himself says so in the same book.[2] [44] . . . [49] Not much later were Ennius and soon after Caecilius and Terence and then also Pacuvius and, when Pacuvius was already old, Accius, and then, rather famous for criticizing their poems, Lucilius.

[2] This book number is challenged by Skutsch 1985, 674–76.

T 85 (= 7 *Ann.* F 21) Gellius, *Attic Nights*

A number of us young men, friends of his, were spending the summer holidays in playful recreation at Puteoli, with literary diversions and modest and honorable pleasures with the rhetorician Antonius Iulianus,[1] a genuinely fine man and of distinguished eloquence. [2] And there it was then announced to Iulianus that a certain professional reader, a man not without learning, was reciting Ennius' *Annals* in a quite refined and sonorous voice to the people in the theater. [3] "Let's go," he said, "to hear that 'Ennianist,' whoever he is": for that was the name by which the man wished to be called.[2] [4] When we had found him already reading to great applause—in fact, he was reading the seventh book of Ennius' *Annals*—, we first heard him delivering these lines incorrectly: "then with great force the four-footed horse [*quadrupes ecus*] and the elephants rush forward," and without adding many more verses after that, he departed to universal praise and applause. [5] Then Iulianus, as he was leaving the theater, said: "What do you think of this reader and the 'four-footed horse'?" For so indeed did he read: "then with great force the four-footed horse [*quadrupes ecus*] and the elephants rush for-

71

phanti / proiciunt sese. [6] ecquid putatis, si magistrum praelectoremque habuisset alicuius aeris, quadrupes ecus dicturum fuisse ac non quadrupes eques, quod ab Ennio ita scriptum relictumque esse nemo unus litterarum veterum diligens dubitavit? [7] cumque aliquot eorum, qui aderant, quadrupes ecus apud suum quisque grammaticum legisse se dicerent et mirarentur, quidnam esset quadrupes eques, vellem vos, inquit optimi iuvenes, tam accurate Q. Ennium legisse, quam P. Vergilius legerat, qui hunc eius versum secutus in georgicis suis equitem pro eco posuit his in versibus [Verg. G. 3.115–17]: frena Pelethronii Lapithae gyrosque dedere / impositi dorso atque equitem docuere sub armis / insultare solo et gressus glomerare superbos. in quo loco equitem, si quis modo non inscite inepteque argutior sit, nihil potest accipi aliud nisi ecum; [8] pleraque enim veterum aetas et hominem equo insidentem et equum, qui insideretur, equitem dixerunt. [9] propterea equitare etiam, quod verbum e vocabulo equitis inclinatum est, et homo eco utens et ecus sub homine gradiens dicebatur. [10] Lucilius adeo, vir adprime linguae Latinae sciens, ecum equitare dicit his versibus [Lucil. 1284–86 M. = 1250–52 W.]: quis hunc currere ecum nos atque equitare videmus, / his equitat curritque: oculis equitare videmus; / ergo oculis equitat. [11] sed enim contentus inquit ego his non fui et, ut non turbidae fidei nec ambiguae, sed ut purae liquentisque esset, ecusne an eques scriptum Ennius reliquisset, librum summae atque reverendae vetustatis, quem fere constabat Lampadionis manu emendatum, studio pretioque multo

---

3 Now generally taken to mean "horseman."

4 C. Octavius Lampadio, a grammarian at Rome in the second century BC (cf. T 73). This book was likely a forgery.

ward." [6] Don't you think that, if he had had a teacher and reading trainer worth a cent, he would have said *quadrupes ecus* and not *quadrupes eques*, which not a single person devoted to old literature doubted was what Ennius wrote and left behind?" [7] And when several of those present said that each had read *quadrupes ecus* with his own grammar teacher and wondered what *quadrupes eques* meant, he said: "I might wish, you fine young men, that you had read Ennius as carefully as Virgil had read him, who, adopting this verse of his [Ennius] in his *Georgics*, substituted *eques* for *ecus* in the following lines: 'The Pelethronian [Thessalian] Lapiths, sitting on horseback, gave us the bridle and the wheeling course and taught the horse[3] to gallop over the ground in arms and to round its proud paces.' In this passage, if only one is not overly clever and subtle to a fault, *eques* cannot be understood in any way other than *ecus* ['horse']; [8] for most people in an earlier age called both the man sitting on a horse and the horse on which he sits *eques.* [9] Therefore *equitare*, too, which is the verb derived from the noun *eques*, was used both of a human riding a horse and of a horse carrying the man. [10] Even Lucilius, a man extremely knowledgeable about the Latin language, says 'a horse rides' in these verses: 'whereby we see this horse race and ride, thereby it rides and races: with eyes we see it ride; therefore with eyes it rides.'" [11] "But," he [the speaker, Sulpicius Apollinaris] said, "I was not satisfied with these examples and, so that it should not be left murky and ambiguous, but clear and apparent whether Ennius had left *ecus* or *eques* in his text, I procured by much effort and expense a book of very great and venerable antiquity, which was almost certainly corrected by Lampadio's[4]

unius versus inspiciendi gratia conduxi et eques, non ecus, scriptum in eo versu inveni. [12] hoc tum nobis Iulianus et multa alia erudite simul et adfabiliter dixit. sed eadem ipsa post etiam in pervulgatis commentariis scripta offendimus.

T 86 Fest., p. 374.3–11 L.

SOLITAURILIA: . . . quod si a sollo et tauris earum hostiarum ductum est nomen antiquae consuetudinis, per unum l enuntiari non est mirum, quia nulla tunc geminabatur littera in scribendo: quam consuetudinem Ennius mutavisse fertur, utpote Graecus Graeco more usus, quod illi aeque scribentes ac legentes duplicabant mutas, semi-<vocales . . .

T 87 *CIL* XIII 3710 B 1

Ennius.

T 88 *Pan. Lat.* 9.7.3 (Eumenius)

aedem Herculis Musarum in circo Flaminio Fulvius ille Nobilior ex pecunia censoria fecit, non id modo secutus

hand, for the sake of examining this one verse, and I found *eques*, not *ecus*, written in this verse." [12] This and many other things did Iulianus then tell us, in a learned and at the same time friendly manner. But later we came across these very remarks written in widely available handbooks.

T 86 Festus

SOLITAURILIA:[1] . . . But if the name of this ancient custom [*solitaurilia*] is derived from *sollus* ["whole"] and *tauri* ["bulls"] among those sacrificial victims, it is not surprising that it is expressed by a single *l*, since no letter was then doubled in writing: Ennius is said to have changed this practice, as a Greek employing a Greek convention, since they, in both writing and reading, used to double mute consonants, half-vowels . . .

[1] A corruption of *suovetaurilia* (a sacrifice consisting of a boar, a ram, and a bull). Ancient grammarians derived it from *sollus*.

T 87 An Inscription

Ennius.[1]

[1] Caption on a mosaic floor ("Monnus Mosaic") found in Trier (Germany) and dated to ca. 3rd cent. AD. Ennius is depicted among other Greek and Roman writers, including Menander, Virgil, and Cicero.

T 88 *Panegyricus Latinus* (Eumenius)

The famous Fulvius Nobilior [censor in 179 BC; cf. T 10] built the temple of Hercules of the Muses in the Circus Flaminius [cf. Macrob. *Sat.* 1.12.16] with the censors' funds, pursuing this not only because he was induced by

quod ipse litteris et summi poetae amicitia duceretur, sed
quod, in Graecia cum esset imperator, acceperat Heraclen
Musageten esse, id est comitem ducemque Musarum,
idemque primus novem signa, hoc est omnium, Camena-
rum ex Ambraciensi oppido translata sub tutela fortissimi
numinis consecravit, ut res est, quia mutuis opibus et
praemiis iuvari ornarique deberent, Musarum quies de-
fensione Herculis et virtus Herculis {et} voce Musarum.

T 89 Arn. *Adv. nat.* 4.29

et possumus quidem hoc in loco omnes istos, nobis quos
inducitis atque appellatis deos, homines fuisse monstrare
vel Agragantino Euhemero replicato, cuius libellos En-
nius, clarum ut fieret cunctis, sermonem in Italum transtu-
lit, vel Nicagora Cyprio vel Pellaeo Leonte vel Cyrenensi
Theodoro vel Hippone ac Diagora Meliis vel auctoribus
aliis mille, qui scrupolosae diligentiae cura in lucem res
abditas libertate ingenua protulerunt.

literature and his friendship with the greatest poet [Ennius], but because he had learned, when he was commander in Greece, that Heracles was Musagetes, i.e., the companion and leader of the Muses. He was also the first to dedicate the nine statues of the Camenae [Muses], that is of all of them, that he had brought from the town of Ambracia under the protection of the strongest divinity [Hercules], as the case is, since they ought to be supported and adorned by mutual resources and rewards, the quiet of the Muses by the protection of Hercules and the virtue of Hercules by the voice of the Muses.

T 89 Arnobius, *Against the Pagans*

And we can indeed show at this point that all those you mention to us and call gods were human beings, either by replicating Euhemerus of Acragas,[1] whose books Ennius translated into the language of Italy to make them well known to all, or Nicagoras of Cyprus[2] or Leon of Pella[3] or Theodoros of Cyrene[4] or Hippo[5] and Diagoras from Melos[6] or a thousand other authors, who, in the interest of scrupulous diligence, have brought hidden things to light with frank liberty.

---

[1] Lat. Agrigentum, a town in Sicily. Only here and in Clement of Alexandria (Clem. Al. *Protr.* 2.24.2) is Euhemerus said to come from Acragas. Elsewhere he is associated with Messene (presumably also in Sicily).   [2] A paradoxographer around 400 BC.   [3] Allegedly an Egyptian priest promoting doctrines about the gods.   [4] A Cyrenaic philosopher (ca. 340–250 BC).   [5] An early natural philosopher.   [6] A lyric poet of the fifth century BC (cf. F 738–39 *PMG*).

T 90 Claud. *Cons. Stil.* III (= *Carm.* 23), Praef. 1–20

maior Scipiades, Italis qui solus ab oris
in proprium vertit Punica bella caput,
non sine Pieriis exercuit artibus arma.
semper erat vatum maxima cura duci.
5   gaudet enim virtus testes sibi iungere Musas;
carmen amat quisquis carmine digna gerit.
ergo seu patriis primaevus Manibus ultor
subderet Hispanum legibus Oceanum,
seu Tyrias certa fracturus cuspide vires
10   inferret Libyco signa tremenda mari:
haerebat doctus lateri castrisque solebat
omnibus in medias Ennius ire tubas.
illi post lituos pedites favere canenti
laudavitque nova caede cruentus eques.
15   cumque triumpharet gemina Carthagine victa
(hanc vindex patri viceret, hanc patriae),
cum longi Libyam tandem post funera belli
ante suas maestam cogeret ire rotas:
advexit reduces secum Victoria Musas
20   et sertum vati Martia laurus erat.

T 91 (cf. T 38, 97) [Aurel. Vict.] *Vir. ill.* 47.1

Marcus Porcius Cato . . . : in praetura Sardiniam subegit,
ubi ab Ennio Graecis litteris institutus.

---

[1] Cato served as praetor in Sardinia in 198 BC, but the connection with Ennius more likely dates to a visit there in 204, when Cato was a quaestor (T 38, 97).

T 90 Claudian, *On Stilicho's Consulship*

The elder Scipio,[1] who single-handedly diverted the Punic War from the Italian shores to their [the Carthaginians'] own capital, wielded arms not without the arts of the Pierides [Muses]: as leader, the cultivation of poets was always very important to him, [5] for prowess enjoys recruiting the Muses as witnesses for itself; whoever does things worthy of a poem loves a poem. Thus, whether, at a young age, he subjected the Spanish ocean to our laws as avenger of his father's shade[2] or whether, to break Tyrian [Carthaginian] forces with a sure lance, [10] he brought to the Libyan sea standards to be feared, learned Ennius clung to his side and was accustomed in all campaigns to go right among the bugles. After the war trumpets, the infantry loved his singing, and the cavalry, bloody with fresh slaughter, praised him. [15] And when he [Scipio] celebrated triumphs, after the twin cities of Carthage[3] had been conquered (one he conquered as avenger of this father, the other of his country), when he at last, after the ruin of a long war, forced mournful Libya to walk before his chariot, Victory brought the returning Muses with her, [20] and Mars' laurel was a garland for the poet.

[1] P. Cornelius Scipio Africanus (ca. 236–183 BC, cos. 205 BC).   [2] P. Cornelius Scipio (cos. 218 BC), fell in Spain in 211 BC fighting the Carthaginians.   [3] Carthago in Africa (near modern Tunis) and Carthago Nova in Spain.

T 91 (cf. T 38, 97) [Aurelius Victor], *On Famous Men*

Marcus Porcius Cato . . . : during his praetorship he conquered Sardinia, where he was instructed in Greek literature by Ennius.[1]

T 92 *Vir. ill.* 52.1–3

Quintus Fulvius Nobilior consul Vettonas Oretanosque
superavit, unde ovans urbem introiit. [2] consul Aetolos,
qui bello Macedonico Romanis affuerant, post ad Antio-
chum defecerant, proeliis frequentibus victos et in Am-
braciam oppidum coactos in deditionem accepit, tamen
signis tabulisque pictis spoliavit; de quibus triumphavit.
[3] quam victoriam per se magnificam Ennius amicus eius
insigni laude celebravit.

T 93 Diom., *GL* I, p. 484.3–7

epos Latinum primus digne scripsit is qui res Romanorum
decem et octo complexus est libris, qui et Annales ‹in›scri-
buntur, quod singulorum fere annorum actus contineant,
sicut publici annales, quos pontifices scribaeque conficiunt,
vel Romani{s},[1] quod Romanorum res gestas declarant.

[1] Romani *Vahlen*: Romanis *codd.*: *an* Roma{n}is (*cf., e.g., The-
bais*) *legendum?*

T 94 Diom., *GL* I, p. 485.32–34

et olim carmen, quod ex variis poematibus constabat, sa-
tira vocabatur, quale scripserunt Pacuvius et Ennius.

T 92 [Aurelius Victor], *On Famous Men*

Quintus Fulvius Nobilior,[1] as consul [189 BC], defeated the Vettones[2] and the Oretani,[3] whence he entered the city [of Rome] celebrating an ovation.[4] [2] As consul, he accepted the surrender of the Aetolians, who had supported the Romans in the Macedonian War [200–197 BC] and later defected to Antiochus,[5] having defeated them in frequent battles and forcing them into the town of Ambracia; he nevertheless stripped them of statues and paintings; he celebrated a triumph over them. [3] This victory, magnificent in itself, his friend Ennius celebrated with memorable praise.

[1] Actually Marcus (a confusion between father and son; cf. T 20).   [2] A Celtic people in Lusitania.   [3] A Celtiberian people in Iberia.   [4] He celebrated an ovation in 191 and a triumph in 187 BC.   [5] King Antiochus III Megas, son of Seleucus II Callinicus.

T 93 Diomedes

He was the first to write a Latin epic worthy of the name, he who covered the affairs of the Romans in eighteen books, which are entitled *Annals* because they include the events of nearly every year in order, just as the public Annals do, which the priests and scribes produce, or *Roman* [*Books*], because they make known the deeds of the Romans.

T 94 Diomedes

And a kind of composition that consisted of various poems was once called satire, such as Pacuvius and Ennius wrote.

81

T 95 Symm. *Ep.* 1.20.2

. . . Ennio ex Aetolicis manubiis captiva tantum chlamys
data Fulvium decolorat . . .

T 96 Symm. *Or.* 3.7

servetur tibi aliquod opus virtutis in posterum, cui nihil
iam remansit ignotum. quas habes laboris indutias? tro-
paeis et litteris occupatus otiosa cum bellicis negotia mis-
cuisti. agnosco in te non adumbrata vestigiis sed expressa
veterum signa virtutum: nempe Fulvium nobilem tam
laude quam nomine inter aquilas cantusque lituorum
praeceptor Accius frequentavit; Africanum illum terra
marique victorem lectionis particeps et laboris Panaetius
non reliquit; cum magno Alexandro mundanam paene
militiam philosophorum comitatus exegit.

T 97 Hieron. *Ab Abr.* 1777 [240 a. C.] (p. 133a Helm)

Quintus Ennius poeta Tarenti nascitur. qui a Catone
quaestore Romam translatus habitavit in monte Aventino
parco admodum sumptu contentus et unius ancillulae
ministerio.

---

[1] Actually Rudiae (T 9, 47b, 48, 53, 57, 71), but a reference to
the "theater capital" in southern Italy might have seemed more
appropriate for Ennius.

T 95 Symmachus, *Correspondence*

[to Ausonius] . . . the gift to Ennius of only a Greek cloak seized from the booty from Aetolia brings shame upon Fulvius[1] . . .

[1] M. Fulvius Nobilior (cos. 189 BC); cf. T 10, 20, 29, 92, 96.

T 96 Symmachus, *Orations*

Some work of virtue may be reserved in future for you,[1] for whom nothing has yet remained unknown. What respite do you have from labor? Engaged with victories and literature, you have mixed the business of leisure with the business of war. I recognize in you signs of the old virtues, not with shadowy traces, but clearly expressed: surely Accius,[2] as tutor, plentifully supplied the noble Fulvius[3] as much with praise as with a name amid eagles and the sounds of war trumpets; Panaetius,[4] engaged in the labor of reading, did not abandon the famous Africanus,[5] victorious on land and sea; with the great Alexander an entourage of philosophers carried out military service practically worldwide.

[1] Flavius Gratianus (359–383, emperor 367–383 AD).   [2] Actually Ennius; cf. T 10, 20, 29.   [3] M. Fulvius Nobilior (cos. 189 BC); cf. T 10, 20, 29, 92, 95.   [4] The Stoic philosopher (ca. 185–109 BC).   [5] P. Cornelius Scipio Aemilianus Africanus (Numantinus) (185/4–129 BC, cos. 147 BC).

T 97 Jerome, on the year 240 BC

The poet Quintus Ennius is born at Tarentum.[1] Having been brought to Rome by the quaestor Cato [cf. T 38], he lived on the Aventine Hill, satisfied with only a modest income and the service of a single maid [cf. T 14].

T 98 Hieron. *Ab Abr.* 1838 [179 a. C.] (p. 138b Helm)

Statius Caecilius comoediarum scriptor clarus habetur, natione Insuber Gallus et Ennii primum contubernalis. . . . mortuus est anno post mortem Ennii et iuxta Ianiculum sepultus.

T 99 Hieron. *Ab Abr.* 1849 [168 a. C.] (p. 140a Helm)

Ennius poeta septuagenario maior articulari morbo perit sepultusque in Scipionis monumento via Appia intra primum ab urbe miliarium. quidam ossa eius Rudiam ex Ianiculo translata adfirmant.

T 100 Hieron. *In Mich.* 2, praef.

si enim criminis est Graecorum benedicta transferre, accusentur Ennius et Maro, Plautus [Ter. *An.* 18–19], Caecilius et Terentius, Tullius quoque et ceteri eloquentes viri, qui non solum versus, sed multa capita et longissimos libros ac fabulas integras transtulerunt.

T 101 Hieron. *In Mich.* 2.7.5/7, ll. 250–54

sed et poeta sublimis—non Homerus alter, ut Lucilius de Ennio suspicatur, sed primus Homerus apud Latinos [cf. Lucil. 1189 M. = 413 W.; Hor. *Epist.* 2.1.50 (T 48a)]—: varium et mutabile semper / femina [Verg. *Aen.* 4.569–70].

T 98 Jerome, on the year 179 BC

Caecilius Statius, a writer of comedies, is considered famous, an Insubrian Gaul by nationality and initially a housemate of Ennius. . . . He died a year after Ennius' death [169 BC] and is buried by the Janiculum.

T 99 Jerome, on the year 168 BC

The poet Ennius died at the age of more than seventy[1] from a joint illness and was buried in the tomb of Scipio on the Via Appia within the first milestone from the city. Some claim that his bones were transferred to Rudiae from the Janiculum.

> [1] Traditionally, Ennius' dates are 239 to 169 BC (T 18, 29, 33, 84), but since his birth is dated to 240 BC in this source (T 97), his life stretches to more than seventy years.

T 100 Jerome, *Commentary on Micah*

For if it is a crime to translate what the Greeks have expressed well, Ennius and Maro [Virgil] should be accused, Plautus, Caecilius, and Terence, also Tullius [Cicero] and other eloquent men, who have translated not only verses, but also many chapters and very long books and entire plays.

T 101 Jerome, *Commentary on Micah*

But the sublime poet too [Virgil]—not another Homer, as Lucilius imagined with regard to Ennius, but the first Homer among the Latins—: "a woman is something fickle and always changing."

T 102 Ser. *Med.* 704–7

. . . , simul et Baccheia dona
705   sumere curabis: nimio sed parcito vino:
Ennius ipse pater, dum pocula siccat iniqua,
hoc vitio tales fertur meruisse dolores.

T 103 Serv. ad Verg. *Aen.* 7.691

at Messapus equum domitor Neptuna proles: hic Messapus per mare ad Italiam venit, unde Neptuni dictus est filius: . . . ab hoc Ennius dicit se originem ducere, unde nunc et cantantes inducit eius socios et eos comparat cycnis.

T 104 Macrob. *Sat.* 6.3.9

nemo ex hoc viles putet veteres poetas, quod versus eorum scabri nobis videntur. ille enim stilus Enniani saeculi auribus solus placebat, et diu laboravit aetas secuta ut magis huic molliori filo adquiesceretur.

T 105 Macrob. *Sat.* 6.9.9

bene inquit Servius haec tibi quaestio nata est ex incuria veteris lectionis. nam quia saeculum nostrum ab Ennio et omni bibliotheca vetere descivit, multa ignoramus, quae non laterent si veterum lectio nobis esset familiaris. . . .

---

[1] The grammarian, one of Macrobius' interlocutors.

T 102 Serenus, *Liber Medicinalis*

At the same time see to taking the gifts of Bacchus, but refrain from too much wine: father Ennius himself, while he drained excessively large goblets, is said to have earned such pains by this vice.[1]

[1] For Ennius' drinking cf. T 44, and for a probable allusion to the consequent gout, T 99, *Sat.* F 13.

T 103 Servius, *Commentary on Virgil*

"but Messapus, tamer of horses, Neptune's offspring": This Messapus came to Italy over the sea, from which fact he was called Neptune's son: . . . Ennius claims to trace his origin from him, and from this he [Virgil] here introduces his [Messapus'] companions singing and compares them to swans [cf. *Aen.* 7.698–702].

T 104 Macrobius, *Saturnalia*

Nobody should regard the ancient poets as unworthy of esteem for the reason that their verses seem rough to us, for that was the only style to please the ears of Ennius' age, and succeeding generations labored long to grow comfortable with this much finer thread.

T 105 Macrobius, *Saturnalia*

"Of course," said Servius,[1] "this question has arisen for you because the ancient texts are neglected: since our age has abandoned Ennius and the whole library of ancient authors, we are ignorant of many things that would not lie hidden if the reading of the ancients were our custom . . ."

T 106 *SHA*, Hadr. (1) 16.5–6

amavit praeterea genus vetustum dicendi. controversias declamavit. [6] Ciceroni Catonem, Vergilio En⟨n⟩ium, Sallustio Coelium praetulit eademque iactatione de Homero ac Platone iudicavit.

T 107 (cf. T 72) Cassiod. *Inst.* 1.1.8

cui et illud convenienter aptari potest quod Vergilius, dum Ennium legeret, a quodam quid ageret inquisitus, respondit: aurum in stercore quaero.

T 108 Isid. *Orig.* 1.22.1

vulgares notas Ennius primus mille et centum invenit.

T 109 (= *Inc.* F 3)

a Isid. *Orig.* 1.39.6

hexametros autem Latinos primum fecisse Ennius traditur; eosque longos vocat.

b Isid. *Orig.* 1.39.15

hic autem vix omnino constat a quo sit inventus [i.e., elegiacus versus], nisi quia apud nos Ennius eum prior usus

T 106 *Historia Augusta*

Moreover, he[1] loved the ancient way of speaking. He declaimed forensic practice speeches [*controversiae*]. [6] He preferred Cato to Cicero, Ennius to Virgil, Coelius[2] to Sallust, and he judged Homer and Plato with the same arrogance.

[1] The emperor Hadrian (r. 117–138 AD).   [2] The historian L. Coelius Antipater (2nd c. BC).

T 107 (cf. T 72) Cassiodorus, *Introduction to Divine and Human Readings*

To whom [Origen] that too could conveniently be applied, namely what Virgil, while reading Ennius, answered when asked by someone what he was doing: "I am looking for gold in the muck."

T 108 Isidore, *Origins*

Ennius was the first to devise 1,100 common symbols.[1]

[1] Apparently stenographic abbreviations.

T 109 (= *Inc.* F 3)

a Isidore, *Origins*

Ennius, moreover, is said to have composed Latin hexameters for the first time, and he calls them "long."

b Isidore, *Origins*

In fact it is scarcely clear by whom it [elegiac verse] was invented, except that among us Ennius was the first to use it. Among the Greeks, the grammarians' controversy re-est. nam apud Graecos sic adhuc lis Grammaticorum pendet ut sub iudice res relegata sit.

T 110 Schol. Bern. ad Verg. *G.* 1.477

pallentia, ut Lucretius ait [1 *Ann.* t 2] pallidum Homerum ad Ennium venisse et loquutum illi hexametris antea Latina lingua inauditis.

T 111 (= 10 *Ann.* F 3) Schol. Bern. ad Verg. *G.* 2.119

"acanthi": Gnifo [F 1 *GRF*] commentatur Annalium libro decimo hanc arborem in insula Cercina regionis Africae esse oportunam tincturae, quae in floris sui colorem lanam tinguat, unde vestis Acanthia appellatur.

T 112 *Gloss.* 2.11 (*CGF* I, p. 73 Kaibel = *Gloss. Lat.* I, p. 568 Lindsay)

tragoedias autem Ennius fere omnes ex Graecis transtulit, plurimas ‹ex› Euripide‹i›s, nonnullas Aristarchiis.

mains unresolved to such an extent that the matter continues to be in dispute [cf. Hor. *Ars P.* 78].

T 110 Scholia Bernensia to Virgil, *Georgics*

"pale" [i.e., images], as Lucretius [1 *Ann.* t 2] says that a pale Homer came to Ennius and spoke to him in hexameters, not previously heard in the Latin language.

T 111 (= 10 *Ann.* F 3) Scholia Bernensia to Virgil, *Georgics*

"acanthus": Gnipho[1] comments on the tenth book of the *Annals* that this tree on the isle of Cercina [near Tunisia] in the region of Africa is suitable for dying; this dyes wool the color of its flower, whence the garment is called "Acanthian."

[1] M. Antonius Gnipho, a teacher of grammar and rhetoric at Rome in the first half of the first century BC (cf. T 71; for testimonia and fragments cf. pp. 98–100 *GRF*).

T 112 *Glossaria Latina*

Moreover, Ennius translated almost all his tragedies from Greek ones, most from those by Euripides, some from those by Aristarchus.[1]

[1] Aristarchus, a Greek tragedian in the time of Euripides (14 *TrGF*); cf. *Ach.* t 1.

T 113 (cf. T 56) *Suda* s.v. Ἔννιος (II, p. 285 Adler, E 1348)

Ἔννιος, Ῥωμαῖος ποιητής· ὃν Αἰλιανὸς ἐπαινεῖν ἄξιόν φησι. Σκιπίωνα γὰρ ᾄδων καὶ ἐπὶ μέγα τὸν ἄνδρα ἐξᾶραι βουλόμενός φησι μόνον ἂν Ὅμηρον ἐπαξίους ἐπαίνους εἰπεῖν Σκιπίωνος. δῆλον δὲ ὡς ἐτεθήπει τοῦ ποιητοῦ τὴν μεγαλόνοιαν καὶ τῶν μέτρων τὸ μεγαλεῖον καὶ ἀξιάγαστον· καὶ ὡς ἐπαινέσαι δεινὸς Ὅμηρός ἐστι καὶ κλέος ἀνδρὸς πυργῶσαί τε καὶ ἆραι, ἐξ ὧν ἐπήνεσε τὸν Ἀχιλλέα καλῶς ἠπίστατο ὁ ποιητὴς ὁ Μεσσάπιος.

T 114 *Anecdoton Parisinum* (GL VII, p. 534.4–6 Keil)

his [i.e., notis] solis in adnotationibus {H}Ennii, Luci⟨li⟩i[1] et historicorum[2] usi sunt Varro, S. Ennius,[3] Aelius[4] aequ{a}e et postremo Probus, qui illas in Virgilio et Horatio et Lucretio apposuit, ut ⟨in⟩ Homero Aristarchus.

[1] *Bergk*
[2] scaenicorum *L. Mueller*
[3] *Timpanaro:* varrus hennius *cod.*
[4] *edd.:* haelius *cod.*

T 113 (cf. T 56) *Suda*

Ennius, a Roman poet, who Aelian[1] says merits praise. Singing of Scipio[2] and wishing to exalt the man to greatness, he [Ennius] says that only Homer could compose praises worthy of Scipio. It is clear that he had been amazed by the poet's genius and the grandeur and worth of his meters, and that the Messapian poet well understood from the way he [Homer] praised Achilles that Homer was capable of praising and of raising to a towering height and exalting the glory of a man.

[1] A sophist of the second century AD.
[2] Probably in the poem named after Scipio.

T 114 *Anecdoton Parisinum*

In the annotations on Ennius, Lucilius, and the historians, Varro, Sextus Ennius[1] and Aelius[2] used only these [critical signs], and so eventually did Probus,[3] who set them in Virgil, Horace, and Lucretius, as Aristarchus[4] did in Homer.

[1] Presumably the so-called grammarian Ennius (T 69), though the text is uncertain.

[2] L. Aelius Stilo Praeconinus (ca. 154–90 BC), a Roman grammarian (cf. T 82).

[3] Valerius Probus, a Roman grammarian of the second half of the first century AD.

[4] The Alexandrian grammarian (ca. 216–144 BC).

EPIC FRAGMENTS

THE *ANNALS*

INTRODUCTION

Ennius' career, like that of so many early Roman poets, began with drama. In 189 BC he accompanied the consul Marcus Fulvius Nobilior to Aetolia as a dramatist and returned as a dramatist, celebrating Fulvius' victory there with a *praetexta* play called *Ambracia*, and he continued to write plays until the very year of his death (T 19). But that was not all. The experience in Aetolia also inspired, or at least helped to shape, a different project, a record in hexameter verse of Rome's story from its founding by Trojan refugees under Aeneas to the grand achievements of Ennius' own day. The resulting poem, the *Annals*, became a major landmark in the history of Roman poetry, and as epic gradually superseded tragedy in prestige, Ennius' reputation came increasingly to rest on his achievement as an epic poet.[1] Though his poem would eventually surren-

[1] Prinzen 1998, 94–205; Goldschmidt 2013, 18–35. The frequency of direct speech in the extant fragments, rightly stressed by Elliott 2007, 43–44, may well be the legacy of Ennius' career as a dramatist. Feeney 2016, 183–95, emphasizes the growing importance of texts and thus text-based genres like epic in the Roman experience of literature, but contrast Wiseman 2015, 63–70, on the possibility of Ennius as public performer.

der to Virgil's *Aeneid* its status as Rome's defining epic, its influence endured for centuries, and its remains have been assiduously collected since the Renaissance. The resulting mass of quotations, paraphrases, allusions, and echoes has enabled subsequent generations of scholars to develop a fairly coherent picture of the *Annals'* content, structure, and style.

The poem appears to have narrated the major events of each year in roughly chronological order, originally filling fifteen book rolls that can be arranged in five groups of three: Books 1 to 3 from the arrival of Aeneas through the expulsion of the Tarquins, Books 4 to 6 from the conquest of Italy through the defeat of Pyrrhus, Books 7 to 9 on the Punic Wars, Books 10 to 12 on affairs in Greece, and Books 13 to 15 on the wars with Seleucus and then, finally, Nobilior's victory at Ambracia. Major proems opened Books 1 (F 1–10) and 7 (F 1–2), with smaller ones introducing Books 6 (F 1) and 10 (F 1). In old age Ennius seems to have returned to the project, introducing with a new preface a final triad dedicated to campaigns of the 170s (16 *Ann.* F 1–5). The work was ambitious in more than mere scale. Abandoning the Saturnian meter of his predecessors Livius Andronicus and Naevius in favor of the dactylic hexameter made available a fuller range of Homeric mannerisms and enabled Ennius to incorporate specific, recognizable echoes of Homeric contexts. His Roman subject matter thus acquired a heroic gloss and openly invited comparison with the Greek poetic tradition. Its metrical innovation also facilitated the technical improvements in diction and verse structure needed to sustain a composition of such length. Yet Ennius might also sacrifice poetic artistry to the demands of chronicle and sometimes struggled, not always successfully, with the awkwardness of contemporary Latin idiom. Nearly two centuries later, Propertius and Ovid would find the *Annals* crude and unkempt (T 51–55), while Virgil, who had clearly ransacked it for useful diction, images, and tropes, was said to have compared the task to seeking gold in a dung heap (T 72, 107).

The poem's orientation in telling this story is traditionally regarded as aristocratic. Its very structure is often said to be modeled on the annual record of events maintained by the Pontifex Maximus, the so-called *Annales Maximi*, with Ennius ever mindful of the interests of the important individuals who supported his work. Most notable among those individuals was Fulvius Nobilior, whose dedication of a temple to Hercules of the Muses with spoils from Ambracia may have provided a fitting climax to the original, fifteen-book endeavor. Ennius had, after all, been swept off to Aetolia like the court poet of some Hellenistic dynast (T 29), and he obliged Fulvius with a celebratory work (*Ambracia*) as once he had indulged Africanus (*Scipio*). Why would the *Annals*, too, not have reflected the obligations of a *poeta cliens*?

This view of the poem's structure, style, and ideology, widely accepted in outline if still debated in points of detail, found its clearest expression in the edition of Otto Skutsch (1985), who dedicated much of his career to establishing as accurately as possible what Ennius wrote and reconstructing as much as he could of the poem's original design. Yet Skutsch's work did not prove definitive. The very clarity and precision of his explication stimulated a new wave of interest in the poem, and this fresh scrutiny challenged in significant ways a century and more of scholarly assumptions. Much truth remains in the traditional view as set out above, and much is still to be learned from the traditional commentaries, but many of the old verities have become much harder to maintain.

First among these is the idea that Ennius modeled his work in some meaningful way on records maintained by the Pontifex Maximus and gave it a title to recall that model. Poem and chronicle were certainly associated by late antiquity (T 93; cf. 4 *Ann.* F 4), but the connection is almost certainly anachronistic. The very existence of so extensive a chronicle for Ennius to consult in the early second century is now widely questioned, replaced by a growing sense that poetic narrative at Rome preceded continuous prose narrative. Ennius' title is, on that view, more likely to be his own coinage than an allusion to a public document, and he was thus, in an important sense, himself Rome's first annalist.[2]

The role that aristocratic connections played in the creation of Ennius' narrative has also been subject to significant revision. The connections themselves are beyond doubt, and it must be acknowledged that no treatment of contemporary events could have avoided political overtones of one kind or another. The further idea that Ennius tailored his narrative to suit the partisan interests of individual patrons is, however, yielding to a more nuanced

[2] The association of poem with priestly annals is made by Skutsch 1985, 2–6; Beck and Walter 2001, 40–41. For recent views of the *Annales Maximi*, still a debated topic, see Rich in *FRHist* 1:141–59, and for their relation to Ennius' poem, Gildenhard 2003; Rüpke 2006, 508–12; Elliott 2013, 23–78, 71–74.

view that recognizes in the very sweep of the story he tells the subordination of personal interests to larger community values.[3]

The methods traditionally employed to reconstruct its narrative by identifying the subject and sequence of its fragments have also come into question. Where Skutsch might confidently cite the context of a Virgilian echo as evidence for an underlying Ennian context or deduce an Ennian context from a narrative detail or a phrase also found in Livy, critics have grown more skeptical of a procedure that postulates echoes and then bases reconstructions upon them.[4] On a more positive note, greater sensitivity to literary nuance has dissolved the artificial distinction between poetic style and chronicle style that long shadowed the evaluation of this poem, while increasing resistance to the teleological bias of traditional literary history has generated greater interest in and more sympathy for what was once dismissed as "archaic" style. Ennius' standing as an artist and innovator has risen accordingly as critics become more willing to understand

[3] Fabrizi 2012, 15–28; Elliott 2013, 40–42; and for the poem's place in a developing literary culture at Rome, Rüpke 2001.

[4] The recovery of lost Ennius from extant Virgil, encouraged by the mass of comparative material preserved by Servius and Macrobius, was a procedure established by Norden 1915, whose comparative method is taken up *passim* by Skutsch. See the table of perceived verbal parallels between *Annals* and *Aeneid* in Goldschmidt 2013, 197–218, whose own study adds an intertextual twist. For the limitations of such Virgiliocentric criticism, see Wigodsky 1972, 55–62; Elliott 2013, 75–134.

and appreciate his literary experiments on their own terms rather than to accept at face value the verdicts of later Roman readers.[5]

Whether the triadic structure observed in the ruin of Ennius' poem was part of its plan from the beginning is unknown. Virgil, so the ancient story goes, outlined his poem in advance and worked from prose summaries of its twelve books, but not even that level of authority survives to support the assumption that Ennius mapped out his entire work before proceeding.[6] The distribution of fragments is too heavily skewed toward Book 1 to reveal more general principles of organization or to identify changes in metrical practice that might suggest an order of composition. To plan from the beginning to write a verse history of Rome in fifteen books, from the arrival of Aeneas to Fulvius at Ambracia, would in any case have been unprec-

[5] Prinzen 1998, 437–47, provides an overview of Ennius' poetic style. For the aesthetic merits of the *Annals* in particular, contrast the circumscribed praise of Otis 1963, 21–23, with the more detailed, sympathetic discussions of Dominik in Boyle 1993, 48–55; Goldberg 1995, 83–110; Gildenhard 2003, 97–102; for changing attitudes toward archaism as a concept in literary history, see Hinds 1998, 52–63; Goldberg 2007a, and from a different perspective, Goldschmidt 2013, 37–50. Among commentaries, that of Flores et al. (2000–2009) is especially sensitive to aesthetic considerations.

[6] Elliott 2013, 298–302, details the triadic structure often claimed for Ennius' poem. The description of Virgil's practice at *Vit. Verg.* 23 may itself have inspired the assumption about Ennius' working method. Cf. Virgil's lament to Augustus about the massiveness of his undertaking at Macrob. *Sat.* 1.24.11.

edented. Neither Livius Andronicus' *Odusseia* nor Nae-
vius' *Bellum Punicum* required more than a single book
roll, and Hellenistic historical poems, more often written
in elegiacs than hexameters, were not especially long.[7]
What became Ennius' monument to Roman achievement
may just as easily have grown from a smaller and more
traditional project, viz. a poem about the siege of Ambra-
cia, which he came to conceive in Homeric terms and for
which he adapted a suitably Homeric medium, the dac-
tylic hexameter. The larger, grander scheme to cast all of
Roman achievement in this form and himself as the Ro-
man Homer could conceivably have evolved from that
initial innovation. An expanding work of this kind would
better align Ennius with his predecessors, making his
achievement more comprehensible but no less remark-
able. Yet whatever its origins, the result was without ques-
tion a work greater in scale and aspiration than any earlier
Roman poem, and it changed forever the way Romans
viewed themselves, their history, and their destiny.[8]

Understanding the poem as Ennius designed it never-

[7] The genre of Hellenistic historical epic as defined by Ziegler
1966 rests in large part on assumptions about Ennius' poem and
received a detailed critique by Cameron 1995, 263–302, fore-
shadowed by Otis 1963, 396–98. For what is now more commonly
thought of as Hellenistic encomium, see Barbantani 2001, and for
Cameron's critique of Ziegler, Kerkhecker 2001, 50–63. The
original length of the first Roman epics is problematic: see Suet.
Gram. et rhet. 2.2, with Kaster 1995, 64–66.

[8] Elliott 2013, 233–94, discusses in detail how Ennius' univer-
salizing tendencies shaped the attitudes of subsequent genera-
tions.

theless poses a challenge: to reconcile scholarly methods and interpretive desires with the inconsistencies and silences of the fragmentary record is no easy task. The problem looms especially large in discussions of *Annals* 15, the likely climax to Ennius' original plan. Some historical facts relevant to its narrative are well established. The Aetolian capital of Ambracia surrendered to Fulvius Nobilior in 189 BC, and in 187 the victorious consul sponsored elaborate victory games on his own initiative before celebrating a triumph. Nor was that all. In the Campus Martius, he refurbished an existing temple to the Muses with a statuary group depicting Hercules as their defender that had come as booty from Ambracia, together with a shrine to the ancient Camenae transferred from an ancient site by the Porta Capena and also a display of *fasti* compiled under his patronage.[9] Uniting Muses and Camenae in this newly styled Temple of Hercules of the Muses and surrounding them with a wall of *fasti* put in material terms a political message closely aligned with the literary one of the *Annals*, which also merged Muses and Camenae and celebrated Roman achievements. The temple would thus seem to represent public expression and public sanction of the same cultural synthesis Ennius sought through the epic, and scholars of otherwise different interpretive

[9] Liv. 38.43–44, 39.4–5, 39.22.1–2 (triumph); Cic. *Arch.* 27; Macrob. *Sat.* 1.12.16 (temple and *fasti*); Serv. ad Verg. *Aen.* 1.8; Liv. 1.21 (Camenae). Extant Livy nowhere mentions the temple, for which also see *LTUR* 3: 17–19. For the Ambracian statues themselves, perhaps originally a choregic monument, see Marabini Moevs 1981, and for their appropriation by Fulvius, Gruen 1992, 107–10.

slants all see in this event a fitting climax to Ennius'
poem.[10] But there is a problem.

Nobilior's demand for a triumph was bitterly opposed
by Marcus Aemilius Lepidus, who as consul in 187 se-
cured a Senate resolution that Ambracia had not been
captured by force, and probably also by Cato, who railed
throughout the 180s over the control of booty by victori-
ous commanders. Only in Lepidus' absence from the city
did Nobilior secure the Senate's authorization for a tri-
umph, which he then hastened to celebrate before Lepi-
dus could return and intervene. The hostility between
them continued unabated until 179, when the two rivals
at last staged a very public reconciliation and were jointly
elected to the censorship. Given the political deadlock of
the 180s, most scholars date Nobilior's temple project to
the censorship of 179.[11] Though Otto Skutsch agreed, he
nevertheless placed the reconciliation with Lepidus,
which we know on Cicero's authority figured in the *An-
nals*, in Book 16, because he could not imagine a single
book long enough to accommodate all the momentous
events of the 180s, which included Cato's censorship
(184), the trial of the Scipios and death of Africanus (183),

[10] So Goldberg 1995, 130–31; Gildenhard 2003, 45–47; Sciar-
rino 2004; Rüpke 2006; Fabrizi 2008. For counterarguments see
Zetzel 2007, 12–14. The temple dedication as celebrated in the
Annals is also important to the arguments of Newlands 1995,
215–18; Feeney 2007, 143–44; Heslin 2015, 202–7. Good sum-
mary of the underlying issues by Rossi and Breed 2006, 408–15.

[11] Full discussion by Martina 1981; Aberson 1994, 199–216;
endorsed by Rüpke 1995, 332–39, and 2006, 490–91; *contra* Fee-
ney 2007, 142–44.

and the growing reputation of Lucius Aemilius Paullus. And that is the problem. If the temple project was not completed until the censorship of 179, either Ennius' narrative in Book 15 was not rigorously chronological, was not inclusive, or did not end with the dedication of the temple.[12] At least one basic assumption about the structure of the poem must be incorrect.

Though no firm and coherent conclusion can be drawn from such evidence, two useful lessons emerge from the very act of articulating this problem. First, the historical record can be as problematic as the literary record, and while the *Annals*, even in its present state, has much to offer the study of both Roman literature and Roman history, using the historical record to understand the fragments is as precarious an undertaking as using the fragments to understand the history. Second, dissatisfaction with the traditional answers to the *Annals*' many interpretive challenges may best be relieved by moving beyond the traditional questions. The old ways of thinking about Ennius and his poem are not the only ways. A wide range of topics concerning style, narrative technique, and reception remain to be explored, as does Ennius' relation to other Greek and Italic literary traditions, his role in the rise of learning among second-century Romans, his influence on their strategies for making sense of their past, and

[12] The summary statements at Skutsch 1985, 144 and 553, are not completely congruent and are difficult to reconcile with his placement of Cicero's testimony about the reconciliation (*Prov. cons.* 20 = 15 *Ann.* t 2) in Book 16. The value of Eumenius' explicit testimony that the temple was financed using censorial funds (*ex pecunia censoria*: *Pan. Lat.* 9.7.3 = T 88) is debated.

his contribution to the development of a new, distinctly Roman literary culture. Such interesting and important lines of inquiry all find a beginning here with the *Annals*.

NOTE ON THE TEXT

When multiple sources preserve a fragment, only the fullest or most important is quoted. The text printed is essentially that of Otto Skutsch, and those familiar with his edition will recognize at once our many debts to it. Fragments explicitly assigned to a book by a source are marked with an asterisk (*). Conjectural placements follow Skutsch, with possible difficulties noted. Line numbers are those of Skutsch's edition; the fragment numbers used here as references are new to this volume.

BOOK I

Nearly a quarter of the fragments that can be securely placed in any book of the Annals *are ascribed to this one, and more general references to its content appear in a wide variety of sources. So unusually rich a mixture of testimony and quotation makes identifying the contents of this book less problematic and significantly more detailed than any other. Ennius apparently established his epic creden-*

TESTIMONIA

Ennius' Dream Vision

Ennius' claim to be Homer reincarnate made a powerful impression on Roman readers, though not always the same impression. Lucretius' recollection of this passage likely incorporates Ennian phrases (t 2); Horace is more skepti-

t 1 Cic. *Rep.* 6.10

hic mihi (credo equidem ex hoc quod eramus locuti; fit enim fere ut cogitationes sermonesque nostri pariant aliquid in somno, tale quale de Homero scribit Ennius, de

BOOK I

tials with an invocation of the Muses (F 1) and then an account of a dream explaining how he came to assume Homer's poetic mantle (t 1–5, F 2–10). The narrative that followed included the story of Aeneas' flight from Troy (F 11–26), the birth of Romulus and Remus (t 6–8, F 27–38), and the subsequent career of Romulus from the founding of Rome to his death and deification (t 9–10, F 39–57).

TESTIMONIA

Ennius' Dream Vision

cal of its poetic conceits (t 3). Among the more general allusions, Propertius' evocation (T 50) sounds serious, while Persius (T 58) is wry: the echoes become increasingly vague and indirect in later centuries (e.g., T 79, 110).

t 1 Cicero, *On the Republic*

Here (I suppose because of what we had discussed; for it often happens that our thoughts and conversations produce something in sleep, of the sort that Ennius writes concerning Homer, about whom he obviously used to

quo videlicet saepissime vigilans solebat cogitare et loqui)
Africanus se ostendit ea forma quae mihi ex imagine eius
quam ex ipso erat notior . . .

t 2 Lucr. 1.112–26

ignoratur enim quae sit natura animai,
nata sit an contra nascentibus insinuetur,
et simul intereat nobiscum morte dirempta
115   an tenebras Orci visat vastasque lacunas
an pecudes alias divinitus insinuet se,
Ennius ut noster cecinit qui primus amoeno
detulit ex Helicone perenni fronde coronam,
per gentis Italas hominum quae clara clueret;
120   etsi praeterea tamen esse Acherusia templa
Ennius aeternis exponit versibus edens,
quo neque permaneant animae neque corpora nostra,
sed quaedam simulacra modis pallentia miris;
unde sibi exortam semper florentis Homeri
125   commemorat speciem lacrimas effundere salsas
coepisse et rerum naturam expandere dictis.

t 3

a Hor. *Epist.* 2.1.50–52

Ennius, et sapiens et fortis et alter Homerus,
ut critici dicunt, † leviter † curare videtur
quo promissa cadant et somnia Pythagorea.

think and speak quite frequently while awake) Africanus[1] presented himself to me in a shape more familiar to me from his portrait bust than from his person . . .

[1] P. Cornelius Scipio Africanus (ca. 236–183 BC, cos. 205 BC), the adoptive grandfather of the speaker, P. Cornelius Scipio Aemilianus Africanus (Numantinus) (185/4–129 BC, cos. 147 BC).

t 2 Lucretius, *On the Nature of Things*

The nature of the soul is unknown, whether it is born or, on the contrary, makes its way into what is being born, and whether it perishes with us, dissolved by death, [115] or visits the darkness and vast caverns of Orcus, or by divine power makes its way into other creatures, as our Ennius sang, who was first to bring a wreath of undying foliage down from lovely Helicon to be celebrated among the Italic races of men. [120] Yet nevertheless, Ennius also explains and sets out in eternal verses that the Acherusian regions indeed exist, where neither our souls nor our bodies endure, but some kind of shades, wondrously pale; he recalls how the image of ever-flourishing Homer [125] arose for him from there and began to pour forth salty tears and unfold in speech the nature of things.

t 3

a Horace, *Epistles*

Ennius, wise and courageous and another Homer, as the scholars say, seems to care little (?) where his promises and Pythagorean dreams end up.

b Porph. ad Hor. *Epist.* 2.1.51

"leviter curare videtur": securus iam de proventu suae lau-
dis est Ennius, propter quam ante sollicitus in principio
Annalium suorum somnio se scripsit admonitum, quod
secundum Pythagorae dogma anima Homeri in suum cor-
pus venisset. facete autem somnia Pythagorea dixit, ut
ipsum etiam Pythagoram † sua sibimet metempsychosi
videre videatur.

t 4 (cf. T 58) Commentum Cornuti in Persium 6.10

"postquam destertuit": . . . [2] sic Ennius ait in Annalium
suorum principio, ubi se dicit vidisse in somnis Homerum
dicentem fuisse quondam pavonem et ex eo translatam in
se animam esse secundum Pytagorae philosophi defini-
tionem, qui dicit animas humanas per palingenesiam, id
est per iteratam generationem, exeuntes de corporibus in
alia posse corpora introire. [3] ideo autem, "quintus" dixit
propter eam opinionem quae dicit animam Pytagorae in
pavonem translatam, de pavone vero ad Euphorbium, de
Euphorbio ad Homerum, de Homero autem ad Ennnium.
[4] vel certe quod cognomento Ennius diceretur.

b Prophyrio, *Commentary on Horace*

"seems to care little": Ennius is now at ease over the growth of his fame, about which he had previously been anxious: he wrote at the beginning of his *Annals* that he was advised in a dream that, according to the doctrine of Pythagoras, Homer's soul had come into his body. He [Horace] wittily called the dreams Pythagorean, as if he [Ennius] seems actually to see Pythagoras himself on account of his metempsychosis [?].

t 4 (cf. T 58) Cornutus, *Commentary on Persius*

"after he had snored off": . . . [2] So Ennius asserts at the beginning of his *Annals*, where he says that he had seen Homer in a dream saying that he had once been a peacock and from that his soul was transferred into him [Ennius] according to the dictates of the philosopher Pythagoras, who says that human souls, through palingenesis, i.e., through repeated births, emerge from their bodies and are able to enter other bodies. [3] And further, he [Persius] said "fifth" because of the belief that says the soul of Pythagoras was transferred into a peacock, from a peacock then to Euphorbus,[1] from Euphorbus to Homer, finally from Homer to Ennius. [4] Or, of course, because Ennius was called by this name [i.e., Quintus, lit. "fifth"].

---

[1] Euphorbus (misspelled "Euphorbius" in the text) was a Dardanian warrior who wounded Patroclus (Hom. *Il.* 16.806–17) and was subsequently killed by Menelaus (Hom. *Il.* 17.45–60). The association of Pythagoras and Euphorbus is mentioned by Diog. Laert. 8.4 and Ov. *Met.* 15.160–64.

t 5 (cf. T 79) Fronto, Ad M. Caesarem et invicem libri, *Ep.* 1.4.5 (p. 8.1–3 van den Hout)

transeo nunc ad Q. Ennium nostrum, quem tu ais ex somno et somnio initium sibi fecisse. sed profecto nisi ex somno suscitatus esset, numquam somnium suum narrasset.

Ilia's Dream (cf. T 54)

t 6 Porph. ad Hor. *Carm.* 1.2.18

Ilia auctore Ennio in amnem Tiberim iussu Amulii regis Albanorum praecipitata Antemnis Anieni matrimonio iuncta est.

The Birth of Romulus and Remus

t 7 *Origo gen. Rom.* 20.3

tum illi quibus id imperatum erat impositos alveo pueros circa radices montis Palatii in Tiberim, qui tum magnis imbribus stagnaverat, abiecerunt, eiusque regionis subulcus Faustulus speculatus exponente, ut vidit relabente flumine alveum in quo pueri erant obhaesisse ad arborem fici puerorumque vagitu lupam excitam quae repente exierat primo lambitu eos detersisse, dein levandorum uberum gratia mammas praebuisse, descendit ac sustulit nutriendosque Accae Larentiae, uxori suae, dedit, ut scribunt Ennius libro primo et Caesar libro secundo.

t 5 Fronto, *Correspondence*

I pass now to our Ennius, whom you say took his start from sleep and a dream. But surely, if he had not been aroused from sleep, he would never have described his dream.

Ilia's Dream (cf. T 54)

t 6 Porphyrio, *Commentary on Horace*

Ilia, according to Ennius, was thrown on the order of Amulius, the Alban king, into the river Tiber at Antemnae and was joined in marriage to the [river] Anio.

The Birth of Romulus and Remus

t 7 *The Origins of the Roman Race*

Then those whose duty it was set the boys in a basket at the foot of the Palatine hill and threw them into the Tiber, which was then overflowing after a great rain. Faustulus, a swineherd of that neighborhood, noticed the abandoned children. As the water receded, he saw that the basket containing the children had lodged by a fig tree and that a she-wolf, who had suddenly come forth aroused by the boys' crying, first licked them clean and then offered her teats for them to nurse. Faustulus came down and picked them up and gave them to his wife, Acca Larentia, to raise, as Ennius writes in his first book and Caesar[1] in his second book.

[1] L. Iulius Caesar (cos. 64 BC) is known to have had antiquarian interests. See *FRHist* 1:641.

t 8 Serv. ad Verg. *Aen.* 8.631

sane totus hic locus [i.e., 8.630–34] Ennianus est:

> fecerat et viridi fetam Mavortis in antro
> procubuisse lupam, geminos huic ubera circum
> ludere pendentis pueros et lambere matrem
> impavidos, illam tereti cervice reflexa
> mulcere alternos et corpora fingere lingua.

Romulus as Sole Ruler

t 9 Varro, *Ling.* 5.55

ager Romanus primum divisus in partis tris, a quo tribus appellata Titiensium, Ramnium, Lucerum: nominatae, ut ait Ennius, Titienses ab Tatio, Ramnenses ab Romulo, Luceres, ut Iunius, ab Lucumone, sed omnia haec vocabula Tusca, ut Volnius, qui tragoedias Tuscas scripsit, dicebat.

t 10 Schol. Bern. ad Verg. *G.* 2.384

Romulus cum aedificasset templum Iovi Feretrio, pelles unctas stravit et sic ludos edidit ut caestibus dimicarent et cursu contenderent, quam rem Ennius in Annalibus testatur.

t 8 Servius, *Commentary on Virgil*

This entire passage [Verg. *Aen.* 8.630–34] is clearly Ennian:

> He [Vulcan] had also made the fertile wolf reclining
>   in Mars'
> verdant grotto: the twin boys at play around her teats,
> hanging on and licking the mother without fear,
> she, bending her shapely neck around, stroking
> each in turn, smoothing their bodies with her tongue.

Romulus as Sole Ruler

t 9 Varro, *On the Latin Language*

The Roman territory was originally divided into three [*tris*] parts, from which the Titienses, the Ramnes, and the Luceres were each called a tribe [*tri-bus*]: the Titienses named from Tatius, as Ennius says, the Ramnenses from Romulus, the Luceres, as Junius[1] says, from Lucumo, but all these terms are Etruscan, as Volnius[2], who wrote Etruscan tragedies, said.

[1] M. Iunius Congus wrote on the Latin language at the time of the Gracchi.   [2] The tragedian Volnius is otherwise unknown.

t 10 Scholia Bernensia to Virgil, *Georgics*

After Romulus erected a temple to Jupiter Feretrius, he spread out greased hides and so established games for men to compete in boxing matches and races, a thing to which Ennius bears witness in his *Annals*.

FRAGMENTS

F 1: Ennius Calls upon the Muses

1 Varro, *Ling.* 7.5–20

dicam in hoc libro de verbis quae a poetis sunt posita, primum de locis . . .

1   Musae, quae pedibus magnum pulsatis Olympum

[20] Caelum dicunt Graeci Olympum, montem in Macedonia omnes, a quo potius puto Musas dictas Olympiadas.

Cf. Serv. ad Verg. *Aen.* 11.660; Varro, *Rust.* 1.1.4.

F 2–9: Ennius' Dream Vision

The poet describes how the shade of Homer appeared to him in a dream and revealed that, through a process of Pythagorean transmigration, his soul had eventually come to be reborn in Ennius. This vision established the Annals' *place in the (still largely Greek) epic tradition, authorized its incorporation of Homeric mannerisms, allusions, and meter, and became a model for subsequent dream visions and discussions of dreams in the emerging Latin tradition. Note, however, that significant pieces of the surviving*

FRAGMENTS

F 1: Ennius Calls upon the Muses

1 Varro, *On the Latin Language*

I shall speak in this book of the words used by poets, first concerning places . . .

Muses,[1] who strike great Olympus with your feet   1

[20] The Greeks call the heaven Olympus. All people call the mountain in Macedonia Olympus, for which reason, I am inclined to think, the Muses were called "daughters of Olympus."

[1] The first attested appearance of this word in Latin: Ennius' predecessors had called them Camenae (cf. Inc. *Ann.* F 38). The programmatic implications of the shift in terminology from Camenae to Muses are explored by Hinds 1998, 56–63. This is not necessarily the opening line of the poem. Cf. Lucretius 1.1–3.

F 2–9: Ennius' Dream Vision

puzzle are placed here by conjecture: F 5 might instead refer to the exposure of Romulus and Remus (Elliott 2013, 149), F 6–7 may belong to the Epicharmus *(Elliott 2013, 144–48). Compare Lucilius' evocation of cosmic phenomena in his condemnation of Lupus (784–90 M. = 805–11 W.). Important modern discussions of the episode and its wider implications for Roman literary culture include Suerbaum 1968, 46–113; Hardie 1986, 76–83; Aicher 1989/90; Barchiesi 1995.*

2 Fronto, Ad M. Caesarem et invicem libri, *Ep.* 4.12.4
(p. 67.3–7 van den Hout)

si quando te

2   somno leni

ut poeta ait,

                    placidoque revinctus

video in somnis, numquam est quin amplectar et exoscu-
ler: tum pro argumento cuiusque somni aut fleo ubertim
aut exulto laetitia aliqua et voluptate. hoc unum ex Anna-
libus sumptum amoris mei argumentum poeticum et sane
somniculosum.

3 (= T 27 = *Epi.* F 1) Cic. *Acad.* 2.51

num censes Ennium cum in hortis cum Ser. Galba vicino
suo ambulavisset dixisse visus sum mihi cum Galba ambu-
lare? at cum somniavit ita narravit:

3   visus Homerus adesse poeta

idemque in Epicharmo [F 1]: nam videbar somniare m{e}d
ego esse mortuum. itaque, simul ut experrecti sumus, visa
illa contemnimus neque ita habemus ut ea quae in foro
gessimus.

Cf. Cic. *Acad.* 2.88; *Rep.* 6.10; Fronto, *Ep.* 2.12 (= T 79).

2 Fronto, *Correspondence*

If ever when

> bound in gentle and peaceful sleep 2

as the poet says, I see you in my dreams, I invariably hug and kiss you fondly. Then, following the course of each dream, I either weep profusely or dance with a kind of happiness and pleasure. This is one proof taken from the annals of my love, poetic and dreamy indeed.[1]

[1] The pun on annals/*Annals* points to Ennius as the poet being quoted. If Fronto's references to tears and to dance echo Ennius' invocations of the Muses and the shade of Homer, the explicit quotation probably derives from this narrative of the poet's dream, since Ilia's sleep (F 28), the other likely source of the phrase, was neither *lenis* nor *placidus*.

3 (= T 27 = *Epi.* F 1) Cicero, *Prior Academics*

Do you suppose that Ennius, when he had gone for a walk in the garden with his neighbor Servius Galba, said "I seemed to walk with Galba"? But when he dreamed, he reported thus:

> the poet Homer seemed to be present 3

and similarly in the *Epicharmus*[1] [F 1]: "for I seemed to dream that I was dead." And so, as soon as we have awakened, we disparage those visions and do not regard them the same way as the things we have done in active life.

[1] See the introduction to that work. Disentangling evidence for the *Epicharmus* from Ennius' treatment of similar ideas in the *Annals'* dream vision can be difficult.

4 Cic. *Acad.* 2.88

nisi vero Ennium non putamus ita totum illud audivisse,

4   O pietas animi

si modo id somniavit, ut si vigilans audiret, experrectus enim potuit illa visa putare ut erant et somnia. dormienti vero aeque ac vigilanti probabantur.

Cf. Donat. ad Ter. *Eun.* 560.

*5 Fest., pp. 354.35–56.1 L.

REMANANT: replent. Ennius lib. I:

5   desunt rivos camposque remanant

Cf. Paul., p. 355.11 L.

6 Varro, *Ling.* 5.60

recte igitur Pacuvius quod ait "animam aether adiugat" et Ennius:

6   terra⟨que⟩ corpus
    quae dedit ipsa capit neque dispendi facit hilum

   que *add. Bergk*

Cf. Varro, *Ling.* 5.111; 9.54.

4 Cicero, *Prior Academics*

Unless of course we do not think that Ennius heard that entire speech:

> O reverent spirit   4

the same way if he only dreamed it as if he heard it while awake, since when wide awake he was able to think those visions were dreams, as indeed they were. They were surely taken to be equally real to him whether asleep or awake.

*5 Festus

remanant: "they replenish." Ennius Book 1:

> [the waters are not?] lacking:[1] they replenish   5
> streams and fields

[1] The meaning is problematic. Warmington, following Scaliger, prints *destituunt rivos*, "they leave the streams," a *lectio facilior*. "Water" was the likely subject of both verbs.

6 Varro, *On the Latin Language*

Pacuvius therefore is right when he says that "the ether adds breath,"[1] and Ennius:

> and earth, which gave the body,   6
> herself takes it back and sustains not the slightest loss

[1] Non., p. 75.8 M. = 105 L. quotes Pacuvius' complete thought: *Mater est terra: ea parit corpus, animam aether adiugat* "Earth is the mother. She gives birth to the body; the ether adds breath" (*Trag.* 94 R.[2-3]). Varro converts to indirect statement what his subsequent citations of these lines show was in Ennius a direct statement: editors thus restore with confidence the direct form reproduced here.

7 Varro, *Ling.* 5.59

haec duo Caelum et Terra, quod anima et corpus. humidum et frigidum terra sive

8 ova parire solet genus pennis condecoratum,
  non animam

ut ait Ennius, et

     post inde venit divinitus pullis
 ipsa anima

sive ut Zeno Citieus, animalium semen ignis isque anima ac mens.

Cf. Diom., *GL* I, p. 383.5–6; Prisc., *GL* II, p. 401.4–5.

8 Charis. *GL* I, p. 98.3–6 = p. 124 B.

"pavos" et "pavo." Ennius:

11   memini me fiere pavom
 et Persius pavo.

 fiere *Vahlen, Skutsch*: fieri *codd.* (*cf.* 10 *Ann.* F 18)

Cf. Donat. ad Ter. *An.* 429 ("memini videre pro vidisse"); *Ph.* 74; *Ad.* 106.

9 Serv. ad Verg. *Aen.* 6.748

"ubi mille rotam volvere per annos": exegerunt statutum tempus per annorum volubilitatem. est autem sermo Ennii.

7 Varro, *On the Latin Language*

These two, Heaven and Earth, are a pair, like life and body. Earth is damp and cold, whether

> the race adorned with feathers is wont to bear eggs,   8
> not life,

as Ennius says, and

>   that life force comes to the chicks afterward
> from the sky

or, as Zeno of Citium [ca. 331–264 BC, founder of the Stoic school] says, the seed of living things is fire, and it is life and mind.

8 Charisius

pavos and *pavo* [peacock]. Ennius:

>   I remember becoming a peacock   11

and Persius uses *pavo*.

9 Servius, *Commentary on Virgil*

"when once for a thousand years they turned [Time's] wheel": i.e., they completed the appointed time through the cycle of years. It is an Ennian phrase.[1]

---

[1] Skutsch 1985, 165, believes that Ennius followed Orpheus and Pythagoras in setting the interval between incarnations at three hundred years. If so, Virgil's "thousand" belongs to him, and the Ennian phrase noted by Servius should therefore be reduced to *rotam . . . annos*. Skutsch treated the phrase as an echo and did not assign it a line number.

F 10: The Poet's Confidence in the Success of His Work

*10 Inc. *De ult syll.*, *GL* IV, p. 231.11–18

neutro genere in casibus supra dictis [nom., acc., voc.] sine ambiguitate brevis est [syllaba finalis] Graecis Latinisque nominibus . . . Graeci etiam nominis exempla subiciamus. Ennius in primo Annali:

12   latos ⟨per⟩ populos res atque poemata nostra
            ⟨. . . clara⟩ cluebunt

suppl. confirmat Lucr. 1.118–19 (t 2)

F 11–26: Aeneas Abandons Troy and Travels to Italy, Where He Establishes Peace with the King of Alba Longa

The Trojan origins of Rome, an idea originally popularized by Greek historians of the West, first gained currency among Romans through versions of Aeneas' story in the history of Fabius Pictor (F 3 FRHist) and the epic of Gnaeus Naevius (BP, F 5–25 Strzelecki), but Ennius' account became the canonical one in the Republic. For the complexities of the developing foundation legend, see Gruen 1992, 6–51.

11 Prisc., *GL* II, p .97.6–9

veterrimus quasi a veter positivo, quod Capri quoque approbat auctoritas et usus antiquissimorum. Ennius:

14   quom veter occubuit Priamus sub Marte Pelasgo

Cf. *Ars Bern.*, *GL* VIII, p. 81.

ANNALS: BOOK I

F 10: The Poet's Confidence in the
Success of His Work

*10 Anonymous grammarian

As for the neuter gender in the cases mentioned above, the final syllable is unambiguously light in Greek and Latin nouns.... Let us also add examples of a Greek noun. Ennius in the first book of *Annals*:

> widely among the peoples[1] will our subject and our   12
>   poetry
>   be brilliantly celebrated

[1] That is, throughout the population of Italy, if Lucretius' echo at 1.119 (t 2) is true to the original. Cf. *Ambracia* F 1 (*per gentes . . . cluebat*), and for Ennius' confidence, the proem to Book 7.

F 11–26: Aeneas Abandons Troy and Travels
to Italy, Where He Establishes Peace
with the King of Alba Longa

11 Priscian

veterrimus as if derived from a positive *veter* [old], which Caper's authority also supports, as does the usage of the most ancient writers. Ennius:

> when aged Priam lay dead beneath the Greek   14
>   onslaught[1]

[1] A characteristically bold Ennian expression (lit., "Pelasgian Mars"), taking Mars figuratively, as Greek uses Ares, for the violence of war and Pelasgus for the first time meaning "Greek," as regularly in subsequent Latin poetry.

12 [Probus] ad Verg. *Ecl.* 6.31 (vol. 3.2, p. 336.4–12 Th.-H.)

cur ibi [Verg. *Aen.* 6.724] Anchisen facit disputantem quod hic Silenum deum, nisi quod poeta Ennius Anchisen augurium [*Sk.*: -ii *codd.*] ac per hoc divini quiddam habuisse praesumit sic,

15   doctus†que Anchisesque Venus quem pulcra dearum
      fari donavit, divinum pectus habere

Naevius *Belli Punici* libro tertio sic "postquam avem aspexit in templo Anchisa . . ." [*BP*, F 25 Strzelecki].

Cf. Schol. Veron. ad Verg. *Aen.* 2.687 (vol. 3.2, p. 427.1–5 Th.-H.).

*13 Fest., p. 218.6–11 L.

ORARE antiquos dixisse pro agere testimonio sunt . . . Ennius quoque cum dixit in lib. I Annalium:

17   face vero quod tecum precibus pater orat

12 [Probus], *Commentary on Virgil*

Why does he there [Verg. *Aen.* 6.724] have Anchises expound what he here has the god Silenus do, if not because the poet Ennius assumed that Anchises knew the art of augury and through this something of divine will? Thus,

> learned Anchises, to whom Venus, splendid among   15
>> goddesses,
> gave the gift of prophecy and a divine heart

So Naevius in the third book of his *Punic War*, "after Anchises observed a bird in the heaven's quadrant . . ." [*BP*, F 25 Strzelecki].

*13 Festus

There is evidence that the ancients said *orare* [to beseech] for *agere* [to urge] . . . So too Ennius when he said in Book 1 of the *Annals*:

> do then what [I?] your father urge[s?] you with   17
>> entreaties[1]

[1] Skutsch, taking the line as part of Anchises' speech, understands the third-person verb as a self-reference, citing the close parallel of Plaut. *Aul.* 153. Warmington, preserving the third person, attributes the line to Venus.

*14 Serv. Dan. ad Verg. *G.* 4.59

"nare per aestatem liquidam" et aliter "nare" pro "volare" ut apud Ennium in primo:

18   transnavit cita per teneras caliginis auras

proprietas tamen vocis aptior est natantibus quam volantibus.

*15 Fest., p. 386.32–35 L.

sos pro eos antiqui dicebant, ut Ennius lib. I:

19   constitit inde loci propter sos dia dearum

*16 Macrob. *Sat.* 6.1.11 (Verg. *Aen.* 1.530, 3.163 "est locus Hesperiam Grai cognomine dicunt")

Ennius in primo:

20   est locus Hesperiam quam mortales perhibebant

*14 Servius Danielis, *Commentary on Virgil*

"to swim through the clear summer air": and elsewhere
nare [to swim] for *volare* [to fly], as in Ennius, in the first
book:

> she[1] floated swiftly through the soft waves of misty   18
> darkness

The connotation of the word nevertheless better suits
those swimming than those flying.

[1] The subject is probably Venus, perhaps on her way to counsel Aeneas.

*15 Festus

The ancients used to say *sos* for *eos* [them], as Ennius
Book 1:

> thereupon she stood, illustrious goddess, close by   19
> them

*16 Macrobius, *Saturnalia* (on Virgil, "there is a place
Greeks call by the name Hesperia")

Ennius in his first book:

> there is a place men used to know as Hesperia[1]   20

[1] That is, "The Western Land."

17 Varro, *Ling.* 5.42

hunc [i.e., Capitolium] antea montem Saturnium appella-
tum prodiderunt et ab eo late

21   Saturniam terram

ut etiam Ennius appellat. antiquom oppidum in hac fuisse
Saturnia scribitur.

Cf. Fest., p. 430.30–34 L.

18 Varro, *Ling.* 7.28

cascum vetus esse significat Ennius quod ait:

22   quam prisci, casci populi, tenuere Latini

Cf. Cic. *Tusc.* 1.27; Hieron. *Epist.* 8.1.

19 Non., p. 197.2–11 M. = 289 L.

CAELUM neutro. masculino Lucretius [2.1097] . . . Varro
Rerum divinarum VI . . . Ennius . . . [Inc. *Ann.* F 97],
idem:

23   Saturno
      quem Caelus genuit

Cf. Charis. *GL* I, p. 72.12–14 = p. 91.14–16 B.

17 Varro, *On the Latin Language*

Previously they called this hill [the Capitol] the Saturnian Hill and by extension from that

the Saturnian land[1]   21

as Ennius also calls it. It is recorded that the ancient town in this land was Saturnia.

[1] The case of Ennius' phrase is uncertain, and it did not necessarily appear at line end.

18 Varro, *On the Latin Language*

Ennius shows that *cascus* means "old" because he says:

> which[1] the original Latins, an ancient people,   22
>   occupied

[1] The antecedent may well be the Saturnian land of F 17.

19 Nonius

caelum [sky] is neuter, masculine in Lucretius [2.1097] . . . Varro, *On Divine Matters*, Book 6 . . . Ennius . . . [Inc. *Ann.* F 97], also:

to Saturn,   23

whom Sky fathered

20 Non., p. 216.31–34 M. = 320 L.

OBSIDIO feminino . . . neutro Ennius:

25   cum † suo obsidio magnus Titanus premebat

suo *codd.*: saevo *Iunius*: sos *Némethy*

*21 Macrob. *Sat.* 6.1.12 (Verg. *Aen.* 8.72 "tuque, o Thybri, tuo, genitor, cum flumine sancto")

Ennius in I:

26   teque pater Tiberine tuo cum flumine sancto

*22 Macrob. *Sat.* 6.1.9 (Verg. *Aen.* 4.482 "axem umero torquet stellis ardentibus aptum")

Ennius in primo:

27   qui caelum versat stellis fulgentibus aptum

23 Serv. Dan. ad Verg. *G.* 3.35

per Assaracum Troianos dicit, nam Assaracus avus Anchisae. Ennius:

28   Assaraco natus Capys optimus isque pium ex se
        Anchisen generat

Cf. Serv. Dan. ad Verg. *Aen.*1.273, 6.777, 8.130.

20 Nonius

obsidio [blockade] is feminine . . . neuter in Ennius:

> great Titan was suppressing with ferocious [?]   25
>   blockade[1]

[1] Text (and sense) are uncertain since loss of context makes it impossible to know whether the line opens with the preposition *cum* [with] or the conjunction *quom* [when]. If the former, the impossible *suo* might be corrected to *saevo* [ferocious]; if the latter, the likely emendation is *sos* [them], that is, "When great Titan was suppressing them . . ." The victims are in either case presumably the sons of Saturn.

*21 Macrobius, *Saturnalia* (on Virgil, "and you, Thybris, parent, with your sacred stream")

Ennius in Book 1:

> and you, Father Tiberinus, with your sacred stream   26

*22 Macrobius, *Saturnalia* (on Virgil, "he spins heaven's vault, studded with blazing stars, on his shoulder")

Ennius in the first book:

> who turns heaven, studded with flashing stars   27

23 Servius Danielis, *Commentary on Virgil*

through Assaracus he says they were Trojans, for Assaracus was the grandfather of Anchises. Ennius:

> to Assaracus was born the excellent Capys, and he in   28
>   turn begat
> faithful Anchises

24 Prisc., *GL* II, pp. 337.26–38.1

Laurentis etiam pro Laurens dicebant. Ennius in Annalibus:

30   quos homines quondam Laurentis terra recepit

25 Atilius Fortun., *GL* VI, p. 284.20–21

maximus qui est versus syllabas habet XVII . . . minimus habet XII ut est Ennianus:

31   olli respondit rex Albai Longai

Cf. Donat., *GL* IV, p. 396.18–19; Pomp., *GL* V, p. 297.20–21; *Ars Bern.*, *GL* VIII, p. 94; *Explan. in Donat.*, *GL* IV, p. 548.2–3.

*26 Macrob. *Sat.* 6.1.13 (Verg. *Aen.* 8.150 "accipe daque fidem, sunt nobis fortia bello pectora")

Ennius in primo:

32   accipe daque fidem foedusque feri bene firmum

24 Priscian

Indeed, they used to say *Laurentis* instead of *Laurens*. Ennius in the *Annals*:

> which men[1] Laurentum's land once received   30

[1] The Trojan refugees under Aeneas are the probable reference. Most fragments cited by Priscian without book number belong to Book 1.

25 Atilius Fortunatianus

The longest verse has seventeen syllables . . . the shortest has twelve, as the Ennian line:

> to him replied the king of Alba Longa[1]   31

[1] A wholly spondaic line made possible by the archaic genitive -*āī*. *olli* (classical *illi*) is also archaic.

*26 Macrobius, *Saturnalia* (on Virgil, "accept and give in exchange this pledge; our hearts are primed for war")

Ennius in his first book:

> accept and give in exchange this pledge and strike a   32
> most firm treaty

F 27–37: The Birth of Romulus and Remus
F 27–28: Ilia's Dream

Aeneas' daughter recounts as if in a dream her abduction
and rape by Mars. In later versions of the story, her name
("the Trojan woman") is often changed to the more Italic
sounding Rhea Silvia, and she is cast as the daughter of the
Alban king Numitor, reflecting a tradition often ascribed
to the first Roman annalist, Fabius Pictor (F 4 FRHist).
Ilia's narrative here in Ennius is much discussed for its

*27 Macrob. *Sat.* 6.1.14 (Verg. *Aen.* 3.587 "et lunam in nimbo nox intempestata tenebat"):

Ennius in primo:

33   quom superum lumen nox intempesta teneret

28 Cic. *Div.* 1.40–42

num te ad fabulas revoco vel nostrorum vel Graecorum poetarum? narrat enim et apud Ennium Vestalis illa:

34   et cita cum tremulis anus attulit artubus lumen,
       talia tum memorat lacrimans, exterrita somno:
       "Eurydica prognata, pater quam noster amavit,
       vires vitaque corpus meum nunc deserit omne.
       nam me visus homo pulcer per amoena salicta

---

[1] This (anachronistic) detail, not confirmed by other testimony concerning Ennius' Ilia, is well established in the later tradition, e.g., Dion. Hal. *Ant.* 1.77–79; Liv. 1.3.11; Serv. Dan. ad Verg. *Aen.* 1.273.   [2] The wife of Aeneas, according to Paus. 10.26.1, citing the *Cypria* and the *Little Iliad*.   [3] His identity as Mars was probably made clear later in the story, but *pulcer*

F 27–37: The Birth of Romulus and Remus
F 27–28: Ilia's Dream

effective representation of dream psychology, its influence on the later epic tradition, and its elusive, highly gendered style. Thematically significant echoes of Ennius' own dream narrative in the prooemium have also been observed at work here. See Krevans 1993; Connors 1994; Goldberg 1995, 96–101; Dangel 1998; Keith 2000; Elliott 2013, 46–50.

*27 Macrobius, *Saturnalia* (on Virgil, "and deepest night was holding back the moon in a cloud")

Ennius in his first book:

> when deepest night held back the light of day 33

28 Cicero, *On Divination*

Need I recall for you the stories both our poets and the Greek poets tell? There's also the famous Vestal[1] in Ennius, who says:

> and quickly the old woman, with limbs atremble, 34
>   brought a light.
> Then, in tears, frightened out of sleep, she recounts
>   these things:
> "Daughter of Eurydice,[2] whom our father loved,
> strength and life now desert my entire body.
> A handsome man[3] seemed to take me through
>   pleasant willows

may itself hint at his divinity. Cf. F 12 *pulcra dearum* (of Venus) and Cic. *Nat. D.* 1.79.

et ripas raptare locosque novos. ita sola
40   postilla, germana soror, errare videbar
tardaque vestigare et quaerere te neque posse
corde capessere: semita nulla pedem stabilibat.
exim compellare pater me voce videtur
his verbis: 'o gnata, tibi sunt ante gerendae
45   aerumnae, post ex fluvio fortuna resistet.'
haec ecfatus pater, germana, repente recessit,
nec sese dedit in conspectum corde cupitus,
quamquam multa manus ad caeli caerula templa
tendebam lacrumans et blanda voce vocabam.
50   vix aegro cum corde meo me somnus reliquit."

haec, etiamsi ficta sunt a poeta, non absunt tamen a con-
suetudine somniorum.

34 etcita *codd.*: excita *edd. pler.*   42 corde *codd.*: corpus
Marx: colla *Vine*

F 29–37: A Council of the Gods Settles Ilia's Fate

*In response to Ilia's prayer, Venus reveals that she will be
married to the river god Anio and her twin sons exposed
and rescued. The divine assembly (F 29–34), famously
parodied in a satire by Lucilius (Book 1), became a model*

29 Tert. *Adv. Valent.* 7

primus omnium Ennius poeta Romanus

51   cenacula maxima caeli

and riverbanks and unfamiliar places. Then alone
awhile, sister true, I seemed to wander and   40
to track with slow foot and seek you but was unable
to embrace you [?]: no path supported my foot.
Then our father seemed to address me with his voice
in these words: 'O child, you must bear great
sorrows before good fortune from the river will end   45
    them.'
So our father spoke, sister, and then quickly
    withdrew,
not putting himself in my sight, though my heart
    yearned for him
as I kept stretching my hands to the azure regions of
    the sky,
weeping and calling out with beseeching voice.
Sleep has only now left me, sick at heart."   50

Though these are a poet's imaginings, they are not far from
the manner of dreams.

F 29–37: A Council of the Gods Settles Ilia's Fate

*for later Latin epic, from Cicero's poem on his consulship
(*Quint.* Inst. 11.1.24) to the opening scene of* Aeneid 10
and beyond. See Wigodsky 1972, 105–7.

29 Tertullian, *Against the Valentinians*

The Roman Ennius was first of all to mention straightfor-
wardly

                    most mighty dining halls of heaven   51

141

simpliciter pronuntiavit elati situs nomine, vel quia Iovem illic epulantem legerat apud Homerum [e.g., *Il.* 1.575, 584].

Cf. Schol. Veron. ad Verg. *Aen.* 10.1 (vol. 3.2, p. 443.6–9 Th.-H.).

30 Serv. ad Verg. *Aen.* 10.5

"considunt tectis bipatentibus": "bipatentibus" physice dixit nam caelum patet ab ortu et occasu. est autem sermo Ennianus, tractus ab ostiis, quae ex utraque parte aperiuntur. unde et modo

52   bipatentibus

apertis intellegimus.

31 Serv. ad Verg. *Aen.* 4.576

"sequimur te, sancte deorum quisquis es": aut distinguendum "sancte" aut "sancte deorum" secundum Ennium dixit:

53   respondit Iuno Saturnia, sancta dearum

Cf. Donat., *GL* IV, p. 394.1–2; *Explan. in Donat.*, *GL* IV, p. 563.19–21; Pomp., *GL* V, p. 291.17; Sacerd., *GL* VI, p. 450.20.

named for their elevated position, or since he had read in Homer that Jupiter dined there [e.g., *Il.* 1.575, 584].

30 Servius, *Commentary on Virgil*

"they sat together in his double-doored hall": He said "double-doored" literally, since heaven lies open from rising to setting. It is, moreover, Ennian language, taken from doors that are opened from both sides. Thus even now we understand

double-doored   52

to mean simply "open."[1]

[1] The doors of the Curia remained open during meetings of the Senate. Divine assemblies in Lucilius, Cicero, and Virgil all echo Roman senatorial procedure, a practice that may have originated with Ennius.

31 Servius, *Commentary on Virgil*

"we follow you, holy divinity, whichever one you are": we must either punctuate after "holy," or he said "holy divinity," following Ennius:[1]

Juno, Saturn's daughter, holy goddess, replied   53

[1] Servius is unsure whether Virgil's *deorum* (of gods) is to be understood with the vocative "holy one" or with *quisquis*, "whichever one."

32 Varro, *Ling*. 7.5–6

dicam in hoc libro de verbis quae a poetis sunt posita . . .
[6] incipiam hinc:

54   unus erit quem tu tolles in caerula caeli
        templa

Cf. Ov. *Met*. 14.806, 814; *Fast*. 2.485.

33 Serv. Dan. ad Verg. *Aen*. 3.333

"morte Neoptolemi regnorum reddita cessit pars Heleno":
"reddita" more veteri pro data accipiendum est; "re" ergo
abundat. Ennius Annalibus:

56   at Ilia reddita nuptum

et alibi . . . [Inc. *Ann*. F 10].

*34 Non., p. 306.26–27 M. = 477 L.

FACESSERE est facere. Ennius Annalibus lib. I:

57   haec ecfatus, ibique latrones dicta facessunt

32 Varro, *On the Latin Language*

I shall speak in this book about words which were put
down by the poets . . . [6] I will begin with this:

> there will be one[1] whom you will raise to the azure 54
>> precincts
> of the sky

[1] Romulus: the emphatic position of *unus* may suggest "the
one but not the other [sc. Remus]."

33 Servius Danielis, *Commentary on Virgil*

"at Neoptolemus' death part of his kingdom was be-
queathed and went to Helenus": *reddita* [bequeathed] in
archaic usage should be understood as "given"; the prefix
re- is therefore superfluous. Ennius in the *Annals*:

> but Ilia, given in marriage 56

and elsewhere . . . [Inc. *Ann.* F 10].

*34 Nonius

facessere means "to do." Ennius, *Annals* Book 1:

> he[1] spoke these things, whereupon his henchmen did 57
>> what he said

[1] The subject is often assumed to be Amulius, ordering the
removal of Ilia. For *latrones* [henchmen, mercenaries], cf. Varro,
Ling. 7.52, and Inc. *Ann.* F 91.

*35 Non., p. 378.15–20 M. = 603 L.

PARUMPER: ut saepe interim et parvo tempore. PARUM-
PER: cito et velociter: Vergilius lib. VI [382] . . . Ennius
Annali lib. I:

58 ted Aeneia, precor, Venus, te genetrix patris nostri,
  ut me de caelo visas, cognata, parumper

  58 ted Aeneia, *Skutsch*: sale nata, *Vahlen*: *alii alia*: te saneneta
codd.

36 Charis., *GL* I, p. 90.24–28 = pp. 114–15 B.

neptis grammatici nolunt dici . . . et advocant Ennium,
quod dixerit ita:

60 Ilia, dia nepos, quas aerumnas tetulisti

Cf. *Explan. in Donat.*, *GL* IV, p. 563.14–16; Non., p. 215.6–8 M.
= 317 L.; Fest., p. 364.4 L.

37 Serv. Dan. ad Verg. *Aen.* 9.653

"cetera" id est "in ceterum." est autem Ennianum:

61   cetera quos peperisti
  ne cures

*35 Nonius

parumper: as often, "meanwhile" and "in a brief time."
parumper: "rapidly" and "quickly":[1] Virgil, Book 6 [382]
. . . Ennius, in Book 1 of the *Annals*:

> I beseech you, Aeneian[2] Venus, you, our father's   58
> parent,
> to look upon me from heaven, kinswoman, for a
> moment

[1] Nonius is mistaken: *parumper* invariably means "for a short time," i.e., *paullisper.*   [2] Skutsch's emendation has great appeal. *Aeneias* was a cult title of Aphrodite that Ennius would have encountered at Ambracia and was easily, if dubiously, associated even there with the hero Aeneas (Dion. Hal. *Ant.* 1.50.4).

36 Charisius

Grammarians disapprove the use of *neptis* [fem. of *nepos*, "grandson," commonly used for both genders] . . . and appeal to Ennius, because he said thus:

> Ilia, divine granddaughter, what troubles you have   60
> borne

37 Servius Danielis, *Commentary on Virgil*

cetera, that is *in ceterum* [for the rest]. It is, moreover, Ennian:

> for the rest, have no concern   61
> for the boys you have borne

F 38–46: The Story of Romulus and Remus
F 38–40: The Twins Are Rescued and Nursed by a
She-Wolf (cf. Inc. Ann. F 6)

38 Fronto, Ad M. Antoninum de orationibus 11 (p. 158.4–6 van den Hout)

Tiber amnis et dominus et fluentium circa regnator undarum. Ennius:

63   postquam constitit † isti fluvius, qui est omnibus princeps
        † qui sub ovilia †
ait.

Cf. Cic. *Orat.* 161.

39 Serv. Dan. ad Verg. *Aen.* 2.355

sane apud veteres "lupus" promiscuum erat, ut Ennius:

65   lupus femina feta repente

Cf. Fest., p. 364.4–5 L.; Quint. *Inst.* 1.6.12.

*40 Non., p. 378.15–24 M. = 603 L.

PARUMPER: cito et velociter. . . . Ennius Annali lib. I . . . [F 35]; idem in eodem:

66   indotuetur ibi lupus femina, conspicit omnis.
      hinc campum celeri passu permensa parumper
      conicit in silvam sese

F 38–46: The Story of Romulus and Remus
F 38–40: The Twins Are Rescued and Nursed by a
She-Wolf (cf. Inc. Ann. F 6)

38 Fronto, *Correspondence*

The Tiber stream is master and ruler of all waters flowing
in the region. Ennius says:

> after the river, which is ruler of all Italian streams [?],   63
> settled down [?][1]

[1] Cicero's allusion to these lines suggests that the phrase
"which is ruler of all" is truly Ennian, but the rest is hopelessly
corrupt. The translation provided is purely *exempli gratia*.

39 Servius Danielis, *Commentary on Virgil*

Among the ancients, *lupus* [wolf] was certainly of either
gender, as Ennius:

> a pregnant she-wolf suddenly   65

***40** Nonius

parumper: "rapidly" and "quickly." . . . Ennius in Book 1
of the *Annals* . . . [F 35]; again in the same:

> Then the she-wolf looks up, catches sight of them all.   66
> From there with quick step she crosses the field in a
>   few moments
> and casts herself into the wood

[1] Dion. Hal. *Ant.* 1.79.4–8, citing Fabius Pictor [F 4 *FRHist*],
tells how shepherds came across the wolf and tried to drive her
from the twins. Ennius perhaps took the story from Fabius Pictor.

F 41–42: The Twins Reach Maturity

41 Non., p. 134.11–13 M. = 195 L.

LICITARI: congredi pugnare. Ennius:

69   pars ludicre saxa
    iactant inter se licitantur

42 Fest., p. 340.22–25 L.

RATUS SUM significat putavi, sed alioqui pro firmo, certo
ponitur ratus et ratum. Ennius:

71   occiduntur. ubi potitur ratus Romulus praedam

*F 43: An Augury Establishes Romulus' Priority as
the City's Founder*

*43 Cic. *Div.* 1.107

atque ille Romuli auguratus pastoralis non urbanus fuit,
nec fictus ad opiniones imperitorum sed a certis acceptus
et posteris traditus. itaque Romulus augur, ut apud En-
nium est, cum fratre item augure:

F 41–42: The Twins Reach Maturity

41 Nonius

licitari: "to join battle," "to fight." Ennius:

> some playfully threw   69
> stones, they competed with each other[1]

[1] Verbal echoes at Ov. *Fast.* 2.365–68 and Verg. *Aen.* 6.642–43 suggest that the context here is the twins exercising with their shepherd companions.

42 Festus

ratus sum means "I thought," but in other contexts *ratus* and *ratum* are used for "firm" and "sure." Ennius:

> they fell. Then [or possibly "when"] stalwart[1]   71
>   Romulus gained the prize

[1] The translation follows Festus, whose gloss is not otherwise attested: *ratus* may instead simply mean "successful" [*OLD* s.v. *ratus* 2b, usually of prophesies and the like], i.e., the opposite of *irritus* [thwarted].

F 43: An Augury Establishes Romulus' Priority as the City's Founder

*__*43** Cicero, *On Divination*

That famous augury of Romulus was a pastoral art, not city bred, nor was it fabricated to sway the opinions of the ignorant, but was accepted by the knowledgeable and handed down to posterity. Thus Romulus, an augur, as he is in Ennius, along with his brother, also an augur:

72   curantes magna cum cura tum cupientes
regni dant operam simul auspicio augurioque.
in Murco Remus auspicio sedet atque secundam
75   solus avem servat. at Romulus pulcer in alto
quaerit Aventino, servat genus altivolantum.
certabant urbem Romam Remoramne vocarent.
omnibus cura viris uter esset induperator.
expectant veluti consul quom mittere signum
80   volt, omnes avidi spectant ad carceris oras
quam mox emittat pictos e faucibus currus:
sic expectabat populus atque ore timebat
rebus utri magni victoria sit data regni.
interea sol albus recessit in infera noctis.
85   exin candida se radiis dedit icta foras lux
et simul ex alto longe pulcerrima praepes
laeva volavit avis. simul aureus exoritur sol
cedunt de caelo ter quattuor corpora sancta
avium, praepetibus sese pulcrisque locis dant.

74 in Murco *Skutsch*: in monte *codd.*

---

[1] The Murcus, later known as the Remuria, was a promontory
on the southeast side of the Aventine hill. Skutsch's emendation,
though not in his text, is almost surely right. [2] Ennius' *sol
albus* is problematic: sun, moon, and morning star have all been
proposed, and all present difficulties. See Skutsch 1985, 231–32;
Meunier 2012, 103–14.

being careful then with great care, each desiring   72
a kingdom, they together take the auspices and
   augury.
On the Murcus[1] Remus sits in wait for a sign and
   watches
alone for a favorable flight; but handsome Romulus   75
   on the high
Aventine seeks and watches for the high-soaring race.
They were competing whether to call the city Roma
   or Remora.
All men were anxious over which would be their
   ruler.
They wait, as when the consul prepares to give
the signal, everyone eagerly looking to the starting   80
   gates
for how soon he sends the painted chariots from the
   barrier:
so the people were waiting, visible on each face a
   concern
for their affairs, to which the victory of supreme rule
   is given.
Meanwhile the sun[2] had set into the depth of night.
Then struck by rays the shining light showed itself   85
   openly
and at once on high from far away a beautifully
   winged
leftward flight advanced. Just as the golden sun
   arises,
there comes descending from the sky a dozen blessed
   bodies
of birds, settling themselves on fine and favorable
   seats.

90   conspicit inde sibi data Romulus esse propritim
          auspicio regni stabilita scamna solumque.

Cf. Gell. *NA* 7.6.9.

F 44–46: A Quarrel Leads to the Death of Remus
(cf. Inc. Ann. F 7)

*44 Fest., p. 312.32–14.1 L.

QUAMDE pro quam usos esse antiquos cum multi veteres
testimonio sunt tum Ennius in primo:

92   Iuppiter ut muro fretus magis quamde manu sim

*45 Non., p. 516.11–14 M. = 830 L.

TORVITER: Pomponius . . . Ennius lib. I:

93   ast hic quem nunc tu tam torviter increpuisti

*46 Macrob. *Sat.* 6.1.15 (Verg. *Aen.* 9.422 "tu tamen in-
terea calido mihi sanguine poenas persolves")

Ennius in primo:

94   nec pol homo quisquam faciet impune animatus
          hoc nec tu: nam mi calido dabis sanguine poenas

      95 dabis *Serv. Dan.*: das *Macrob.*

Cf. Serv. Dan. ad Verg. *Aen.* 9.422.

Thus Romulus sees that given to himself alone, 90
approved by auspices, were the base and bulwark of a
   kingdom.

F 44–46: A Quarrel Leads to the Death of Remus
(cf. Inc. Ann. F 7)

*44 Festus

Many old writers attest that the ancients used *quamde* for
quam [than], including Ennius in his first book:

> Jupiter[1] that I am supported by my wall more than by 92
>   my arm

[1] "Jupiter" is probably the subject of a preceding verb, e.g.,
"ordains" or "forbids." The uncertain context makes it impossible
to know whether the speaker is Romulus or Remus.

*45 Nonius

torviter [fiercely]: Pomponius . . . Ennius Book 1:

> but this one, whom now you have so fiercely berated 93

*46 Macrobius, *Saturnalia* (on Virgil, "well then, you will
pay me back with your life's blood")

Ennius in his first book:

> no living man at all will do this with impunity, 94
> nor will you, for you will pay me the penalty with
>   your life's blood

F 47–57: Romulus as Sole Ruler
F 47–53: The Reconciliation of Romans and Sabines (?)

*47 Fest., p. 416.35–18.1 L.

STOLIDUS: stultus. Ennius lib. I:

96   nam vi depugnare sues stolidi soliti sunt

*48 Fest., p. 384.25–27 L.

SUM pro eum usus est Ennius lib. I:

97   astu non vi sum summam servare decet rem

*49 Fest., p. 432.21–25 L.

SAS Verrius putat significare eas teste Ennio qui dicat in lib. I:

98   † virgines nam sibi quisque domi Romanus habet sas

cum "suas" magis videatur significare.

F 47–57: Romulus as Sole Ruler
F 47–53: The Reconciliation of Romans and
Sabines (?)

*47 Festus

stolidus: "mindless." Ennius Book 1:

> for mindless boars are wont to settle disputes by   96
> force

*48 Festus

Ennius used *sum* for *eum* [him] in Book 1:

> it is right that he guide important affairs of state by   97
> cleverness, not force

*49 Festus

Verrius thinks *sas* means *eas* ["them," fem.], citing Ennius as a witness, who says in Book 1:

> maidens, for each Roman has one of them for himself   98
> at home

although it seems rather to mean "their own."[1]

---

[1] Verrius' gloss is correct. The line as quoted is problematic: the required scansion *virginĕs* by iambic shortening would be unprecedented in epic verse. Alternatives have been proposed, but the truth is lost in the preceding line. The context is almost certainly the abduction of the Sabine women.

F 50–51: A Prayer to Mars and Quirinus

The "consorts" provided for them here are in origin abstract attributes: Valor (Nerio), Will (Herie), and Exhortation (Hora). Ovid's metamorphosis of Romulus' wife Hersilia into Quirinus' consort Hora (Met. 14.829–51) cannot be traced back to Ennius.

*50 Gell. *NA* 13.23.18

Ennius autem in primo Annali in hoc versu,

99 ⟨te Mavors, te⟩ Nerienem Mavortis et Heriem

si, quod minime solet, numerum servavit, primam syllabam intendit, tertiam corripuit.

suppl. Skutsch

*51 Non., p. 120.1–2 M. = 172 L.

HORA: iuventutis dea. Ennius Annali lib. I:

100 ⟨teque⟩ Quirine pater veneror Horamque Quirini

suppl. Columna

*52 Charis., *GL* I, p. 196.16–17 = p. 255 B.

"concorditer": Ennius ann. lib. I:

101 aeternum seritote diem concorditer ambo

F 50–51: A Prayer to Mars and Quirinus

*50 Gellius, *Attic Nights*

[On the scansion of Nerio] Ennius, moreover, in his first book of *Annals*, in this verse:

⟨you, Mars, you,⟩ Nerio, consort of Mars, and Herie[1]   99

if he has preserved the meter, which he is not always accustomed to do, has lengthened the first syllable and shortened the third.

[1] Nerio and Herie are in origin attributes rather than proper names, "valor" and "will," respectively. So too Hora in F 51, from the same (Oscan) root as Herie. Gellius identifies Nerio as Sabine. They are the objects here of the speaker's prayer.

*51 Nonius

Hora: the goddess of youth. Ennius, Book 1 of the *Annals*:

⟨and you,⟩ Father Quirinus, I beseech, and Hora,   100
    consort of Quirinus

*52 Charisius

concorditer: Ennius, Book 1 of the *Annals*:

see that both of you join eternal days harmoniously   101
    together

*53 Non., p. 111.39–12.2 = 160 L.

FORTUNATIM: prospere. Ennius Annali lib. I:

102   quod mihi reique fidei regno vobisque, Quirites,
       se fortunatim feliciter ac bene vortat

54 (cf. *Inc.* F 1) *Rhet. Her.* 4.18

compositio est verborum constructio quae facit omnes
partes orationis aequabiliter perpolitas. ea conservabitur
si fugiemus crebras vocalium concursiones . . . et si vita-
bimus eiusdem litterae nimiam adsiduitatem, cui vitio
versus hic erit exemplo—nam hic nihil prohibet in vitiis
alienis exemplis uti:

104   O Tite, tute, Tati, tibi tanta, tyranne, tulisti

Cf. Prisc., *GL* II, p. 591.13; *GL* III, p. 492.25; Pomp., *GL* V,
p. 303.33–34, 287.29; *Explan. in Donat.*, *GL* IV, p. 565; Isid. *Orig.*
1.36.14; Charis., *GL* I, p. 282.8 = p. 370 B.; Donat., *GL* IV,
p. 398.20–21; Mart. Cap. 5.514; Sacerd., *GL* VI, p. 454.29–30.

55 Cic. *Rep.* 1.64

iusto quidem rege cum est populus orbatus,

105   pectora [diu] . . . tenet desiderium

sicut ait Ennius post optimi regis obitum,

                                simul inter
       sese sic memorant: O Romule, Romule die,
       qualem te patriae custodem di genuerunt!
       O pater, O genitor, O sanguen dis oriundum!

*53 Nonius

fortunatim: "prosperously." Ennius, Book 1 of the *Annals*:

> that this may turn out prosperously, happily, and well   102
>   for me,
> our affairs, treaty, kingdom, and for you, Quirites

54 (cf. *Inc.* F 1) *Rhetorica ad Herennium*

Artistic composition is an arrangement of words that makes every part of the discourse equally polished. It will be maintained if we avoid the frequent clash of vowels . . . and if we shun excessive repetition of the same letter, for which fault this verse will be an example—for here nothing prevents using examples from the faults of others:

> you, O Titus Tatius, tyrant, took on yourself such   104
>   great troubles

55 Cicero, *On the Republic*

Indeed, when a people is bereft of a just king,

> longing . . . occupies their breasts   105

as Ennius says after the death of a most excellent king,

>   among themselves
> together they thus speak out: "O Romulus, Romulus
>   divine,
> what a guardian of the fatherland the gods created in
>   you!
> O father, O sire, O bloodline descended from the
>   gods!"

non "eros" nec "dominos" appellabant eos quibus iuste paruerant, denique ne "reges" quidem, sed "patriae custodes," sed "patres," sed "deos;" nec sine causa. quid enim adiungunt?

tu produxisti nos intra luminis oras

vitam honorem decus sibi datum esse iustitia regis existimabant.

105 diu *Ennio neg. Vahlen*

Cf. Lactant. *Inst.*1.15.30; Prisc., *GL* II, p. 250.15–16.

56 Serv. ad Verg. *Aen.* 6.763

"aevum" . . . proprie aeternitas est quae non nisi in deos venit. Ennius:

110   Romulus in caelo cum dis genitalibus aevom
        degit

Cf. Cic. *Tusc.* 1.28.

*57 Fest., p. 278.27–30 L.

PERTU‹SUM dolium› . . . ‹Ennius› lib. I . . .:

112   (de ruit) ç mu

Not "masters" nor "lords" did they call those they justly
obeyed, and indeed, not even "kings," but "guardians of
the fatherland," "fathers," "gods," and not without reason.
What do they say next?

> you have led us to the realms of light

They believed that life, honor, and distinction were given
to them by the justice of their king.

56 Servius, *Commentary on Virgil*

aevum . . . is properly "eternity," which comes only to the
gods. Ennius:

> Romulus passes eternity in heaven with the gods who   110
> begat him[1]

[1] The line may be parodied by Lucilius (1357 M., not in W.).
See Skutsch 1968, 109–12; Connors 2005, 126.

*57 Festus

a worn‹out jug› . . . Ennius, Book 1:

> (de ruit) ç mu[1]   112

[1] Skutsch 1985, 263: "The passage is hopelessly mutilated. . . .
All we know is that a line from *Annals* I, which near the end could
have contained the letters *c mu*, was quoted for the sake of a word
beginning with *p*."

BOOK II

Fragments explicitly attributed to this book by their sources confirm that Annals 2 *covered the reigns of the three kings Numa Pompilius (F 1–4), Tullus Hostilius (F 5–11), and Ancus Marcius (F 12–19), but identification of specific lines with specific events is highly problematic.*

1 Varro, *Ling.* 7.42

apud Ennium:

113   olli respondit suavis sonus Egeriai

olli valet dictum illi ab olla et ollo . . .

2 Varro, *Ling.* 7.43–44

apud Ennium:

114   mensas constituit idemque ancilia

dicta ab ambecisu, quod ea arma ab utraque parte ut Thracum incisa. [44]

libaque, fictores, Argeos, et tutulatos

---

[1] The *ancilia* are the ritual figure-eight shields of the Salian priests.

BOOK II

Tullus' destruction of Alba Longa as described in this book may be echoed by Virgil in Aeneid 2: cf. Servius ad 2.313, 486, whose comment ("de Albano excidio . . . translatus") led Vahlen to place Inc. Ann. F 9 here as well.

1 Varro, *On the Latin Language*

In Ennius:

> to him answered Egeria's sweet voice   113

olli has the force of *illi*, dative of feminine *olla* and masculine *ollus* . . .

2 Varro, *On the Latin Language*

In Ennius:

> he established the sacrificial tables and likewise the   114
>   sacred shields[1]

the term is from *ambecisus* [an incision on both sides], because those arms were cut in at both edges like those of Thracians. [44]

> and sacrificial cakes, shapers, Argei, and priests with
>   conical caps

165

liba quod libandi causa fiunt. fictores dicti a fingendis libis. Argei ab Argis; Argei fiunt e scirp[e]is, simulacra hominum XXVII; ea quotannis de ponte sublicio a sacerdotibus publice deici solent in Tiberim. tutulati dicti hi qui in sacris in capitibus habere solent ut metam.

Cf. Fest., pp. 484.35–86.2 L.; Paul., p. 485.12–14 L.; Serv. Dan. ad Verg. *Aen.* 2.683.

3 Varro, *Ling.* 7.45

eundem Pompilium ait fecisse flamines, qui cum omnes sunt a singulis deis cognominati, in quibusdam apparent ἔτυμα, ut cur sit Martialis et Quirinalis; sunt in quibus flaminum cognominibus latent origines ut in his qui sunt versibus plerisque:

116   Volturnalem
       Palatualem Furinalem Floralemque
       Falacrem⟨que⟩ et Pomonalem fecit hic idem

quae obscura sunt; eorum origo Volturnus, diva Palatua, Furrina, Flora, Falacer pater, Pomo[rum]na[m].

118 que *add. Skutsch*

liba [cakes] because they are made for libations [i.e., offerings]. They are called "shapers" because they shape the cakes. The Argei are named for Argos: Argei are made from rushes, the images of twenty-seven men. Every year they are accustomed to be thrown publicly by the priests from the Pile Bridge[2] into the Tiber. These priests are called *titulati* because in performing the ritual they are accustomed to have on their heads something like a turning point.[3]

[2] The *pons sublicius* connected the city with the Janiculum and was the *pons* from which the term *pontifex* was often thought to have derived (Varro, *Ling.* 5.83).   [3] The turning points (*metae*) at a racecourse were conical.

3 Varro, *On the Latin Language*

He [Ennius] says that this same [Numa] Pompilius established the *flamens*. Since they are all called by the names of the individual gods they serve, in some cases the etymology is quite clear for why one is called Martial or Quirinal;[1] there are some *flamens* for whose names the origins are unclear, as with most in these verses:

> [priests] of Volturnus,   116
> Palatus, Furina, and Flora,
> Falacer and Pomona he likewise created

which are obscure. Their origins are Volturnus, the divine Palatine, Furrina, Flora, father Falacer, Pomona.[2]

[1] That is, the special priests of Mars and Quirinus (the deified Romulus).   [2] Of these minor divinities, Volturnus, Furrina, and Falacer remain obscure.

*4 Fest., pp. 152.16–18 L.

ME pro mihi dicebant antiqui ut Ennius cum ait lib. II:

119 si quid me fuerit humanitus, ut teneatis

5 Quint. *Inst.* 1.5.12

nam duos in uno nomine faciebat barbarismos Tinga Placentinus, si reprehendenti Hortensio credimus, "preculam" pro "pergula" dicens, et immutatione, cum *c* pro *g* uteretur, et transmutatione, cum *r* praeponeret antecedenti. at in eadem vitii geminatione

120   Mettoeo‹que› Fufetioeo

dicens Ennius poetico iure defenditur.

 sic rest. Ritschl: alii alia in loco valde corrupto

6 Serv. Dan. ad Verg. *Aen.* 10.6

"quianam": cur [quare *add. Serv. Dan.*] Ennianus sermo est. [*add. Serv. Dan.*:]

121   quianam legiones caedimus ferro

*4 Festus

The ancients used to say "me" [ablative or accusative] instead of "to me" [dative], as when Ennius says in Book 2:

> if something human befalls me, [see] that you   119
>   maintain

5 Quintilian, *The Orator's Education*

Tinga of Placentia committed two barbarisms in a single word, if we believe Hortensius' criticism, in saying *preculam* for *pergula* [market stall], by substitution in using *c* for *g* and by transposition when he put *r* before *e*. But Ennius, saying

> ⟨and⟩ of Mettus Fufetius[1]   120

is acquitted of the same double fault by poetic license.

[1] Mettus Fufetius ruled Alba after the death of its king, Cluilius. His punishment by Tullus for treachery may be the subject of F 9 and 10. Liv. 1.23–28 tells the story. Ennius' Homeric genitive is a marked Grecism.

6 Servius Danielis, *Commentary on Virgil*

quianam: "why?," "for what reason?" It is an Ennian expression:

> why do we cut down legions with the sword[1]   121

[1] Vahlen and Skutsch, for no particularly good reason, assign this fragment to Book 2. Warmington more cautiously places it among the fragments *Incertae sedis.*

*7 Fest., pp. 312.32–14.2 L.

QUAMDE pro quam usos esse antiquos cum multi veteres testimonio sunt tum Ennius in primo [F 44] . . . secundo:

122   quamde tuas omnes legiones ac popularis

*8 Fest., pp. 188.27–90.2 L.

OCCASUS: interitus, vel solis cum decidit a superis infra terras. quo vocabulo Ennius pro occasione est usus in lib. II:

123   hic occasus datus est, at Horatius inclutus saltu

9 *Macrob. exc. Bob.*, *GL* V, p. 651.34

tractare saepe trahere et habitare saepe habere . . . Ennius:

124   tractatus per aequora campi

10 Prisc., *GL* II, pp. 206.22–7.2

vetustissimi tamen etiam homo homonis declinaverunt. Ennius:

125   volturus in †spineto† miserum mandebat homonem:
heu quam crudeli condebat membra sepulcro

nam et vultur et vulturus et vulturius dicitur.

Cf. Charis., *GL* I, p. 147.15 = p. 187.5 B.; Ps.-Prob. (*Att. Accad. Torino* 19 [1884] 446); Serv. ad Verg. *Aen.* 6.595.

170

*7 Festus

Many old writers attest that the ancients used *quamde* for *quam* [than], including Ennius in his first book [F 44] . . . and in his second:

> than all your legions and countrymen   122

*8 Festus

occasus: removal, as of the sun when it drops from the heavens below the earth. Ennius used this word in place of *occasio* [opportunity] in Book 2:

> here an opportunity was given, but renowned   123
> Horatius[1] with a leap

[1] Probably the last of the Horatii (not Horatius Cocles), the "opportunity" being the momentary advantage of the three Curiatii. So Skutsch 1985, 274–75, citing Liv. 1.25.8. Cf. Prop. 3.3.7 (T 50).

9 *Excerpts from Macrobius*

tractare, "to drag often," and *habitare*, "to hold often" [iterative forms] . . . Ennius:

> dragged back and forth over the surface of   124
> the plain

10 Priscian

The oldest writers nevertheless declined *homo* [man] with a genitive *homonis.* Ennius:

> a vulture devoured the wretched man [hanging?]   125
> Alas! in how cruel a tomb it buried his limbs

for *vultur* and *vulturus* and *vulturius* are used.

*11 Fest., p. 362.19–24 L.

"rigido‹que Calore" idem› Ennius [Inc. *Ann.* F 31] ioca-
tus videtur . . . et lib. II cum ait:

127   ‹. . . Cael›i caerula prata

Caelium montem dicit,

> Caeli *suppl. Lindsay*

*12 Fest., p. 312.7–11 L.

QUAESO ut significat idem quod rogo, ita quaesere ponitur
ab antiquis pro quaerere, ut est apud Ennium lib. II:

128   Ostia munita est. idem loca navibus pulcris
             munda facit, nautisque mari quaesentibus vitam

Cf. Paul. *Fest.*, pp. 127.1; 313.4 L.

*13 Fest., p. 490.5–9 L.

TOLERARE: patienter ferre . . . Ennius lib. II:

130   ferro se caedi quam dictis his toleraret

*14 Fest., p. 184.17–18 L.

NINGULUS: nullus ut Ennius lib. II:

131   qui ferro minitere atque in te ningulus

Cf. Paul., p. 185.4 L.

172

*11 Festus

"and by the stiff Calor" [Inc. *Ann.* F 31] Ennius appears to have made a similar joke . . . also when in Book 2 he says:

> the blue-green meadows of ⟨the Caelian⟩   127

he speaks of the Caelian hill.[1]

[1] Ennius plays on the similarity of common words to less obvious proper names: *calor* [heat] and the river Calor, *caelum* [heaven] and the hill of Rome.

*12 Festus

As *quaeso* [request] means the same as *rogo* [*ask*], so *quaesere* [to request] is used by the ancients instead of *quaerere* [to request], as it is in Ennius, Book 2:

> Ostia was established. He[1] also improved the channel   128
> for fine ships and for sailors seeking a livelihood at sea

[1] Ancus, the traditional founder of Ostia (Cic. *Rep.* 2.5; Liv. 1.3.39).

*13 Festus

tolerare: "to bear with patience" . . . Ennius, Book 2:

> that he endure falling by the sword than by these   130
>   words

*14 Festus

ningulus: "no one," as Ennius, Book 2:

> [you] who threaten with the sword, while against you   131
>   no one

*15 Prisc., *GL* II, p. 504.13–27

vetustissimi inveniuntur etiam produxisse et eruo erūi, arguo argūi, annuo annūi. Ennius in II:

132   adnuit sese mecum decernere ferro

*16 Prisc., *GL* III, p. 3.4–6.

sic ἐμοῦ σοῦ οὗ mei tui sui, ἐμοῦς σοῦς οὖς mis tis sis. sed propter supra dictum causam [*scil.* ne verbum esse putetur] tacitus est tertiae huiuscemodi genetivus. Ennius in II:

133   ingens cura †mis cum† concordibus aequiperare

*17 Fest., p. 446.13–15 L.

SPERES antiqui pluraliter dicebant, ut Ennius lib. II:

134   et simul effugit. speres ita funditus nostras

*18 Fest., p. 384.26–29 L.

SUM pro eum usus est Ennius lib. I . . . [F 48] et lib. II:

135   at sese sum quae dederat in luminis oras

Cf. Paul., p. 385.5 L.

174

*15 Priscian

Very ancient writers are found even to have lengthened
the penultimate vowel also [in the perfect of] *eruo, erūi*
[to uproot], *arguo, argūi* [to accuse], *annuo, annūi* [to
agree]. Ennius in Book 2:

he agreed to settle with me by the sword   132

*16 Priscian

So in this way [the singular genitives] ἐμοῦ σοῦ οὗ corre-
spond to *mei tui sui* [and the plurals] ἐμοῦς σοῦς οὗς to
mis tis sis, but for the reason mentioned above [i.e., lest it
be mistaken for a verb] the genitive of the third of this type
is not expressed. Ennius in Book 2:

a great concern for us [?] to equal my comrades   133

*17 Festus

The ancients used to say *speres* [hopes] in the plural,[1] as
Ennius, Book 2:

and simultaneously fled. So our hopes utterly   134

[1] Nominative and, as in the verse cited, accusative.

*18 Festus

Ennius used *sum* for *eum* [him] in Book 1 [F 48] . . . and
Book 2:

but herself, who had brought him into the realms of   135
    light

*19 Fest., p. 480. 29–32 L.

ᴛ⟩ᴜᴅɪᴛᴀɴᴛᴇꜱ: tundentes ⟨negotium, id est ag⟩entes sig-
nificare ait Cincius ⟨de verbis priscis. E⟩nnius lib. II:

136   haec inter se totum ⟨. . . tuditan⟩tes

Cf. Paul., p. 481.7 L.

*19 Festus

tuditantes: "hammering out" ⟨a matter⟩ means, as Cincius[1] ⟨*On Archaic Words*⟩ says, "conducting a matter." Ennius, Book 2:

> thoroughly hammering out these things . . . among 136
> themselves[2]

[1] L. Cincius Alimentus, an Augustan antiquarian, not to be confused with the historian of the same name, a younger contemporary of Fabius Pictor.   [2] For the sense, cf. Inc. *Ann.* F 104, but the construction is obscured by the lacuna. The exact sense thus remains problematic.

BOOK III

*This book took up the story from the death of Ancus (F 1)
and probably continued to the expulsion of the Tarquins,
making three books to carry the narrative from the found-
ing of Rome to the end of the monarchy. There are hints
among the fragments of the auspicious omen marking the*

1 Fest., p. 388.3–7 L.

SOS . . . interdum pro suos ponebant, ut cum per dativum
casum idem Ennius effert:

137   postquam lumina sis oculis bonus Ancus reliquit

Cf. Paul., p. 387.12–14 L.

*2 Fest., p. 386.20–24 L.

SOLUM: terram. Ennius lib. III:

138   Tarquinio dedit imperium simul et sola regni

et aliubi "sed sola terrarum . . ." [Inc. *Ann.* F 18].

BOOK III

elder Tarquin's entry to Rome (F 3; cf. Liv. 1.34.8), the flame seen around the head of Servius Tullius (F 7–8; cf. Liv. 1.39), and the funeral of Tarquin (F 9, 10?), but nothing is certain.

1 Festus

sos . . . they occasionally used in place of *suos* [their own], as when Ennius puts it in the dative case:[1]

> after good Ancus left the light with his eyes   137

[1] The phrase is in fact almost certainly (instrumental?) ablative, as at Inc. *Ann.* F 86, *corde relinquite somnum.*

*2 Festus

solum: "land." Ennius, Book 3:

> [the people] gave Tarquin command along with the   138
> bedrock of rule

and elsewhere "but the surfaces of the earth . . ." [Inc. *Ann.* F 18].

*3 [Prob.] ad Verg. *Ecl.* 6.31 (vol. 3.2, p. 341 Th.-H.)

pro aere venti hic extrinsecus accipiuntur: ad quod argumentum collegimus Ennii exemplum de Annalium tertio:

139   et densis aquila pennis obnixa volabat
       vento quem perhibent Graium genus aera lingua

*4 Fest., p. 386.32–36 L.

sos pro eos antiqui dicebant, ut Ennius . . . lib. III:

141   circum sos quae sunt magnae gentes opulentae

*5 Macrob. *Sat.* 1.4.18

quo in loco animadvertendum est non solum quod "noctu concubia" sed quod "qua noctu" dixerit [Ennius]. et hoc posuit in Annalium septimo [F 14], in quorum tertio clarius idem dixit:

142   hac noctu filo pendebit Etruria tota

*6 Macrob. *Sat.* 6.1.16 (Verg. *Aen.* 7.520–21 "concurrunt undique telis / indomiti agricolae")

Ennius in tertio:

143   postquam defessi sunt stare et spargere sese
       hastis ansatis, concurrunt undique telis

    143 stare et *Vahlen*: stant et *codd.*: stantes *Fruter*

*3 [Probus], *Commentary on Virgil*

"Winds" are understood here by implication instead of "air." In support of this interpretation we adduce an example from the third book of Ennius' *Annals*:

> and an eagle came flying, battling with close-packed   139
>   wings
> the wind, which the Greek race in its tongue calls *aer*

*4 Festus

The ancients used to say *sos* for *eos* [them], as Ennius . . . Book 3:

> around them, who are great peoples and wealthy   141

*5 Macrobius, *Saturnalia*

Here we should note that he said not only *noctu concubia* but also *qua noctu*. He did this in the seventh book of the *Annals* [F 14], in the third of which he said the same thing more clearly:

> on this night all of Etruria will hang by a thread   142

*6 Macrobius, *Saturnalia* (on Virgil, "from all sides the undaunted farmers charge with their spears")

Ennius in Book 3:

> after growing weary of standing firm and showering   143
>   each other
> with javelins sent whirling, from all sides they charge
>   with their spears

*7 Macrob. *Sat.* 6.1.9 (Verg. *Aen.* 4.482, 6.797 "axem umero torquet stellis ardentibus aptum")

Ennius in primo [F 22] . . . et in tertio:

145   caelum prospexit stellis fulgentibus aptum

*8 Non., p. 51.7–12 M. = 72 L.

LAEVUM significari veteres putant quasi a levando. . . . Ennius Annali lib. III:

146   olli de caelo laevom dedit inclutus signum

olli *Passerat*: olim *codd.*

9 Donat. ad Ter. *Hec.* 135

uxor dicitur . . . vel quod lotos maritos ipsae ungebant, cuius rei Ennius testis est:

147   exin Tarquinium bona femina lavit et unxit

Cf. Serv. ad Verg. *Aen.* 6.219 ("lavant frigentis et ungunt"): versus Ennii qui ait . . .

*10 Fest., p. 254.22–24 L.

PRODINUNT: prodeunt, ut Ennius Annali lib. III:

148   prodinunt. famuli tum candida lumina lucent

Cf. Paul., p. 255.8–9 L.

*7 Macrobius, *Saturnalia* (on Virgil, "he spins heaven's vault, studded with blazing stars, on his shoulder")

Ennius in the first book [F 22] . . . and in the third book:

> [Tanaquil?] looked out on heaven, studded with 145
> shining stars

*8 Nonius

Old critics think *laevum* [favorable] takes its meaning as if from *levando* [relieving]. . . . Ennius in *Annals*, Book 3:

> the renowned one[1] gave [her?] a favorable sign from 146
> heaven

[1] Perhaps Jupiter, but possibly the eagle of F 3, if the line refers to that earlier omen. Editors from Merula to Skutsch, recalling *Aen.* 2.679–94, identify F 7–8 with the omen Tanaquil received concerning Servius Tullius, but note the hesitation of Wigodsky 1972, 46–47 (reading *olim*, not *olli*).

9 Donatus, *Commentary on Terence*

uxor [wife] is so called . . . perhaps because they anoint their husbands themselves after they are washed, of which fact Ennius is a witness:

> then the good woman washed and anointed [the body 147
> of?] Tarquin

*10 Festus

prodinunt: "they go forth," as Ennius in *Annals*, Book 3:

> [they] go forth. Then the household servants beamed 148
> bright lights

*11 Gell. *NA* 1.22.14–16

an autem superesse dixerint veteres pro restare et per-
ficiendae rei deesse quaerebamus. [15] nam Sallustius in
significatione ista non superesse sed superare dicit [*Iug.*
70.2] . . . [16] sed invenimus in tertio Ennii Annalium in
hoc verso,

149   inde sibi memorat unum super esse laborem

id est reliquum esse et restare, quod, quia id est, divise
pronuntiandum est, ut non una pars orationis esse videa-
tur sed duae.

*11 Gellius, *Attic Nights*

We also wondered if the ancients used *superesse* to mean "to remain and be lacking to complete a thing," [15] for Sallust uses in that sense not *superesse* but *superare* [*Iug.* 70.2] . . . [16] but we find in this verse in the third book of Ennius' *Annals*:

> then he declares that one task remains for him   149

that is, "is left and remains undone," but this is because it is divided and should be pronounced not as one part of speech [i.e., the verb *superesse*] but as two [i.e., adverb *super* + verb *esse*], which it is.

BOOK IV

This book dealt with the early days of the Republic, but specific references are difficult to identify. Anxur (F 3) was captured by the Romans in 406, 400, and 329 BC. The solar eclipse of F 4 must have been that of June 21, 400 BC.

1 Fest., pp. 310.35–12.4 L.

QUADRATA ROMA in Palatio ante templum Apollinis dicitur, ubi reposita sunt quae solent boni ominis gratia in urbe condenda adhiberi, quia saxo finitus [*Wiseman*: munitus *edd. pler.*: minitus *cod.*] est initio in speciem quadratam. eius loci Ennius meminit cum ait:

150   et qui se sperat Romae regnare Quadratae?

   et qui se sperat *Salmasius*: quis est erat *cod.*

BOOK IV

Skutsch heard echoes in F 5 of Camillus' famous speech opposing relocation to Veii after the Gallic sack in 390 (Liv. 5.51–54).

1 Festus

Roma Quadrata [i.e., Square Rome] is said to be [a site?] on the Palatine before the temple of Apollo, where the things customarily used to secure a favorable omen in founding the city are stored, since it was originally marked out by stone in the shape of a square. Ennius recalls this place when he says:

and who hopes to rule as king at Roma Quadrata?[1]   150

[1] Three men aspired to kingship in the early days of the Republic: Sp. Cassius (485 BC), Sp. Maelius (439 BC), and M. Manlius Capitolinus (384 BC). If Liv. 4.15.3 echoes this verse, the reference here is likely to Maelius, but certainty is impossible. Warmington instead placed the verse in Book 1 (123 W.) in the context of Romulus' succession. For the epithet *quadrata*, cf. Solin. 1.17–18 (citing Varro); Dion. Hal. *Ant.* 1.88.2; Plut. *Rom.* 9.4; Tzetzes on Lycoph. *Alex.* 1232, and the discussion by Wiseman 2015b, 114–20.

*2 Macrob. *Sat.* 6.1.17 (Verg. *Aen.* 12.552 "summa nituntur opum vi")

Ennius in quarto:

151   Romani scalis: summa nituntur opum vi

3 Paul. *Fest.*, p. 20.22–23 L.

ANXUR vocabatur quae nunc Tarracina dicitur Vulscae gentis, sicut ait Ennius:

152   Volsculus perdidit Anxur

4 Cic. *Rep.* 1.25

id autem [*scil.* solem lunae opposito deficere] postea ne nostrum quidem Ennium fugit, qui ut scribit anno quinquagesimo ⟨et⟩ CCC fere post Romam conditam,

153   Nonis Iunis soli luna obstitit et nox

atque in hac re tanta inest ratio atque sollertia ut ex hoc die quem apud Ennium et in Maximis Annalibus consignatum videmus superiores solis defectiones reputatae sunt usque ad illam quae Nonis Quintilibus fuit regnante Romulo.

---

[1] This passage is central to the debate over the relationship between Ennius' poem and the *Annales Maximi* (F 5 *FRHist*). See Elliott 2013, 23–30, and Rich, *FRHist* 3:6–7.

*2 Macrobius, *Saturnalia* (on Virgil, "they strive with all their might and main")

Ennius in the fourth book:

> the Romans on ladders: they strive with all their   151
>   might and main

3 Paul the Deacon, *Epitome of Festus*

The town of the Vulscian tribe now called Tarracina used to be called Anxur, as Ennius says:

> the Volscian[1] lost Anxur   152

[1] What appears to be an unflattering diminutive ("the wretched Volscians," Warmington) may be no more than an ethnic label. See Skutsch 1968, 143–44. Lucilius occasionally uses such forms without semantic function, e.g., *vetulus*, "old" (282, 826, 1066 M. = 306, 952, 1029 W.), *aureolus*, "golden" (290 M. = 323 W.) or as a collective, e.g., *servuli*, "slaves as a whole" (730 M. = 738 W.).

4 Cicero, *On the Republic*

But afterward, it [a solar eclipse] did not escape the notice even of our own Ennius, since he writes that in about the three hundred and fiftieth year after the founding of Rome:

> on the fifth of June the moon and night   153
>   obscured the sun

Indeed, so much skilled calculation has been applied to this matter that from the date we see recorded in Ennius and in the *Annales Maximi* previous solar eclipses have been reckoned all the way back to the one that occurred on the fifth of July when Romulus was king.[1]

5 Varro, *Rust.* 3.1.2–3

etenim vetustissimum oppidum cum sit traditum Grae-
cum Boeotiae Thebae, quod rex Ogygos aedificarit, in agro
Romano Roma quam Romulus rex: nam in hoc nunc de-
nique est ut dici possit, non cum Ennius scripsit

154   septingenti sunt, paulo plus aut minus, anni
       augusto augurio postquam incluta condita Roma est

[3] Thebae, quae ante cataclysmon Ogygi conditae dicun-
tur, eae tamen circiter duo milia annorum et centum sunt.

Cf. Suet. *Aug.* 7 (155).

5 Varro, *On Agriculture*

The most ancient Greek city, according to tradition, is
Boeotian Thebes, which king Ogygos built. In Roman ter-
ritory it is Rome, which king Romulus built: for in this
matter now at last it can be said and not when Ennius
wrote,

> seven hundred years, a little more or less,   154
> since by august augury renowned Rome was
>   founded[1]

[3] Thebes, however, which is said to have been founded
before the flood called after Ogygos, is some 2,100 years
old.

---

[1] Whether Ennius is speaking in his own voice, as Varro im-
plies, or the lines belong to Camillus, as Skutsch 1985, 314–15
suggests, is unclear, as is Ennius' date for the founding of Rome.
For the problem see Feeney 2007, 100–103; Elliott 2013, 272–74.

BOOK V

This book is traditionally believed to have covered events from 385 to the end of the Samnite Wars ca. 295 BC, but only F 3 and F 5 suggest a specific context. Skutsch confidently attributed F 1 to a speech in 340 BC by the consul Manlius justifying the notorious order to execute his own

1 August. *Civ.* 2.21

sicut etiam ipse Tullius non Scipionis nec cuiusquam alterius sed suo sermone loquens in principio quinti libri [*de Rep.*], commemorato prius Ennii poetae versu quo dixerat

156   moribus antiquis res stat Romana virisque

quem quidem ille versum, inquit, vel brevitate vel veritate tamquam ex oraculo quodam mihi esse effatus videtur.

Cf. SHA, *Avid. Cass.* 5.7 (*Divi Marci epistula*).

2 *Fragm. de metr.*, *GL* VI, pp. 611.24–12.6

hexameter heroicus . . . totus ex spondiis:

157   cives Romani tunc facti sunt Campani

BOOK V

son for insubordination (cf. Liv. 8.7), but Warmington more cautiously kept it among the fragments Incertae sedis *(467 W.). Other identifications are purely conjectural. (Skutsch relocated line 166, assigned to this book by Festus, to Book 6.)*

1 Augustine, *City of God*

Just as even Cicero himself, at the beginning of the fifth book [of his *Republic*], speaking not in the words of Scipio or of anyone else but in his own, having previously recalled the verse of the poet Ennius, where he had said

> on old-time ways the Roman state stands fast and on   156
> its men

remarks, "he seems to me to have spoken this verse in its brevity and truth as if by some oracle."

2 *Anonymous metrical treatise*

a heroic hexameter . . . entirely of spondees:

> the Campanians were then made Roman citizens[1]   157

[1] The citizens of Capua received the *civitas sine suffragio* in the 330s BC.

3 Ekkehartus in Oros. *Hist.* 3.9.5 ("anno autem post hunc subsequente Minucia virgo Vestalis ob admissum incestum damnata est vivaque obruta in campo qui nunc sceleratus vocatur")

supra ruta . . . nunc *Ekkehartus addidit* Ennius:

158   quom nihil horridius umquam lex ulla iuberet

      quom [cum] *Ekkehart*: quo *mavult Skutsch*

*4 Fest., pp. 188.27–90.3 L.

OCCASUS: interitus . . . quo vocabulo Ennius pro occasione est usus in lib. II [F 8] . . . ; item in lib. V:

159   inicit inritatus: tenet occasus, iuvat res

5 Ps.-Acro ad Hor. *Epist.* 2.2.98

"lento Samnites ad lumina prima duello": sensus, invicem odiosi sumus fallendo nos et mala carmina praedicantes et hoc sine fine facimus. ut Romani quondam pugnavere cum hostibus Samnitibus usque ad noctem: unde Ennius:

160   bellum aequis {de} manibus nox intempesta diremit

      de *del. Fabricius*

3 Ekkehart on Orosius, *Histories* ("In the year following this [i.e., 337 BC], the Vestal Virgin Minucia was condemned on a charge of incest and buried alive in the field now called 'accursed.'")[1]

above "buried . . . now" *Ekkehart added*: Ennius:

since nothing more horrible did any law ever demand   158

[1] Ekkehart IV, a learned monk of St. Gall, recorded two quotations from Ennius in his library's manuscript of Orosius (cod. Sangall. 621): this one and 7 *Ann.* F 3. (An earlier reader of the same ninth-century manuscript is responsible for Inc. *Ann.* F 28.) See Skutsch 1985, 25–26.

*4 Festus

occasus: removal . . . Ennius used this word in place of *occasio* [opportunity] in Book 2 [F 8] . . . , likewise in Book 5:

rushes in provoked: opportunity holds [him?],   159
    circumstance helps

5 Ps.-Acro, *Commentary on Horace*

"like Samnites in a weary duel until nightfall": The sense is, we in turn grow tiresome by fooling ourselves and declaiming terrible poetry, and this we do without end. So once the Romans fought with their enemy the Samnites until nightfall, from which Ennius:

deepest night broke off the battle evenly drawn[1]   160

[1] Skutsch tentatively refers the line to the battle of Lautulae in 315 BC, citing Liv. 9.23.4. Horace's allusion, which the scholiast seems to have misunderstood, is not to soldiers but to the heavily armed gladiators known as Samnites.

*6 Non., p. 556.19–20 M. = 893 L.

ANSATAE: iaculamenta cum ansis. Ennius lib. V:

161   ansatas mittunt de turribus

*7 Prisc., *GL* II, p. 428.13–15

sed magis a misereo est, quo vetustissimi sunt usi, ut supra dictum est. Ennius in V Annalium:

162   cogebant hostes lacrumantes ut misererent

*8 Macrob. *Sat.* 6.4.4

agmen pro actu et ductu quodam ponere non inelegans est, ut "leni fluit agmine Thybris" [Verg. *Aen.* 2.782]; immo et antiquum est. Ennius enim ⟨in⟩ quinto ait:

163   quod per amoenam urbem leni fluit agmine flumen

*6 Nonius

ansatae: missiles with thongs. Ennius, Book 5:

> they send down thonged missiles from the towers   161

*7 Priscian

But it [distinctions among active, deponent, and inceptive forms] is even more the case with *misereo* [I take pity], which the oldest writers used, as mentioned above. Ennius in *Annals* 5:

> in tears they compelled the enemy to take pity   162

*8 Macrobius, *Saturnalia*

Using *agmen* [column] to mean *actus* [movement] and a kind of *ductus* [directed motion] is not inelegant, as in "the Tiber flows with gentle column" [Verg. *Aen.* 2.782]; indeed, it is also ancient. So Ennius says in Book 5:

> the river that flows with gentle column through the   163
>   pleasant city

BOOK VI

This book centered on the war with Pyrrhus, king of
Epirus, who invaded Italy in 280 BC at the invitation of
Tarentum. Ennius' version of these events clearly had
great appeal to Cicero (F 1, 4, 11, 15), but the identifi-
cation of specific references in the fragments is largely
conjectural. Cicero's witticism as reported by Quintilian
suggests that F 1 was the book's opening line. Other cogent
suggestions: Tarentum's initial appeal for aid (F 2), the
battle of Heraclea and its aftermath (F 8–11), the self-
sacrifice (devotio) of the consul P. Decius Mus at the battle
of Aesculum in 279 (F 12; cf. Cic. Fin. 2.61; Tusc. 1.89),

*1 Quint. Inst. 6.3.86

dissimulavit Cicero cum Sex. Annalis testis reum laesisset
et instaret identidem accusator "dic M. Tulli siquid potes
de Sexto Annali": versus enim dicere coepit de libro Ennii
Annali sexto

164   quis potis ingentis oras evolvere belli

Cf. Macrob. Sat. 6.1.18; Serv. ad Verg. Aen. 9.528; Diom., GL I,
pp. 385.31–86.1.

BOOK VI

the speech of Appius Claudius Caecus opposing peace (F 15).

For the importance of this book to the poem as a whole and its abiding interest for later readers, see Suerbaum 1995; Fantham 2006; Fabrizi 2012, 119–50. Its imitation by Virgil in Aeneid *6 has brought special attention to F 9, e.g., Goldberg 1995, 101–2; Elliott 2013, 167–69; Goldschmidt 2013, 160–61. The methods used by Kleve 1990 to identify fragments of this book in P. Herc. 21 are now regarded as questionable; his readings should be treated with extreme caution.*

*1 Quintilian, *The Orator's Education*

Cicero used dissimulation when a witness named Sextus Annalis had damaged his client and the prosecutor kept pressing him with "What have you to say, Marcus Tullius, concerning Sextus Annalis?" He began reciting lines from the sixth book of Ennius' *Annals*:

who can unroll the vast boundaries of the war   164

*2 Fest., p. 168.3–6 L.

NAVUS: celer et strenuus a navium velocitate videtur dictus. Ennius lib. VI:

165 navos repertus homo, Graio patre, Graius homo, rex

*3 Fest., p. 412.13–23 L.

STIR‹PEM hominum in masculino gene›re antiqui . . . ‹Ennius in sexto›:

166 nomine Burrus uti memorant a stirpe supremo

  nomine *Fest.*: homines *Non.*   Burrus *ap. Cic. Orat.* 160: Pyrrhus *vel* Pyrrus *codd.*

Cf. Non. p. 226.32–33 M. = 336 L.

4 Cic. *Div.* 2.116

Herodotum cur veraciorem ducam Ennio? num minus ille potuit de Croeso quam de Pyrrho fingere Ennius? quis enim est qui credat Apollinis ex oraclo Pyrrho esse responsum:

167 aio te Aeacida Romanos vincere posse

primum Latine Apollo numquam locutus est; deinde ista sors inaudita Graecis est; praeterea Pyrrhi temporibus iam Apollo versus facere desierat; postremo, quamquam semper fuit, ut apud Ennius est, "stolidum . . ." [F 14], tamen hanc amphiboliam versus intellegere potuisset "vincere te Romanos" nihilo magis in se quam in Romanos valere.

Cf. Quint. *Inst.* 7.9.6; Vel. Long., *GL* VII, p. 55.17–24; Porph. ad Hor. *Ars P.* 403; Prisc., *GL* III, pp. 234.18–35.4.

*2 Festus

navus: "swift" and "vigorous," seems to derive from the speed of ships. Ennius, Book 6:

> a vigorous man was found, a Grecian man from a   165
>   Grecian father, a king

*3 Festus

stirps [scion] of men, ancient writers use in the masculine . . . Ennius in Book 6:

> Pyrrhus[1] by name, a man of highest stock, so they say   166

[1] Here and at Inc. *Ann.* F 29 editors restore the spelling *Burrus* in the Latin on the strength of Cic. *Orat.* 160, *Burrum semper Ennius, numquam Pyrrhum* "Ennius always wrote *Burrus*, never *Pyrrhus*." Cf. *Trag.* F 154.

4 Cicero, *On Divination*

Why should I accept Herodotus as more truthful than Ennius? Surely he was no less able to invent stories about Croesus than Ennius was about Pyrrhus? Who could believe that the response of Apollo's oracle to Pyrrhus was

> I say that you, Aeacus' descendant, the Romans can   167
>   defeat

First, Apollo never spoke in Latin. Second, that prophecy is unknown to the Greeks. Third, in Pyrrhus' day Apollo had ceased making verses, and finally, although it was always the case, as in Ennius, that "obtuse is the race of the Aeacids . . ." [F 14], he would nevertheless have been able to understand that this ambiguous verse "the Romans you defeat" could as easily apply to himself as to the Romans.

*5 Fest., p. 384.18–21

⟨SUMMU⟩SSI dicebantur ⟨murmuratores⟩. Naevius . . . [F 47 *TrRF*], Ennius in sexto:

168   ⟨. . .⟩ntus in occulto mussabat

   intus *Colonna*: Quintus *Merula*: sic irata Tarentus *Skutsch*, *e.g.*

*6 Macrob. *Sat.* 6.1.54 (Verg. *Aen.* 7.625 "pulverulentus eques furit: omnes arma requirunt")

Ennius in sexto:

169   balantum pecudes quatit: omnes arma requirunt

7 Gell. *NA* 16.10.1–5

otium erat quodam die Romae in foro a negotiis et laeta quaedam celebritas feriarum, legebatur in consessu forte conplurium Enni liber ex Annalibus [cf. T 85]. in eo libro versus hi fuerunt:

170   proletarius publicitus scutisque feroque
         ornatur ferro. muros urbemque forumque
         excubiis curant

[2] tum ibi quaeri coeptum est quid esset proletarius. . . . [5] nam Q. Ennius verbum hoc ex duodecim tabulis vestris accepit . . .

---

   [1] Skutsch, following Vahlen, associates this fragment with the army raised from the *proletarii* by the magistrate Marcius Philippus in 281 or 280 BC (Cassius Hemina, F 24 *FRHist*). Warmington places it among the fragments *Incertae sedis* (526–28 W.).

*5 Festus

sumussi are said to be "murmurers." Naevius . . . [F 47 *TrRF*], Ennius in his sixth book:

> [the Tarentine people?[1]] grumbled in secret   168

[1] Skutsch's suggested supplement reflects a suggestion by Vahlen 1903, clxxv, that the context is Tarentine disaffection with Pyrrhus.

*6 Macrobius, *Saturnalia* (on Virgil, "the dusty horseman rages: all look for their weapons")

Ennius in Book 6:

> makes the bleating flocks tremble: all look for their   169
>   weapons

7 Gellius, *Attic Nights*

One day there was a general suspension of business in the forum at Rome and quite a joyous celebration of the holiday. It happened that a book of Ennius' *Annals* was being read before a rather large gathering [cf. T 85]. In that book were these lines:[1]

> the proletariat at public cost with shields and savage   170
>   sword was armed. The walls and city and forum
>   they protect by standing guard

[2] Then the question arose what "proletariat" meant. . . .
[5] For Ennius took the word from your Twelve Tables . . .

Cf. Non., p. 155.19–23 M. = 228 L.: proletarii cives dice-
bantur qui in plebe tenuissima erant et non amplius quam
mille et quingentos aeris in censum deferebant. Ennius
Annali: "proletari ut publicitus scutaque ferique ornatus
ferro."

*8 Macrob. *Sat.* 6.1.53 (Verg. *Aen.* 12.492–3 "apicem ta-
men incita summum / hasta tulit")

Ennius in sexto:

173 †decimo tamen induvolans secum abstulit hasta
     insigne

    decimo *Macrobius*: decisum *Skutsch*: de corno *Fordyce*

*9 Macrob. *Sat.* 6.2.27 (Verg. *Aen.* 6.179–82 "itur in anti-
quam silvam . . . ornos")

Ennius in sexto:

175 incedunt arbusta per alta, securibus caedunt,
     percellunt magnas quercus, exciditur ilex,
     fraxinus frangitur atque abies consternitur alta,
     pinus proceras pervortunt: omne sonabat
     arbustum fremitu silvai frondosai.

Cf. Nonius: *proletarii* are said to be citizens, who were at the lowest class among the common people and reported no more than 1,500 asses in the census. Ennius in the *Annals*: "of the fierce proletariat armed at public expense with a shield and sword."[2]

[2] Nonius had no direct knowledge of the *Annals*, and his excerpts from it are often, as here with *scutaque ferique*, corrupt.

*8 Macrobius, *Saturnalia* (on Virgil, "yet the speedy spear took off the topmost peak of his helmet")

Ennius in Book 6:

⟨. . .⟩ yet the spinning spear carried off with itself   173
    the emblem[1]

[1] At the battle of Heraclea, a soldier named Dexius killed Megacles and carried off the cloak and helmet of Pyrrhus, which Megacles was wearing (Plut. *Pyrrh.* 17.4). Skutsch therefore places this fragment here. Vahlen and Warmington, understanding Macrobius' "in sexto decimo" as the book number, place it in Book 16 (see 425–26 W.), but that reading is almost certainly an intrusion from *Sat.* 6.1.50 (16 *Ann.* F 15).

*9 Macrobius, *Saturnalia* (on Virgil, "they go into an ancient wood . . . the mountain ash")

Ennius in Book 6:

They stride through the lofty copses. They slash with   175
    their axes:
they send great oaks flying, the holm oak is cut down,
the ash is smashed and the towering fir laid low,
they overturn tall pines: the whole copse
resounds with the leafy wood's rumbling.

10 Oros. *Hist.* 4.1.14 [de pugna Heracleensi]

sed Pyrrhus atrocitatem cladis quam hoc bello exceperat
dis suis hominibusque testatus est adfigens titulum in tem-
plum Tarentini Iovis, in quo haec scripsit:

180   qui antehac
    invicti fuere viri, pater optume Olympi,
    hos ego vi pugna vici victusque sum ab isdem

et cum a sociis increpitaretur cur se victum diceret qui
vicisset respondisse fertur: ne ego si iterum eodem modo
vicero sine ullo milite Epirum revertar.

11 Cic. *Off.* 1.38

Pyrrhi quidem de captivis reddendis illa praeclara:

183   nec mi aurum posco nec mi pretium dederitis:
    non cauponantes bellum sed belligerantes
    ferro, non auro vitam cernamus utrique.
    vosne velit an me regnare era quidve ferat Fors

10 Orosius, *Histories* (on the battle of Heraclea)

But Pyrrhus bore witness before his gods and before men
to the horrific slaughter he sustained in this battle, placing
an inscription in the temple of Jupiter at Tarentum, in
which he wrote these lines:[1]

> men who previously   180
> had been unvanquished, best father of Olympus,
> those I vanquished by force in battle and was by the
>   same men vanquished

and when he was rebuked by his allies, asking why he, who
had vanquished, said he had been vanquished, he is said
to have replied, "Well, if I were victorious a second time
in that way, I would return to Epirus with not a single
soldier."

[1] The inscription is as much a poetic invention as the oracle
of F 4. Orosius reports it in prose: the hexameters printed are the
result of editorial intervention, as is the attribution to Ennius.
Warmington puts the fragment among the *Varia* (21–22 W.).

11 Cicero, *On Duties*

Indeed, the famous words of Pyrrhus concerning the re-
turn of prisoners are outstanding:

> I do not ask for gold for myself, nor should you give   183
>   me a ransom:
> not hawking war but waging war,
> with iron, not with gold let both sides resolve the vital
>   question.
> Whether you or me Dame Fortune wants to rule, or
>   whatever she brings,

virtute experiamur, et hoc simul accipe dictum:
quorum virtuti belli fortuna pepercit
eorundem me libertati parcere certum est.
190   Dono—ducite—doque—volentibus cum magnis dis.

regalis sane et digna Aeacidarum genere sententia.

Cf. Serv. ad Verg. *Aen.* 10.532.

*12 Non., p. 150.5–10 M. = 218 L.

PROGNARITER: strenue, fortiter et constanter. . . . Ennius
Annalium lib. VI:

191   divi hoc audite parumper:
ut pro Romano populo prognariter armis
certando prudens animam de corpore mitto,
⟨sic⟩

194 *add. Skutsch*

*13 Schol. Veron. ad Verg. *Aen.* 5.473 (vol. 3.2, p. 434.12–
16 Th.-H.)

"hic victor superans animis tauroque superbus": Ennius in
VI:

195   aut animo superant atque asp   rima
    – ◡ fera belli spernunt

asperrima *Mai*: aspera prima *Keil*

let us put to the test by valor. And understand this
    saying, too:
Those whose valor the fortune of war has spared,
their liberty it is certain that I spare.
I offer them—take them—I give them up, as is the   190
    great gods' will.

It is a kingly sentiment and worthy of the race of Aeacus.

*12 Nonius

prognariter: "actively," "bravely," and "steadfastly." . . . Ennius, *Annals* Book 6:[1]

              Gods, hear this prayer a moment: 191
Just as I knowingly send the spirit from my body
in contest of arms on behalf of the Roman people,
⟨so⟩

[1] Nonius' gloss is incorrect. Ennius substitutes *prognariter . . . prudens* for the metrically intractable *sciens prudens* in the formula for *devotio.*

*13 Scholia Veronensia to Virgil, *Aeneid*

"here the towering victor, proud in spirit over the bull":
Ennius in Book 6:

either they tower in spirit and . . .   195
– ∪ cruelties of war they spurn

14 Cic. *Div.* 2.116

. . . postremum, quamquam semper fuit, ut apud Ennium est

197   stolidum genus Aeacidarum:
          bellipotentes sunt magis quam sapientipotentes

15 Cic. *Sen.* 16

ad Appii Claudii senectutem accedebat etiam ut caecus esset; tamen is, cum sententia senatus inclinaret ad pacem cum Pyrrho foedusque faciendum, non dubitavit dicere illa quae versibus persecutus est Ennius:

199   quo vobis mentes, rectae quae stare solebant
          antehac, dementes sese flexere †via

ceteraque gravissime; notum enim vobis carmen est; et tamen ipsius Appi extat oratio.

200 via *codd.*: viai *Lambinus*: vietae *Scaliger (approbat Skutsch)*

*16 Donat. ad Ter. *Phorm.* 821

"parare in animo cupiditates": vetuste[1] additum animo. Ennius in sexto:

201   sed ego hic animo lamentor

    [1] *Klotz*: venuste *codd.*

14 Cicero, *On Divination*

. . . finally, although it was always the case, as it is in Ennius, that

<blockquote>

obtuse is the race of the Aeacids: 197
they are much better at fighting than at thinking

</blockquote>

15 Cicero, *On Old Age*

There was also added to the old age of Appius Claudius the fact that he was blind. Nevertheless, when opinion in the Senate was inclining toward peace with Pyrrhus and making a treaty, he did not hesitate to say what Ennius renders in verse:

<blockquote>

down what road [?] have your senses, which before   199
    used to
stand upright, wandered off senseless

</blockquote>

and the rest most solemnly, for you know the poem. And anyway, the speech of Appius himself survives.

*16 Donatus, *Commentary on Terence*

"entertain desires in your heart": the addition of *animo* is archaic. Ennius in Book 6:

<blockquote>

but I grieve here in my heart   201

</blockquote>

17 Varro, *Ling.* 7.41

apud Ennium:

202   orator sine pace redit regique refert rem

orator dictus ab oratione: qui enim verba haberet publice adversus eum quo legabatur ab oratione orator dictus. cum res maior oratione ⟨egebat⟩ legabantur potissimum qui causam commodissime orare poterant.

*18 Macrob. *Sat.* 6.1.10 (Verg. *Aen.* 10.2 "conciliumque vocat divum pater atque hominum rex")

Ennius in sexto:

203   tum cum corde suo divom pater atque hominum rex
        effatur

*19 Macrob. *Sat.* 6.1.8 (Verg. *Aen.* 2.250 "vertitur interea caelum et ruit Oceano nox")

Ennius libro sexto:

205   vertitur interea caelum cum ingentibus signis

17 Varro, *On the Latin Language*

In Ennius:

> the envoy returns without a peace and refers the 202
>> matter to the king

orator [envoy] is derived from "oration," for one who spoke publicly before the one to whom he was sent is called an "orator" because of his oration. When a quite serious matter required a speech, those most particularly were selected, who were able to plead the case most effectively.

*18 Macrobius, *Saturnalia* (on Virgil, "the father of gods and king of men summons a council")

Ennius in Book 6:

> then from his heart the father of gods and king of 203
>> men[1]
> speaks out

[1] Variants on the Homeric formula πατὴρ ἀνδρῶν τε θεῶν τε also appear in Inc. *Ann.* F 123 and F 124. An active role for divinities in the narrative is not necessarily confined to mythological contexts. See Elliott 2013, 45–51.

*19 Macrobius, *Saturnalia* (on Virgil, "meanwhile, the heavens revolve and night rushes on from Ocean")

Ennius, Book 6:

> meanwhile, the heavens with their vast constellations 205
>> revolve

BOOK VII

This book is thought to have opened with a proem in which Ennius simultaneously acknowledged his predecessor Naevius' success in memorializing Rome's first struggle with Carthage and asserted the artistic superiority of his own achievement as the first creator of a Latin epic in hexameters (F 1–2). The historical narrative that followed this introduction appears to have begun with an ethnography of Carthage (F 3–5) and, in tacit deference to Naevius, made only passing mention of the First Punic War (F 6–9).

F 1–2: A Prooemium

This programmatic introduction has long attracted attention for the light it appears to shed on Ennius' poetic aspirations and the place he claimed for himself in Latin literary history (e.g., Suerbaum 1968, 249–95; Habinek 2006; Wiseman 2006). Though Varro also quotes it (Ling. 7.36), Cicero's evident fondness for the passage (Brut. 71, 76; Orat. 157, 171; Div. 1.114) probably explains its recollection by so many subsequent authors (e.g., Quint. Inst. 9.4.115; Serv. Dan. ad Verg. G. 1.11; Orig. 4.4–5; Fest., p. 432.13–20 L.; Mar. Victorin., GL VI, pp. 138.32–39.1).

BOOK VII

References to battles with Celts (F 14–16) and Illyrians (F 17) are discernible, but most fragments are assigned with varying degrees of probability to an account of the second (Hannibalic) war with Carthage. The book probably carried the story down to events of 217 BC in the aftermath of the Roman defeat at Lake Trasimene. For its relation to Virgil's account of another war in Italy, see Norden 1915, 153–73; Goldschmidt 2013, 127–48.

F 1–2: A Prooemium

If read as a "proem in the middle," it may itself be evidence for Alexandrian influence on Latin literature at this seminal stage of development (Conte 2007, 226–29; cf. Goldschmidt 2013, 55–61). Its echo of the poet's dream-vision in Book 1 must have developed the claim to poetic authority made there, but the fragments are so deeply embedded in the specific literary argument of Cicero's Brutus *that they are difficult to extract and understand on their own terms (Goldberg 2009, 643–47). The sequence of lines in what follows is likely but not certain.*

1 (= T 18)

a Cic. *Brut.* 75–76

tamen illius, quem in vatibus et Faunis adnumerat Ennius,
bellum Punicum quasi Myronis opus delectat. sit Ennius
sane, ut est certe, perfectior: qui si illum, ut simulat, con-
temneret, non omnia bella persequens primum illud Puni-
cum acerrimum bellum reliquisset. sed ipse dicit cur id
faciat.

206   scripsere [inquit] alii rem
    vorsibus

et luculente quidem scripserunt, etiam si minus quam tu
polite. nec vero tibi aliter videri debet, qui a Naevio vel
sumpsisti multa, si fateris, vel, si negas, surripuisti.

b Cic. *Brut.* 71

et nescio an reliquis in rebus omnibus idem eveniat: nihil
est enim simul et inventum et perfectum; nec dubitari
debet quin fuerint ante Homerum poetae, quod ex eis
carminibus intellegi potest, quae apud illum et in Phaea-
cum et in procorum epulis canuntur. quid, nostri veteres
versus ubi sunt?

        quos olim fauni vatesque canebant

cum

208   neque Musarum scopulos
      nec dicti studiosus [quisquam erat] ante hunc

   quisquam erat *Ciceroni tribuit Skutsch*

216

1 (= T 18)

a Cicero, *Brutus*

The *Bellum Punicum* of that poet, whom Ennius counts among the soothsayers and Fauns, nevertheless gives pleasure as a work of Myron does. Granted that Ennius is more polished, as he surely is: if, as he pretends, he faulted him, he would not in recounting all our wars have left that first, most bitter Punic war alone. But he himself says why he does so.

> others [says he] have written about this subject 206
> in verses

and they wrote about it splendidly, even if not in as polished a way as you did. Nor in fact should it seem any different to you, who either appropriated, if you confess it, or, if you deny it, stole much from Naevius.

b Cicero, *Brutus*

Something similar undoubtedly happens in all other remaining endeavors, for nothing is simultaneously both invented and perfected. There were without doubt poets before Homer, as can be understood from those poems performed in his epics at the banquets of the Phaeacians and of the suitors. Well, where are our own ancient verses,

> which once the fauns and bards used to sing,[1]

when

> neither the Muses' peaks 208
> nor [anyone] careful of speech [existed] before him

[1] Ennius refers to the old Saturnian meter of Naevius' poem. For the connotations of this passage, see Suerbaum 1968, 265–77; Hinds 1998, 63–71; Wiseman 2006.

217

ait ipse de se nec mentitur in gloriando: sic enim sese res habet.

c Cic. *Orat*. 171

ergo Ennio licuit vetera contemnenti dicere "vorsibus quos olim Fauni vatesque canebant," mihi de antiquis eodem modo non licebit? praesertim cum dicturus non sim "ante hunc," ut ille, nec quae sequuntur:

210   nos ausi reserare

*2 Fest., p. 432.20–30 L.

SAS Verrius putat significare eas teste Ennio qui dicat in lib. I [F 49] "virgines . . . sas," cum "suas" magis videatur significare. sicuti eiusdem lib. VII fatendum est eam significari cum ait:

211   nec quisquam sophiam,

quae doctrina latina lingua nomen habet

                          sapientia quae perhibetur,
      in somnis vidit prius quam sam discere coepit

Cf. Paul. *Fest*., p. 433.4–5 L.: sam eam. idem Ennius "ne quisquam philosophiam in somnis vidit prius quam sam discere coepit."

F 3–5: Carthaginian Ethnography

3 Ekkehartus in Oros. *Hist*. 4.6.21 ("Carthaginienses . . . Hamilcarem quendam cognomento Rhodanum virum facundia sollertiaque praecipuum ad perscrutandos Alexandri actus direxerunt"):

So he says about himself and does not lie in his boasting: that's the fact of it.

c Cicero, *Orator*

Since Ennius was allowed, in disparaging old poetry, to say "in verses which once the fauns and bards used to sing," shall I not be allowed to speak the same way about old writers? especially since I am not about to say "before him," as he did, nor what follows,

> we dared unbar . . .   210

*2 Festus

Verrius thinks *sas* means *eas* ["them," fem.], citing Ennius as a witness, who says in Book 1 [F 49] "maidens . . . them," although it seems rather to mean "their own." So in the same poet's Book 7, it must be admitted that *eam* is meant when he says:

> nor did anyone else see the wisdom,   211

which is what learning is called in Latin

> which is called knowledge,
> in his dreams before he began to acquire it

F 3–5: *Carthaginian Ethnography*

3 Ekkehart on Orosius, *Histories* (". . . the Carthaginians directed a certain Hamilcar, surnamed Rhodanus, an especially articulate and shrewd individual, to discover Alexander's intentions") *supra lineam quae est* "tandos . . . direxerunt" *Ekkehartus addidit* Ennius:

213   quantis consiliis quantumque potesset in armis

4 Fest., pp. 290.35–92.2 L.

PUELLI per deminutionem a pueris dicti sunt. itaque et Ennius ait:

214   Poeni soliti suos sacrificare puellos

divis *post* suos *add. Non.*: divis *del. Richter*: suos soliti dis *Vahlen, Warmington*

Cf. Paul. *Fest.*, p. 291.5–6 L.; Non., pp. 158.14–30 M. = 232–33 L.

5 Varro, *Ling.* 5.182

militis stipendia ideo quod eam stipem pendebant; ab eo etiam Ennius scribit:

215   Poeni stipendia pendunt

F 6–9: First Punic War, 264–241 BC

6 Cic. *Inv.* 1.27

narratio est rerum gestarum aut ut gestarum expositio. . . . historia est gesta res, ab aetatis nostrae memoria remota, quod genus:

216   Appius indixit Carthaginiensibus bellum

220

above the line "direct . . . to discover," *Ekkehart added* Ennius:[1]

> with how many counsels he excelled and how much   213
> in arms

[1] For Ekkehart, see 5 *Ann.* F 3.

4 Festus

puelli is derived as a diminutive of *pueri*. And so too Ennius says:

> Carthaginians accustomed to sacrifice their   214
> small sons

5 Varro, *On the Latin Language*

thus the soldier's "stipend" because they weigh out this *stips* [coin]; so too from this Ennius writes:

> the Carthaginians pay out the stipends   215

F 6–9: First Punic War, 264–241 BC

6 Cicero, *On Invention*

The narrative is the exposition of events that have occurred or are supposed to have occurred. . . . History is the account of what has occurred remote from the memory of our own age, such as of the type:

> Appius declared war on the Carthaginians   216

*7 Prisc., *GL* II, pp. 485.17–86.14

in *-geo* desinentia, *l* vel *r* antecedentibus, *-geo* in *si* conversa faciunt praeteritum perfectum, ut *indulgeo indulsi, fulgeo fulsi, algeo alsi, urgeo ursi* . . . Ennius in VII Annalium:

217   urserat huc navim conpulsam fluctibus pontus

   urserat Z: *approbavit Skutsch*: mulserat *ceteri*

*8–9 Fest., p. 488.32–36 L.

TONSAM Ennius significat remum, quod quasi tondeatur ferro, cum ait lib. VII:

218   poste recumbite vestraque pectora pellite tonsis

   item:

219   pone petunt, exim referunt ad pectora tonsas

F 10–13: Hostilities Are Resumed, Spurred by a Fury

(The association of these fragments is much discussed, from Norden 1915, 10–33, to Fabrizi 2012, 155–63.)

10 [Prob.] ad Verg. *Ecl.* 6.31 (vol. 3.2, p. 340.16–22 Th.-H.)

si ergo caelum pro igni acceperimus superest ut in eo quod ait "spiritus intus alit" [*Aen.* 6.726] aerem dictum praesumamus. . . . hoc illud et Ennius appellavit in Annalibus:

*7 Priscian

verbs ending in *-geo* preceded by *l* or *r* turn *-geo* to *-si* to
form the perfect, as *indulgeo indulsi, fulgeo fulsi, algeo
alsi, urgeo ursi* . . . So Ennius in Book 7 of the *Annals*:

> the sea had driven the ship, buffeted by the waves, to   217
> this place

*8–9[1] Festus

Ennius uses *tonsa* for "oar" because it is as if cut by a knife,
as he says in Book 7:

> then lean back and drive your chests from the oars   218

similarly:

> they reach back, and then pull the oars to their chests   219

[1] "Part of a command to rowers, followed soon after (219) by
a description of its execution." So Skutsch 1985, 390, a possible,
though hardly certain, interpretation of two lines that may be
from the same passage.

*F 10–13: Hostilities Are Resumed,
Spurred by a Fury*

10 [Probus], *Commentary on Virgil*

If, therefore, we understand "heaven" as "fire," it follows
that where he says "the spirit nourishes within" [*Aen.*
6.726], we should understand "air" as meant. . . . Ennius
too calls it this in the *Annals*:

220   corpore tartarino prognata Paluda virago
cui par imber et ignis, spiritus et gravis terra

220 corpore tartarino *Varro, Fest.*: corpora tartareo *Prob.*
paluda *Varro*: palude *Prob.*

Cf. Varro, *Ling.* 7.37; Fest., p. 494.7–8 L.; Paul., p. 495.4 L.

*11 Prisc., *GL* II, pp. 222.11–23.63

Nar quoque Naris monosyllabum similiter producit *a* in
genetivo et est proprium fluvii. nam si nasum velimus sig-
nificare, haec naris huius naris similem genetivo nomina-
tivum proferimus . . . sed Nar servavit *a* productam etiam
in obliquis. Ennius in vii Annalium:

222   sulpureas posuit spiramina Naris ad undas

*12 Serv. Dan. ad Verg. *G.* 2.449

buxum lignum non arborem dicit, quamvis Ennii exemplo
et arborem potuerit dicere neutro genere. ille enim sic in
septimo:

223   longique cupressi
stant rectis foliis et amaro corpore buxum

224 corpore *codd.*: cortice *Merula, fortasse recte*

224

the warrior maiden Paluda[1], of hellish body born,   220
to whom showers and fire, spirit and weighty earth
    are equal

[1] Presumably the Fury's name, perhaps from *paludamentum*, "a commander's cloak" (so Varro, guessing), or from *palus*, "swamp" (Skutsch, tentatively).

*11 Priscian

The monosyllable Nar similarly has a long *a* in the genitive Naris and is specific to the river. For if we want to indicate the nose, we pronounce the nominative *naris* [nostril] like the genitive of Nar. . . . but Nar maintains the long *a* even in the oblique cases. Ennius in *Annals* 7:

he placed the blowholes of the Nar[1] by its sulfurous   222
    waters

[1] An Umbrian river (mod. Nera), a tributary of the Tiber known for its sulfurous springs. Ennius probably puns on the ambiguous form *naris*.

*12 Servius Danielis, *Commentary on Virgil*

"box" means a wood, not a tree, although on Ennius' example he could also have meant a tree in the neuter. So he [Ennius] says in his seventh book:

        and slender cypresses   223
stand with leaves straight and with bitter body the
    box

13 Hor. *Sat.* 1.4.60–62

225   non ut si solvas "postquam Discordia taetra
       Belli ferratos postes portasque refregit,"
       invenias etiam disiecti membra poetae.

Cf. Serv. ad Verg. *Aen.* 7.622 (226: "Ennii versum").

*F 14–16: A Gallic Threat Repelled, 225 BC
Recalling the Gallic Catastrophe of 390 BC*

*14 Macrob. *Sat.* 1.4.17–18

reliqua autem verba quae Avieno nostro nova visa sunt
veterum nobis sunt testimoniis adserenda. Ennius enim—
nisi cui videtur inter nostrae aetatis politiores munditias
respuendus—"noctu concubia" dixit his versibus:

227   qua Galli furtim noctu summa arcis adorti
       moenia concubia vigilesque repente cruentant

quo in loco animadvertendum est non solum quod "noctu
concubia" sed quod etiam "qua noctu" dixerit. et hoc po-
suit in Annalium septimo, in quorum tertio clarius idem
dixit . . . [3 *Ann.* F 5].

13 Horace, *Satires*

it's not as if you scattered

> "after loathsome Discord   225
> broke open the ironbound posts and portals of War,"

where you'd still find the limbs of a dismembered poet.[1]

[1] Servius' note identifies the poet in question as Ennius. Skutsch 1985, 402–3, citing Varro, *Ling.* 5.165, associates the "portals of War" with the *Ianus Geminus*; cf. Liv. 1.19.2.

F 14–16: A Gallic Threat Repelled, 225 BC
Recalling the Gallic Catastrophe of 390 BC

14 Macrobius, *Saturnalia

As for the other words that seemed novel to our friend Avienus, we must defend them with the testimony of the ancients. For Ennius—unless someone thinks he should be denied a place in the more refined elegance of our age—said *noctu concubia* in these lines:

> at the time for bedding down at night [*noctu*   227
>   *conubia*], the Gauls slipped stealthily
> over the citadel's highest walls and suddenly bloodied
>   the guard

Here we should note that he said not only *noctu concubia* but also *qua noctu.* He did this in the seventh book of the *Annals*, in the third of which he said the same thing more clearly . . . [3 *Ann.* F 5].

A Marshaling of Roman Allies

15 Diom., *GL* I, p. 446.24–26

schesis onomaton est cum singulis nominibus epitheta
coniuncta sunt ut

229   Marsa manus, Paeligna cohors, Vestina virum vis

Cf. Charis., *GL* I, p. 282.5–6 = p. 370.21–23 B.; Donat., *GL* IV,
p. 398.17–19; Pomp., *GL* V, p. 303.19–21.

The Battle of Telamon (?)

*16 Fest., pp. 386.32–88.2 L.

sos pro eos antiqui dicebant, ut Ennius . . . lib. VII:

230   dum censent terrere minis hortantur ibe sos

An Incident of the Second Illyrian War (?),
219 BC

17 Fest., p. 362.19–25 L.

rigido‹que Calore idem› [Inc. *Ann.* F 31] Ennius iocatus
videtur . . . et alibi

A Marshaling of Roman Allies

15 Diomedes

The patterning of names is when epithets are joined with individual nouns as,

> Marsian band, Paelignian cohort, Vestinian mass of men[1]　　229

[1] The Marsi, Paeligni, and Vestini were peoples to the east of the Sabine country and firm allies of Rome.

The Battle of Telamon (?)

*16 Festus

The ancients used to say *sos* for *eos* ["them," masc.], as Ennius . . . Book 7:

> in electing to cow them with threats[1], they instead incite them　　230

[1] The Gauls were especially notorious for taunting their enemy, e.g., Polyb. 2.29.6, and the famous story of T. Manlius' single combat with a Gaul told by Claudius Quadrigarius (F 6 *FRHist*) and Liv. 7.10.5.

An Incident of the Second Illyrian War (?), 219 BC

17 Festus

similarly with "the unyielding Calor" [Inc. *Ann.* F 31] Ennius appears to be punning . . . and so elsewhere

231   inde Parum ‹caute procedere se sim›ulabant

Parum insulam refert.

suppl., e.g., Heraeus

F 18–20: *From Speeches by Hannibal (?)*

*18 Macrob. *Sat.* 6.1.19 (Verg. *Aen.* 12.565 "ne qua meis dictis esto mora: nunc Iuppiter hac stat")

Ennius in septimo:

232   non semper vostra evortit: nunc Iuppiter hac stat

*19 Macrob. *Sat.* 6.1.62 (Verg. *Aen.* 10.254 "audentes fortuna iuvat")

Ennius in septimo:

233   fortibus est fortuna viris data

20 (= T 11) Cic. *Balb.* 51

neque enim ille summus poeta noster Hannibalis illam magis cohortationem quam communem imperatoriam voluit esse:

234   hostem qui feriet †erit [inquit] mi† Carthaginiensis
        quisquis erit, cuiatis siet

versus amplius corrupti: hostem qui feriet is mi Carthaginiensis civis erit *Skutsch, e.g.*

---

1 Cf. Shakespeare, *Henry* V 4.3.61–63: "For he that sheds his blood with me / shall be my brother; be he ne'er so vile, / this day shall gentle his condition."

from there they pretended ‹to advance cautiously› to   231
    Pharos[1]

Pharos refers to the island.

[1] Since Ennius' orthography did not distinguish between aspirated and unaspirated consonants (e.g., Gk. φ and π), he could pun on "to Pharos," the island, and *parum*, "not enough."

F 18–20: From Speeches by Hannibal (?)

*18 Macrobius, *Saturnalia* (on Virgil, "Let no delay meet my words: Jupiter now stands on our side")

Ennius in Book 7:

he does not always thwart your endeavors: now   232
    Jupiter stands on our side

*19 Macrobius, *Saturnalia* (on Virgil, "Fortune favors the bold")

Ennius in Book 7:

good fortune has been given to bold men   233

20 (= T 11) Cicero, *Pro Balbo*

For our greatest poet [Ennius] did not want this to be so much an exhortation for Hannibal as for commanders in general:[1]

he who strikes an enemy will be Carthaginian with   234
    me,
whoever he is, from whatever country

F 21: Battle of the Trebia, 218 BC?

*21 Macrob. *Sat.* 6.9.9–10

omnes enim antiqui scriptores ut hominem equo insi-
dentem, ita et equum, cum portaret hominem, "equitem"
vocaverunt, et "equitare" non hominem tantum sed
equum quoque dixerunt. Ennius libro Annalium septimo
ait,

236   denique vi magna quadrupes, eques atque elephanti
        proiciunt sese

numquid dubium est quin equitem in hoc loco ipsum
equum dixerit, cum addidisset illi epitheton quadrupes?

236 (ac non) quadrupedes equites *Nonius*

Cf. Gell. *NA* 18.5.4–7 (T 85); Non., p. 106.29–30 M. = 152 L.;
Serv. Dan. ad Verg. *G.* 3.116.

F 22–23: The Carthaginian Threat to Lilybaeum?

*22 Fest., pp. 166.32–68.32 L.

NARE a nave ductum Cornificius ait, quod aqua feratur
natans ut navis. Ennius lib. VII:

238   alter nare cupit, alter pugnare paratust

F 21: Battle of the Trebia, 218 BC?

*21 Macrobius, *Saturnalia*

All ancient writers used *eques* for a man sitting on a horse
as well as for a horse when carrying a man, and the verb
equitare not just of a man riding, but also of the horse
carrying. Ennius in Book 7 of the *Annals* says:

> then with a great rush the quadruped forces, cavalry   236
>   and elephants,
> hurled themselves forward[1]

Can there be any doubt that he used *eques* in this passage
of the horse itself, since he added to it the epithet "four-
footed"?

[1] Polyb. 3.74 and Liv. 21.55.9 report that the performance of
the Carthaginian cavalry and elephants at the Trebia was decisive.

F 22–23: The Carthaginian Threat to Lilybaeum?

*22 Festus

Cornificius says that *nare* [to swim, to be afloat] is derived
from *navis* [ship] because a swimmer is borne by water as
is a ship. Ennius, Book 7:

> one ‹side?› wishes to be afloat, the other is prepared   238
>   to fight ‹on land?›[1]

[1] A pun on *nare* and *pugnare* is likely, the alliteration of *pug-
nare paratust* only a secondary effect.

*23 Non., p. 116.2–7 M. = 166 L.

GRACILITUDO {et gracilens pro gracilis et gracilentum pro gracili et gracilium, *secl. On.*} pro gracilitas. . . . Ennius lib. VII:

239   deducunt habiles gladios filo gracilento

F 24: Introduction of the di consentes, *217 BC*

24 Apul. *De deo Soc.* 2

est aliud deorum genus . . . quorum in numero sunt illi duodecim nudo positu nominum in duo versus ab Ennio coartati,

240   Iuno Vesta Minerva Ceres Diana Venus Mars
        Mercurius Iovis Neptunus Volcanus Apollo

Cf. Mart. Cap. 1.42.

F 25–28: Unidentified Fragments

25 Macrob. *Sat.* 6.1.22 (Verg. *Aen* 8.596 "quadrupedante putrem sonitu quatit ungula campum")

Ennius in sexto:

242   explorant Numidae, totam quatit ungula terram

---

[1] Since no suitable event in Book 6 has been identified, editors posit an error or corruption in Macrobius' designation and reassign this fragment to Book 7. Numidian cavalry were prominent at the Trebia, but not only there.

*23 Nonius

[on synonyms for "slenderness" and "slender"] *gracilitudo*
{and *gracilens* for *gracilis*, and *gracilentum* for *gracili*, and
gracilium} for *gracilitas*. . . . Ennius, Book 7:[1]

> they forge handy swords like slender thread[2]   239

[1] Nonius' sequence seems illogical. Skutsch suggests *gracili-
tudo pro gracilitas, et gracilens pro gracilis, et gracilentum et
gracilium pro gracili*.   [2] The famously well-tempered Span-
ish sword may be meant. Cf. Liv. 22.46.5.

F 24: Introduction of the di consentes, 217 BC

24 Apuleius, *De Deo Socratis*

There is another class of gods . . . which includes the fa-
mous twelve whose names are fitted in stark arrangement
in two lines by Ennius:

> Juno Vesta Minerva Ceres Diana Venus Mars   240
> Mercury Jove Neptune Vulcan Apollo[1]

[1] Liv. 22.10.9, recording the ritual banquet (*lectisternium*)
and introduction of the twelve great gods (*di consentes*) as re-
sponses to the precarious military situation in 217 BC, suggests a
possible context for these lines. Cf. F 21.

F 25–28: Unidentified Fragments

25 Macrobius, *Saturnalia* (on Virgil, "the hoof shakes the
crumbling ground with its four-footed beat")

Ennius in Book Six:[1]

> the Numidians investigate, the hoof everywhere   242
>   shakes the ground

*26 Non., pp. 385.5–16 M. = 614–15 L.

RUMOR: favor, auxiliatio. . . . Ennius Annali lib. VII:

243   legio †redditu †rumore †ruinas
       mox auferre domos populi rumore secundo

> redditu rumore *codd.*: rediit murumque *Vahlen*: reddit ur-
> bemque *Ribbeck, alia alii*   ruinas *codd.*: rapinas *dubitanter*
> *Skutsch*

*27 Charis., *GL* I, p. 130.29–30 = p. 166.16–17 B.

frus, haec frus quia sic ab Ennio est declinatum Annalium
libro VII,

245   russescunt frundes

non frondes.

*28 Fest., p. 306.25–31 L.

QUIANAM pro quare et cur positum est apud antiquos ut
Navium . . . et Ennium in lib. VII:

246   quianam dictis nostris sententia flexa est?

Cf. Paul., p. 307.9–10 L.

*26 Nonius

rumor [rumor]: support, aid. . . . Ennius in *Annals*, Book
7:

> the legion ‹. . . . .›[1]   243
> soon carries off toward home, with the people's
>   support

[1] The corruption conceals at least one verb and the object of
"carry off."

*27 Charisius

frus [foliage], feminine *frus*, since it is declined this way
by Ennius, *Annals*, Book 7:

> the foliage begins to turn red   245

not *frondes* [the classical form].

*28 Festus

quianam [why ever?] is found for *quare* and *cur* in ancient
writers, as in Naevius . . . and Ennius in Book 7:

> why ever has your opinion been changed by our   246
>   words?

BOOK VIII

*This book centered on the Hannibalic war, including the
battle of Cannae and the delaying tactics of Q. Fabius
Maximus, but stopping before the victory of Livius Salina-
tor at the Metaurus in 207 BC. F 16 must refer to Fabius'
reelection to the consulship in 214 BC (Liv. 24.8–9), but
while independent sources mention other events likely to
have been included at this point in the poem (T 50, t 1–2),
most associations of specific fragments with specific events
are speculative. Among the more likely: the account of
Cannae at Liv. 22.44–50 has encouraged identification of
F 4 to 12 with that battle. F 15 may refer to a Campanian*

TESTIMONIA

T 50 Prop. 3.3.9–11

et [Ennius] cecinit . . .

> vitricesque moras Fabii pugnamque sinistram
>   Cannensem et versos ad pia vota deos,
> Hannibalemque Lares Romana sede fugantes

BOOK VIII

attack on Cumae in 215 BC (Liv. 23.35), F 18 to Hanni-
bal's march from Capua to the outskirts of Rome in 211
BC (Liv. 26.7.3). The famous description of the "Good
Companion" (F 12) probably belongs to the narrative of
Cannae, where the proconsul Cn. Servilius Geminus
fought with distinction. That passage is much discussed,
in no small part for its reportedly autobiographical content
(Williams 1968, 691–93; Badian 1972, 172–83; Goldberg
1995, 120–23; Gildenhard 2003, 109–11; Hardie 2007;
Elliott 2013, 228–32).

TESTIMONIA

T 50 Propertius, *Elegies*

and [Ennius] sang of

> Fabius' victorious delays and the unlucky battle
> of Cannae and the gods attentive to pious vows
> and the Lares driving Hannibal to flight from their
> Roman seat

t 1 Serv. ad Verg. *Aen.* 1.20

"[Iuno] audierat": a Iove aut a fatis . . . et perite "audierat";
in Ennio enim inducitur Iuppiter promittens Romanis ex-
cidium Carthaginis.

t 2 Serv. ad Verg. *Aen.* 1.281

bello Punico secundo, ut ait Ennius, placata Iuno coepit
favere Romanis.

FRAGMENTS

*1

a Cic. *Mur.* 30

etenim, ut ait ingeniosus poeta et auctor valde bonus,
proeliis promulgatis [247 Sk.] "pellitur e medio" non so-
lum ista vestra verbosa simulatio prudentiae sed etiam ipsa
illa domina rerum "sapientia . . ."

b Gell. *NA* 20.10.3–5

"ex Ennio ergo" inquam "est, magister, quod quaero. En-
nius enim verbis hisce [ex iure manum consertum] usus
est." [4] cumque ille demiratus aliena haec esse a poetis
et haud usquam inveniri in carminibus Ennii diceret, tum
ego hos versus ex octavo Annali absentes dixi . . .

248   pellitur e medio sapientia, vi geritur res;

t 1 Servius, *Commentary on Virgil*

"[Juno] had heard": either from Jupiter or the Fates . . .
and "had heard" is skillful, for in Ennius Jupiter is intro-
duced promising Romans the destruction of Carthage.

t 2 Servius, *Commentary on Virgil*

At the time of the Second Punic War, as Ennius says, Juno
was appeased and began to favor the Romans.

FRAGMENTS

*1

a Cicero, *Pro Murena*

In fact, as a talented poet and very fine author says, *once
battles are declared* [247 Sk.][1] "driven from view" is not
just your wordy imitation of discretion but also that very
mistress of affairs, "good sense . . ."

  [1] This phrase is almost certainly Ennian, but the original syn-
tax uniting it with what follows is unrecoverable.

b Gellius, *Attic Nights*

"Well, Master," I said, "what I am asking about is from
Ennius, for Ennius used these words [to lay claim by law]."
[4] And when he said in considerable surprise that this
expression was foreign to poets and not to be found any-
where in the poetry of Ennius, then I recited from mem-
ory these verses from the eighth book of the *Annals* . . .

> good sense is driven from view, by force are affairs   248
>   managed,

spernitur orator bonus, horridus miles amatur;
250   haud doctis dictis certantes, nec maledictis
miscent inter sese inimicitias agitantes;
non ex iure manu consertum, sed magis ferro—
rem repetunt regnumque petunt—vadunt solida vi

[5] cum hos ego versus Ennianos dixissem, "credo" inquit grammaticus "iam tibi. sed tu velim credas mihi Quintum Ennium didicisse hoc non ex poeticae litteris, set ex iuris aliquo perito."

Cf. Cic. *Fam.* 7.13.2; *Att.* 15.7; Lact. *Inst.* 5.1.1.

*2 Fest., pp. 188.27–90.5 L.

OCCASUS: interitus, vel solis cum descidit a superis infra terras; quo vocabulo Ennius pro occasione est usus in lib. II [F 8] . . . ; item in lib. V [F 4]; item in lib. VIII:

⟨monuit res⟩
255   aut occasus ubi tempusve audere, repressit

monuit res *suppl. Skutsch*

Cf. Paul. *Fest.*, p. 189.13 L.

3 Paul. *Fest.*, p. 507.20–25 L.

VEL conligatio quidem est disiunctiva, sed non earum rerum quae natura disiuncta sunt, in quibus "aut" coniunctione rectius utimur, ut "aut dies est aut nox," sed

---

[1] This fragment is sometimes assigned to the *Scipio*.

the honest advocate is spurned, the uncouth soldier
loved,
not striving with learned speech nor with insulting   250
speech
do they contend among themselves, stirring up
hatred;
not to lay claim by law, but rather by the sword—
they press claims and seek mastery—they rush on
with force unchecked

[5] When I had recited these lines of Ennius, the gram-
marian said, "Now I believe you. But I would like you to
believe me that Ennius learned this not from the study of
poetry, but from someone knowledgeable about law."

*2 Festus

occasus: removal, as of the sun when it drops from the
heavens below the earth. Ennius used this word in place
of *occasio* [opportunity] in Book 2 [F 8] . . . ; likewise in
Book 5 [F 4]; likewise in Book 8:

when ⟨circumstances⟩[1]
or the opportunity or the moment ⟨advised⟩ daring,   255
he stifled

[1] Skutsch's supplement, conceived with Fabius Cunctator in
mind, is speculative. The line in Festus could mean simply "or
when the opportunity or the moment stifled daring."

3[1] Paul the Deacon, *Epitome of Festus*

vel is in fact a dissociative conjunction, but not of those
things which are separated by nature, for which we more
correctly use the conjunction *aut*, as "it is either day or

earum rerum quae non sunt contra, e quibus quae eligatur
nihil interest, ut Ennius,

256   vel tu dictator vel equorum equitumque magister
        esto vel consul

*4 Macrob. *Sat.* 6.2.16 (Verg. *Aen.* 11.425–27 "multa dies
variusque labor mutabilis aevi / rettulit in melius: multos
alterna revisens / lusit et in solido rursus fortuna locavit")

Ennius in octavo:

258   multa dies in bello conficit unus . . .
        et rursus multae fortunae forte recumbunt:
260   haud quaquam quemquam semper fortuna secuta est

*5 Non., p. 150.18–20 M. = 219 L.

PRAECOX {et} PRAECOCA: quod est inmatura. Ennius An-
nali lib. VIII:

261   praecox pugna est

*6 Diom., *GL* I, p. 382.11–12

verum apud veteres et abnueo dictum annotamus, ut En-
nius octavo Annalium:

262   certare abnueo. metuo legionibus labem

night," but of those things that are not opposed, for which it makes no difference which is selected, as Ennius:

> you be dictator or master of the horses and of cavalry   256
> or consul

*4 Macrobius, *Saturnalia* (on Virgil, "time and the varied toils that the changeable seasons bring / have made many things better: fortune, returning now in this guise, now / in that has mocked many, then given them back their footing")

Ennius in Book 8:

> one day accomplishes much in war . . .   258
> and many fortunes chance to sink back again:[1]
> Fortune has attended almost no one at every   260
>   moment.

[1] A preceding line noting the *rise* of many fortunes has probably been lost.

*5 Nonius

praecox {and} *praecoca*: is what is premature. Ennius, *Annals*, Book 8:

> battle is premature   261

*6 Diomedes

But we note that among the ancients *abnueo* [refuse] was also said, as Ennius in the eighth book of the *Annals*:

> I refuse to engage. I fear ruin for the legions   262

*7 Macrob. *Sat.* 6.1.22 (Verg. *Aen.* 8.596 "quadrupedante putrem sonitu quatit ungula terram")

Ennius in sexto [*Ann.* 7 F 25] . . . , idem in octavo:

263   consequitur. summo sonitu quatit ungula terram

*8 Non., p. 217.8–10 M. = 320 L.

PULVIS generis masculini, ut saepe. feminini. Ennius lib. VIII Annalium:

264   iamque fere pulvis ad caeli vasta videtur

idem lib. IX [F 12] . . .

> caeli *Ernout*: caelum *codd.*

*9 Fest., p. 210.11–14 L.

OBSTIPUM: obliquum, Ennius lib. XVI [F 17] . . . et in lib. VIII:

265   amplius exaugere obstipo lumine solis

*10 Macrob. *Sat.* 6.1.52 (Verg. *Aen.* 12.284 "ac ferreus ingruit imber")

Ennius in octavo:

266   hastati spargunt hastas; fit ferreus imber

*11 Prisc, *GL* II, p. 480.5–6

denseo denses et denso densas . . . a denso Ennius in VIII:

267   densantur campis horrentia tela virorum

*7 Macrobius, *Saturnalia* (on Virgil, "the hoof shakes the crumbling ground with its four-footed beat")

Ennius in Book Six [*Ann.* 7 F 25] . . . , also in Book Eight:

> [the cavalry?] follows. Their hoof strikes the ground   263
> with a great din

*8 Nonius

pulvis [dust], as often, is masculine in gender. Feminine in Ennius, Book 8 of the *Annals*:

> and around now a dust cloud is seen [extending?] to   264
> the far reaches of heaven

also in Book 9 [F 12] . . .

*9 Festus

obstipum [lit., "bent"]: *obliquum* [slanting]. Ennius, Book 16 [F 17] . . . and in Book 8:

> to make much greater by the slanting sunlight   265

*10 Macrobius, *Saturnalia* (on Virgil, "and an iron rain comes rushing down")

Ennius in Book 8:

> the spearmen discharge their spears; an iron rain   266
> results

*11 Priscian

denseo denses and *denso densas* . . . [conjugated] from *denso* [thicken], Ennius in Book 8:

> the men's bristling spears crowd thickly on the plain   267

247

12 (= T 82) Gell. *NA* 12.4

descriptum definitumque est a Q. Ennio in Annali septimo
graphice admodum sciteque sub historia Gemini Servili,
viri nobilis . . . qualibus denique ad minuendas vitae mo-
lestias fomentis levamentis solaciis amicum esse conveniat
hominis genere et fortuna superioris. . . . [4] quapropter
adscribendos eos [versus] existimavi si quis iam statim de-
sideraret:

268	haece locutus vocat quocum bene saepe libenter
	mensam sermonesque suos rerumque suarum
270	consilium partit, magnam quom lassus diei
	partem fuisset de summis rebus regundis
	consilio indu foro lato sanctoque senatu;
	quoi res audacter magnas parvasque iocumque
	eloqueretur †et cuncta† malaque et bona dictu
275	evomeret si qui vellet tutoque locaret;
	quocum multa volup
	gaudia clamque palamque;
	ingenium quoi nulla malum sententia suadet
	ut faceret facinus levis aut mala: doctus, fidelis,
280	suavis homo, iucundus, suo contentus, beatus,
	scitus, secunda loquens in tempore, commodus,
	verbum

268 quocum *codd.*: quicum *Hug, adprobat Skutsch*
270 consilium partit *Skutsch*: comiter inpertit *codd.*
280 iucundus *Skutsch*: facundus *codd.*

---

[1] "We are thus forced . . . to assume that Gellius made a mis-
take in assigning this fragment to Book VII instead of Book VIII,
which contains the account of Cannae" (Skutsch 1985, 448).

12 (= T 82) Gellius, *Attic Nights*

In the seventh book of the *Annals*[1] Ennius describes and
defines very vividly and skillfully in the story of Servilius
Geminus, a man of distinction . . . what remedies, forms
of relief and solace for abating the annoyances of life the
friend of a man superior in social class and fortune ought
to have. . . . [4] I therefore thought these [verses] worth
quoting, in case anyone desired to see them immediately.

Having said these things, he summons the man with whom very often	268
he cared to share his table and conversation and his thoughts	
on private matters when exhausted from having spent the greater part	270
of the day managing the highest affairs of state,	
giving advice in the forum and the sacred Senate.	
To him he would speak with confidence of matters great and small,	
of jests and of matters bad and good alike to say	
he would unburden, if he wished, and keep them in safety,	275
with whom much pleasure[2]	
joys privately and openly;	
whose character no frivolous or evil thought induces	
to do an evil deed; a learned, loyal,	
accommodating man, delightful, content with what he has, happy,	280
discerning, with the right word at the right time, obliging, of few	

---

[2] The half-foot missing here indicates a gap of almost certainly
two half-lines or more.

paucum, multa tenens antiqua, sepulta vetustas
quae facit, et mores veteresque novosque †tenentem
multorum veterum leges divomque hominumque
285   prudentem qui dicta loquive tacereve posset.
hunc inter pugnas conpellat Servilius sic:

[5] L. Aelium Stilonem dicere solitum ferunt Q. Ennium
de semet ipso haec scripsisse picturamque istam morum
et ingenii ipsius Q. Ennii factam esse.

13 Paul. *Fest.*, p. 397.7–9 L.

SUPPERNATI dicuntur quibus femina sunt succisa in mo-
dum suillarum pernarum. Ennius:

287   his pernas succidit iniqua superbia Poeni

Cf. Fest., p. 396.22–27 L.

***14** Macrob. *Sat.* 6.1.20 (Verg. *Aen.* 12.565 "invadunt
urbem somno vinoque sepultam")

Ennius in octavo:

288   nunc hostes vino domiti somnoque sepulti

words, retaining much ancient lore, which time has
buried, and retaining customs old and new,
the laws of many ancient gods and men,
a prudent man, able to speak or keep still on matters   285
    spoken.
This man amid the fight Servilius[3] addresses thus:

[5] They say that Lucius Aelius Stilo[4] was accustomed to
say that Ennius wrote these words about none other than
himself, and that this was a description of Ennius' own
character and disposition.

[3] Cn. Servilius Geminus (cos. 217 BC), killed in the battle.
[4] L. Aelius Stilo Praeconinus (ca. 154–90 BC), an early Roman
grammarian and teacher of Varro.

13 Paul the Deacon, *Epitome of Festus*

Men whose thighs are cut through in the manner of pigs'
haunches are called "hamstrung." Ennius:

Punic harsh arrogance severed their thighs[1]   287

[1] Liv. 22.51.7 records such mutilations on the field at Cannae.
Cf. Val. Max. 9.2.ext.2.

***14** Macrobius, *Saturnalia* (on Virgil, "they attack a city
buried in sleep and drink")

Ennius in Book 8:

now the enemy was overcome by drink and buried in   288
    sleep

15 Paul. *Fest.*, p. 110.19–20 L.

MEDDIX apud Oscos nomen magistratus est. Ennius:

289   summus ibi capitur meddix, occiditur alter

16 Gell. *NA* 10.1.6

verba M. Varronis ex libro disciplinarum quinto haec sunt: "aliud est 'quarto' praetorem fieri et 'quartum,' quod 'quarto' locum significat ac tres antefactos, 'quartum' tempus adsignificat et ter ante factum. igitur Ennius recte quod scripsit:

290   Quintus pater quartum fit consul

et Pompeius timide quod in theatro, ne adscriberet 'consul tertium' aut 'tertio,' extremas litteras non scripsit."

Cf. Non., p. 435.12–13 M. = 701 L.

17 Fest., p. 218.12–13 L.

OSCOS quos dicimus ait Verrius Opscos antea dictos teste Ennio quom dicat:

291   de muris rem gerit Opscus

18 (cf. *Inc.* F 19) Fest., p. 188.1–3 L.

Ennius:

292   ob Romam noctu legiones ducere coepit

Cf. Paul. *Fest.*, p. 187.11–12 L.; Fest., p. 206.24–26 L.

252

15 Paul the Deacon, *Epitome of Festus*

meddix is the name of a magistrate among the Oscans.
Ennius:

> there the chief *meddix* is captured, the other killed   289

16 Gellius, *Attic Nights*

Marcus Varro's words in Book 5 of his *Instructions* are
these: "It is one thing to be elected praetor *quarto* [fourth]
and another to be praetor *quartum* [for the fourth time],
because *quarto* indicates the order with three elected be-
fore, *quartum* indicates time and three previous elections.
Therefore what Ennius wrote was correct:

> Quintus his father is elected consul for the fourth   290
>   time

and Pompey was timid when, to avoid writing either 'con-
sul for the third time' or 'third' on his theater, he did not
write the final letters."[1]

[1] The ambiguous abbreviation TERT. on the dedicatory in-
scription was, Gellius goes on to say (10.1.7), Cicero's suggestion.

17 Festus

Those we call "Oscans" Verrius says were previously called
"Opscans," citing Ennius, since he says:

> the Opscan conducts his business from   291
>   the walls

18 (cf. *Inc.* F 19) Festus

Ennius:

> he began marching his legions toward Rome at night   292

*19 Schol. Bern. ad Verg. *G.* 4.72

"auditur fractos sonitus imitata tubarum": inde Ennius in VIII ait:

293   tibia Musarum pangit melos

*20 Non., p. 151.18–26 M. = pp. 221–22 L.

PORTISCULUS proprie est hortator remigum, id est, qui eam perticam tenet, quae portisculus dicitur, qua et cursum et exhortamenta moderatur. . . . Ennius lib. VIII Annalium:

294   tonsamque tenentes
        parerent observarent portisculus signum
        quom dare coepisset

    294 tonsamque *Carrio*: tonsam ante *Scaliger*: tusam ante *Lindsay*: tusante *codd.*

*21 Prisc., *GL* II, p. 210.6–11

quod autem Ionis et Calypsonis et Didonis dicitur, ostendit hoc etiam Caesellius Vindex in stromateo his verbis: Calypsonem. ita declinatum est apud antiquos. Livius: "Calypsonem" [*Od.* F 13 M.]. Ennius in VIII:

297   Poenos Didone oriundos

*19 Scholia Bernensia to Virgil, *Georgics*

"[a voice] is heard imitating the faint sound of trumpets":
so Ennius in Book 8 says:

> the pipe[1] sang the Muses' melody 293

[1] The relation of lemma to gloss may suggest an original contrast in Ennius between sounding the *tuba* of war and the *tibia* of peace.

*20 Nonius

The *portisculus* is, strictly speaking, the oarsmen's time-beater, i.e., the one who holds the hammer called the *portisculus*, with which he regulates their speed and rhythm . . . Ennius, Book 8 of the *Annals*:

> and holding tight the oar 294
> they attended, they watched as the timekeeper
> began to give the signal

*21 Priscian

As to the fact that one says *Ionis*, *Calypsonis*, and *Didonis* [genitives] Caesellius Vindex [early second-century AD grammarian] also shows this in his *Miscellany* with these words: *Calypsonem.* So it was declined among the ancients. Livius, *Calypsonem* [*Od.* F 13 M.]. Ennius in Book 8:

> the Carthaginians born from Dido 297

BOOK IX

This book continued the narrative of the war against Hannibal and, since Book 10 almost certainly opened with an introduction to the Second Macedonian War (F 1, 2), probably climaxed with Scipio's decisive victory over Hannibal at Zama. The fragments include likely references to Livius Salinator's victory at the Metaurus in 207 BC (F 2), the invasion of Africa (F 4, 7), and the election of consuls

*1 Non., p. 472.5–6 M. = 757 L.

LUCTANT pro luctantur. Ennius lib. IX:

298   – ∪ viri varia validis † viribus luctant

       viri varia *Housman*: defessi varie *Flores*: varia *codd. nonnulli*   vice *post* validis *Housman*: cum *Dousa*: ut *Lindsay*

2 Serv. Dan. ad Verg. *Aen.* 9.641

mactus autem apud veteres etiam mactatus dicebatur, ut Ennius:

299   Livius inde redit magno mactatus triumpho

---

[1] M. Livius Salinator, together with his co-consul C. Claudius Nero, won a decisive victory over Hasdrubal at the Metaurus in 207 BC. Salinator celebrated a triumph; Nero claimed only an

BOOK IX

for the year 204 BC (F 6), but aside from other generic (and disparaging) references to Carthaginians (F 5, 8), nothing else is at all certain. Identification of the Cyclops simile (F 15) with Philip V of Macedon is purely speculative: the possibility is thoroughly discussed by Tomasco in Flores 2006, 4:39–139, and Fabrizi 2012, 151–77.

*1 Nonius

luctant [active: "they struggle"] for *luctantur* [deponent]. Ennius Book 9:

> men struggle [with?] stout strength [in doubtful   298
> battle?]

2 Servius Danielis, *Commentary on Virgil*

mactus [honored], among the ancients *mactatus* was also used, as Ennius:

> thence Livius returned honored with a great   299
> triumph[1]

ovatio since the battle was fought in his colleague's province (Liv. 28.9.2–18; Val. Max. 4.1.9).

257

*3 Non., p. 66.18–24 M. = 92 L.

POLITIONES: agrorum cultus diligentes, ut polita omnia dicimus exculta et ad nitorem deducta. Ennius Satyrarum lib. III [F 6] . . . idem Annali lib. IX:

300   rastros dente †fabres capsit causa poliendi
            agri

      dentifabres *Turnebus*: dentiferos Hug | *ante* agri *lacunam posuit Skutsch*

4 Cic. *Tusc.* 1.45

qui ostium Ponti viderunt et eas angustias per quas penetravit ea quae est nominata "Argo . . ." [*Trag.* F 89.5–6] aut ii qui Oceani freta illa viderunt

302   Europam Libyamque rapax ubi dividit unda

Cf. Cic. *Nat. D.* 3.24.

5 Gell. *NA* 6.12.6–7

Vergilius quoque tunicas huiuscemodi [manicatas] quasi femineas probrosas criminatur. "et tunicae" inquit "manicas . . ." [*Aen.* 9.616]. [7] Q. quoque Ennius Carthaginiensium

303   tunicata iuventus

non videtur sine probro dixisse.

*3 Nonius

politiones: the diligent cultivation of fields, just as we call all things *polita* that are carefully made and brought to a high gloss. Ennius in Book 3 of his *Satires* [F 6] . . . and Book 9 of his *Annals*:

> have him take toothed rakes for harrowing   300
> the field[1]

---

[1] Text and context are uncertain. *capsit* (old optative of *capio*) is probably jussive.

4 Cicero, *Tusculan Disputations*

Those who have seen the entrance to Pontus and the narrows through which the ship called Argo passed . . . [*Trag.* F 89.5–6] or those who saw the well-known straits of Ocean,

> where the greedy swell parts Europe and Libya   302

5 Gellius, *Attic Nights*

Virgil too disparages tunics of this type [long-sleeved] as effeminate and shameful: "and sleeves on the tunic," he says, ". . ." [*Aen.* 9.616]. [7] Ennius also seems to have spoken of the Carthaginians'

> tunic-clad youth   303

not without scorn.

*6 (= T 17) Cic. *Brut.* 57–60

quem vero exstet et de quo sit memoriae proditum elo-
quentem fuisse et ita esse habitum, primus est M. Corne-
lius Cethegus, cuius eloquentiae est auctor et idoneus
quidem mea sententia Q. Ennius, praesertim cum et ipse
eum audiverit et scribat de mortuo; ex quo nulla suspicio
est amicitiae causa esse mentitum. [58] est igitur sic apud
illum in nono ut opinor Annali:

304   additur orator Cornelius suauiloquenti
        ore Cethegus Marcus Tuditano collega
        Marci filius

et oratorem appellat et suaviloquentiam tribuit . . . sed est
ea laus eloquentiae certe maxima:

            is dictus popularibus ollis
        qui tum vivebant homines atque aevom agitabant
        Flos delibatus populi

[59] probe vero; ut enim hominis decus ingenium, sic in-
geni ipsius lumen et eloquentia, qua virum excellentem
praeclare tum illi homines florem populi esse dixerunt

                Suadaique medulla

Πειθώ quam vocant Graeci, cuius effector est orator, hanc
Suadam appellavit Ennius; eius autem Cethegum medul-
lam fuisse vult, ut, quam deam in Pericli labris scripsit
Eupolis sessitavisse [F 102 *PCG*], huius hic medullam
nostrum oratorem fuisse dixerit. [60] at hic Cethegus con-
sul cum P. Tuditano fuit bello Punico secundo . . . et id

306 popularibus ollis *Merula*: ollis popularibus olim *codd.*

*6 (= T 17) Cicero, *Brutus*

Of those, however, who are certainly on record and known to have been eloquent and recognized as such, the first is Cornelius Cethegus [cos. 204 BC], of whose eloquence Ennius is a witness and indeed, in my view, a suitable one, especially since he had heard him himself and writes about him after his death; there is thus no suspicion that he lied for the sake of friendship. [58] There is thus the following, according to him in, I believe, the ninth book of the *Annals*:

> there is added the orator Cornelius of mellifluent   304
> speech Cethegus Marcus to Tuditanus as colleague,
> Marcus' son

He calls him orator and attributes mellifluence to him . . . but this is surely the greatest praise of his eloquence:

> he was pronounced by those countrymen
> who were then alive and living out their years
> the choicest Flower of the people.

[59] Truly well put, for just as a man's distinction is his talent, so the glory of his talent is eloquence, and someone surpassingly great in eloquence was called by the men of that time the flower of the people

> and the marrow of Persuasion

What the Greeks call Peitho, which the orator brings about, Ennius here called Persuasion. He wishes Cethegus to have been the marrow of this, so he said our orator had been the marrow of the goddess, who Eupolis wrote had dwelt on the lips of Pericles [F 102 *PCG*]. [60] Now this Cethegus was consul with Publius Tuditanus at the

ipsum nisi unius esset Enni testimonio cognitum, hunc
vetustas, ut alios fortasse multos, oblivione obruisset.

Cf. Cic. *Sen.* 50; Quint. *Inst.* 2.15.4, 11.3.31; Gell. *NA* 12.2.3;
Serv. Dan. ad Verg. *Aen.* 8.500.

7 Cic. *De or.* 3.167

illa quidem traductio atque immutatio in verbo quandam
fabricationem habet: in oratione

309   Africa terribili tremit horrida terra tumultu

pro Afris est sumpta Africa, neque factum est verbum . . .
[Dubia *Ann.* F 10] neque translatum . . . [Pac. *Trag.* 77
R.$^{2-3}$], sed ornandi causa proprium proprio commutatum.

Cf. Cic. *Fam.* 9.7.2; *Orat.* 93; Fest., p. 138.16–18 L.

8 Columna, p. 239 (148 H.)

310   perculsi pectora Poeni

hoc fragmentum mihi e Cosenia Fabius Aquinas misit.
quod a quodam suo vetustissimo Statii interprete MS ex-
cerpsit. cuius nomen, cum in illius libri principio et fine
multae desiderentur paginae, prorsus ignoratur. constat
tamen ex collatione non esse Lactantium.

---

1 The fragment first appears with this note in Colonna's 1590
edition of Ennius. Its authenticity is not beyond question and its
attribution to Book 9 entirely conjectural. For its history see To-
masco in Flores 2006, 4:92–96.

time of the Second Punic War . . . and antiquity would have buried him in oblivion (as perhaps it has buried many others) were he not known through the testimony of Ennius alone.[1]

[1] It is knowledge of Cethegus' eloquence that survives only through Ennius' testimony. His public career (cens. 209, cos. 204, both with P. Sempronius Tuditanus as colleague) is in fact well attested. On the artistry of this fragment, see Gildenhard 2003, 98–100.

7 Cicero, *On the Orator*

Even the transfer and metonymy of single words has a certain artfulness: in the utterance

Africa, wild[1] land, trembles with a terrible tumult   309

"Africa" is adopted for "Africans." The word is neither manufactured . . . [Dubia *Ann.* F 10] nor metaphorical . . . [Pac. *Trag.* 77 R.$^{2-3}$], but for the sake of imparting distinction an appropriate word is substituted for another appropriate word.

[1] Skutsch understands "shuddering," taken closely with *tremit*.

8 Colonna

the Carthaginians struck to the heart   310

Colonna:[1] Fabius Aquinas sent this fragment to me from Cosenza. He excerpted it by hand from a certain very old commentator on Statius. Since at the beginning and end of this book many pages were lacking, his name is completely unknown. It is evident from the collation, however, that he is not Lactantius.

*9 Macrob. *Sat.* 6.4.17

inseruit operi suo e Graeca verba, sed non primus hoc est ausus; auctorum enim veterum audaciam secutus est. "dependent lychni laquearibus aureis" [*Aen.* 1.726], sicut Ennius in nono:

311   lychnorum lumina bis sex

*10 Non., p. 110.8–10 M. = 157 L.

FAMUL: famulus. Ennius lib. IX:

312   mortalem summum Fortuna repente
         reddidit † summo regno famul † ut † optimus esset

*11 Prisc., *GL* II, p. 278.10–19

apud illos [Graecos] enim si in *x* desinentia nomina habent verba cum *g*, nominum quoque genitivus per *g* declinatur . . . unde frux etiam frugis facit genitivum, quia ἀπὸ τοῦ "φρύγω" Graeco verbo nascitur. Ennius in XVI Annali [F 21] . . . ; idem in IX pro frugi homo frux ponit, quod est adiectivum:

314   sed quid ego haec memoro? dictum factumque facit
              frux

id est frugi homo.

---

1 The nominative *frux* is in fact rare. Cf. Varro, *Ling.* 9.76.

2 A proverbial expression like "no sooner said than done." Cf. Ter. *Haut.* 760: *dictum ac factum reddidi* "I carried it out as soon as it was said."

*9 Macrobius, *Saturnalia*

He [Virgil] also inserted words from Greek in his work, but he was not the first to dare this, for he was following the boldness of ancient authors: "*lychni* [lamps] hang from the gold-coffered ceiling" [*Aen.* 1.726], just like Ennius in Book Nine:

twice six lights of lychni   311

*10 Nonius

famul: *famulus* ["household slave"]. Ennius in Book 9:

Fortune suddenly casts the highest mortal   312
from the highest power to be the lowest [?] slave[1]

[1] The general sense is clearer than the surviving text, for which various, not entirely satisfactory emendations have been proposed. Lucr. 3.1035 seems to echo the problematic line end *proinde ac famul infimus esset* "as if to be the lowest slave."

*11 Priscian

Among them [the Greeks], if nouns ending in *x* have verbs with *g*, the genitive of the nouns is also declined with *g* . . . from which *frux* [fruit] too makes as its genitive *frugis*,[1] since it derives from the Greek verb *phrygo* [to parch]. Ennius in *Annals* Book 16 [F 21] . . . ; again in Book 9 he puts *frux*, which is an adjective, in place of *frugi homo* [an honest man]:

but why do I mention these things? The honest man   314
    makes the word the deed.[2]

that is, "an honest man."

*12 Non., p. 217.7–11 M. = 320 L.

PULVIS generis masculini, ut saepe. feminini Ennius lib. VIII Annalium [F 8] . . . idem lib. IX:

315 pulvis fulva volat

   pulvis: iamque fere pulvis fulva volat *Nonius, correxit Hug*

*13 Brev. Expos. ad Verg. *G.* 2.437 (vol. 3.2, pp. 311.21–12.1 Th.-H.)

"undantem": abundantem. Ennis in libro VIIII Annalium:

316   praeda exercitus undat

*14 Non., p. 150.37–40 M. = 220 L.

PERPETUASSIT: † sit perpetua, aeterna. Ennius Annali lib. IX:

317   libertatemque ut perpetuassint
   †que †maximae

   317 perpetuassint *Merula*: *alia alii*: perpetias sint *vel* perpetuitas sint *codd.*

*15 Prisc., *GL* II, pp. 485.17–86.17

in *geo* desinentia *l* vel *r* antecedentibus *geo* in *si* conversa faciunt praeteritum perfectum ut . . . urgeo ursi, turgeo tursi, tergeo tersi . . . Ennius in VII Annalium [F 7] . . . , idem in VIIII:

319 Cyclopis venter velut olim turserat alte
  carnibus humanis distentus

*12 Nonius

pulvis [dust], as often, is masculine in gender. Feminine in Ennius, Book 8 of the *Annals* [F 8] . . . also in Book 9:

tawny dust flies up   315

*13 Scholia to Virgil, *Georgics*

undantem: *abundantem* [abounding]. Ennius in Book 9 of the *Annals*:

the army swells with booty   316

*14 Nonius

perpetuassit: may it be perpetual [?], ‹meaning› enduring forever. Ennius, *Annals*, Book 9:

and that they preserve liberty forever   317
and [?][1]

[1] The phrase is hopelessly corrupt. Of the many conjectures, Müller's *quaeque axim* (adopted by Warmington, "and all that I may have done") is the most appealing. The construction suggests a prayer.

*15 Priscian

verbs ending in *-geo* preceded by *l* or *r* turn *-geo* to *si* to form the perfect, as *urgeo ursi, turgeo tursi, tergeo tersi* . . . Ennius in Book 7 of the *Annals* [F 7] . . . , the same in Book 9:

just as the Cyclops' belly had once swelled high,   319
stretched tight with human flesh

*16 Non., p. 95.30–31 M. = 136 L.

DEBILO: debilis. Ennius lib. IX:

321   † debilo homo

    debil *Lipsius*: debile *dubitanter Skutsch*

*16 Nonius

debilo: *debilis* [feeble]. Ennius Book 9:

a feeble creature   321

BOOK X

The surviving invocation (F 1) confirms that this book dealt with the Second Macedonian War of 200 to 197 BC. Identifiable topics include the consular elections for 200 (F 2) and 198 (F 5, probably), together with the levy of additional troops authorized for that year by the Senate (F 6;

1 Gell. *NA* 18.9.3–6

"'insequenda' enim scribi," inquit [grammaticus] "⟨oportuit⟩ [apud Catonem], non 'insecenda,' quoniam 'insequens' significat ***, traditumque esse 'inseque,' quasi 'perge dicere' et 'insequere,' itaque ab Ennio scriptum in his versibus,

322   insece Musa manu Romanorum induperator
      quod quisque in bello gessit cum rege Philippo

[4] alter autem ille eruditior nihil mendum sed recte atque integre scriptum esse perseverabat et Velio Longo, non homini indocto, fidem esse habendam, qui in commentario quod fecisset de usu antiquae lectionis scripserit non "inseque" apud Ennium legendum esse sed "insece" . . . [5] ego arbitror et a M. Catone "insecenda" et a Q. Ennio

BOOK X

cf. Liv. 32.8.2). *The story of the Epirote shepherd who provided Flamininus with a tactical advantage at the Aous seems the possible subject of F 8 and F 9 (if the latter is indeed a fragment of Ennius). Other contexts suggested for various fragments of this book are less secure.*

1 Gellius, *Attic Nights*

"[In Cato] *insequenda* ought to be written," [the grammarian] said, "not *insecenda*, since *insequens* means ***, and *inseque* has come down to us as 'proceed to say' and 'press on,' and thus was written by Ennius in the following lines:

> proceed, Muse, to say what deeds of arms each
> > Roman
> commander accomplished in the war with King Philip

322

[4] But the other, more learned man insisted there was no error, but that it was written correctly and appropriately and that we ought to trust Velius Longus,[1] a man not without learning, who in the commentary he prepared on the use of archaic terms wrote that not *inseque* should be read in Ennius but *insece* . . . [5] I think Cato wrote *insecenda*

---

[1] Grammarian of the early second century AD (*GL* VII, pp. 48–81).

271

"insece" scriptum sine "u" littera. offendi enim in bibliotheca Patrensi librum verae vetustatis Livii Andronici, qui inscriptus est Ὀδύσσεια, in quo erat versus primus hoc verbo sine "u" littera, "virum mihi, Camena, insece versutum" [F 1 *FPL*⁴] . . . [6] illic igitur aetatis et fidei magnae libro credo.

Cf. Paul. *Fest*., p. 99.10 L.

2 Isid. *Orig.* 1.36.3

zeugma est clausula dum plures sensus uno verbo clauduntur. quae fit tribus modis. nam aut in primo aut in postremo aut in medio id verbum ponitur quod sententias iungit. in primo ut . . . [Lucil. 139 M. = 132 W.], in medio

324   Graecia Sulpicio sorti data, Gallia Cottae

in postremo . . . [Ter. *An.* 68].

and Ennius wrote *insece* without the letter *u*, for in the library at Patras I came upon a book of undoubted antiquity by Livius Andronicus called *Odussia*, the first line of which has this verb without the letter *u*, "proceed, Camena, to tell me of the versatile man" [*Od.* F 1 *FPL*⁴].² . . . On such a point, then, I trust a book of great age and reliability.

² Ennius thus seems deliberately to echo Livius Andronicus' calque on Homeric ἔννεπε (Goldberg 1995, 64–65; Hinds 1998, 58–63; Feeney 2016, 53–56). Whether he actually wrote *insece* or *inseque* is uncertain.

2 Isidore, *Origins*

Zeugma is a sentence end when multiple senses are completed by a single verb. It comes about in three ways: the verb that joins the thoughts is placed in either the first, final, or middle position. In the first position, as . . . [Lucil. 139 M. = 132 W.], in the middle position,

> Greece was assigned by lot to Sulpicius, Gaul to   324
>   Cotta¹

in the final position . . . [Ter. *An.* 68].

¹ Provinces allotted to the consuls of 200 BC, P. Sulpicius Galba and C. Aurelius Cotta. Sulpicius thus took command of the war with Macedon. Cotta's province was in fact *Italia*, but he joined the praetor Furius Purpurio in suppressing a serious threat from Gaul (Liv. 31.6.1–2, 11.2–3).

*3 (= T 111) Schol. Bern. ad Verg. *G.* 2.119

"acanthi": Gnifo commentatur Annalium libro decimo hanc arborem in insula Cercina regionis Africae esse oportunam tincturae, quae in floris sui colorem lanam tingit, unde vestis Acanthia appellatur.

325   acanth⟨us⟩

Ennio redd. Buecheler

*4 Serv. Dan. ad Verg. *G.* 4.188

mussant hic murmurant, quae vox ponitur et in tacendi significatione . . . mussant autem murmurant Ennius in X sic ait:

326   aspectabat virtutem legionis suai
        expectans si mussaret quae denique pausa
        pugnandi fieret aut duri ⟨finis⟩ laboris

     327 pausa *Bergk*: causa *Dousa*: causam *codd.*   328 finis
add. Bergk: pausa *Dousa*

5 (cf. T 13) Cic. *Rep.* 1.30

in ipsius paterno genere fuit noster ille amicus, dignus huic ad imitandum

329   egregie cordatus homo, catus Aelius Sextus

----

[1] The speaker is Laelius, but since a significant lacuna precedes this passage, its context is uncertain.

*3 (= T 111) Scholia Bernensia to Virgil, *Georgics*

"acanthus": Gnipho[1] comments in the tenth book of the *Annals* that this tree on the island of Cercina [near Tunisia] in the region of Africa is suitable for dying; this dyes wool the color of its flower, whence the garment is called "Acanthian."

acanth⟨us⟩[2]   325

[1] M. Antonius Gnipho tutored the young Caesar and then founded a school at Rome. Cicero as praetor in 66 BC attended his lectures. Whether Gnipho wrote a full-fledged commentary on the *Annals* is uncertain. See Kaster 1995, 116–22.   [2] Or quite possibly, as suggested by Bücheler, Acanthus, a town in Thrace, with a pun on the name of the tree. Cf. 7 *Ann.* F 17.

*4 Servius Danielis, *Commentary on Virgil*

mussant [they murmur] here for *murmurant* [they mutter], a word which is also employed for indicating silence . . . Ennius in Book 10 thus says *mussant* for *murmurant*:

he was observing his troops' morale,   326
wondering if they would mutter, what rest at last
there would be from fighting or end to hard labor

5 (cf. T 13) Cicero, *On the Republic*

That friend of ours[1] belonged to his father's family, a man worthy of his emulation,

a man outstandingly wise, shrewd Sextus Aelius[2]   329

[2] Sex. Aelius Paetus, famous for his legal knowledge, was consul in 198 BC with T. Quinctius Flamininus, who would defeat Philip the following year at Cynoscephalae.

qui "egregie cordatus" et "catus" fuit et ab Ennio dictus
est non quod ea quaerebat quae numquam inveniret, sed
quod ea respondebat quae eos qui quaesissent et cura et
negotio solverent.

Cf. Cic. *De or.* 1.198; *Tusc.* 1.18; Varro, *Ling.* 7.46; Pomp. *Dig.*
1.2.2.38; August. *Ep.* 19.

*6 Prisc., *GL* II, p. 30.1–6

finalis dictionis subtrahitur *m* in metro plerumque, si a
vocali incipit sequens dictio . . . vetustissimi tamen non
semper eam subtrahebant. Ennius in x Annalium:

330 insignita fere tum milia militum octo
duxit delectos bellum tolerare potentes

330 *an* militis? *Skutsch*

*7 Fest., p. 184.3–8 L.

NICTIT: canis in odorandis ferarum vestigiis leviter gan-
niens, ut Ennius in lib. X:

332 veluti quando vinclis venatica velox
apta dolet si forte ⟨feras⟩ ex nare sagaci
sensit, voce sua nictit ululatque ibi acute

unde ipsa gannitio.

333 dolet *Baehrens*: canis *Ribbeck*: solet *codd.*   feras *add.*
Müller   334 acute *Scaliger*: acta et *codd.*

Cf. Paul. *Fest.*, p. 185.1–3 L.

who was "outstandingly wise" and "shrewd" and was called so by Ennius not because he would seek out things he could not discover, but because he would reply with answers that would free those who had asked from anxiety and trouble.[3]

[3] Cicero alludes to the formal replies (*responsa*) of the jurisconsult.

*6 Priscian

The final *m* of a word is frequently dropped in scansion if the following word begins with a vowel . . . nevertheless, the oldest poets did not always drop it. Ennius in Book 10 of the *Annals*:[1]

> then some eight thousand decorated soldiers   330
> he led, chosen men able to endure war

[1] Hiatus, though explicitly attested here by Priscian, is generally avoided in the *Annals*: Inc. *Ann.* F 61 is the only clear parallel. Skutsch thus suggests *militis octo* for *militum octo*.

*7 Festus

nictit:[1] of a dog whimpering gently when it scents the tracks of wild animals, as Ennius in Book 10:

> just as when a swift hunting dog held by a chain   332
> complains if it chances to pick up a scent of ‹wild
>   animals?› with its
> keen nose: it whimpers with its own voice and then
>   whines keenly

From that comes [the noun] "whimpering."

[1] The verb (*nictire*) is otherwise unattested.

8 Cic. *Sen.* 1

337   O Tite, si quid ego adiuero curamve levasso
      quae nunc te coquit et versat in pectore fixa,
      ecquid erit praemi?

licet enim mihi versibus eisdem adfari te, Attice, quibus
adfatur Flamininum

335   ille vir haud magna cum re sed plenus fidei

quamquam certo scio non ut Flamininum

336   sollicitari te Tite sic noctesque diesque

novi enim moderationem animi tui et equitatem, teque
non cognomen solum Athenis deportasse, sed humanita-
tem et prudentiam intellego.

Cf. Donat. ad Ter. *Phorm.* 34.

9 Varro, *Rust.* 2.2.1

sed quoniam nos nostrum pensum absolvimus ac limitata
est pecuaria quaestio, nunc

340   rursus vos reddite nobis,
      O Epirotae . . .

de unaquaque re ut videamus quid

      pastores a Pergamide Maledove potis sint

---

1 Observing the archaism of *potis sint* and that the phrases
rursus . . . nobis, O Epirotae, and *pastores . . . sint* can be scanned
as dactylic, Skutsch claims these phrases as fragments of the *An-
nals,* while the reference to shepherds leads him to associate them
with F 8 and claim them for Book 10; arguments in Skutsch
1978.   2 Both, presumably, locations in Epirus, though Perga-
mis is uncertain and Maledus (or Maledum) otherwise unknown.

8 Cicero, *On Old Age*

> Titus, if I should provide some aid or lighten the care 337
> which, now fixed in your breast, sears and unsettles
>   you,
> will there be some reward?

For I may address you, Atticus, with those very lines with
which Flamininus is addressed by

> that man of no great wealth but full of loyalty[1] 335

although certainly I understand that it is not, like Flamini-
nus,

> that you, Titus, are thus tormented night and day 336

for I know the control and balance of your mind, and I
realize that you have brought back from Athens not only
a cognomen[2] but sensibility and discretion.

[1] There is no strong reason to assume with Skutsch (following
Baehrens) that in Ennius (the evident source of the lines quoted)
this description of the speaker preceded his speech.   [2] Cic-
ero's friend Titus Pomponius gained the cognomen Atticus from
his extended residence in that city.

9[1] Varro, *On Agriculture*

Since we have completed our task and the subject of cattle
raising has been sketched out, now

>   return once more to us, 340
>   O Epirotes,

so we can see concerning each matter what

> shepherds from Pergamis or Maledus[2] can
>   accomplish.

*10 Donat. ad Ter. *Phorm.* 287

"columen vero familiae": Ennius X:

343   regni versatum summam venere columnam

*11 Macrob. *Sat.* 6.1.60 (Verg. *Aen.* 7.295–96 "num capti potuere capi? num incensa cremavit / Troia viros?")

Ennius in decimo, cum de Pergamis loqueretur:

344   quae neque Dardaniis campis potuere perire
        nec quom capta capi nec quom combusta cremari

*12 Prisc., *GL* II, p. 541.13–17

"cambio" ἀμείβω ponit Charisius et eius praeteritum "campsi," quod ἀπὸ τοῦ κάμπτω ἔκαμψα Graeco esse videtur. unde et "campso campsas" solebant vetustissimi dicere. Ennius in X:

346   Leucatan campsant

*10 Donatus, *Commentary on Terence*
"the very pillar of my household": Ennius Book 10:

> they have come to overturn the lofty pillar of the   343
>   kingdom

*11 Macrobius, *Saturnalia* (on Virgil, "Could they not stay captive once captured? Could Troy in flames not have consumed her heroes?")

Ennius in Book Ten, when speaking about Pergamum [the Trojan citadel]:

> which could neither perish on the Dardanian plains   344
>   nor stay captive when captured nor when set on fire
>   burn

*12 Priscian

Charisius says *cambio*, "I exchange" [Gk.], and its perfect *campsi*, which appear to be from Greek κάμπτω ἔκαμψα [I bend, I have bent], from which the oldest writers were accustomed to say *campso*, *campsas* [present and perfect]. Ennius in Book 10:

> they doubled Leucata[1]   346

[1] The southwest promontory of the island of Leucas (Lefkas), on the route into the Corinthian Gulf from the north and the west. L. Flamininus, the consul's brother, would have passed it in 197 BC on his way to besiege Leucas, the capital of Acarnania (Liv. 33.17), but other contexts are imaginable. The Latin verb is a calque on the Greek nautical term for rounding a promontory.

*13 Diom., *GL* I, p. 382.21–26

hortatur quod vulgo dicimus veteres nonnulli "horitur" dixerunt, ut Ennius sexto decimo Annalium . . . [F 22]. idem in decimo:

347   horitatur   induperator

quasi specie iterativa.

*14 Macrob. *Sat.* 6.1.9 (Verg. *Aen.* 4.482 "axem umero torquet stellis ardentibus aptum")

Ennius in primo [F 22] . . . et in tertio . . . [F 7], in decimo

348   hinc nox processit stellis ardentibus apta

*15 Non., p. 370.19–23 M. = 589 L.

PASSUM: extensum, patens, unde et passus dicimus quod gressibus mutuis pedes patescunt. Ennius Annalium lib. X:

349   aegro corde, comis passis

*16 Diom., *GL* I, p. 373.3–6

apud veteres reperimus etiam *n* littera addita pinso quod est tundo et pinsit secundum tertium ordinem, ut Ennius decimo Annalium:

350   pinsunt terram genibus

*13 Diomedes

For *hortatur* [urges], which we commonly say, some old writers said *horitur*, as Ennius in Book sixteen of the *Annals* . . . [F 22]. Likewise in Book ten:

> . . . keeps cheering them on . . . the commander[1]   347

as a kind of iterative form.

[1] *induperator* [commander] normally ends a verse in Ennius, but here could possibly open the following one.

*14 Macrobius, *Saturnalia* (on Virgil, "he spins heaven's vault, studded with blazing stars, on his shoulder")

Ennius in Book One [F 22] . . . and in Book Three [F 7], and in Book Ten:

> then night continued on, studded with blazing stars   348

*15 Nonius

passum: "stretched out," "spreading open," from which we also say *passus* [steps] because the feet spread apart with each step. Ennius in Book 10 of the *Annals*:

> sick at heart, with hair spread in disarray   349

*16 Diomedes

Among the ancients we even find the letter *n* added, as *pinso*, which is "I beat," and *pinsit* following the third conjugation, as Ennius in Book 10 of the *Annals*:

> they beat the ground with their knees   350

*17 Fest., p. 514.20–22 L.

veruta pila dicuntur quod ‹velut verva› habent praefixa.
Ennius lib. X:

351   verut-

*18 *Macrob. exc. Bob.*, *GL* V, p. 645

a fio fiere esse deberet; et licet usus aliter obtinuerit—fieri
enim nunc dicitur—Ennius tamen in X Annalium

352   fiere

dixit, non fieri.

*17 Festus

Javelins are called *veruta* because they have, as it were, spits [*verva*] attached. Ennius Book 10:

javelin [351

*18 *Excerpts from Macrobius*

fiere [bring about] ought to be the infinitive of *fio*. And granted that another usage occurs, for *fieri* now is said, but Ennius nevertheless in *Annals* 10 said

fiere 352

not *fieri*.

BOOK XI

The content of this book is uncertain, and none of its (largely generic) fragments can be securely identified. Skutsch thought the narrative concluded the Second Macedonian War down through Flamininus' famous declaration of Greek freedom at the Isthmian Games in 196 BC. Warm-

*1 Fest., p. 306.21–23 L.

QUIPPE significare quidni testimonio est Ennius lib. XI[1]:

353   quippe solent reges omnes in rebus secundis

> [1] XI *Ursinus:* XL *codd.*

*2 Fest., pp. 344.35–46.2 L.

⟨RIMA⟩RI: quaere⟨re valde ut in rimis quoque⟩ . . . qui te riman . . . Ennius lib. XI:

354   ⟨rimantur⟩ utrique

> rimantur *suppl. Spangenberg*

BOOK XI

ington, following a different scheme, hypothesized a narrative running through the 190s BC that included the opening of hostilities with Antiochus III and Cato's campaigns in Spain.

*1 Festus

That *quippe* [surely] means *quidni* [lit., "why not?"] is attested by Ennius in Book 11:

> surely all kings in favorable circumstances are 353
>   accustomed

*2 Festus

⟨*rima*⟩*ri* is to seek ⟨earnestly, as even in crannies⟩ . . . who seeks (?) you . . . Ennius, Book 11:

> both sides ⟨earnestly seek⟩[1] 354

[1] Festus' text is itself fragmentary. *utrique* [both sides] was certainly part of the verse he quoted, and the remains of his gloss make it likely that *rimantur* was its verb. Nothing else about the line is known.

*3 Prisc., *GL* II, p. 445.7–8

sono sonas et sonis. Ennius in XI Annalium:

355   tum clipei resonunt et ferri stridit acumen

Cf. Prisc., *GL* II, pp. 473.22–74.1.

*4 Prisc., *GL* II, p. 419.16–17

a strido quoque alii stridui, alii stridi protulerunt. Ennius in Annalium XI:

356   missaque per pectus dum transit striderat hasta

*5 Fest., pp. 386.32–88.3 L.

sos pro eos antiqui dicebant, ut Ennius l. I [F 15] . . . et lib. III [F 4] . . . , lib. VII [F 16] . . . , lib. XI:

357   contendunt Graecos, Graios memorare solent sos

     Graecos, Graios *Vahlen*: Graios, Graecos *Festus*

Cf. Fest., p. 362.11–12 L.

*3 Priscian

sono [I sound] yields *sonas* and *sonis* [i.e., either first or third conj.]. Ennius in *Annals* 11:

> then the small shields resound and the sword's edge   355
> whizzes

*4 Priscian

From *strido* [I shriek], too, some conjugated *stridui* [i.e., second conj. perf.], others *stridi* [i.e., third conj. perf.]. Ennius in *Annals* 11:

> and the spear, sent through his chest, shrieked as it   356
> passed through

*5 Festus

The ancients used to say *sos* for *eos* [them], as Ennius Book 1 [F 15] . . . , Book 3 [F 4] . . . , Book 7 [F 16] . . . , and Book 11:

> they claim [compare?] the Greeks, Grecians are men   357
> accustomed to call them[1]

[1] Roman poetry prefers the form *Graius* to the prosaic *Graecus*: thus Vahlen's transposition of *Graios, Graecos*. The topic is widely assumed to be Roman kinship with the Greeks and the speaker to be Flamininus at the Isthmian Games (cf. Inc. *Ann.* F 17), but the sense is in fact uncertain.

*6 Fest., p. 226.12–15 L.

petrarum genera sunt duo, quorum alterum naturale saxum prominens in mare, cuius Ennius meminit lib. XI:

358   alte delata petrisque ingentibus tecta

et Laevius in Centauris [F 10 Courtney] "ubi ego saepe petris"; alterum manu factum . . .

*7 Non., p. 195.10–13 M. = 287 L.

CRUX generis feminini saepe. masculini, Ennius Annalium lib. XI:

359   malo cruce, fatur, uti des,
       Iuppiter

Cf. Fest., p. 136.12–13 L.

*8 Non., p. 483.1–2 M. = 775 L.

LACTE, nominativo casu, ab eo quod est lac. Ennius lib. XI:[1]

361   et simul erubuit ceu lacte et purpura mixta

       [1] X *codd. det.*

*9 Non., p. 149.27–29 M. = 218 L.

PENICULAMENTUM a veteribus pars vestis dicitur. Ennius lib. XI[1] Annalis [*sic*]:

362   pendent peniculamenta unum ad quemque pedum

       [1] XII *cod.*

*6 Festus

There are two kinds of rocks, one of which is natural stone
jutting into the sea, the kind Ennius recalls in Book 11:

> carried deep and covered with immense rocks 358

and Laevius in *The Centaurs* [F 10 Courtney], "where I
often with stones"; the other kind is made by hand . . .

*7 Nonius

crux [cross] often of feminine gender. Masculine, Ennius,
Annals, Book 11:

> "Give them," says he, "utter ruin, 359
> Jupiter"

*8 Nonius

lacte, as the nominative case, derived from *lac* [milk]. En-
nius in Book 11:

> and at once blushed like milk and crimson mixed 361

*9 Nonius

Peniculamentum [from *peniculus*, "a little tail" or "brush"]
is said by the ancients to be a part of a garment. Ennius,
Annals Book 11:

> the hems hang down to each and every foot 362

BOOK XII

The content of this book is uncertain. Q. Fabius Maximus Verrucosus (dict. 217, cos. V 209 BC), the great Cunctator, died in 203 BC, and since the book number provided for F 1 by Macrobius is reliable, the famous praise of Fabius there must be retrospective, but the occasion for it is unknown. Whether F 2 describes a specific episode (Skutsch) or makes a general statement about the exhaustion of even a victorious army (Vahlen) cannot be determined.

*1 Cic. *Off.* 1.84

illa [sc. plaga] pestifera, qua, cum Cleombrotus invidiam timens temere cum Epaminonda conflixisset, Lacedaemoniorum opes corruerunt. quanto Q. Maximus melius, de quo Ennius:

363   unus homo nobis cunctando restituit rem.
    noenum rumores ponebat ante salutem.
365   ergo postque magisque viri nunc gloria claret.

    364 noenum *Lachmann*: non enim *Cicero*

Cf. Cic. *Sen.* 10 (363–65); Macrob. *Sat.* 6.1.23 (363); Serv. ad Verg *Aen.* 6.845 (363); allusions at Cic. *Att.* 2.19.2; Liv. 30.26.7; Ov. *Fast.* 2.240; Sen. *Ben.* 4.27.2; Suet. *Tib.* 21; Seren. Sammon. 1092; fainter echoes at Polyb. 3.105.8; Plin. *HN* 22.10.

BOOK XII

Gellius clearly states on Varro's authority (T 84) that Ennius composed this book in his sixty-seventh year (i.e., 172 BC), a fact difficult to reconcile with the widely held view that Ennius added a sixteenth book to his Annals to relate events of the early 170s BC. For the problem, which assumes that Ennius composed his books in chronological sequence, see Skutsch 1985, 674–76; Paladini in Flores 2006, 4:308–10; Zetzel 2007, 13–14.

*1 Cicero, *On Duties*

That other blow was disastrous, by which, when Cleombrotus, fearing unpopularity, had rashly joined battle with Epaminondas, the Lacedaemonians' power collapsed. How much better was Quintus [Fabius] Maximus, of whom Ennius [wrote]:

> one man by delaying restored the state to us.   363
> He did not put popular opinion above safety:
> so now the man's glory shines ever brighter with   365
>   passing time.

*2 Prisc., *GL* II, pp. 152.18–53.14

acer et alacer et saluber et celeber quamvis acris et alacris
plerumque faciant et salubris et celebris feminina, in utra-
que tamen terminatione communis etiam generis inveni-
untur prolata . . . Ennius in XVI [F 18] . . . idem in XII:

366   omnes mortales victores, cordibus vivis
         laetantes, vino curatos somnus repente
         in campo passim mollissimus perculit acris

*2 Priscian

Although *acer* and *alacer* and *saluber* and *celeber* for the most part form as a feminine *acris* and *alacris* and *salubris* and *celebris*, nevertheless in both terminations they are also found inflected the same way . . . Ennius in 16 [F 18] . . . The same in 12:

> all men in victory, with hearts elated, 366
> rejoicing, tended by wine, the softest sleep
> suddenly fells helter-skelter on the plain, however
>   vigilant.[1]

[1] Priscian clearly reads *acris* as nominative, i.e., sleep "dazzling" as well as "extremely soft," but, as Skutsch observes, an accusative plural ("[men] however vigilant") makes for much easier syntax.

BOOK XIII

Roman tradition included numerous stories casting the defeated Hannibal as a "wise advisor" at the court of Antiochus III (e.g., Nep. Han. 2; Gell. NA 5.5). In recalling this narrative motif, F 3 confirms that this book dealt with Antiochus and the outbreak of hostilities with Rome in

1 Varro, *Ling.* 7.21

"quasi Hellespontum et claustra," quod Xerxes quondam eum locum clausit; nam ut Ennius ait:

369   isque Hellesponto pontem contendit in alto

2 Serv. Dan. ad Verg. *Aen.* 2.173

"salsusque per artus sudor iit": "salsus sudor" iudicium commoti numinis fuisse dicitur. Probo sane displicet "salsus sudor" et supervacue positum videtur. hoc autem Ennius de lamis dixit:

370   salsas   lamas

BOOK XIII

*192/1 BC, but its content is otherwise uncertain. The refe-
rence to Xerxes in F 1 is often taken to reflect Roman an-
xiety in 192 BC over a possible invasion across the Helles-
pont (cf. Liv. 35.23, 41). The contexts suggested for other
fragments are even more problematic.*

1 Varro, *On the Latin Language*

"as it were the Hellespont and its barriers," because Xer-
xes once barricaded this place, for as Ennius says:

and he stretched a bridge over the deep Hellespont   369

2 Servius Danielis, *Commentary on Virgil*

"and salty sweat ran down its limbs": "salty sweat" is said
to have been an expression of the divinity's agitation. Pro-
bus,[1] admittedly, disliked "salty sweat" and thought its use
superfluous. Ennius, however, said this about marshes:

salty   marshes   370

[1] For the great grammarian M. Valerius Probus, much re-
spected by Servius (and Donatus before him), see Kaster 1995,
242–50.

*3 Gell. *NA* 6.2.3–12

scripsit autem Caesellius Q. Ennium in XIII. Annali "cor" dixisse genere masculino. [4] verba Caeselli subiecta sunt: "masculino genere, ut multa alia, enuntiavit Ennius. nam in XIII. Annali *quem cor* dixit." [5] ascripsit deinde versus Ennii duo: "Hannibal audaci cum pectore de me hortatur / ne bellum faciam, quem credidit esse meum cor?" [6] Antiochus est, qui hoc dixit, Asiae rex. is admiratur et permovetur, quod Hannibal Carthaginiensis bellum se facere populo Romano volentem dehortetur. [7] hos autem versus Caesellius sic accipit, tamquam si Antiochus sic dicat: "Hannibal me, ne bellum geram, dehortatur; quod cum facit, ecquale putat cor habere me et quam stultum esse me credit, cum id mihi persuadere vult?" [8] hoc Caesellius quidem, sed aliud longe Ennius. [9] nam tres versus sunt, non duo, ad hanc Ennii sententiam pertinentes, ex quibus tertium versum Caesellius non respexit:

371   Hannibal audaci cum pectore de me hortatur
            ne bellum faciam, quem credidit esse meum cor
            suasorem summum et studiosum robore belli

[10] horum versuum sensus atque ordo sic, opinor, est: Hannibal ille audentissimus atque fortissimus, quem ego credidi—hoc est enim "cor meum credidit," proinde atque diceret "quem ego stultus homo credidi"—summum fore suasorem ad bellandum, is me dehortatur dissua-

---

[1] L. Caesellius Vindex, a second-century grammarian. Gell. *NA* 11.15.2 notes another, equally foolish mistake by him.

[2] The syntax of *studiosum robore* is unexplained. The phrase may be corrupt.

298

*3 Gellius, *Attic Nights*

Caesellius[1] wrote that Ennius, in the thirteenth book of his *Annals*, used *cor* in the masculine gender. [4] Caesellius' words follow: "Ennius used *cor*, like many other words, in the masculine gender; for in *Annals* 13 he said *quem cor*." [5] He then cited two verses of Ennius: "Hannibal, of audacious heart, urges me not to make war: what heart did he think was mine?" [6] The speaker is Antiochus, king of Asia. He is surprised and indignant that Hannibal, the Carthaginian, discourages his desire to make war on the Roman people. [7] Now, Caesellius understands these lines as if Antiochus were saying: "Hannibal dissuades me from making war. When doing so, what kind of heart does he think I have, and how foolish does he believe me to be, when he wishes to persuade me of this?" [8] So Caesellius; but Ennius' meaning was quite different. [9] For there are three verses, not two belonging to this utterance of Ennius, of which Caesellius overlooked the third verse:

> Hannibal of audacious heart urges me   371
> not to wage war, whom my heart took to be
> the greatest advocate and zealous mainstay [?][2] of war

[10] The meaning and arrangement of these verses I believe to be this: "Hannibal, that boldest and most valiant man, who I believed (for that is the meaning of *cor meum credidit*,[3] exactly as if he had said 'who I, foolish man, believed') would strongly advise war, discourages and dis-

---

[3] Gellius is correct. Ennius' periphrasis avoids the unmetrical *crēdidī.*

detque, ne bellum faciam. [11] Caesellius autem forte
ῥαθυμότερον iunctura ista verborum captus "quem cor"
dictum putavit et "quem" accentu acuto legit, quasi ad cor
referretur, non ad Hannibalem. [12] sed non fugit me, si
aliquis sit tam inconditus, sic posse defendi "cor" Caeselli
masculinum, ut videatur tertius versus separatim atque
divise legendus, proinde quasi praecisis interruptisque
verbis exclamet Antiochus: "suasorem summum!" sed non
dignum est eis, qui hoc dixerint, responderi.

373 robore: roboris *Bergk*

Cf. Non., p. 195.17–20 M. = 287 L.

*4 Gell. *NA* 18.2.12–16

hoc quaesitum est verbum "verant," quod significat "vera
dicunt," quisnam poetarum veterum dixerit . . . [16] nemo
. . . commeminerat dictum esse a Q. Ennio id verbum in
tertio decimo Annalium in isto versu

374   satin vates verant aetate in agunda

suades me from making war." [11] Caesellius, however, somewhat carelessly misled by that combination of words, assumed that Ennius said *quem cor*, reading *quem* with an acute accent, as if it belonged with *cor* and not with Hannibal. [12] But it does not escape me that, if anyone should have so little understanding, one might defend Caesellius' masculine *cor* by maintaining that the third verse should be read separately and apart from the others, as if Antiochus had exclaimed in broken and abrupt language, "a mighty adviser!" But those who would argue thus do not deserve a reply.

*4 Gellius, *Attic Nights*

The question was raised about which one of the early poets had used the verb *verant*, which means "they speak the truth"?[1] . . . [16] No one remembered that the word was used by Ennius in the thirteenth book of his *Annals* in this line:

> Really now, do seers speak the truth with respect to   374
> their own lives?

[1] The verb is otherwise unattested.

BOOK XIV

This book likely concluded the narrative of Rome's war with Antiochus III: F 4, describing the appearance of a distant fleet under sail, could belong to an account of the battle of Myonnesus in 190 BC (cf. Liv. 37.29.7, 30.7) and F 8 to a speech by Antiochus after his defeat at Magnesia, but no other identifications are even this likely. And in-

*1 Prisc., *GL* II, pp. 473.22–74.3

haec tamen ipsa et secundum tertiam vetustissimi protulisse inveniuntur coniugationem, ut Ennius in XI Annali [F 3] . . . , idem in XIV:

375   litora lata sonunt

*2 Macrob. *Sat.* 6.1.51 (Verg. *Aen.* 8.91 "labitur uncta vadis abies")

Ennius in XIV:

376   labitur uncta carina, volat super impetus undas

*3 Gell. *NA* 2.26.21–23

sed cum omnia libens audivi, quae peritissime dixisti, tum maxime, quod varietatem flavi coloris enarrasti fecistique,

BOOK XIV

deed, Skutsch's suggested emendation of the syntactically difficult fero *to* foro *in F 8 would require an entirely different context for these lines in a quite different narrative, perhaps a speech by P. Scipio in 184 BC, answering the political attacks on him.*

*1 Priscian

Nevertheless, the oldest writers are found to have used these same verbs also inflected in the third conjugation, as Ennius in *Annals* 11 [F 3] . . . , and again in Book 14:

> the broad beaches echo   375

*2 Macrobius, *Saturnalia* (on Virgil, "the greased keel glides over the shallows")

Ennius in Book 14:

> the greased keel glides, its onrush flies over the waves   376

*3 Gellius, *Attic Nights*

But not only have I listened with pleasure to all your very learned remarks, but in particular that you explained the diversity of the color *flavus* and allowed me to understand

ut intellegerem verba illa ex Annali quarto decimo Ennii amoenissima, quae minime intellegebam:

377   verrunt extemplo placidum mare: marmore flavo
    caeruleum spumat sale conferta rate pulsum

[22] non enim videbatur "caeruleum mare" cum "marmore flavo" convenire. [23] sed cum sit, ita ut dixisti, flavus color e viridi et albo mixtus, pulcherrime prorsus spumas virentis maris "flavom marmor" appellavit.

377 placidum *Parrhasius*: placide *codd.*   378 sale *Prisc.*: mare *Gellius*

Cf. Prisc., *GL* II, p. 171.11–13.

*4 Macrob. *Sat.* 6.5.10 (Verg. *Aen.* 1.224 "despiciens mare velivolum")

Laevius in Helena "tu qui permensus ponti maria alta velivola" [F 11 Courtney]. Ennius in quarto decimo,

379   quom procul aspiciunt hostes accedere ventis
    navibus velivolis

those very charming lines from the fourteenth book of Ennius' *Annals*, which before I did not understand at all well:

> they forthwith swept the gentle sea: with yellow   377
>   marble
> its green salt[1] foamed, beaten by the thronging ships

[22] For "green sea" did not appear compatible with "yellow marble." [23] But since, as you said, *flavus* is a color mixing green and white, he quite beautifully called the foam of the green sea "yellow marble."

---

[1] Reading *sale* with Skutsch (and Priscian); Gellius read *mare*.

*4 Macrobius, *Saturnalia* (on Virgil, "looking down on the swift-sailing sea")

Laevius in *Helen*, "you who have traversed the sea's deep, swift-sailing expanses" [F 11 Courtney]. Ennius in Book Fourteen:

> when far off they see the enemy advance with the   379
>   winds
> on swift-sailing ships[1]

---

[1] For *velivolus* describing ships, not the sea that conveys them (a distinction noted by Serv. ad Verg. *Aen.* 1.224), cf. *Trag.* 33; Lucr. 5.1442; Ov. *Pont.* 4.542.

*5 Gell. *NA* 10.25.4

item

381   rumpia

genus tali est Thraecae nationis, positumque hoc vocabulum in Quinti Enni Annalium XIV.

*6 Prisc., *GL* II, p. 501.10–16

deponentia in -rior desinentia, "orior" et "morior" tam secundum tertiam quam secundum quartam coniugationem declinaverunt auctores. . . . Lucanus in IIII: "non gratis moritur . . ." [275: *sic Prisc.*, "vincitur haud gratis" *Luc. codd.*]. Ennius in XIIII Annalium:

382   nunc est ille dies quom gloria maxima sese
           nobis ostentat, si vivimus sive morimur

*7 Macrob. *Sat.* 6.4.6 (Verg. *Aen.* 11.601–2 "tum [late] ferreus hastis / horret ager")

"horret" mire se habet; sed et Ennius in quarto decimo:

384   horrescit telis exercitus asper utrimque

et in *Erectheo* [*Trag.* F 51] . . . et in *Scipione* [F 6] . . .

*8 Prisc., *GL* II, p. 518.13–16

vetustissimi tamen tam producebant quam corripiebant supradicti verbi ["tutudi"] paenultimam. Ennius in XIIII:

385   infit: "O cives, quae me fortuna fero sic
           contŭdit indigno bello confecit acerbo

           385 fero sic *codd.*: foro sic *Skutsch*: ferox *Columna*: *alia alii*

306

*5 Gellius, *Attic Nights*

So too

rumpia   381

is a kind of lance of the Thracian nation: this word appears
in Book 14 of Ennius' *Annals.*

*6 Priscian

Authors inflected the deponent verbs ending in -*rior*, *orior*
and *morior*, according to both the third and fourth conju-
gations. . . . Lucan in Book 4: "he dies not for nothing . . ."
[275]. Ennius in Book 14 of the *Annals*:

> now is the day when the greatest glory presents   382
> itself to us, whether we live or die

*7 Macrobius, *Saturnalia* (on Virgil, "then the field, full
of iron, bristles with spears")

"bristles" is a remarkable usage, but so too Ennius in Book
Fourteen:

> on both sides the fierce army bristles with lances   384

and in *Erectheus* [*Trag.* F 51] . . . and in *Scipio* [F 6] . . .

*8 Priscian

The oldest writers nevertheless as often lengthened as
shortened the penultimate syllable of the above-mentioned
word [*tutudi*]. Ennius in Book 14:

> says he: "O Countrymen, what fortune has thus   385
> bruised me and destroyed me with undeserved,
>   fierce, bitter war

*9 Fest., p. 218.21–25 L.

OB praepositione antiquos usos esse pro "ad" testis est Ennius cum ait lib. XIIII:

387   omnes occisi occensique in nocte serena

id est accensi . . .

*9 Festus

That the ancients used the preposition *ob* for *ad* has Ennius as a witness, since he says in Book 14:

all slaughtered and burned in the tranquil night   387

that is, "burned up" . . .

BOOK XV

*Significantly more is conjectured about this book than is
actually known. In 189 BC Ennius accompanied the con-
sul M. Fulvius Nobilior on his campaign in Aetolia (T 10,
20, 29) and eventually wrote in praise of Roman success
there in capturing Ambracia, the Aetolian capital (T 92).
Glorification of Nobilior's achievement certainly took the
form of a praetexta play posterity knew as* Ambracia
*(Flower 1995, 184–86), but these events must also have
figured prominently in what seems originally to have been
conceived as the concluding book of the* Annals. *The bitter
siege implied by t 1 and F 1–2 is congruent with historical
accounts of events at Ambracia (Polyb. 21.27–30; Liv.
38.3.9–11.9), but the widely held view that this book, and
thus the poem, climaxed with Nobilior's triumph and sub-
sequent dedication of a shrine to Hercules Musarum with
spoils from that city is unattested and fraught with dif-
ficulties. The triumph came in 187 BC, but the temple
probably not until Nobilior's censorship in 179 BC, when
reconciliation with his bitter rival M. Aemilius Lepidus
brought a necessary change in the political climate. The*

TESTIMONIA

t 1 Macrob. *Sat.* 6.2.32

item de Pandaro et Bitia aperientibus portas [Verg. *Aen.*

310

BOOK XV

reconciliation is attested for the Annals (t 2), and the temple dedication is surely the action referred to in T 10 (and probably also Inc. Ann. *F 38), but these hints are themselves problematic. Much may turn on whether Cicero's phrase "Martis manubias Musis" (T 10) is Ennian and whether its apparently iambo-trochaic shape indicates an origin in the* Ambracia *(so Timpanaro 1949, 198–200) or it is in fact dactylic (by synizesis) and belongs to the* Annals.[1] *No other direct traces remain, though Ovid's decision to end* Fasti 6 *with the Augustan renovation of this temple by L. Marcius Philippus quite possibly alludes to Ennius' finale (Newlands 1995, 215–18). See the Introduction for the historical background and for the challenge posed by the possibility of what would be a highly compressed narrative to our understanding of the poem's overall design.*

[1] A limited sample size makes the norms of Ennius' metrical practice difficult to discern: synizesis is certain in 1 *Ann.* F 43.89 and 4 *Ann.* F 4. Cicero quotes and alludes to the *Annals* often. The *Ambracia* is otherwise cited only by Nonius Marcellus.

TESTIMONIA

t 1 Macrobius, *Saturnalia*

Similarly, the passage about Pandarus and Bitia opening

311

9.672–818] locus acceptus est ex libro quinto decimo Ennii, qui induxit Histros duos in obsidione erupisse porta et stragem de obsidente hoste fecisse.

t 2 Cic. *Prov. cons.* 20

an vero M. ille Lepidus, qui bis consul et pontifex maximus fuit, non solum memoriae testimonio, sed etiam Annalium litteris et summi poetae voce laudatus est, quod cum M. Fulvio collega, quo die censor est factus, homine inimicissimo, in campo statim rediit in gratiam, ut commune officium censurae communi animo ac voluntate defenderent?

T 10 Cic. *Arch.* 27

iam vero ille qui cum Aetolis Ennio comite bellavit Fulvius non dubitavit Martis manubias Musis consecrare.

the gates [Verg. *Aen.* 9.672–818] was taken over from Book Fifteen of Ennius, who introduced two Istrians breaking out of the gate under siege and wreaking havoc among the besieging enemy.

t 2 Cicero, *De Provinciis Consularibus*

Was not the famous Marcus Lepidus, who was twice consul and pontifex maximus, praised not only by the record of memory but also in literary annals and by the voice of the greatest poet because, on the day he was elected censor, in the Campus Martius he immediately reconciled with his colleague Marcus Fulvius, his most bitter foe, so they would exercise the mutual responsibility of the censorship with mutual good spirit and goodwill?[1]

[1] The reconciliation is recounted in detail by Liv. 40.45.6–46, and cited as a moral exemplum by Val. Max. 4.2.1 and Gell. *NA* 12.8.5–6. For its position in this book of the *Annals* rather than (with Skutsch) in Book 16, see the Introduction.

T 10 Cicero, *Pro Archia*

And furthermore, he who fought against the Aetolians with Ennius as his companion, that famous Fulvius, did not hesitate to dedicate the spoils[1] of Mars to the Muses.

[1] Such spoils (*manubiae*) were the booty from a campaign that remained within the victorious commander's control, in this case including the statuary group from Ambracia that Fulvius eventually set in the Temple of Hercules of the Muses. See the Introduction.

FRAGMENTS

*1 Non., p. 114.5–8 M. = 163 L.

FALAE turres sunt ligneae. Ennius lib. XV:

388   malos defindunt, fiunt tabulata falaeque

haec [tabulata] sunt et in circo quae aput veteres propter
spectatores e lignis erigebantur.

diffindunt *Merula*: defigunt *Vahlen*

*2 Prisc., *GL* II, p. 281.2–9

vetustissimi tamen etiam praecipis genetivum qui a nomi-
nativo praeceps est secundum analogiam nominativi pro-
tulerunt . . . Ennius in XV Annali:

389   occumbunt multi letum ferroque lapique
       aut intra muros aut extra praecipe casu

Cf. Prisc., *GL* II, p. 250.9–11.

*3 Macrob. *Sat.* 6.3.2–4

Homerus de Aiacis forti pugna ait [*Il.* 16.102–11] . . . hunc
locum Ennius in quinto decimo [XII *codd. meliores*] ad
pugnam C. Aelii [*Merula*: Caelii *codd.*] tribuni his versibus
transfert:

391   undique conveniunt velut imber tela tribuno:
       configunt parmam, tinnit hastilibus umbo,

       392 *post* umbo *lacunam suspiciunt nonnulli*

---

[1] Association of this passage with the siege of Ambracia is
based largely on presumptions about Macrobius' thought se-
quence and the consequent emendation of his text. See Wigodsky

ANNALS: BOOK XV

FRAGMENTS

*1 Nonius

falae are wooden towers. Ennius, Book 15:

> they trimmed the uprights, platforms and towers are   388
> made

These are also in the circus [i.e., the platforms], which among the ancients were erected of wood for spectators.

*2 Priscian

The oldest writers nevertheless also displayed a genitive *praecipis*, which from the noun *praeceps* followed on analogy from the nominative. . . . Ennius in *Annals* 15:

> many meet death by sword and by stone   389
> in headlong fall within the walls or without

*3 Macrobius, *Saturnalia*

About Ajax' heroic fighting Homer says [*Il.* 16.102–11] . . . In Book fifteen Ennius applies this passage to the fighting of the tribune Gaius Aelius, with these lines:[1]

> From all sides the missiles converge like a rainstorm   391
> on the tribune:
> they pierce his small shield, the boss rings from the
> shafts,

1972, 61–62; Paladini and Salvatore in Flores 2006, 4:393–94. A tribune named Gaius Aelius figures, together with his brother Titus, in Livy's story not of Ambracia but of the Istrian War of 178/7 BC (Liv. 41.1.7, 3.6–8, 4.3), leading Warmington to set the fragment in Book 16.

aerato sonitu galeae, sed nec pote quisquam
undique nitendo corpus discerpere ferro.
395   semper abundantes hastas frangitque quatitque.
totum sudor habet corpus, multumque laborat,
nec respirandi fit copia: praepete ferro
Histri tela manu iacientes sollicitabant.

hinc Vergilius eundem locum de incluso Turno gratia ele-
gantiore composuit . . . [*Aen.* 9.806–14].

*4 Prisc., *GL* II, pp. 258.20–59.10

alia omnia eiusdem generis [i.e. masculini] Latina . . . se-
cundae sunt declinationis . . . excipitur arcus, quod dif-
ferentiae causa quidam tam secundae quam quartae pro-
tulerunt. de caelesti enim [i.e. de Iride] Cicero dicens . . .
"cur autem arci species . . ." invenitur tamen apud veteres
etiam feminini generis, secundum quod bene quartae est
declinationis. Ennius in XV Annali:

399   arcus ubi aspicitur, mortalibus quae perhibetur
    ⟨Iris⟩

    399 aspicitur *Columna*: aspiciunt *codd.*: {ubi} subspiciunt
Vahlen   perhibetur *vel* perhibentur *codd.*
    400 Iris *suppl. Skutsch*

with the helmet's bronze echoing, but neither can
    anyone
though pressing from all sides tear his body with a
    blade.
All the while he breaks and brandishes the showering   395
    shafts.
Sweat possesses his entire body, and he strains
    greatly,
nor is there a chance to catch a breath. With winged
    steel
the Istrians[2] harry him as they hurl their spears.

Virgil drew on this when he wrote with charm and greater
finesse a similar passage about Turnus surrounded . . .
[*Aen.* 9.806–14].

[2] According to Florus 1.26, Istrians fought on the Aetolian
side in 189 BC.

*4 Priscian

All other Latin words of the same [masculine] gender . . .
are of the second declension . . . *arcus* [bow] is the excep-
tion, because for variety some use it in the second as well
as the fourth declension. Concerning a divinity [Iris] Cic-
ero says . . . "why a kind of rainbow. . . ." Among the an-
cients even a feminine is found, which follows the pattern
of the fourth declension. Ennius in *Annals* 15:

where a rainbow is observed, which among mortals is   399
    called
⟨Iris⟩[1]

[1] Skutsch compares *Aen.* 9.803–5, where Iris is sent to order
Turnus' retreat from the Trojan camp.

BOOK XVI

What Pliny (t 1) knew about this book almost certainly derived from Ennius' own writing; F 1 to 5 are thus plausibly imagined as part of a proem in which the aged poet announced the resumption of his labors. The Caecilii said to have inspired him, however, are unknown, and confusion somewhere along the line of transmission with the exploits of the brothers Titus and Gaius Aelius recorded by Livy (41.1.7, 3.6–8, 4.3) and/or the Aelius (codd. Caelius) of 15 Ann. F 3 is quite possible. F 10 and F 15 may derive from a single combat described in Homeric terms, but the larger military context for it is unknown. Restoration of the Istrian names Bradylis (F 6) and (A)Epulo (F 7) suggests an account of the Roman campaigns in Istria of

TESTIMONIUM

t 1 Plin. *HN* 7.101

Q. Ennius T. Caecilium Teucrum fratremque eius praecipue miratus propter eos sextum decimum adiecit Annalem.

BOOK XVI

178–177 BC, and the capture of Nesactium may be the context of F 8 (cf. Liv. 41.11.4–5), but the military references in this book are largely generic and thus impossible to place. The descriptive flourishes in F 13, 14, 17, and 18 and the touch of tragic history in F 8 and 16 suggest a poet working with what has become a well-established epic idiom.

For the proem to Book 16 and its wider ramifications, see Suerbaum 1968, 113–67. The reconstruction by Badian 1972, 185–87, and Martina 1979 of the politics that motivated Ennius' addition of this book, invoked passim by Skutsch, should be treated with caution.

TESTIMONIUM

t 1 Pliny the Elder, *Natural History*

Ennius especially admired Titus Caecilius Teucer and his brother and because of them added the sixteenth book of his *Annals*.

FRAGMENTS

*1 Non., p. 219.14–15 M. = 324 L.

PIGRET. Ennius lib. XVI:

401   post aetate pigret sufferre laborem

*2 Charis., *GL* I, p. 132.4–6 = p. 168.15–17 B.

hebem Caecilius in Ὑποβολιμαίῳ "subito res reddent hebem" [*Com.* 81 R.$^{2-3}$]. Ennius XVI, ubi Fl. Caper: "non ut adiunctivo sed appellativo est locutus":

402   hebem

*3 Fest., p. 306.21–25 L.

QUIPPE significare quidni testimonio et Ennius lib. XI [F 1] . . . , idem XVI:

403   quippe vetusta virum non est satis bella moveri

*4 Macrob. *Sat.* 6.1.17 (Verg. *Aen.* 12.552 "summa nituntur opum vi")

Ennius in quarto [F 2] . . . et in sexto decimo:

FRAGMENTS

*1 Nonius

pigret [to be reluctant]. Ennius in Book 16:

> he [?] is reluctant to take up the task in advanced age   401

*2 Charisius

Caecilius used *hebem* [weak] in *Hypobolimaeus* [*The Sub-stitute Son*],[1] "The facts will quickly render him weak" [*Com.* 81 R.[2–3]]. Ennius, Book 16, where Flavius Caper[2] comments "he used it not as an adjective but as a noun":

> weak   402

[1] Caecilius Statius' play became a classic of the comic reper-toire (Varro, *Rust.* 2.11.11; Cic. *Rosc. Am.* 46) and was then fre-quently cited by later grammarians.   [2] A grammarian of the second century AD. He is known to have written on standards of Latinity and on Latin morphology, but none of his works survives.

*3 Festus

That *quippe* [surely] means *quidni* [lit., "why not?"] is at-tested by Ennius, Book 11 [F 1] . . . and 16:

> surely it is not enough that the ancient wars of men   403
> be told

*4 Macrobius, *Saturnalia* (on Virgil, "they strive with all their might and main")

Ennius in the fourth book [F 2] . . . and in the sixteenth:

404   reges per regnum statuasque sepulcraque quaerunt,
         aedificant nomen, summa nituntur opum vi

*5 Gell. *NA* 9.14.5

Q. Ennius in XVI Annali "dies" scripsit pro "diei" in hoc versu:

406   postremo longinqua dies confecerit aetas

       confecerit *codd. complures*: quod fecerit *codd. nonnulli*

*6 Fest., p. 348.15–18 L.

REGIMEN pro regimento usurpant poetae. Ennius lib. XVI:

407   primus senex Bradylis regimen, bellique peritus

       Bradylis *Bergk*: bradyn in *codd.*

*7 Fest., p. 446.2–5 L.

SPICIT quoque sine praepositione dixerunt antiqui . . . et spexit. Ennius lib. XVI:

408   quos ubi rex Epulo spexit de cotibus celsis

       Epulo *Schegkius, Bergk*: pulo *Festus*: <q>uos epulo postquam *Varro*

Cf. Varro, *Ling.* 6.82.

322

kings throughout their reign seek statues and   404
    memorials,
they build a name, they strive with all their might and
    main

*5 Gellius, *Attic Nights*

Ennius in Book 16 of the *Annals* wrote *dies* [day] for *diei*
[genitive] in this verse:

in the end, the long age of day will destroy   406

*6 Festus

Poets use *regimen* [rule] for *regimentum*. Ennius, Book
16:

first to rule [was] Bradylis,[1] an old man and   407
    experienced in war

[1] If the emendation is correct, this would be the Bradylis who
founded the Istrian dynasty (Polyb. 39.2.4). Festus' *bradyn* [sic]
in regimen ["slow to rule"?] balances *bellique peritus*, but with
awkward syntax and an unparalleled Graecism.

*7 Festus

Ancient writers also use *spicit* [spies] without a preposi-
tion . . . and *spexit* [spied]. Ennius, Book 16:

when the king Epulo[1] spied them from the high crags   408

[1] An Istrian chieftain who fought against the Romans in 178–
177 BC (Liv. 41.11.1).

*8 Fest., p. 514.2–3 L.

VAGOREM pro vagitu: Ennius lib. XVI:

409   qui clamos oppugnantis vagore volanti

*9 Prisc., *GL* II, p. 518.13–18

vetustissimi tamen tam producebant quam corripiebant supradicti verbi ["tutudi"] paenultimam. Ennius in XIIII [F 8] . . . ecce hic corripuit. idem in XVI:

410   ingenio forti dextra latus pertudit hasta

*10 Macrob. *Sat.* 6.1.24 (Verg. *Aen.* 10.488 "corruit in vulnus. sonitum super arma dederunt")

Ennius in sexto decimo:

411   concidit et sonitum simul insuper arma dederunt

*8 Festus

vagor for *vagitus* [wailing]: Ennius, Book 16:

> which clamor with winged wailing the besiegers[1]　　409

[1] "Clamor" was the subject and "the besiegers" the direct object of the missing verb.

*9 Priscian

The oldest writers nevertheless as often lengthened as shortened the penultimate syllable of the above-mentioned word [*tutudi*]. Ennius in Book 14 . . . [F 8]. See, here he has shortened it. So too in Book 16:

> the spear [sent?] with firm will by the right hand　　410
> 　　pierced his side[1]

[1] Syntax and sense are uncertain. (The text may well be corrupt.) The translation follows Flores. Priscian seems to be mistaken in claiming a perf. form *tūdit*; Inc. *Ann.* F 66 should probably read *contu‹n›dit*.

*10 Macrobius, *Saturnalia* (on Virgil, "he fell forward on his wound; his armor clattered atop him")[1]

Ennius in Book Sixteen:

> he tumbled down, and his armor clattered atop him　　411

[1] Servius ad loc. quotes Hom. *Il.* 4.504: δούπησεν δὲ πεσών, ἀράβησε δὲ τεύχε᾽ ἐπ᾽ αὐτῷ "He fell forward with a thud, and his armor clattered about him."

*11 Fest., p. 168.3–7 L.

NAVUS: celer et strenuus, a navium velocitate videtur dictus. Ennius lib. VI [F 2] . . . et lib. XVI:

412   navorum imperium servare est induperantum

*12 Fest., p. 254.30–33 L.

PRODIT: memoriae porro dat, et fallit; item ex interiore loco procedit; item perdit, ut Ennius lib. XVI:

413   non in sperando cupide rem prodere summam

*13 Fest., p. 310.28–33 L.

⟨QUANDO cum gravi voce pro⟩nuntiatur significat ⟨quoniam, acuta est temporis adverbium⟩ ut Plautus [*Men.* 78; *Pseud.* 257] . . . et Ennius lib. XVI:

414   nox quando mediis signis praecincta volabit

*11 Festus

navus: "swift" and "vigorous," seems to derive from the speed of ships. Ennius, Book 6 [F 2] . . . and Book 16:

> vigorous commanders must maintain command   412

*12 Festus

prodit [advances]: "consigns to memory," and "is mistaken"; likewise "brings out from an inner place"; likewise "ruins," as Ennius, Book 16:

> not to endanger[1] great affairs of state by eagerly   413
> hoping

[1] Festus' gloss appears to confuse *prodere* with *perdere*, i.e., not "to ruin" but "to expose to ruin." Skutsch cites Liv. 22.44.7 (of the legions at Cannae), *proiectis ac proditis ad inconsultam atque improvidam pugnam* "thrust out and exposed to an ill-advised and imprudent battle."

*13 Festus

‹*quando* when pro›nounced ‹with a grave accent› means ‹"since"; with an acute accent it is an adverb of time›, as Plautus [*Men.* 78; *Pseud.* 257] . . . and Ennius, Book 16:

> when Night will fly girded with constellations around   414
> her middle[1]

[1] That is, at midnight. Night drives a chariot across the sky, cf. *Andromeda*, *Trag.* F 34.

***14** Macrob. *Sat.* 6.4.19

et quod dixit "nec lucidus aethra / siderea polus" [Verg. *Aen* 3.585–86] Ennius prior dixerat in sexto decimo:

415   interea fax
     occidit Oceanumque rubra tractim obruit aethra

***15** Macrob. *Sat.* 6.1.50 (Verg. *Aen.* 3.175 "tum gelidus toto manabat corpore sudor")

Ennius in sexto decimo:

417   tunc timido manat ex omni corpore sudor

***16** Serv. Dan. ad Verg. *G.* 1.18

favens pro volens . . . favere enim veteres etiam velle dixerunt. Ennius:

418   matronae moeros complent spectare faventes

Cf. Serv. Dan. ad Verg. *G.* 4.230: apud eundem Ennium in XVI [F 23].

***17** Fest., p. 210.11–14 L.

OBSTIPUM: obliquum. Ennius lib. XVI:

419   montibus obstipis obstantibus, unde oritur nox

*14 Macrobius, *Saturnalia*

And his expression "nor the vault of heaven alight with starry brilliance" [Verg. *Aen.* 3.585–86], Ennius previously said in his sixteenth [book]:

> meanwhile the torch[1]   415
> sets and a reddening brilliance slowly covers the
>   Ocean

[1] That is, the sun. Cf. *Medea (exul)*, *Trag.* F 98.

*15 Macrobius, *Saturnalia* (on Virgil, "then a clammy sweat trickled over his entire body")

Ennius in his sixteenth [book]:

> then in his fear sweat trickles from all his body   417

*16 Servius Danielis, *Commentary on Virgil*

favens [favoring] for *volens* [wishing] . . . for the ancients too used *favere* for *velle*. Ennius:

> the matrons crowd the walls, wishing to observe   418

*17 Festus

obstipum [lit., "bent"]: *obliquum* [slanting]. Ennius, Book 16:

> with slanting [i.e., steep] mountains standing in the   419
>   way, from which night rises

*18 Prisc., *GL* II, pp. 152.17–53.10

acer et alacer et saluber et celeber quamvis acris et alacris plerumque faciant et salubris et celebris feminina, in utraque tamen terminatione communis etiam generis inveniuntur prolata . . . Ennius in XVI:

420   aestatem autumnus sequitur, post acer hiems it

idem in XII [F 2] . . .

> it *vel* sit *codd. Servii:* fit *Fabricius*

Cf. Serv. ad Verg. *Aen.* 6.685; *Explan. in Donat., GL* IV, p. 491.26–27.

*19 Fest., p. 446.12–15 L.

SPERES antiqui pluraliter dicebant, ut Ennius lib. II . . . [F 17] et lib. XVI:

421   spero si speres quicquam prodesse potis sunt

*20 Fest., p. 432.20–34 L.

SAS Verrius putat significare eas teste Ennio qui dicat in lib. I [F 49] . . . sicuti lib. VIII fatendum est eam significari cum ait [F 2] . . . idem cum ait sapsam, pro ipsa nec alia ponit in lib. XVI:

422   quo res sapsa loco sese ostentatque iubetque

*18 Priscian

Although *acer* and *alacer* and *saluber* and *celeber* for the most part form as a feminine *acris* and *alacris* and *salubris* and *celebris*, nevertheless in both terminations they are found inflected the same way . . . Ennius in 16:

> autumn follows on summer, after it comes keen   420
>   winter

the same in 12 [F 2] . . .

*19 Festus

The ancients used to say *speres* [hopes] in the plural, as Ennius, Book 2 [F 17] . . . and Book 16:

> I hope, if hopes can do some kind of good at all   421

*20 Festus

Verrius thinks *sas* means *eas* [them], citing Ennius, who says in Book 1 [F 49] . . . just as in Book 8 it must be admitted that *eam* [her] is meant when he says [F 2] . . . Likewise, when he says *sapsam*, he uses it instead of *ipsa nec alia* [that and nothing else] in Book 16:

> in which place the very situation reveals itself and   422
>   commands

*21 Prisc., *GL* II, p. 278.10–15

apud illos [Graecos] enim si in *x* desinentia nomina habent
verba cum *g*, nominum quoque genitivus per *g* declinatur
. . . unde *frux* etiam *frugis* facit genitivum, quia ἀπὸ τοῦ
φρύγω Graeco verbo nascitur. Ennius in XVI[1] Annali:

423   si luci si nox si mox si iam data sit frux

     [1] XVII *codd. duo, fortasse recte*

*22 Diom., *GL* I, p. 382.21–26

hortatur quod vulgo dicimus veteres nonnulli horitur dixe-
runt, ut Ennius sexto decimo Annalium,

424   prandere iubet horiturque

idem in decimo [F 13] . . .

*23 Serv. ad Verg. *G.* 4.230

"ore fave": cum religione ac silentio accede. in XVI En-
nius:

425   hic insidiantes vigilant, partim requiescunt
       succincti gladiis, sub scutis, ore faventes

ponitur eadem vox et pro velle apud eundem Ennium in
XVI . . . [F 16].

    425 hic insidiantes *codd.*: insidiantes hi, *Skutsch*
    426 succincti *Bergk*: tecti *codd.*: tecti cum *Baehrens*: contecti
Merula

Cf. Serv. Dan. ad Verg. *G.* 1.18.

*21 Priscian

Among them [the Greeks], if nouns ending in *x* have verbs with *g*, the genitive of the nouns is declined with *g* . . . from which *frux* [fruit] too makes its genitive *frugis*, since it derives from the Greek verb φρύγω [to parch]. Ennius in Book 16 [17?] of the *Annals*:

> if by daylight, if at night, if soon, if now there were an advantage   423

*22 Diomedes

For *hortatur* [urges], which we commonly say, some ancients said *horitur*, as Ennius in Book sixteen of the *Annals*:

> he urges and encourages [them?] to eat   424

so too in ten [F 13] . . .

*23 Servius, *Commentary on Virgil*

ore fave: approach with reverent silence. Ennius in Book 16:

> here in ambush they keep watch: some at rest, equipped with swords, keeping silent behind their shields   425

the same expression is also used for *velle* [to wish] by the same Ennius in Book 16 . . . [F 16].

*24 Fest., p. 444.2–7 L.

‹SCITAE alias quae sunt› bona facie, a‹li›as bonis ‹artibus mulieres a› poetis usurpantur. Te‹rentius in Phormion›e [110]: "satis inquit scite"; et ‹in Heautontimo›rumeno [764]: "at si scias quam scite ‹in mentem vene›rit." Ennius in lib. ‹X›VI:

| 427 | lumen | scitus agaso |

lumen *codd.*: iumen‹ta *nonnulli*

*24 Festus

scitae is sometimes applied by poets to women of good
looks, sometimes to women of good accomplishments.
Terence in *Phormio* [110], "she looks, he says, good
enough," and in *The Self-Tormentor* [764], "But if you
knew how cleverly it came to mind." Ennius in Book < 1 >6:

  light   the skillful groom   427

BOOK XVII

Though it is entirely possible that Books 16 to 18 were conceived as a triad, what is known of Book 16 provides no clue to the content of the remaining books. The Homeric simile of F 5 (cf. Il. 9.4–8, 16.765–11), presumably

*1 Macrob. *Sat.* 6.1.21 (Verg. *Aen.* 11.745 "tollitur in caelum clamor, cunctique Latini")

Ennius in septimo decimo:

428   tollitur in caelum clamor exortus utrimque

*2 Non., pp. 222.25–23.1 M. = 329 L.

SPECUS genere masculino . . . feminino Ennius Annalium lib. XVII:

429   tum cava sub monte late specus intus patebat

     tum cava *Priscian*: tum causa *Festus*: concava *Nonius*   late
Priscian: latet *Nonius*: alte *Festus*

Cf. Prisc., *GL* II, p. 260.1–3; Fest., p. 462.16–20 L.; Serv. ad Verg. *Aen.* 7.568.

BOOK XVII

*introducing a battle narrative, is of a piece with Ennius'
technique elsewhere; other lines, descriptive or morali-
zing, are generic.*

*1 Macrobius, *Saturnalia* (on Virgil, "a cry is raised to
heaven, and all the Latins")

Ennius in his seventeenth [book]:

> a cry begun on both sides is raised to heaven   428

*2 Nonius

specus [cavern] is of masculine gender . . . feminine, En-
nius, *Annals*, Book 17:

> then a hollow cavern opened wide inward under the   429
> mountain

*3 Prisc., *GL* II, pp. 198.6–99.6

primae declinationis feminorum genetivum etiam in *-as* more Graeco solebant antiquissimi terminare . . . Ennius in XVII Annali,

430   dux ipse vias

pro "viae."

*4 Macrob. *Sat.* 6.1.22 (Verg. *Aen.* 8.596 "quadrupedante putrem sonitu quatit ungula campum")

Ennius in sexto [F 25] . . . , idem in octavo [F 7] . . . , idem in septimo decimo:

431   it eques et plausu cava concutit ungula terram

*5 Macrob. *Sat.* 6.2.28 (Verg. *Aen.* 2.416–18 "diversi magno [adversi rupto *Verg.*] ceu quondam turbine venti / confligunt Zephyrusque Notusque et laetus Eois / Eurus equis")

Ennius in septimo decimo,

432   concurrunt veluti venti, quom spiritus Austri
          imbricitor Aquiloque suo cum flamine contra
          indu mari magno fluctus extollere certant

*3 Priscian

Very ancient writers were also accustomed to terminate the genitive of first declension feminine nouns in *-as*, in the manner of Greek . . . Ennius in *Annals* 17:

the leader himself of the route[1]   430

for [classical] *viae*.

[1] Priscian may be mistaken. Skutsch observes that ancient grammarians mistook accusative *custodias* at Sall. *Hist.* 3 F 79 (Ramsey) for an archaic genitive.

*4 Macrobius, *Saturnalia* (on Virgil, "the hoof shakes the crumbling ground with its four-footed beat")

Ennius in Book Six [F 25] . . . , so too in Book Eight [F 7] . . . , so too in Book Seventeen:

the cavalry passes, and the hollow hoof shakes the   431
    ground with its beat

*5 Macrobius, *Saturnalia* (on Virgil, "just as in a great cyclone winds from different quarters clash, the West Wind, the South Wind, and the East Wind that delights in the horses of Dawn")

Ennius in Book Seventeen:

they clash like the winds, when the South Wind's   432
    gust,
bringing rain, and the North Wind with its own
    counterblast
compete to raise swells on the mighty main

***6** Serv. Dan. ad Verg. *G.* 4.188

mussant hic murmurant, quae vox ponitur et in tacendi
significatione, ut apud Ennium in XVII:

435   noenu' decet mussare bonos qui facta labore
       enixi † militiam peperere

> 435 noenu' decet *Ribbeck*: non decet *Festus*: non possunt
> *Servius*   bonos *Festus*: boni *Servius*

Cf. Fest., p. 131.9–11; Serv. Dan. ad Verg. *Aen.* 12.657.

***7–8** Non., p. 134.18–23 M. = 195 L.

LONGISCERE: longum fieri vel frangi [*sic Lindsay*: fran-
gere *codd.*]. Ennius lib. XVII:

437   neque corpora firma
    longiscunt quicquam

idem:

439   quom soles eadem facient longiscere longe

> cum soles eadem *Vahlen*: cum sola est eadem *codd.*: *alia alii*

*6 Servius Danielis, *Commentary on Virgil*

mussant [they mumble] here means *murmurant* [they murmur], which is a term also used in the sense of being silent, as in Ennius, in Book 17:

it is not meet that good men acquiesce in silence,   435
    who with effort
strove in battle [?] to bring forth great deeds

*7–8[1] Nonius

longiscere: "to grow long" or "to be shattered." Ennius, Book 17:

nor do firm bodies   437
    grow long at all

the same poet:

when sunny days will make these same grow long at   439
    length

[1] These two lines do not necessarily derive from the same passage, though some editors have sought to connect them. Nonius' logic is unclear: *frangi* [to be shattered] in his text may be the wrong verb.

BOOK XVIII

The content of this book is unknown, though Ennius' death in 169 BC (T 19, 98, 99) provides a terminus ante quem *for the historical narrative. Some kind of valedictory epilogue to the work is sometimes imagined—thus Flores, for*

*1 Gell. *NA* 13.21.14

contra vero idem Ennius in Annali duodevicesimo

440   aere fulva

dixit, non fulvo, non ob id solum quod Homerus ἠέρα βαθεῖαν dicit, sed quod hic sonus, opinor, vocalior est visus et amoenior.

Cf. Gell. *NA* 2.26.11.

*2 Non., p. 63.4–10 M. = 87 L.

GRUMAE sunt loca media, in quae directae quattuor congregantur et conveniunt viae. est autem gruma mensura quaedam, qua fixa viae ad lineam deriguntur, ut est agri-

BOOK XVIII

example, reassigns 4 Ann. F 5 *to this book—but such efforts have not won wide acceptance. See Suerbaum 1968, 143–46; Esposito in Flores 2006, 4:449–51.*

*1 Gellius, *Attic Nights*

But on the other hand [cf. Inc. *Ann.* F 58], this same Ennius in the eighteenth book of the *Annals* said,

with tawny mist 440

[*fulva*, feminine], not *fulvo* [masculine], not only because Homer says "deep mist" [feminine], but because this sound, I think, seemed more sonorous and agreeable.[1]

[1] Though Skutsch ad loc. calls this explanation "somewhat fanciful" and later "sheer fancy" (p. 665, on Inc. *Ann.* F 58), that a native speaker of Latin like Gellius should so interpret the difference in grammatical gender is itself of interest.

*2 Nonius

grumae are the middle points, along which the four roads laid out converge and meet. The *gruma* is also a kind of measuring tool, by which, when in position, roads are laid out in straight lines, such as used by land surveyors and

343

mensorum et talium.—Ennius lib. XVIII gruma derigere dixit:

441 degrumare forum

Lucilius lib. III [99–100 M. = 96–97 W.]: "viamque / degrumabis uti castris mensor facit olim."

degrumare forum *Vahlen*: degrumari ferrum *Non*.

the like.—Ennius, Book 18, said of marking out with the *gruma*:

to mark out a forum[1] 441

Lucilius, Book 3 [99–100 M. = 96–97 W.]: "and you will lay out the route as a surveyor sometimes does for a camp."

[1] The terms are equally appropriate to the laying out of a town or a military camp.

ANNALIUM SEDIS INCERTAE
FRAGMENTA

Modern editors assign some 181 additional lines or partial lines to the Annals (442–623 Sk.), most often on the authority of the sources that preserve them, but occasionally by implication or inference from their apparent content or metrical shape. Lines ascribed to Ennius by an ancient source are indicated below by an asterisk (*), and those explicitly ascribed to the Annals by two asterisks (**). Problematic attributions are identified in the notes.

*1 Serv. ad Verg. *Aen.* 2.274–75

442   ei mihi, qualis erat, quantum mutatus ab illo
        Hectore . . .

Ennii versus.

*2 Non., p. 64.29 M. = 90 L.

PROPAGES est series et adfixio continua vel longe ducta. pages enim conpactio, unde conpages. et propagare genus iuge longe mittere. Pacuvius Antiope [*Trag.* 20 R.$^{2–3}$] . . . , Ennius:

UNPLACED FRAGMENTS OF
THE *ANNALS*

Though firm assignment of any of these fragments to specific books is impossible, Skutsch made the following tentative suggestions: Book 1: F 1–8; Book 2: F 9–11; Book 4: F 12; Book 5: F 13; Book 6: F 14–15; Book 7: F 16–27; Book 8: F 28–33; Book 9: F 34; Book 10: F 35; Book 13: F 36; Book 14: F 37–38; Book 15: F 39; Book 16: F 40.

*1 Servius, *Commentary on Virgil*

Ah me, how he was, how much changed from that Hector . . .   442

A verse of Ennius.[1]

---

[1] Some, but probably not all of Verg. *Aen.* 2.274 is Ennian; an echo of tragedy rather than epic is possible.

*2 Nonius

propages is a series and joining continuous or at length, for *pages* is a thing fitted together, from which comes *conpages* [a structure]. And *propagare* [to propagate] is to bring forth a consistent species for a long time. Pacuvius in *Antiope* [*Trag.* 20 R.[2–3]] . . . , Ennius:

443   nobis unde forent fructus vitaeque propagmen

Cf. Non., p. 221.8 M. = 326 L.

3 Prisc., *GL* III, p. 205.17–25

tertia vero possessiva etsi naturam habeat ut per vocati-
vum dici possit . . . possumus enim etiam ad alienam pos-
sessionem dirigere sermonem, ut

444   O genitor noster, Saturnie, maxime divom

usus tamen deficit.

*4 Prisc., *GL* III, p. 192.14–17

per species ut Ennius:

445   optima caelicolum, Saturnia, magna dearum

magna dixit pro maxima, positivum pro superlativo, cum
aptissime superius "optima caelicolum" dixisset.

whence there may be benefits for us and prolongation   443
    of life

3 Priscian

[discussing ways to express possession] In fact, a third possessive, though it has a nature that can be used as a vocative . . . we are able to employ even for expressing possession of another, as

O our begetter, Saturn's son, greatest of the gods   444

The usage is nevertheless passé.[1]

[1] So too in Livius Andronicus, nouns in *-ius* have a vocative in *-ie* instead of *-ī*, e.g., *filie* (*Od.* F 2 M.), *Laertie* (*Od.* F 38 M.), probably intended as a Graecism. Ennius' line reproduces Hom. *Il.* 8.31 [Athena speaking]: ὦ πάτηρ ὑμέτερε, Κρονίδη, ὕπατε κρειόντων "our father, son of Kronos, greatest of the mighty ones." The assumption that fragments relating to the gods must derive from one of the early, "mythological" books of the poem is challenged by Elliott 2013, 45–51.

*4 Priscian

[on the five ways authors use variation] through likeness, as Ennius:

best of the heaven dwellers, Saturn's daughter, great   445
    among goddesses

He said "great" for "greatest," the positive for the superlative, since just before he had quite appropriately said "best of the heaven dwellers."[1]

[1] The punctuation reflects Priscian's interpretation, but the line could be understood as "best of the heaven-dwelling goddesses, great daughter of Saturn."

*5 Serv. Dan. ad Verg. *Aen.* 1.254

"subridens": laetum ostendit Iovem et talem qualis esse solet cum facit serenum. poetarum enim est elementorum habitum dare numinibus, ut supra de Neptuno dictum est. [*add. Serv. Dan.*] Ennius:

446 Iuppiter hic risit tempestatesque serenae
   riserunt omnes risu Iovis omnipotentis

*6 Iul. Roman. ap. Charis., *GL* I, p. 128.30–32 = p. 163 B.

itaque Plinius Secundus recte arborem ita [ficu] dici ait, pomum vero per o litteram dici. fici Ennius:

448 fici dulciferae lactantes ubere toto

7 Non., p. 418.3–12 M. = 674 L.

URGUERE est premere, cogere. Vergilius *G.* lib. III [523] . . . et [222] . . . ; Lucilius lib. XXIX [820 M. = 961 W.] . . . ; Varro antiquitate rerum humanarum,

449 qua murum fieri voluit urguemur in unum

*5 Servius Danielis, *Commentary on Virgil*

subridens [smiling]: he presents Jupiter as pleased and the way he is accustomed to be when he creates calm weather, for the poets' custom is to give divine powers the appearance of the elements, as was said above of Neptune. Ennius:

> Jupiter here laughed and all the weathers at ease 446
> laughed with the laugh of Jupiter the all-powerful

*6 Julius Romanus

Thus [the elder] Pliny says the tree is correctly called thus [*ficu*, i.e., fourth declension]; the fruit, though, is denoted by the letter *o* [*fico*, i.e., second declension]. *fici* [i.e., nom. pl.] in Ennius:

> sweet-bearing figs dripping milk from the whole 448
> udder

7 Nonius

urguere is to squeeze, to compel. Virgil, *Georgics*, Book 3 [523] . . . and [222] . . . ; Lucilius, Book 29 [820 M. = 961 W.] . . . ; Varro in *The Antiquity of Human Affairs*:[1]

> where he has wished a wall to be we are squeezed 449
> together

[1] A hexameter quoted by Varro on a Roman theme (Remus complaining of Romulus?) is often identified as Ennian, but Warmington relegates this one to his *Spuria* (25).

*8 Varro, *Ling.* 7.46

apud Ennium:

450   iam cata signa fere sonitum dare voce parabant

cata: acuta. hoc enim verbo dicunt Sabini. quare "catus
Aelius Sextus" [10 *Ann.* F 5] non ut aiunt sapiens sed
acutus; et quod est "tunc coepit memorare simul cata
dicta" [Inc. *Ann.* F 83] accipienda acuta dicta.

*9 Prisc., *GL* II, p. 450.2–8

in nominationibus, id est in ὀνοματοποιία, sive nominum
seu verborum novis conformationibus non omnes declina-
tionis motus sunt quaerendi ut . . . taratantara. Ennius:

451   at tuba terribili sonitu taratantara dixit

Cf. Serv. ad Verg. *Aen.* 9.503 "at tuba terribilem sonitum":
hemistichium Ennii. nam sequentia iste mutavit. ille enim
ad exprimendum tubae sonum ait "taratantara dixit."

*10 Serv. Dan. ad Verg. *Aen.* 3.333

"regnorum reddita cessit pars Heleno": reddita more ve-
teri pro data accipiendum est; re ergo abundat. Ennius
Annalibus "at Ilia reddita nuptum" [1 *Ann.* F 33] et alibi:

*8 Varro, *On the Latin Language*

In Ennius:

> around then the shrill signals were preparing to   450
>   resound

cata: "sharp." The Sabines use this word. That is why "*catus Aelius Sextus*" [10 *Ann.* F 5] means not, as they say, "wise," but "shrewd"; and "then at the same time he began to recall *cata dicta*" [Inc. *Ann.* F 83] should be understood as "shrewd sayings."

*9 Priscian

In *nominationes*, i.e., in onomatopoeia, whether of nouns or verbs, with unusual forms not every inflectional ending should be looked for as . . . *taratantara.* Ennius:

> and the trumpet with terrifying tone sounded   451
>   *taratantara*

Compare Servius on Virgil, "and the trumpet a terrifying tone . . .": a half-line of Ennius, for he [Virgil] changed what follows. He [Ennius], to bring out the trumpet's tone, says "it sounded *taratantara*."

*10 Servius Danielis, *Commentary on Virgil*

"part of his kingdom was bequeathed and went to Helenus": *reddita* [bequeathed] in archaic usage should be understood as "given": the prefix *re-* is therefore superfluous. Ennius in the *Annals*, "but Ilia, given in marriage" [1 *Ann.* F 33], and elsewhere:

452   isque dies post †aut marcus† quam regna recepit

pro accepit; aut reddita quod Heleno debebatur impe-
rium.

(postquam) Ancus Marcius *Ilberg*: aut Ancus (. . . aut obiit
Tullus) *Vahlen*: Antiocus *Mariotti*

*11 Macrob. *Sat.* 6.4.3 (Verg. *G.* 2.462, "mane salutan-
tum totis vomit aedibus undam")

pulchre "vomit undam" et antique. nam Ennius ait:

453   et Tiberis flumen ‹flavom› vomit in mare salsum

flavom *hic addidit Skutsch, post* et *Ilberg*

*12 Plin. *HN* 18.84

pulte autem non pane vixisse longo tempore Romanos
manifestum quoniam et pulmentaria hodieque dicuntur
et Ennius antiquissimus vates obsidionis famem expri-
mens offam eripuisse plorantibus liberis patres comme-
morat.

454   erip ∪ – ∪ patres pueris plorantibus offam

versum sic rest. Bergk: *fortasse* eripiunt- (eriperent-)que *pos-
tul.* Skutsch: offam eripuisse plorantibus liberis patres *Plinius*

and this day when Ancus Marcius [?] received the   452
    kingship

for *accepit*; or "given back" because power was owed to
Helenus.

*11 Macrobius, *Saturnalia* (on Virgil, "spews a wave of
morning callers from the whole palace")

"spews a wave" is lovely and ancient, for Ennius says:

and the Tiber spews its ‹yellow[1]› stream into the   453
    salty sea

[1] This adjective, a common epithet of the Tiber, is the most
obvious supplement to complete the line.

*12 Pliny the Elder, *Natural History*

Moreover, it is clear that the Romans lived for a long time
on porridge [*puls*], not bread since we speak of *pulmen-
taria* [foodstuffs] even today, and Ennius, a very archaic
poet, describing hunger during a siege records that fathers
snatched a morsel away from their crying children.

fathers [snatched?] a morsel from their crying   454
    children[1]

[1] Alternatively, reversing *plorantibus liberis* in Pliny's para-
phrase produces an iambic senarius plus one foot, in which case
the fragment would come from a play, not the *Annals* (so Warm-
ington, *Trag. inc.* 395–96). *liberis*, however, is more likely to be
Pliny's substitution for *pueris*, which by his day had ceased to be
the common generic for children of either sex. Since *offa*, literally,
"a flour dumpling," came to mean any bit of food, the line quoted
does not in fact illustrate Pliny's point very well.

**13 Charis., *GL* I, p. 240.5–8 = p. 313 B.

EUAX. Plautus in *Bacchidibus* [247] . . . Ennius quoque
Annalium libro:

455   aqua est aspersa Latinis

  euax *supra* libro *cod., non credendum*

14 Cic. *Rep.* 3.6

ex qua vita [civili] sic summi viri ornantur ut vel M.'
Curius,

456   quem nemo ferro potuit superare nec auro

**15 Gell. *NA* 7.6.6

cur autem non Q. quoque Ennium reprehendit [Hyginus],
qui in Annalibus non pennas Daedali (ut Vergilius prae-
petes dicit), sed longe diversius,

457   Brundisium [inquit] pulcro praecinctum praepete
              portu

Cf. Gell. *NA* 9.4.1.

*16 Serv. Dan. ad Verg. *Aen.* 8.361

"lautis mugire carinis": carinae sunt aedificia facta in cari-
narum modum . . . [*add. Serv. Dan.*] alii dicunt carinas

**13 Charisius

euax! [hurrah![1]] Plautus in *Bacchides* [247] . . . Ennius, too, in a book of the *Annals*:

> the Latins were refreshed[2]   455

[1] The exclamation of Charisius' lemma appears in Plautus but is difficult to interpret in the Ennian line as quoted.   [2] Lit., "water was splashed upon the Latins." The metaphorical sense is common and also appears in the Plautine line Charisius cites.

14 Cicero, *On the Republic*

From such a [public] life the greatest men win honor, as for example Manius Curius,[1]

> whom none could overcome by sword or by gold   456

[1] Manius Curius Dentatus (cos. 290, 275, 274 BC), victor over Pyrrhus, for which reason the fragment is often assigned to Book 6.

**15 Gellius, *Attic Nights*

Furthermore, why does he [Hyginus] not also fault Ennius, who in the *Annals* calls not the wings of Daedalus *praepes* [favorable], as Virgil does, but something quite different:

> Brundisium [he says] belted by a handsome,   457
>   hospitable harbor

*16 Servius Danielis, *Commentary on Virgil*

"to bellow in the elegant Carinae district": *carinae* are buildings made in the form of ships' keels [*carinae*]: . . .

357

montem nominatum quod ager suburbanus ante portam
carus erat. alii lauta loca legatorum . . . alii quod ibi Sabini
nobiles habitaverint quorum genus invidere et carinare
solebat. carinare autem est obtrectare. Ennius . . . [Inc.
Ann. F 111]; alibi:

458   neque me decet hanc carinantibus edere cartis

res *vel* rem *suppl. Skutsch*

---

*17 Fest. p. 362.9–13 L.

⟨REGALE est di⟩gnum rege. ⟨Romanos in lib. XI Annal.
Graio⟩s appellat Enni⟨us

459   ⟩cos Grai memo
li⟩ngua longos per

---

*18 Fest., p. 386.20–24 L.

SOLUM: terram Ennius l. III [F 2] . . . et aliubi:

461   sed sola terrarum postquam permensa parumper

Cf. Varro, *Ling.* 5.22.

*19 G. Valla (ed. 1486) ad Juv. 7.134 ("spondet enim Ty-
rio stlattaria purpura filo")

stlataria Probus exponit illecebrosa. Ennius:

462   et melior navis quam quae stlataria portat

i.e., multi sonalis quae dicitur vulgo batalaria.

Others say the *carinae* were named for a mountain, which was a desirable area outside the city by the gate, others that it was an elegant district for ambassadors . . . , others that the Sabine nobility lived there, a class accustomed to envy and to revile. *carinare* is to revile. Ennius . . . [Inc. *Ann.* F 111]; elsewhere:

> nor does it suit me to publish this on abusive pages[1]   458

[1] The sentiment recurs at *Satires* F 12, where this line might perhaps be placed. The metonymy of page for work is taken up by Lucilius 1085 M. = 1013 W.

*17 Festus

‹regal means w›orthy of a king. Ennius calls ‹the Romans in *Annals* Book 11 Greek›s

Festus' damaged text makes no clear sense: what Skutsch prints as 459 may conceal a garbled version of 11 *Ann.* F 5. For the history of conjecture, see Skutsch 1985, 616–18; Jackson in Flores 2009, 5:92–97.

*18 Festus

solum: "land." Ennius, Book 3 [F 2] . . . and elsewhere:

> but after she had passed over the surfaces of the   461
> earth for a short while

*19 Valla on Juvenal, *Satires* ("the imported purple with Tyrian thread wins credit")

Probus explains *stlataria* as "alluring." Ennius:

> and a better ship than one carrying foreign fripperies   462

i.e., a multidecked ship [?], which is commonly called a warship [?].

*20 Schol. Bern. ad Verg. *G.* 1.512

"ut cum carceribus sese effudere quadrigae": carceribus
ianuis. Ennius ait:

463   quom a carcere fusi
     currus cum sonitu magno permittere certant

21 Charis., *GL* I, p. 272.22–27 = p. 359 B.

metaphorae quaedam sunt communes quae a Graecis aco-
luthoe appellantur, ut "Tiphyn aurigam celeris fecere cari-
nae," quia quemadmodum in navi auriga dici potest, ita et
in curru gubernator, ut

465   quomque gubernator magna contorsit equos vi

Cf. Diom., *GL* I, p. 457.27–29; Quint. *Inst.* 8.6.9; Sacerd., *GL* VI,
p. 466.27–29.

*22 Fest., p. 498.1–4 L.

TERMONEM Ennius Graeca consuetudine dixit, quem nos
nunc terminum, hoc modo:

466   ingenti vadit cursu qua redditus termo est

et

467   hortatore bono prius quam sam finibus termo

sam *Skutsch*: qui *Vahlen*: iam *Fest.*

---

1 Festus' order of quotation probably reflects the order of
these lines in the *Annals*, but they do not necessarily originate in
the same passage, nor is it clear whether they derive from nar-
rated events or similes.   2 Lit., *hortator*, presumably the one
who sets the cadence for oarsmen (cf. F 59). Lacking verb and

*20 Scholia Bernensisia to Virgil, *Georgics*

"as when chariots pour out from the starting gates": *carceribus* means "from the starting gates." Ennius says:

> when poured from the gate 463
> the chariots with a mighty clamor strive to hurl

21 Charisius

Some metaphors, which are called by the Greeks *acoluthoi*, are interchangeable, as "they made Tiphys driver of the swift ship,"[1] since in the same way a driver can be said to be in a ship, so too a steersman can be in a chariot, as

> and when the steersman turned his horses with a 465
> mighty pull[2]

[1] This line is ascribed to the *Argonautica* of Varro Atacinus [fr. 4 Courtney] on the basis of its correspondence to Ap. Rhod. 1.400–401.   [2] The quotation of this line by Quintilian, whose range of epic citations is limited, strongly suggests its attribution to Ennius.

*22[1] Festus

Ennius said *termo*, following Greek usage, when we now say *terminus* [turning post], in this way:

> with immense speed it goes to where the turning post 466
> is duly set

and

> with a good coxswain[2] before it at the boundaries the 467
> turning post

a clear subject, the syntax of the line is uncertain. Skutsch's *sam* ["it," i.e., a ship] would provide the object of a temporal clause.

**23 Prisc., *GL* II, p. 482.2–5

detondeo, detondi. vetustissimi tamen etiam detotondi
protulerunt. Ennius in Annalibus:

468   et detondit agros laetos atque oppida cepit

> detotondit *codd. plerique*: deque totondit *Merula*

*24 Brev. Expos. ad Verg. *G.* 2.43 (vol. 3.2, p. 285.1–3
Th.-H.)

"non mihi si linguae centum": Homericus sensus Graeci
poetae, sicut et Ennius:

469   non si lingua loqui saperet quibus, ora decem sint
        in me, tum ferro cor sit pectusque revinctum

> 469 quibus *Vahlen*: at *cod.*   470 in me, tum *Müller*: in
> metrum *cod.*

Cf. Schol. Bern. ad loc.

**25 Charis., *GL* I, p. 200.22–23 = p. 260 B.

HISPANE: Ennius Annalium libro:

471   Hispane non Romane memoretis loqui me

Cf. Fest. p. 362.13–14 L.

*26 [Probus] ad Verg. *G.* 2.506 (vol. 3.2, p. 374.11–14
Th.-H.)

Tyriam purpuram vult intellegi Sarranum ostrum. Tyron
enim Sarram appellatum Homerus docet, quem etiam
Ennius sequitur auctorem cum dicit:

472   Poenos Sarra oriundos

Cf. Serv. ad loc.

**23 Priscian

detondeo, *detondi* [I shear, I have sheared]. The oldest writers nevertheless also use *detotondi* [a reduplicated perfect]. Ennius in the *Annals*:

> and he sheared the joyful fields, and he captured   468
> towns

*24 Scholia to Virgil, *Georgics*

"not if I had one hundred tongues . . .": a conceit of the Greek poet Homer, and so too Ennius:[1]

> not if there were ten mouths in me, from which my   469
> tongue
> knew how to speak, and my heart and breast were
> bound in iron

[1] The image, going back to Homer, *Il.* 2.488–90, becomes something of a topos in Latin poetry. See Hinds 1998, 34–39; Gowers 2007.

**25 Charisius

Hispane: Ennius in [a?] Book of the *Annals*

> report[1] that I speak in Spanish fashion, not Roman   471

[1] Whether the verb is an injunction or an ironic invitation ("you may report") is impossible to determine without context.

*26 [Probus], *Commentary on Virgil*

He wants "Sarranian shell dye" to be understood as Tyrian purple, for Homer shows that Tyre was called Sarra, whom Ennius also follows as an authority when he says:

> Carthaginians sprung from Sarra   472

*27 Paul. *Fest.*, p. 51.3 L.

473   consiluere

Ennius pro conticuere posuit.

*28 Glossator ad Oros. *Hist.* 4.14.13 [de Hannibale] ("odio Romani nominis . . . fidelissime, alias infidelissimus . . .")

in bello dicitur in quo erat infidus animo longe leviori quam Pyrrus. de quo Ennius:

474   at non sic dubius fuit hostis
Aeacida Burrus

    475 Eacida Phyrrus *cod.*

*29 Fest., p. 516.8–11 L.

VENEN- - - di⟩cebant antiqui cuius color inficiendo mutabatur, ut Ennius cum ait:

476   quom illud quo iam semel est imbuta veneno

*27 Paul the Deacon, *Epitome of Festus*

they fell silent   473

Ennius put [*consiluere*, lit., "they grew quiet"] for *conti-cuere*.

*28 An annotator of Orosius, *Histories* [on Hannibal] ("entirely faithful to his hatred of the Roman name . . . entirely deceitful in other things . . .")[1]

in the war in which he was deceitful he is said to have been far more fickle of mind than Pyrrhus, about whom Ennius wrote:

> but not so untrustworthy a foe was   474
> Pyrrhus,[2] sprung from Aeacus

[1] One manscript of Orosius, the ninth-century codex Sangallensis, contains two interlinear annotations by the tenth-century monk Ekkehart of St. Gall [5 *Ann.* F 3, 7 *Ann.* F 3] and this one by a somewhat older commentator. For details, see Skutsch 1985, 25–26.   [2] For the spelling, see 6 *Ann.* F 3.

*29 Festus

The ancients spoke of poison [?], the color of which was changed by adulteration, as when Ennius says:

> when that poison, with which it[1] has once been   476
> imbued

[1] The subject is *lana* [wool] if Skutsch, citing Hor. *Carm.* 3.5.27–28, is right to identify the line with the story of Regulus after the battle of Cannae (Liv. 22.60.6–27).

*30 Porph. ad Hor. *Sat.* 1.10.30

"Canusini̇́more bilinguis": ‹bilinguis› dixit quoniam utra-
que lingua usi sunt sicut per omnem illum tractum Italiae,
quoniam ex maiore parte Graeci ibi incoluerunt . . . ideo
ergo et Ennius et Lucilius [1124 M. = 142 W.] dixerunt.

477   Bruttace bilingui

Cf. Paul. *Fest.*, p. 31.25–27 L.

*31 Fest., p. 362.19–24 L.

478   rigido‹que Calore›

Ennius iocatus videtur . . . et alibi [7 *Ann.* F 17].

   suppl. *Heraeus*

*32 Paul. *Fest.*, p. 453.20–21 L.

SICIL[IC]ES: hastarum spicula lata. Ennius:

479   incedit veles volgo sicilibus latis

*33 *Bell. Hisp.* 23.2

hic dum in opere nostri distenti essent complures ex su-
periore loco adversariorum decucurrerunt nec detinenti-

*30 Porphyrio, *Commentary on Horace*

"in the manner of bilingual Canusians": He said bilingual since they used either language, as throughout that entire region of Italy [Apulia], since Greeks for the most part inhabited it . . . and so both Ennius and Lucilius [1124 M. = 142 W.] said:

> the bilingual Bruttian[1]   477

[1] Ennius' case is ablative, its function indeterminable. "Bilingual" in Latin often carries connotations of treachery, and the Bruttii of Calabria, speakers of Oscan and Greek, came to be reviled for their early defection to Hannibal (Gell. *NA* 10.3.19).

*31 Festus

> and by the stiff Calor   478

Ennius appears to be punning[1] . . . and elsewhere [7 *Ann.* F 17].

[1] The pun is on Calor, a river flowing from the Apennines into the Volturnus, and *calor* = heat.

*32 Paul the Deacon, *Epitome of Festus*

sicilices: the broad points of lances. Ennius:

> the skirmishers advanced as customary with their   479
> broad points

*33 Anonymous, *On the Spanish Campaign*

At this point, while our men were occupied with the work, a number of our adversaries ran down from a higher eleva-

bus nostris multis telis iniectis complures vuneribus affe-
cere. hic tum, ut ait Ennius [adtennius *plerique*],

480   nostri cessere parumper

*34 Varro, *Ling.* 7.103

multa ab animalium vocibus tralata in homines, partim
quae sunt aperta, partim obscura. perspicua ut Ennii

481   animusque in pectore latrat

   -que in *Scaliger*: cum *cod.*

*35 *Macrob. exc. Bob.*, *GL* V, p. 651.34–36

eructo etiam a quo principali veniat quaeritur. et est a
verbo erugit. Ennius:

482   contempsit fontes quibus ex erugit aquae vis

   Cf. *Macrob. exc. Par.*, *GL* V, p. 626.20–21.

*36 Serv. ad Verg. *Aen.* 10.396

"semianimesque micant digiti ferrumque retractant":
Ennii est ut

483   oscitat in campis caput a cervice revolsum
         semianimesque micant oculi lucemque requirunt

   quem versum ita ut fuit transtulit ad suum carmen Varro
   Atacinus.

tion and by casting many javelins wounded a number of
our men, who were unable to restrain them. Then, as
Ennius says,

> our men gave way for a little while   480

*34 Varro, *On the Latin Language*

Many terms are transferred from the cries of animals to
people, some of which are obvious, some obscure. Clear
terms, as Ennius'

> and the spirit in his breast growled[1]   481

[1] Cf. Hom. *Od.* 20.13 [Odysseus' anger at the treacherous
maidservants]: κραδίη δὲ ἔνδον ὑλάκτει "the heart within him
growled."

*35 *Excerpts from Macrobius*

From what root *eructo* [I vomit forth] comes is also sought.
And it is from the verb *erugit* [gurgles]. Ennius:

> he scorned the springs from which a rush of water   482
>   gurgles

*36 Servius, *Commentary on Virgil*

"and the fingers half-alive twitch and grasp at the sword":
The idea is Ennius', as

> the head, torn from the neck, gapes on the plain,   483
>   and half-alive, the eyes twitch and seek the light

a verse Varro Atacinus [F 2 Courtney] transferred as it was
to his own poem.

*37 Lactant. ad Stat. *Theb*. 11.56

"carmen tuba sola peregit": Ennius:

485   quomque caput caderet carmen tuba sola peregit
      et pereunte viro raucum sonus aere cucurrit

38 Varro, *Ling*. 7.25–26

cornua a curvore dicta quod pleraque curva. [26]

487   Musas quas memorant nosce nos esse Camena‹s

Casmenar›um [*suppl. Pomponius Laetus*] priscum voca-
bulum ita natum ac scriptum est alibi. Carmenae ab ea-
dem origine sunt declinatae. in multis verbis {in} quod
antiqui dicebant *s* postea dicunt *r*.

Musas *Scaliger*: curvamus ac *cod*.

*39 Serv. Dan. ad Verg. *Aen*. 11.19

"vellere signa": . . . vellere proprie dixit, quia Romana
signa figebantur in castris . . . [*add. Serv. Dan*.]: alii vellere
movere accipiunt. Ennius:

370

*37 Lactantius, *Commentary on Statius*

"the trumpet finished its song alone": Ennius:[1]

> and when his head fell, the trumpet finished its song   485
>   alone,
> and as the man perished, a hoarse sound raced from
>   the bronze

[1] This is the only echo of Ennius that has been identified in
Statius.

38 Varro, *On the Latin Language*

cornua [horns] is said from *curvor* [curvature] because
most horns are *curva* [curved]. [26]

> learn that we, whom they call Muses, are the   487
>   Camenae[1]

Casmenae is the early name as it originated and is written
elsewhere. Carmenae is formed from the same origin. In
many words, what the ancients pronounced as *s* they later
pronounce as *r.*

[1] The text of Varro that preserves this famous line is prob-
lematic, and while the verse as restored is widely accepted, some
uncertainty remains. For the restoration, see Skutsch 1968, 20–
22, and for the placement of the verse in either *Annals* 1 (editors
from Merula to Vahlen) or 15 (Skutsch), see Jackson in Flores
2009, 5:157–64.

*39 Servius Danielis, *Commentary on Virgil*

"to pull up the standards": . . . he said *vellere* [to pull up]
literally, since Roman standards were fixed in the camp
. . . : Others take *vellere* as "to move." Ennius:

488   rex deinde citatus

convellit sese

*40 Non., p. 370.19–24 M. = 589 L.

PASSUM: extensum patens: unde et passus dicimus quod
gressibus mutuis pedes patescunt. Ennius Annalium lib. X
. . . [F 15]:

490   ⟨passis⟩ late palmis pater

passis ait palmis patentibus et extensis.

**41 Prisc., *GL* II, pp. 334.18–35.1

celeris . . . ex quo celerissimus pro celerrimus superlati-
vum protulerunt. Cn. Matius in *Iliade* "celerissimus advo-
lat Hector." Ennius in Annalibus,

491   exin per terras postquam celerissimus rumor

*42 Varro, *Ling.* 7.12

tueri duo significat, unum ab aspectu ut dixi, unde est
Enni [enim *cod.*] illud [*Trag.* F 169] . . . et

492   quis pater aut cognatus volet nos contra tueri

       nos *an* vos *nonnulli disputant*

*43 Non., p. 230.15–16 M. = 341 L.

VULTUS masculino genere appellatur. Vergilius [*Aen.*
5.848] . . . , neutro Lucretius [4.1213] . . . , Ennius:

493   avorsabuntur semper vos vostraque volta

> then the king, aroused,   488
> pulled himself up

*40 Nonius

passum: "stretched out," "spreading open," from which we also say *passus* [steps] because the feet spread apart with each step. Ennius in Book 10 of the *Annals* . . . [F 15];

> with hands ‹spread› wide the father   490

he says "with hands spread" meaning "wide open and out-stretched."

**41 Priscian

celeris [swift] . . . from which they produce the superlative *celerissimus* instead of *celerrimus*. Gnaeus Matius[1] in his *Iliad*: "most swift Hector flies up." Ennius in the *Annals*:

> then, after most swift Rumor through the lands   491

[1] An author quoted by Varro, Gellius, and the later grammarians, but otherwise unknown.

*42 Varro, *On the Latin Language*

tueri [to look at, to protect] has two meanings, one from looking at, as I have said, whence that verse of Ennius [*Trag.* F 169] . . . and

> who, either father or kinsman, will want to look upon   492
> us

*43 Nonius

vultus [face] is mentioned in the masculine gender. Virgil [*Aen.* 5.848] . . . , neuter, Lucretius [4.1213] . . . , Ennius:

> you and your faces will always be turned away   493

*44 Porph. ad Hor. *Sat.* 1.2.37

"audire est operae pretium procedere recte / qui moechis non vultis ut omni parte laborent": urbane abutitur Ennianis versibus:

494   audire est operae pretium procedere recte,
          qui rem Romanam Latiumque augescere voltis

sed illud urbanius quod, cum Ennius "vultis" dixerit, hic "non vultis" intulerit.

Cf. Varro, *Men.* 542 B., ap. Non., p. 478.16 M. = 767 L.; Mart. Cap. 3.272; Mar. Vict., *GL* VI, p. 67.4–7.

*45 Charis., *GL* I, p. 201.10–16 = p. 261 B.

in mundo pro palam et in expedito ac cito. Plautus [*Pseud.* 500] . . . , Caecilius [*Com.* 276, 278 R.[2–3]] . . . , Ennius:

496   tibi vita
          seu mors in mundo est

46 *Rhet. Her.* 4.18

compositio . . . conservabitur . . . si non utemur continenter similiter cadentibus verbis, hoc modo:

*44 Porphyrio, *Commentary on Horace*

"It is worth your while, you who wish no straightforward progress for adulterers, to hear how they struggle on all sides": He wittily twists lines of Ennius:[1]

> it is worth your while to listen, you who wish   494
> straightforward progress for Roman affairs and
>   Latium to increase

but that is wittier because, when Ennius said "you wish," he [Horace] introduced "you do not wish."

[1] If Ennius' apparent solemnity is taken ironically, these lines might equally suit the satires (cf. *Satires* F 19), but a parody is more likely to have targeted the *Annals*.

*45 Charisius

in mundo for openly and readily and quickly. Plautus [*Pseud.* 500] . . . , Caecilius [*Com.* 276, 278 R.$^{2-3}$] . . . , Ennius:[1]

> whether life   496
> or death is readily in store for you

[1] The phrase *in mundo* is otherwise attested only in comedy. This could possibly be a dramatic fragment, but Charisius rarely quotes from Ennius' plays.

46 *Rhetorica ad Herennium*

Artistic composition . . . will be preserved . . . if we do not use a continuous series of words with similar case endings [homoeoptoton], in this way:

498   flentes plorantes lacrumantes obtestantes

> flentes plorantes *Rhet. Her.*: merentes flentes *grammatici*
> obtestantes *Rhet. Her.*: ac miserantes *Diomedes, Charisius*:
> commiserantes *Donatus et al.*

Cf. Diom., *GL* I, p. 447.16–19; Charis., *GL* I, p. 282.12–13 =
p. 371 B.; Donat., *GL* IV, p. 398.22–23; *Explan. in Donat.*, *GL* IV,
p. 565; Pomp., *GL* V, p. 304.3–5.

*47 Lactant. ad Stat. *Theb.* 6.27

"et cornu fugiebat somnus inani": sic a pictoribus simula-
tur ut liquidum somnum e cornu super dormientes vidatur
effundere [cf. Serv. Dan. ad Verg. *Aen.* 1.692]. sic Ennius:

499   quom sese exsiccat somno Romana iuventus

*48 Donat. ad Ter. *Phorm.* 1028

"faxo tali sum mactatum": sum modo pro eo quod est eum.
sic frequenter veteres. Ennius:

500   omnes corde patrem debent animoque benigno
            circum sum

*49 Serv. ad Verg. *Aen.* 4.404

"it nigrum campis agmen": hemistichium Ennii de ele-
phantis dictum, quo ante Accius usus est de Indis:

502   it atrum campis agmen

> atrum *Skutsch*: nigrum *Servius*

sobbing, imploring, weeping, protesting[1]   498

[1] The line as quoted is likely to be Ennian. The apparent textual variants in the later grammarians have been explained as versions of a different line, as metrical "corrections" of this one, or as their own illustrative inventions. Between 2 and 3 percent of Ennius' surviving epic hexameters end, as here, with a double spondee (*spondiazon*).

*47 Lactantius, *Commentary on Statius*

"and Sleep with empty horn fled": Somnus [Sleep] is represented thus by painters, so that he seems to be pouring out liquid sleep from a horn over those sleeping. So Ennius:

when the Roman youth dry themselves off from sleep   499

*48 Donatus, *Commentary on Terence*

"I'll have him afflicted in such a way": *sum* [pronoun] here for *eum* because it is "him." Thus frequently in old writers. Ennius:

all should their father with affection [?] and goodwill   500
around him[1]

[1] The construction (and thus the sense) is obscure. Donatus' reading of archaic *sum* in Terence, not found in the Terentian manuscripts, is supported by *circum sos* in 3 *Ann.* F 4.

*49 Servius, *Commentary on Virgil*

"the black column in the field moves": a half-line of Ennius said about elephants, which Accius previously used about Indians:

the dark column in the field moves   502

377

*50 Paul. *Fest.*, p. 363.1 L.

REDINUNT: redeunt.
. . . Ennius . . . ‹*28 fere litt.*›:

503   redinunt

Cf. Fest., p. 362.3–4 L.

*51 Serv. Dan. ad Verg. *Aen.* 11.326

"texamus . . . naves": quidam texamus proprie dictum tra-
dunt quia loca in quibus naves fiunt Graece ναυπήγια,
Latine textrina dici. Ennius dicit:

504   idem campus habet textrinum navibus longis

navalia enim non esse ναυπήγια sed νεώρια.

Cf. Cic. *Orat.* 157.

*52 Isid. *Orig.* 19.1.22

celoces quae Graeci κέλητας vocant, id est veloces bire-
mes vel triremes agiles et ad ministerium classis aptae.
Ennius:

505   labitur uncta carina per aequora cana celocis

Cf. *CIL* VIII 27790 = *CLE* 2294.

*50 Paul the Deacon, *Epitome of Festus*

redinunt: *redeunt* [they return].

. . . Ennius . . . :

> they return   503

*51 Servius Danielis, *Commentary on Virgil*

"let us build . . . ships": Some maintain that *texamus* [let us build] is used appropriately since the places in which ships are made are called in Greek *naupēgia*, in Latin *textrina*. Ennius says:

> this selfsame plain contains a shipyard for warships   504

since dockyards are not *naupēgia* but *neōria*.[1]

[1] Greek distinguishes between shipyards for construction (*naupēgia*) and docks for storage (*neōria*). Latin *navalia* stood for both: Ennius' use of *textrinum* (lit., "a weaver's shop") for a shipyard is otherwise unattested.

*52 Isidore, *Origins*

celoces are what Greeks call *kelētas*, i.e., swift biremes or triremes, nimble and suitable for the service of a fleet. Ennius:

> the cutter's greased keel slips o'er the white waves   505

*53 Fest., p. 356.32–33 L.

RESTAT pro distat ait Verrius Ennium ponere cum {h}is dicat:

506   impetus haud longe mediis regionibus restat

   haud *Turnebus*: aut *codd.*

*54 Serv. Dan. ad Verg. *Aen.* 9.327

temere . . . significat sine causa. Ennius:

507   haud temere est quod tu tristi cum corde gubernas

*55 Isid. *Orig.* 19.2.12

clavus est quo regitur gubernaculum. de quo Ennius:

508   dum clavom rectum teneam navemque gubernem

   dum *Quintilian*: ut *Isidorus*

Cf. Quint. *Inst.* 2.17.24.

*56 Fest., p. 138.13–21 L.

METONYMIA est tropos cum . . . significatur . . . a superiore re inferior, ut Ennius:

509   cum magno strepitu Volcanum ventus vegebat

*53 Festus

Verrius says that Ennius uses *restat* [comes to a halt] for *distat* [stands at a distance] when he says:

> the attack halts not far from the middle ground[1] 506

[1] The construction is uncertain, as is the subject (a military maneuver? a ship on its course?) and the action (stops en route? in midfield?).

*54 Servius Danielis, *Commentary on Virgil*

temere [lit., "rashly"] . . . means "without cause." Ennius:

> it is hardly without cause that you steer with heavy 507
> heart

*55 Isidore, *Origins*

clavus is that with which a rudder is controlled. About which Ennius says:

> so long as I hold the tiller straight and steer the ship 508

*56 Festus

Metonymy is the trope when . . . a lesser thing is indicated by a greater, as Ennius:

> with a mighty blast the wind aroused Vulcan[1] 509

[1] Some kind of conflagration is presumably meant.

**57 Charis., *GL* I, p. 19.1–2 = p. 16 B.

dicunt quidam veteres in prima declinatione solitos no-
mina . . . proferre . . . dativo per *-i* . . . item adhuc morem
esse poetis in dativo casu, ut "aulai medio" Vergilius,

510   terrai frugiferai

Ennius in Annalibus.

Cf. Charis., *GL* I, p. 538.26–28 = p. 16 B.; Sacerd., *GL* VI,
p. 449.1–3; *Fragm. Bob.*, *GL* V, p. 555.1–3; Mart. 11.90.5.

*58 Gell. *NA* 13.21.13

Ennius item "rectos cupressos" dixit contra receptum vo-
cabuli genus hoc versu:

511   capitibus nutantis pinos rectosque cupressos

firmior ei credo et viridior sonus esse vocis visus est, rectos
dicere cupressos quam rectas.

Cf. Non., p. 195.21 M. = 287 L.

*59 Isid. O*rig.* 19.2.4

agea viae sunt loca in navi per qua ad remiges hortator
accedit. de qua Ennius:

512   multa foro ponet et agea. longa repletur

**57 Charisius

Some say that in the first declension old writers were accustomed to produce nouns with a dative in *-i* . . . and further that poets also had this habit in the dative case, as Virgil's *aulai medio* ["in the middle of the hall," *Aen.* 3.354], and Ennius'

> of the fruit-bearing earth   510

in the *Annals.*[1]

  [1] Skutsch 1985, 663: "it is a mystery how Charisius could have mistaken *aulai* and *terrai* for datives." They are archaic genitives.

*58 Gellius, *Attic Nights*

So too Ennius said *rectos cupressos*, contrary to the accepted gender of the word, in this verse:

> pines with nodding heads and upright cypresses[1]   511

The sound of the expression seemed stronger to him, I believe, and more vigorous by saying *rectos cupressos* rather than *rectas.*

  [1] The initial resolved *longum* of *căpĭtĭbŭs* is problematic. An alternative scansion might be *căptibus* by syncope, or the text may be corrupt. For the gender of *cupressus*, cf. 7 *Ann.* F 12.

*59 Isidore, *Origins*

agea are ramps, the places in a ship along which the coxswain approaches the rowers. On this Ennius has:

> much will he load on deck and gangway. The warship   512
>   [?] is again filled

*60 Serv. Dan. ad Verg. *Aen.* 11.306

"invictisque viris gerimus": atqui supra egimus "bis capti Phryges" [9.599]. sed invictis ideo dicit quia sequitur "nec victi . . . ferro." "possunt" autem "absistere" mire ait ac si diceret: etiam si velint, eos a bellis discedere natura non patitur. [*add. Serv. Dan.*] Ennius:

513   qui vincit non est victor nisi victus fatetur

Varro et ceteri invictos dicunt Troianos quia per insidias oppressi sunt. illos enim vinci affirmant qui se dedunt hostibus.

*61 Fest., p. 394.6–9 L.

SUPERESCIT significat supererit. Ennius:

514   dum quidem unus homo Romanus toga superescit

quidem *codd.*: cui dem *Skutsch metri causa*   homo Romanus toga *Fest.*: homo Romae *Paulus*: homo vestitus *Havet*

Cf. Paul. *Fest.*, p. 395.1–2 L.

*62 Serv. Dan. ad Verg. *Aen.* 1.123

"imber" dicitur umor omnis ut Lucretius [1.715] . . . [*add. Serv. Dan.*]: veteres enim omnem aquam imbrem dicebant. Ennius imbrem pro aqua marina:

515   ratibusque fremebat
imber Neptuni

Cf. Serv. Dan. ad Verg. *Aen.* 11.299; *G.* 1.12.

*60 Servius Danielis, *Commentary on Virgil*

"and we wage [war] with unconquered men": and yet above we dealt with "Phrygians captured twice" [9.599]. But he says "unconquered" because of what follows, "not conquered . . . by the sword." Moreover, he says wonderfully "they are able to abstain" as if he were saying: even if they wanted to, their nature does not permit them to abandon war. Ennius:

> he who conquers is not a conqueror unless the   513
>   conquered acknowledges it

Varro and others say the Trojans were unconquered because they were overcome by ambush. They maintain that those are conquered who surrender themselves to the enemy.

*61 Festus

superescit means "will survive." Ennius:

> so long indeed as one togate Roman survives   514

*62 Servius Danielis, *Commentary on Virgil*

The word *imber* is used of all types of moisture, as Lucretius [1.715]: . . . For old writers used to say *imber* for all water. Ennius uses *imber* for sea water:

> and Neptune's water   515
>   rumbled with ships

*63 Isid. *Orig.* 19.2.14

tonsilla uncinus ferreus vel ligneus, ad quem in litore de-
fixum funes navis inligantur. de quo Ennius:

517   tonsillas apiunt, configunt litus, aduncas

*64 Serv. ad Verg. *Aen.* 6.545

"explebo numerum": ut diximus supra "explebo" est mi-
nuam. nam ait Ennius:

518   navibus explebant sese terrasque replebant

*65 Serv. ad Verg. *Aen.* 9.678

"armati ferro": aut bene instructi armis aut, ut Asper dicit,
ferrea corda habentes, i.e. dura et cruenta cogitantes; ut
Ennium sit secutus, qui ait:

519   succincti corda machaeris

**66 Prisc., *GL* II, pp. 517.22–18.22

tundo, tutudi: paenultima a plerisque correpta, a quibus-
dam autem etiam producta . . . vetustissimi tamen tam
producebant quam corripiebant supra dicti verbi paenul-
timam. Ennius in XIIII [F 8] . . . ecce hic corripuit. idem
in XVI [F 9] . . . idem in Annalibus:

*63 Isidore, *Origins*

tonsilla, a hook of iron or wood to which, when fixed on the shore, a ship's hawsers are tied. On this Ennius:

> they pierce the beach, they tie up to the hooked poles 517

*64 Servius, *Commentary on Virgil*

"I will fill out the number": as we said above,[1] *explebo* is "I will diminish," for Ennius says:

> they unfilled themselves from the ships and refilled 518
> the land

[1] No such note survives in the extant texts of Servius, who seems to misunderstand Virgil's phrase.

*65 Servius, *Commentary on Virgil*

"armed with iron": either well equipped with weapons or, as Asper says,[1] having hearts of iron, i.e., bent on harsh and bloody deeds; as if he followed Ennius, who says:

> girt at their breasts with swords 519

[1] Aemilius Asper, a second-century commentator on Virgil. The Ennian parallel, if apt, might better suggest that Virgil's phrase simply means "armed with swords."

**66 Priscian

tundo, *tutudi*: the penultimate syllable is shortened by many, though by some also lengthened . . . The oldest writers nevertheless as often lengthened as shortened the penultimate syllable of the above-mentioned word. Ennius in Book 14 [F 8] . . . See, here he has shortened it. So too in Book 16 [F 9] . . . So too in the *Annals*:

520   viresque valentes

contu‹n›dit crudelis hiems

hic produxit paenultima.

521 contundit *Baehrens*: contudit *Priscianus*: contutudit *Mueller*

*67 Cic. *Sen.* 14

sua enim vitia insipientes et suam culpam in senectutem conferunt, quod non faciebat is cuius modo mentionem feci Ennius:

522   sicuti fortis equos spatio qui saepe supremo
         vicit Olympia nunc senio confectus quiescit

equi fortis et victoris senectuti comparat suam.

*68 (= T 103, cf. T 67) Serv. ad Verg. *Aen.* 7.691

"at Messapus equum domitor Neptunia proles": hic Messapus per mare ad Italiam venit . . . ab hoc Ennius dicit se originem ducere, unde nunc et cantantes inducit eius socios et eos comparat cycnis.

524   Messap‹us›

> and their sturdy strength   520
cruel winter crushes

Here he has lengthened the penultimate syllable.[1]

[1] Priscian is thought to be mistaken: thus the emendation of perfect *contudit* to present *contundit*.

*67 Cicero, *On Old Age*

Fools attribute their own faults and their own error to old age, a thing he, whom I just mentioned, was not accustomed to do, Ennius:

> just as a brave horse, who often in the last lap   522
> was victorious at Olympia, now, exhausted by age, is
>   at rest

He is comparing his own old age to that of a brave and victorious horse.[1]

[1] For other statements about old age in the *Annals*, cf. 16 *Ann.* F 1 and Gell. *NA* 17.21.43 (T 84).

*68 (= T 103, cf. T 67) Servius, *Commentary on Virgil*

"but Messapus, tamer of horses, Neptune's offspring": This Messapus came to Italy over the sea . . . Ennius claims to trace his origin from him, and from this he [Virgil] here introduces his [Messapus'] companions singing and compares them to swans [cf. *Aen.* 7.698–702].

Messap⟨us?⟩[1]   524

[1] Servius' statement implies that the name Messapus appeared in the *Annals*, though in what case cannot be determined.

69 Cic. *De or.* 3.168

videtis profecto genus hoc totum, cum inflexo immuta-
toque verbo res eadem enuntiatur ornatius. cui sunt fini-
tima . . . cum intellegi volumus . . . aut ex uno plures ut "at
Romanus homo . . . trepidat" [Inc. *Ann.* F 98] aut cum ex
pluribus intellegitur unum:

525   nos sumus Romani qui fuimus ante Rudini

*70 Paul. *Fest.*, p. 453.10–11 L.

SYBINAM appellant Illyri telum venabuli simile. Ennius:

526   Illyrii restant sicis sybinisque fodentes

*71 Paul. *Fest.*, p. 46.16–17 L.

CRACENTES: graciles. Ennius:

527   succincti gladiis, media regione cracentes

*72 Serv. Dan. ad Verg. *Aen.* 5.37

"occurrit Acestes / horridus in iaculis et pelle Libystidis
ursae": in iaculis in hastis. Ennius:

528   levesque sequuntur in hastis

69 Cicero, *On the Orator*

No doubt you understand this whole category, when by an adapted and transferred word the same thing is formulated more ornately. Close to this . . . is when we want . . . either the many to be understood from the one, as "yet the Roman . . . trembles" [Inc. *Ann.* F 98] or when out of many one is understood:

> we are Romans, who formerly were Rudini[1]   525

[1] Ennius' origin at Rudiae is well established in the ancient biographical tradition: T 9, 57, 67, 99. This line, though unattributed, is thus widely taken to be an autobiographical statement—Cicero's *unum* may well be Ennius—but whether it was actually spoken *in propria persona* remains uncertain.

***70** Paul the Deacon, *Epitome of Festus*

The Illyrians call *sybina* a missile similar to a hunting spear. Ennius:

> the Illyrians stand firm, stabbing with daggers and   526
> sybinae

***71** Paul the Deacon, *Epitome of Festus*

cracentes: "slender." Ennius:

> girt with swords, around the waist slender   527

***72** Servius Danielis, *Commentary on Virgil*

"Acestes rushes up, bristling with javelins and with the hide of a Libyan she-bear": *in iaculis* [with javelins] means "with lances." Ennius:

> and the light-armed troops follow with lances   528

*73 Non., p. 223.32 M.= 331 L.

SAGUM generis neutri ut plerumque. masculini Ennius:

529   tergus † igitur sagus pinguis opertat

*74 Charis., *GL* I, p. 105.17–18 = p. 134 B.

"sagum" neutro genere dicitur, sed Afranius in *Deditione* [*Tog.* 44 R.$^{2-3}$] masculine dixit "quia quadrati sunt sagi"; et Ennius:

530   sagus caerulus

*75 Fest., p. 444.23–29 L.

SPIRA dicitur et basis columnae unius tori aut duorum, et genus operis pistori, et funis nauticus in orbem convolutus, ab eadem omnes similitudine. Pacuvius . . . [*Trag.* 385 R.$^{2-3}$]. Ennius quidem hominum multitudinem ita appellat cum ait:

531   spiras legionibus nexit

*76 Serv. Dan. ad Verg. *Aen.* 9.163 [165]

"indulgent vino et

532   vortunt crateras aenos"

potantes exhauriunt; et est hemistichium Ennianum.

392

*73 Nonius

sagum [cloak] is generally of neuter gender. Masculine, Ennius:

> a thick cloak therefore [?] covers his back   529

*74 Charisius

sagum is said to be of neuter gender, but Afranius in *The Surrender* [*Tog.* 44 R.²⁻³] used a masculine form in the phrase "since cloaks are square," and Ennius:

> a blue cloak   530

*75 Festus

spira is a word for the base of a column with one molding or two, and a kind of millstone, and a ship's cable wound in a coil, all for their shared similarity. Pacuvius . . . [*Trag.* 385 R.²⁻³]. Indeed, Ennius calls a large body of men thus when he says:

> he wove coils in with his legions[1]   531

[1] In addition to the obvious wordplay on weaving, Ennius may be punning on *spira* [coil] and the Hellenistic tactical unit called a σπεῖρα (Polybius' term for a maniple). The reference might then be the use of auxiliary units in support of Roman legions.

*76 Servius Danielis, *Commentary on Virgil*

> "they indulge in wine, and
>
>   they tilt up the bronze bowls"   532

They drained at a draft; it is also an Ennian half-line.

*77 Serv. Dan. ad Verg. *Aen.* 1.69

"incute vim ventis": duplex sensus est. incute enim si inice significat, ventis dativus est casus . . . si autem fac, septimus casus est et erit sensus fac vim Troianis per ventos. [*add. Serv. Dan.*] hoc est, per ventos vim in Troianos incute. Ennius:

533   dictis Romanis incutit iram

*78 Serv. ad Verg. *Aen.* 12.499

"irarum habenas": hic moderate locutus est. nam Ennius ait:

534   irarum effunde quadrigas

     irarum effunde *F*: effundit irarum *ceteri codd.*

*79 Macrob. *Sat.* 6.3.7–8

Homerica descriptio est equi fugientis in haec verba [*Il.* 6.506–11 = 15.263–68]:

     ὡς δ' ὅτε τις στατὸς ἵππος ἀκοστήσας ἐπὶ φάτνῃ
     δεσμὸν ἀπορρήξας θείῃ πεδίοιο κροαίνων
     εἰωθὼς λούεσθαι ἐϋρρεῖος ποταμοῖο
     κυδιόων· ὑψοῦ δὲ κάρη ἔχει, ἀμφὶ δὲ χαῖται
     ὤμοις ἀΐσσονται· ὃ δ' ἀγλαΐηφι πεποιθὼς
     ῥίμφά ἑ γοῦνα φέρει μετά τ' ἤθεα καὶ νομὸν ἵππων

*77 Servius Danielis, *Commentary on Virgil*

"strike violence into your winds": There is a double sense, for if *incute* means *inice* [strike], *ventis* is dative case . . . if, on the other hand, it means *fac* [make], *ventis* is instrumental ablative and the sense will be "make violence against the Trojans by means of the winds." That is, through your winds make violence against the Trojans. Ennius:

> he arouses anger in the Romans by his speech   533

*78 Servius, *Commentary on Virgil*

"the reins of anger": here he spoke with moderation, for Ennius says:

> pour out the chariots of anger[1]   534

[1] The textual alternative in the manuscripts of Servius, with an indicative rather than imperative verb, turns the line into the first half of an iambic octonarius, which would indicate an origin in drama, not epic.

*79 Macrobius, *Saturnalia*

A Homeric description of a fleeing horse is in these words:

> as when a stabled horse, well-fed at his fodder,
> snaps his tether and gallops over the plain,
> accustomed to bathe in the fine-flowing river,
> exulting: he holds his head high, and about his
> shoulders his mane flutters. He is confident in his
>   glory
> as his legs carry him swiftly to the haunts and
>   pastures of horses.

Ennius hinc traxit:

535   et tum, sicut equos qui de praesepibus fartus
     vincla suis magnis animis abrumpit et inde
     fert sese campi per caerula laetaque prata
     celso pectore; saepe iubam quassat simul altam,
     spiritus ex anima calida spumas agit albas

Vergilius: "qualis . . . vinclis" et cetera [*Aen.* 11.492–97].

*80 Fest., p. 362.26–28 L.

item [Ennius]:

540   unus surum Surus ferre, tamen defendere possent

SURI autem sunt fustes, et hypocoristicos surculi.

    unus surum Surus *Reichardt*: unum usurum surus *Fest.*,
p. 362

Cf. Fest., p. 382.25–33 L.; Paul. *Fest.*, p. 383.12–14 L.

*81 Cic. *Div.* 2.82

ad nostri augurii consuetudinem dixit Ennius:

541   tum tonuit laevom bene tempestate serena

Cf. Varro, *Men.* 103 B.

Ennius drew on these lines:

> and then, just like a horse, stuffed full at the manger,   535
> that in high spirits snaps his tether and then
> takes himself through the green and fertile pastures
>   of the field
> with chest high: he often shakes his mane loftily,
> his breath sends white foam from his heated soul

Virgil: "as when . . . from his tether" and so on [*Aen.* 11.492–97].[1]

---

[1] The simile, also taken up at Ap. Rhod. 3.1259–62, is thoroughly discussed by von Albrecht 1969.

*80 Festus

Similarly [Ennius]:

> one Syrian to carry a stake, nevertheless they could   540
>   defend[1]

suri are stakes, and the diminutive is *surculi.*

---

[1] Text, and thus syntax and sense, are problematic, though wordplay on *surus* [stake] and *Surus* [Syrian?] is evident. It may be relevant that, according to Cato (ap. Plin. *HN* 8.11 = F 115 *FRHist*), an especially brave Carthaginian war elephant with a single tusk was called Surus.

*81 Cicero, *On Divination*

It was in reference to our practice of augury that Ennius said:

> then it thundered on the left, favorably, in a clear sky   541

*82 Varro, *Ling.* 7.32

dubitatur . . . utrum primum una canis aut canes sit appel-
lata: dicta enim apud veteres una canes. itaque Ennius
scribit:

542   tantidem quasi feta canes sine dentibus latrat

Lucilius: "nequam et magnus homo, laniorum immanis
canes ut" [1221 M. = 1175 W.]. impositio unius debuit esse
canis, plurimum canes. sed neque Ennius consuetudinem
illam sequens reprehendendus nec is qui nunc dicit "canis
caninam non est" . . . sic dictum a quibusdam ut una canes
una "trabes remis rostrata per altum."

*83 Varro, *Ling.* 7.46

apud Ennium "iam cata signa . . ." [Inc. *Ann.* F 8]: cata
acuta. hoc enim verbo dicunt Sabini. quare "catus Aelius
Sextus" [10 *Ann.* F 5] non ut aiunt sapiens sed acutus, et
quod est

543   tunc coepit memorare simul cata dicta

accipienda acuta dicta.

*82 Varro, *On the Latin Language*

There is doubt . . . whether originally a single female dog was called *canis* or *canes*, for among old authors the expression in the singular was *canes*. So Ennius writes:

> as much as if a pregnant, toothless bitch barks   542

Lucilius: "a worthless, big man, like the butchers' monstrous dog" [1221 M. = 1175 W.]. Applied to one, it should have been *canis*, to many *canes*, but Ennius should not be faulted for following the old practice, nor should he who now says "a dog [*canis*] does not eat dog meat [*canina*]" . . . just as some have said, like feminine *canes* in the singular, in the singular "the beaked ship with oars across the deep."[1]

---

[1] This second anonymous phrase is claimed for Ennius by Vahlen (616); Skutsch, finding the attribution unlikely, places it among his *Spuria* (9). The attested line of Ennius could instead belong to a satire.

*83 Varro, *On the Latin Language*

In Ennius, "around then the shrill signals . . ." [Inc. *Ann.* F 8]. *cata*, "sharp." The Sabines use the word. That is why *"catus* Aelius Sextus" [10 *Ann.* F 5] means not, as they say, "wise," but "shrewd," and

> then at the same time he began to recall *cata dicta*   543

should be understood as "shrewd sayings."

***84** Paul. *Fest.*, p. 103.26–28 L.

LITUUS appellatus quod litis sit testis. est enim genus
bucinae incurvae, quo qui cecinerit dicitur liticen. Ennius:

544   inde loci lituus sonitus effudit acutos

***85** Varro, *Ling.* 7.103–4

multa ab animalium vocibus tralata in homines . . . pers-
picua ut Ennii "animusque in pectore latrat" [Inc. *Ann.*
F 34] . . . [104] minus aperta ut . . . Ennii . . . [Inc. *Ann.*
F 126]; eiusdem ab haedo:

545   clamor ad caelum volvendus per aethera vagit

***86** Fest., p. 462.5–10 L.

SULTIS si voltis significat, composito vocabulo ita ut alia
sunt: ‹sodes› si audes, sis si vis . . . Ennius:

546   pandite sulti genas et corde relinquite somnum

Cf. Paul. *Fest.*, pp. 463.1–2; 83.15–16 L.

*84 Paul the Deacon, *Epitome of Festus*

The *lituus* is so called because it is a witness to strife [*lis*].[1]
It is, to be sure, a kind of curved horn, from which one
who plays it is called a *liticen*. Ennius:

> thereupon the trumpet poured forth sharp sounds　　544

[1] Derivation of *lĭtuus* from *lĭs* is impossible. This word for both
the augur's curved staff and a kind of military horn may be Etrus-
can in origin.

*85 Varro, *On the Latin Language*

Many terms are transferred from the cries of animals to
people . . . clear terms, as Ennius' "and the spirit in his
breast growled" [Inc. *Ann.* F 34] . . . [104] less clear, as . . .
Ennius' . . . [Inc. *Ann.* F 126], and of the same poet, from
a goat:

> a clamor, rolling to the heavens, cries[1] through the　　545
> 　　aether

[1] The verb is more commonly used of infants, but Mart.
3.58.37 uses it of a young goat.

*86 Festus

sultis means *si voltis* [if you please], a contracted expres-
sion, as are others [of similar sense]: ⟨*sodes*⟩, *si audes; sis,
si vis* . . . Ennius:

> open your eyelids, if you please, and remove sleep　　546
> 　　from your heart[1]

[1] Plural imperatives. The plural *sultis*, apparently read by Fes-
tus without the final -*s*, is rare.

87 Fest., p. 426.5–14 L.

SAGACES appellantur multi ac sollertis acuminis. Afranius in Brundisina "quis tam sagaci corde atque ingenio unico" [*Tog.* 15 R²⁻³]. Lucretius l. II "nec minus haec animum cognoscere ⟨posse sagacem" [840]. sagacem⟩ etiam canem ⟨indagatorem Ennius dicit⟩

547   invictus ca⟨nis nare sagax et vi⟩ribus fretus

suppl. Vahlen

*88 Paul. *Fest.*, p. 504.14–16 L.

TRIFAX telum longitudinis trium cubitorum, quod catapulta mittitur. Ennius:

548   aut permarceret paries percussus trifaci

**89 Gell. *NA* 3.14.5

Varro . . . disserit . . . ac dividit subtilissime quid dimidium dimiato intersit, et Q. Ennium scienter hoc in Annalibus dixisse ait:

549   sicuti siquis ferat vas vini dimidiatum

sicuti pars quae deest ei vaso non "dimidiata" dicenda est sed "dimidia."

87 Festus

People with plenty of sharp cunning are called *sagaces*. Afranius in *The Girl from Brindisi*, "who with such a shrewd heart and rare talent" [*Tog.* 15 R²⁻³]. Lucretius in Book 2 "that the keen mind is no less able to recognize these things" [840]. ‹Ennius also calls a keen hunting› dog

> an invincible hound, keen of nose and buoyed by   547
>   strength[1]

[1] Scansion suggests an early hexameter poet, thus most likely Ennius. Cf. the simile at 10 *Ann.* F 7. The supplements are supported by related definitions (minus the quotations) at Cic. *Div.* 1.54; Paul. Fest., pp. 303.2–4, 427.1–2 L.

*88 Paul the Deacon, *Epitome of Festus*

A *trifax* is a missile three cubits long, which is shot from a catapult. Ennius:

> or the wall[1] pelted by the *trifax* might crumble   548

[1] Strictly speaking, a house wall and not a fortification. Contrast Inc. *Ann.* F 90.

**89 Gellius, *Attic Nights*

Varro . . . discusses . . . and distinguishes most acutely the difference between "a half" and "halved," and says that Ennius said this knowledgeably in the *Annals*:

> as if someone were to bring a halved cup of wine   549

just as the part missing from this cup should be spoken of not as "halved" but "a half."

**90 Gell. *NA* 10.29.2–3

"atque" particula . . . si gemina fiat, auget intenditque rem de qua agitur, ut animadvertimus in Q. Enni Annalibus, nisi memoria in hoc versu labor:

550   atque atque accedit muros Romana iuventus

cui significationi contrarium est quod itidem a veteribus dictum est, "deque ‹deque›(?)."

Cf. Non., p. 530.2 M. = 850 L.

*91 Non., pp. 134.29–34 M. = 195–96 L.

LATROCINARI: militare mercede. Plautus [*Cornicularia*, F 61 L.] . . . Ennius:

551   fortunasque suas coepere latrones
          inter se memorare

*92 Serv. ad Verg. *G.* 2.424

"gravidas, cum vomere, fruges": cum abundat, nam hoc dicit: subministrat fruges vomere, id est per vomerem. Ennius:

553   effudit voces proprio cum pectore sancto

id est proprio pectore, nam cum vacat.

**90 Gellius, *Attic Nights*

The particle *atque* . . . if it is made double, increases and intensifies the thing being dealt with, as we notice in the *Annals* of Ennius, unless in this line my memory is faulty:

> up to and to[1] the walls the Roman youth approach   550

Opposite to this meaning is what was said in the same way by old writers, *deque deque* [away and away from].

[1] *atque* here = adverbial *ad* + *-que*.

*91 Nonius

latrocinari: "to serve as a soldier for pay." Plautus [*Cornicularia*, F 61 L.] . . . Ennius:

> and the mercenaries began to recall   551
> among themselves their fortunes

*92 Servius, *Commentary on Virgil*

"heavy fruits when [laid open] by the plow": *cum* [when] is redundant, for he is saying this: it [i.e., the earth] provides fruit with a plow, i.e., by means of a plow. Ennius:

> he poured forth speech with his own blessed heart[1]   553

that is *proprio pectore*, for *cum* is superfluous.[2]

[1] The subject is a god if, as 1 *Ann.* F 21, 31, 43.88 suggest, *sanctus* in Ennius is characteristic of divinity.

[2] Servius reads Ennius correctly, but misreads Virgil, whose *cum* parallels *cum recluditur* in the preceding line and is thus the conjunction, not the preposition.

93 Varro, *Ling.* 7.7

quaqua intuiti erant oculi a tuendo primo templum dictum; quocirca caelum quoad tuimur dictum templum sic:

554   contremuit templum magnum Iovis altitonantis

*94

a Serv. Dan. ad Verg. *Aen.* 1.31

arcebat: prohibebat. significat autem et "continet." Ennius:

555   qui fulmine claro
omnia per sonitus arcet

id est continet.

b [Probus] ad Verg. *Ecl.* 6.31 (vol. 3.2, p. 343.13–14 Th.-H.)

et alio loco [*i.e., Lucr. haud recte*]: omnia per sonitus arcet,

                terram mare caelum

*95 Non., p. 555.14 M. = 891 L.

FALARICA telum maximum. Vergilius lib. IX [705] . . . Ennius:

557   quae valide veniunt . . . falarica missa

93 Varro, *On the Latin Language*

Whatever the eyes had gazed on was originally called a
templum [precinct] from *tueri* [to gaze]; therefore the sky,
as far as we gaze on it, is called a *templum*, thus:

> the great precinct of high-thundering Jupiter 554
> trembled

*94

a Servius Danielis, *Commentary on Virgil*

arcebat: "kept off." It also, however, means "encom-
passes." Ennius:

> who, with bright thunderbolt 555
> encompasses all things with its sound

that is, it "encompasses."

b [Probus], *Commentary on Virgil*

and in another place: encompasses all things with its
sound:

> earth, sea, sky[1]

[1] The anonymous commentator seems to attribute the line to
Lucretius, but it is clearly a fuller form of the second Ennian line
quoted by Servius.

*95 Nonius

A *falarica* is an extremely large missile. Virgil, Book 9
[705] . . . Ennius:

> which come sturdily . . . the *falarica* hurled 557

*96 Isid. *Nat. rer.* 12.3

partes autem eius [sc. caeli] haec sunt: cohus axis cardines convexa poli hemisphaeria. cohus est quo caelum continetur. unde Ennius:

558 vix solum complere cohum torroribus caeli

axis linea recta quae per mediam pilam caeli tendit.

  torroribus *Baehrens*: terroribus *codd.*

*97 Non., p. 197.2–8 M. = 289 L.

CAELUM . . . masculino Lucretius ". . . caelos omnis . . ." [2.1091]; Varro rerum divinarum VI deum significans, non partem mundi ". . . Caelus, Tellus"; Ennius:

559 fortis Romani ⟨sunt⟩ quamquam caelus profundus

  sunt *add. Merula*: stant *Mariotti*

Cf. Charis., *GL* I, p. 72.12–14 = p. 91 B.

98 Cic. *De or.* 3.168

. . . cum intellegi volumus aliquid aut ex parte totum, ut pro aedificiis cum parietes aut tecta dicimus; aut ex toto partem, ut cum unam turmam equitatum populi Romani dicimus; aut ex uno pluris:

560 at Romanus homo, tamenetsi res bene gesta est,
  corde suo trepidat

aut cum ex pluribus intellegitur unum: . . . [Inc. *Ann.* F 69].

*96 Isidore, *On the Nature of Things*

The parts of it [the sky] are these: hollow, axis, hinges, vaults, poles, hemispheres. The hollow is what holds in the sky, from which Ennius says:

> scarcely to fill the single hollow of the sky with   558
> firebrands

The axis is a straight line, which extends through the central pole of the sky.

*97 Nonius

caelum [heaven] . . . masculine in Lucretius, ". . . all the heavens . . ." [2.1091]; Varro, *On Divine Matters*, Book 6 meaning a god, not part of the world ". . . heaven, earth"; Ennius:

> Romans are as brave as the heaven is high   559

98 Cicero, *On the Orator*

[on varieties of synecdoche] . . . when we want either some totality to be understood from a part, as when we say "walls" or "roofs" for buildings; or a part from the whole, as when we say "one squadron" for the cavalry of the Roman people; or many from one:

> yet the Roman, despite affairs having gone well,   560
> trembles at heart

or when from the many one is understood: . . . [Inc. *Ann.* F 69].

*99 Non., p. 214.7–10 M. = 315 L.

METUS masculino. feminino Naevius: "magnae metus tumultus pectora possidit" [*BP*, F 53 Strzelecki]. Ennius:

562   nec metus ulla tenet, freti virtute quiescunt

*100 Donat. ad Ter. *Phorm.* 465

"cum istoc animo" pro "huius animi." Ennius:

563   optima cum pulcris animis Romana iuventus

*101 Serv. Dan. ad Verg. *Aen.* 1.81

"cavum conversa cuspide montem impulit in latus": ordo est: conversa cuspide cavum montem in latus impulit. et alibi "in latus . . . contorsit" [2.51]. [*add. Serv. Dan.*]: alii in latus pro latus accipiunt. Ennius:

564   nam me gravis impetus Orci
         percutit in latus

*102 Non., p. 211.10–13 M. = 311 L.

LAPIDES et feminino genere dici possunt ut apud Ennium:

566   tanto sublatae sunt
         a‹u›gmine tunc lapides

ad Homeri similitudinem, qui genere feminino lapides posuit.

augmine *Wakefield*: agmine *codd.*

*99 Nonius

metus [fear] in the masculine. In the feminine Naevius: "an upsurge of great fear possesses his breast" [*BP*, F 53 Strzelecki]. Ennius:

> nor does any fear hold them; they rest secure in their 562
> courage

*100 Donatus, *Commentary on Terence*

"with that sort of spirit" for "of this spirit." Ennius:

> the best Roman youth with fine spirits 563

*101 Servius Danielis, *Commentary on Virgil*

"with point reversed he struck the mountain's hollow in the side": the order is, "with point reversed into the hollow mountainside he struck," and elsewhere "into the side . . . he twisted" [2.51]. Others take "into the side" as "the side." Ennius:

>   for the heavy onslaught of Death 564
> strikes into my side

*102 Nonius

lapides [stones] can also be used in the feminine gender, as in Ennius:

>   in such a mass 566
> were the stones then raised up

on the model of Homer, who used "stones" in the feminine gender [*Il.* 12.287; *Od.* 19.494].

*103 Serv. Dan. ad Verg. *Aen.* 9.327

temere significat et "facile": Plautus [*Bacch.* 85] . . . significat et "subito." Ennius:

568   quo tam temere itis

*104 Serv. ad Verg. *Aen.* 12.709

"inter se coiisse viros et cernere ferro": vera et antiqua haec est lectio. nam Ennium secutus est qui ait:

569   olli cernebant magnis de rebus agentes

Cf. Serv. ad Verg. *Aen.* 11.236: olli illi secundum Ennium.

*105 Serv. ad Verg. *G.* 3.76

"mollia crura reponit": Ennius de gruibus:

570   perque fabam repunt et mollia crura reponunt

Cf. Schol. Bern. ad loc.

**106 Prisc., *GL* II, p. 170.6–9

iubar quoque tam masculinum quam neutrum proferebant. Ennius in Annalibus:

571   interea fugit albus iubar Hyperionis cursum

*103 Servius Danielis, *Commentary on Virgil*

temere [rashly] also means "easily": Plautus [*Bacch.* 85]
. . . It also means "suddenly." Ennius:

where do you go so suddenly   568

*104 Servius, *Commentary on Virgil*

"that the men had come together and decide by the
sword": This is a correct and ancient usage, for he followed
Ennius, who says:

they were determining in discussing momentous   569
    affairs

*105 Servius, *Commentary on Virgil*

"places pliant legs": Ennius about cranes:

they pick their way through the bean field and place   570
    pliant legs

**106 Priscian

iubar [the morning star] they also used to put in both the
masculine and the neuter.[1] Ennius in the *Annals*:

meanwhile the pale morning star flees Hyperion's   571
    course

---

[1] *iubar* is properly the morning star (e.g., Varro, *Ling.* 6.6;
Serv. ad Verg. *Aen.* 4.130); its description here parallels the re-
treat of the *sol albus* at 1 *Ann.* F 43.84.

*107 Isid. *Orig.* 18.36.3

rotis quadrigas currere dicunt sive quia mundus iste circuli sui celeritate transcurrit sive propter solem quia volubili ambitu rotat, sicut ait Ennius:

572   inde patefecit radiis rota candida caelum

*108 Prisc., *GL* II, p. 470.21–23

proprie necatus ferro, nectus vero alia vi peremptus dicitur. Ennius:

573   hos pestis necuit, pars occidit illa duellis

*109 August. *Ep.* 231.3

ego autem quod ait Ennius:

574   omnes mortales sese laudarier optant

partim puto approbandum, partim cavendum.

Cf. August. *De Trin.* 13.3.6.

110 Sen. *Ep.* 102.16

laudat qui laudandum esse iudicat. cum tragicus ille apud nos ait magnificum esse "laudari a laudato viro" [Naev. F 14 *TrRF*], laude digno ait. et cum aeque antiquus poeta ait:

575   laus alit artis

non laudationem dicit, quae corrumpit artes.

---

[1] The quotations, both probably drawn second-hand from Cicero's *Hortensius*, are abridged. The second, almost certainly Ennian, can be scanned as either dactyls or anapests, and so might possibly derive instead from either a tragedy or a satire.

*107 Isidore, *Origins*

They say that a four-horse team runs "on wheels" either because this universe of ours runs its course by the swiftness of its orbit or because of the sun, since it "wheels" in a circular rotation, as Ennius says:

> thereupon the bright wheel [i.e., the sun] reveals the   572
> sky with its rays

*108 Priscian

necatus is properly said of one killed by the sword, but *nectus* of one taken off by some other violent means. Ennius:

> these a plague killed, that other part fell in wars   573

*109 Augustine, *Letters*

For my part, what Ennius says:

> all men wish themselves to be praised   574

I think should be partly approved, partly avoided.

110 Seneca, *Epistles*

He praises who judges that one should be praised. When that well-known tragic poet of ours [Naevius] says it is a wonderful thing "to be praised by a praiseworthy man" [Naev. F 14 *TrRF*], he says that he is deserving of praise. And when the equally ancient poet says:[1]

> praise nourishes the arts   575

he is not speaking of panegyric, which corrupts the arts.

*111 Serv. Dan. ad Verg. *Aen.* 8.361

"lautis mugire carinis": carinae sunt aedificia facta in cari-
narum modum . . . [*add. Serv. Dan.*] alii dicunt carinas
montem nominatum quod ager suburbanus ante portam
carus erat. alii lauta loca legatorum . . . alii quod ibi Sabini
nobiles habitaverint quorum genus invidere et carinare
solebat. carinare autem est obtrectare. Ennius:

576   contra carinantes verba atque obscena profatus

alibi . . . [Inc. *Ann.* F 16].

> atque *codd.*: aeque *Castricomius ap. Merulam*

*112 Cassiod., *GL* VII, p. 207.1–3

"cum" praepositio per *c* scribenda est, "quum" adverbium
temporis, quod significat quando, per *q* scribendum est
discretionis causa, ut apud Ennium:

577   cum legionibus quom proficiscitur induperator

*113 Schol. Bemb. ad Ter. *Haut.* 257

"interea loci": "loci" parhelcon, nam loci omni significa-
tioni addi solet. Ennius:

578   flamma loci postquam concussa est turbine saevo

---

[1] In the Terentian phrase, *loci* is actually partitive genitive,
indicating a point in time, not place (*OLD* 25b). The syntax of
Ennius' isolated line is unclear; *loci* is unlikely to qualify *postquam*.

*111 Servius Danielis, *Commentary on Virgil*

"to bellow in the elegant Carinae district": *carinae* are buildings made in the form of ships' keels [*carinae*]: . . . Others say the *carinae* were named for a mountain, which was a desirable area outside the city by the gate, others that it was an elegant district for ambassadors . . . , others that the Sabine nobility lived there, a class accustomed to envy and to revile. Indeed, *carinare* is to revile. Ennius:

> having uttered against those speaking abuse words   576
> indecent [and?][1]

elsewhere: . . . [Inc. *Ann.* F 16].

[1] It is difficult to see what is joined by *atque*. The Renaissance emendation *aeque* (i.e., "words equally indecent") is possible. Alternatively, *obscena* might be constructed as a neuter noun, *verba atque obscena* = *verba obscena*.

*112 Cassiodorus

cum as preposition should be written with a *c*; the temporal adverb *quum*, which means "when," should be written with a *q* to make the distinction,[1] as in Ennius:

> when the commander departs with the legions   577

[1] So too Quint. *Inst.* 1.7.5. The distinction reflects different etymologies and, in Ennius' time, slightly different pronunciations.

*113 Bembine Scholia to Terence

"in the meantime": *loci* is redundant, for it is customarily added to every indication of a place.[1] Ennius:

> the flame [there?] after it was aroused by a fierce   578
> whirlwind

*114 Consent., *GL* V, p. 400.2–11

scire debemus metaplasmos hos vel a poetis ipsis positos iam in ipsa scriptura fieri, vel nobis, cum ita scandendi aut pronuntiandi necessitas urgebit, faciendos relinqui. poetae faciunt metaplasmos cum ipsi iam scripturam relinquunt corruptam, ut est "relliquias Danaum" [Verg. *Aen.* 1.30] et "tanton me crimine dignum duxisti" [Verg. *Aen.* 10.668]: addit enim unam litteram per metaplasmum *l*, item contra dempsit unam litteram per metaplasmum *e*; sic ut Lucilius "atque ore corupto" [1243 M. = 1255–56 W.]: dempsit enim unam litteram per metaplasmum *r*; et Ennius:

579   huic statuam statui maiorum † orbatur † athenis

et hic quoque per metaplasmum dempsit litteram *r*.

*115 Ps.-Acro ad Hor. *Epist.* 1.13.10

"viribus uteris per clivos flumina lamas": lamas lacunas maiores continentes aquam caelestem. Ennius:

580   silvarum saltus latebras lamasque lutosas

lama est aqua in via stans ex pluvia.

*114 Consentius

We need to understand that these metaplasms [i.e., misplaced letters] either occur in the writing itself already set by the poets themselves or left for us to manufacture when the requirements of scansion or pronunciation so demand. Poets create metaplasms when they themselves leave an error in the text, as is "the lleavings of the Danaans" [Verg. *Aen.* 1.30] and "hav you found me guilty of so great a crime" [Verg. *Aen.* 10.668], for he adds one letter for a metaplasm with *l*, and again, the other way, he removed one letter for a metaplasm with *e*; as so Lucilius "and with corupt mouth" [1243 M. = 1255–56 W.]: he removed one letter for a metaplasm with *r*; and Ennius:

> that to this one of the ancestors a statue is erected [?]   579
>   at Athens [?]

and he too removed the letter *r* for a metaplasm.[1]

[1] The missing *r* must have been felt in what is now the hopelessly corrupt *orbatur. statui*, translated here as a present passive infinitive, could equally well be perfect active indicative, i.e., "I erected a statue to this ancestor." The line is sometimes assigned to the *Scipio*. See Suerbaum 1968, 247–48.

*115 Ps.-Acro, *Commentary on Horace*

"use your strength over hills, streams, bogs": *lamae* [bogs] are rather large pools containing rain water. Ennius:

> woodland glades and remote places and muddy bogs   580

lama is rain water standing on the surface.

*116 Schol. Veron. ad Verg. *Aen.* 5.241 (vol. 3.2, p. 433.17 Th.-H.)

"et pater ipse manu magna Portunus euntem impulit": Ennius:

581   atque manu magna Romanos impulit amnis

*117 Comm. Bern. in Lucan. 1.6

"infestisque obvia signis signa pares aquilas et pila minantia pilis": Ennii versus:

582   pila retunduntur venientibus obvia pilis

*118 Varro, *Ling.* 7.100

apud Ennium

583   decretum est stare ‹et fossari› corpora telis

hoc verbum Ennii dictum a fodiendo; a quo fossa.

    et fossari *add. Bergk*

*119 *Bell. Hisp.* 31.6–7

ita cum clamor esset intermixtus gemitu gladiorumque crepitus auribus oblatus, imperitorum mentes timore praepediebat. [7] hic, ut ait Ennius:

584   premitur pede pes atque armis arma teruntur

adversariosque vehementissime pugnantes nostri agere coeperunt.

*116 Scholia Veronensia to Virgil, *Aeneid*

"and Father Portunus himself with a mighty hand drove him on as he went": Ennius:

> and with a mighty hand the stream drove on the   581
> Romans

*117 Commenta Bernensia on Lucan

"with standards against hostile standards, eagles matched, and javelins threatening javelins": a verse of Ennius:

> the javelins facing the oncoming javelins are blunted   582

*118 Varro, *On the Latin Language*

In Ennius:

> it was decided to stand ‹and be dug through› their   583
> bodies by missiles

This word was used by Ennius from *fodere* [to dig], from which comes *fossa* [ditch].

*119 Anonymous, *On the Spanish Campaign*

And so, as shouting was mingled with groans and the clatter of swords struck the ears, the raw troops' minds were impeded by fear. [7] Here, as Ennius says:

> foot is pressed against foot, and weapons ground   584
> down on weapons

and our men began to drive back their opponents, though they fought fiercely.

421

*120 Auson. *Technop*. 13.3

Ennius ut memorat repleat te

585   laetificum gau

liquida mens hominum concretum felle coquat pus . . .
[17] unde Rudinus ait

586   divom domus, altisonum cael

et cuius de more quod adstruit

587   endo suam do

aut de fronde loquens cur dicit

588   populea frun-

et quod nonnumquam praesumit "laetificum gau."

 588 populea fruns *Ausonius*: populeas frundes *e.g., Skutsch*

Cf. Charis., *GL* I, p. 278.21–24 = p. 367 B.; Diom., *GL* I,
p. 441.31–34; Mar. Victorin., *GL* VI, p. 56.6–9; Inc. *De ult. syll.*,
GL IV, p. 263.12–13; Consent. *De barb.*, *GL* V, p. 388.22–24.

*121 Cic. *Att*. 6.2.8

ain tandem, Attice, laudator integritatis et elegantiae nos-
trae?

589 ausus es hoc ex ore tuo

inquit Ennius . . .

*120 Ausonius, *Technopaegnion*

As Ennius says, let

joy-making happi[1]   585

fill you. Let the jaundiced minds of men concoct gall-clotted pus . . . [17] How is it that the man from Rudiae says

home of the gods, high-sounding heav   586

and what he heaps on in his characteristic way,

into his dom   587

or, speaking of a leaf, why he says,

poplar folia-   588

and because he sometimes anticipates "joy-making happi."

[1] The authenticity of this phrase is questionable; the others are more likely to be genuine. The apocope of *do*[*mus*] probably intends to sound Homeric. Hellenistic effects are suspected in the other examples: see Zetzel 1974, and Skutsch ad loc. Given Ennius' inclination toward the parody of epic diction in the *Satires* (F 3, 5, 15, 19), assignment of these fragments to the *Annals* cannot be certain.

*121 Cicero, *Letters to Atticus*

Do you really mean it, Atticus, you encomiast of my fastidious rectitude?

you have dared this from your own lips   589

as Ennius says . . .

*122 Cic. *Rep.* 1.3

quemadmodum

590   urbes magnas atque imperiosas

ut appellat Ennius, viculis et castellis praeferendas puto,
sic . . .

*123 Varro, *Ling.* 5.65

idem hi dei Caelum et Terra Iuppiter et Iuno, quod, ut ait
Ennius "istic est is Iuppiter . . ." [Inc. F 9]. quod hinc om-
nes et sub hoc, eundem appellans dicit:

591   divomque hominumque pater, rex

*124 Cic. *Nat. D.* 2.4

quod ni ita esset, qui potuisset adsensu omnium dicere
Ennius . . . [*Trag.* F 134], illum vero et Iovem et domina-
torem rerum et omnia nutu regentem, et, ut idem Ennius:

592   patrem divomque hominumque

et praesentem ac praepotentem deum.

Cf. *Ibid.* 64; Min. Fel. *Oct.* 19.

*125 Varro, *Ling.* 7.41

apud Ennium "orator . . ." [6 *Ann.* F 17]. orator dictus ab
oratione. qui enim verba {orationum} haberet publice
adversus eum quo legabatur ab oratione orator dictus.
cum res maior oratione ‹egebat› [*Stroux*: maiore ratione

*122 Cicero, *On the Republic*

For the same reason that

cities great and powerful 590

as Ennius calls them, are, I think, to be ranked above small villages and strongholds, thus . . .

*123 Varro, *On the Latin Language*

These same gods Sky and Earth are Jupiter and Juno because, as Ennius says, "That one is Jupiter . . ." [Inc. F 9]. Because all things come from him and are under him, he says, addressing the same god:

of gods and men father, king 591

*124 Cicero, *On the Nature of the Gods*

If this were not so, how could Ennius have said with everyone's approval . . . [*Trag.* F 134]; he is indeed Jupiter and ruler of the universe, governing all things by his nod and, as the same Ennius says:

father of gods and of men 592

both an ever-present and ever-powerful god.

*125 Varro, *On the Latin Language*

In Ennius "the envoy . . ." [6 *Ann.* F 17]. *orator* [envoy] is derived from "oration," for one who spoke publicly before the one to whom he was sent is called an "orator" because of his oration. When a quite serious matter required a

cod.], legabantur potissimum qui causam commodissime orare poterant. itaque Ennius ait:

593   oratores doctiloqui

*126 Varro, *Ling*. 7.103–4

multa animalium vocibus tralata in homines, partim . . . aperta, partim obscura. perspicua ut Ennius . . . [Inc. *Ann.* F 34] . . . ; [104] minus aperta ut . . . Ennii a vitulo . . . [Inc. F 14]; eiusdem a bove:

594   clamore bovantes

eiusdem a leone:

595   pausam fecere fremendi

eiusdem ab ⟨ha⟩edo . . . [Inc. *Ann.* F 85].

*127 Paul. *Fest*., p. 6.4–6 L.

ADGRETUS: apud Ennium

596   adgretus fari

pro eo quod est adgressus ponitur; quod verbum venit a Graeco ⟨ἐγείρομαι⟩, surgo.

*128 Paul. *Fest*., p. 317.11–12 L.

RUNA genus teli significat. Ennius:

597   runata recedit

id est proeliata.

speech, those most particularly were selected, who were able to plead the case most effectively. And so Ennius says:

> envoys learned of speech 593

*126 Varro, *On the Latin Language*

Many terms are transferred from the cries of animals to people, some of which . . . are obvious, some obscure. Clear terms, as Ennius' . . . [Inc. *Ann.* F 34] . . . ; [104] less clear as . . . Ennius' from a calf . . . [Inc. F 14]; and of the same poet from an ox:

> bellowing with the clamor 594

of the same poet from a lion:

> they made a stop to the roaring 595

of the same poet from a goat . . . [Inc. *Ann.* F 85] .

*127 Paul the Deacon, *Epitome of Festus*

adgretus: in Ennius:

> having stepped forward to speak 596

is put in place of *adgressus*, which word comes from the Greek ‹ἐγείρομαι›, i.e., *surgo* [I rise up].

*128 Paul the Deacon, *Epitome of Festus*

runa means a type of spear. Ennius:

> the *runa*-equipped gives way[1] 597

that is, having given battle.

---

[1] The subject is feminine, probably a military unit, *cohors* or *manus*.

**129 Paul. *Fest.*, p. 388.25–36 L.

SOSP<ES salvum significat>. omnes fer{r}e auc<tores sic
utuntur>: Afranius [*Tog.* 132 R.^{2–3}] . . . <Vergilius. . .> [*Aen.*
8.470] . . . ; Enn<ius [*Trag.* F 186] . . . ; Acc<ius [*Trag.* 695
R.^{2–3}] . . .>. set Ennius vid<etur servatorem signi>ficare
cum dix<it l. Iove

598   sospite> liber

quo sospite *suppl. Orsini*: Iove sospite *Skutsch*

Cf. Paul. *Fest.*, p. 389.6–7 L.

*130 Charis., *GL* I, p. 83.21–25 = p. 105 B.

celer celerior celerrimus facit. nam quod Ennius ait:

599   equitatus iit celerissimus

barbarismus est.

iit *Baehrens*: ut *codd.*

*131 Charis., *GL* I, p. 141.24–27 = p. 179 B.

Caesar in analogicis harum partum . . . et Ennius:

600   iamque fere quattuor partum

quoniam ab hac parte facit et has partes.

**129 Paul the Deacon, *Epitome of Festus*

sosp⟨es means "safe"⟩. Nearly all authors use it this way:
Afranius [*Tog.* 132 R.$^{2-3}$] . . . ; ⟨Virgil⟩ [*Aen.* 8.470] . . . ;
Ennius [*Trag.* F 186] . . . ; Acc⟨ius [*Trag.* 695 R.$^{2-3}$] . . .⟩.
But Ennius seems ⟨to mean one who saves⟩ when he said
⟨in Book—, Jupiter

savior⟩ free   598

*130 Charisius

celer [swift] produces *celerior, celerrimus* [swifter, swift-
est], for what Ennius says:

the cavalry went most swiftly   599

is a barbarism.[1]

[1] Untrue. The correct explanation of this apparently incorrect
superlative is provided by Priscian, Inc. *Ann.* F 41.

*131 Charisius

Caesar in his work on analogy has "of these parts" [*partum*,
an uncommon genitive pl.] . . . and Ennius:

and at about then of the four parts   600

since from "this part" he also makes "these parts."

*132 Serv. ad Verg. *Aen.* 1.51

"furentibus Austris": figura est celebrata apud Vergilium
et est species pro genere. legerat apud Ennium

601   furentibus ventis

sed quasi asperum fugit et posuit austris pro ventis.

*133 Serv. ad Verg. *Aen.* 6.705

"praenatat" praeterfluit, et contrarie dictum est. nam non
natant aquae sed nos in ipsis natamus. Ennium igitur secu-
tus est qui ait:

602   fluctusque natantes

*134 Serv. ad Verg. *Aen.* 9.37

"hostis adest heia": hic distinguendum ut "heia" militum
sit properantium clamor. et est Ennianum qui ait:

603   heia machaeras

ergo heia ingenti clamore dicentes ad portas ruebant. alii
"hostis adest, heia" legunt.

*132 Servius, *Commentary on Virgil*

"with raging Austers [South Winds]": This is a well-known figure in Virgil, and is naming the specific for the general. He had read in Ennius

with raging winds   601

but he avoided it as harsh and put *Austris* for "winds."[1]

[1] Virgil also avoided the archaic scansion *furēntĭbŭs vēntīs*, as in Inc. *Ann.* F 136.

*133 Servius, *Commentary on Virgil*

praenatat [swims by], *praeterfluit* [flows by]. The expression is also reversed, for waters do not swim, but we swim in them. He therefore followed Ennius, who says:

and swimming billows   602

*134 Servius, *Commentary on Virgil*

"the enemy is here, hey": Here it should be punctuated so that *heia* is the clamor of the soldiers rushing forward. It comes from Ennius, who says:

hey! the swords   603

Thus, while saying "hey" with an immense clamor, they began rushing to the gates. Others read, "The enemy is here! Hey!"[1]

[1]Servius wrestles with the fact that the force of exclamatory *heia*, which ranges from concession to astonishment to urgency, can be hard to pin down . . . much less to translate.

*135 Non., p. 190.20–21 M. = 280 L.

ARMENTA genere neutro plerumque, feminino Ennius:

604   ipsus ad armentas eosdem

*136 Serv. ad Verg. *Aen.* 11.27–28

"quem non virtutis egentem / abstulit atra dies et funere mersit acerbo": Ennii versus est:

605   (quem?) non virtutis egentem

*137 Serv. ad Verg. *Aen.* 12.115

"lucemque elatis naribus efflant": Ennianus versus est ordine commutato. ille enim ait:

606   funduntque elatis naribus lucem

Cf. Mar. Victorin., *GL* VI, p. 28.3–7.

*138 Serv. Dan. ad Verg. *Aen.* 12.294

"teloque . . . trabali": Ennius:

607   teloque trabali

*139 Gloss. Philox. *AP* 7

APLUSTRA: πτερὸν πλοίου ὥς Ἔννιος:

608   aplustra

Paul. *Fest.*, p. 9.10–11 L.

---

[1] That is, the fan-shaped sternpost, curving back toward the bow, its ribs both recalling the feathers of a wing and explaining the plural form for what is in fact a single object. The term is borrowed from Greek, ἄφλαστον (pl. at Hdt. 6.114).

*135 Nonius

armenta [cattle] mostly in the neuter gender, Ennius has it in the feminine:

> he himself to the cattle, the same men[1]   604

[1] Sense and syntax are obscure, and no proposed emendation has won wide acceptance.

*136 Servius, *Commentary on Virgil*

"whom, not lacking in courage, black day took away and plunged in bitter death": It is a verse of Ennius:

> (whom?)[1] not lacking in courage   605

[1] Whether Virgil's relative pronoun was part of the phrase he borrowed is uncertain, nor is it clear from Servius' comment that the Ennian echo ended with *egentem*.

*137 Servius, *Commentary on Virgil*

"and light from uplifted nostrils they breathe out": It is an Ennian verse with the order reversed. For he says:

> and they pour out from uplifted nostrils light   606

*138 Servius Danielis, *Commentary on Virgil*

"and with a spear stout as a beam": Ennius:

> and with a spear stout as a beam   607

*139 *A Glossary*

aplustra: the fan [lit., "wing"] of a ship, as Ennius:

> the sternpost[1]   608

*140 Serv. ad Verg. *Aen.* 7.683

"gelidumque Anienem": Anio fluvius haud longe ab urbe est. sed hic euphoniam secutus est; nam Ennius

609   Anionem

dixit iuxta regulam.

*141 Paul. *Fest.*, p. 4.20–23 L.

AMBACTUS apud Ennium lingua Gallica servus appellatur. am praepositio loquelaris significat circum, unde supra ambactus id est circumactus dicitur.

610   ambactus

Cf. *Gloss. Philox. AM 11 ambactus*: δοῦλος μισθωτὸς ὡς Ἔννιος ("a slave for hire, as in Ennius").

*142 Isid. *Orig.* 10.270

teterrimus pro fero nimium. tetrum enim veteres pro fero dixerunt, ut Ennius:

611   tetros elephantos

*143 Porph. ad Hor. *Carm.* 1.9.1

"vides ut alta stet nive . . .": stet autem plenum sit significat, ut Ennius:

612   stant pulvere campi

et Vergilius "iam pulvere caelum / stare vident" [*Aen.* 12.407–8].

*140 Servius, *Commentary on Virgil*

"and the cool Anio": The Anio is a river not far from the city, but here he pursued euphony, for Ennius said:

the Anio

609

following the rule.[1]

---

[1] At issue is the declension of the name, whether *Anio, Anionis* (Ennius) or *Anien, Anienis* (Virgil).

*141 Paul the Deacon, *Epitome of Festus*

ambactus in Ennius is a word for a slave in the Gallic language. The prepositional prefix *am* in that language means "around"; from which comes the above *ambactus*, i.e., one driven around.

ambactus

610

*142 Isidore, *Origins*

teterrimus for something extremely fierce, for the ancients said *tetrum* for *ferus* [fierce], as Ennius:

ferocious elephants

611

*143 Porphyrio, *Commentary on Horace*

"do you see how thick with snow stands . . .": *stet* [stands] indicates "is full," as Ennius:

the plains stand thick with dust

612

and Virgil: "now they see the sky appear thick with dust" [*Aen.* 12.407–8].

435

*144 Diom., *GL* I, p. 385.15–30

possum tamen nonnulli veterum et passiva declinatione
figurant, potestur et possuntur; et quitur et quitus sum
apud nonnullos veterum reprimus . . . Accius quitus sum
ponit [*Trag.* 662 R.$^{2-3}$] . . . Caecilius "si non sarciri quitur"
[*Com.* 279 R.$^{2-3}$]. item potestur apud Ennium reperimus:

613   nec retrahi ∪ ∪ – ∪ potestur
imperiis

*145 Schol. Bern. ad Verg. *G.* 4.7

"laeva": prospera. "numina laeva" secundum haruspici-
nam dixit sinistrum prosperum, ut in secundo "intonuit
laevum" [*Aen.* 2.693], quia sinistra nostra dextera sunt ei
et dextera nostra sinistra sunt ei, ut Ennius ait:

615   ab laeva rite probatum

**146 Schol. Veron. ad Verg. *Aen.* 10.8 (vol. 3.2, p. 443.16
Th.-H.)

(abnueram: E)nnius Anna(lium):

616   haec abnu⟨eram⟩

    suppl. Mai

*144 Diomedes

Some ancients nevertheless also conjugate *possum* [I can] with the passive forms *potestur* and *possuntur*; we also find *quitur* and *quitus sum* among some ancients . . . Accius uses *quitus sum* [*Trag.* 662 R.[2-3]] . . . Caecilius "if it cannot [*quitur*] be fixed" [*Com.* 279 R.[2-3]]. Similarly, we find *potestur* in Ennius:

> nor is he enabled . . . to be drawn back   613
> by commands[1]

[1] The meter is uncertain. If scanned as dactylic, the *Annals* is the likely source, but bacchiacs or trochees would suggest a play, a satire, or perhaps the *Scipio*.

*145 Scholia Bernensia to Virgil, *Georgics*

laeva [on the left]: favorable. "Favorable powers" he said in accord with divination that the left is favorable, as in the second book "thundered on the left" [*Aen.* 2.693], since our left is his right and our right is his left, as Ennius says:[1]

> from the left duly approved   615

[1] For the left as the favorable side for an omen, cf. Cic. *Div.* 1.12, and Inc. *Ann.* F 81.

**146 Scholia Veronensia to Virgil, *Aeneid*

("I had refused": E)nnius in the *Anna(ls)*

> ⟨I had⟩ refused these things   616

147 Sacerd., *GL* VI, p. 468.1–6

synecdoche est oratio plus minusve dicens quam neces-
saria postulat significatio . . . per id quod dicitur illud quod
sequitur:

617   rex ambas ultra fossam protendere coepit

subauditur enim manus.

> protendere *Lachmann*: retinere *codd.*

148 Pomp., *GL* V, p. 291.3–5

[fiunt soloecismi] per genera verborum, si utaris passiva
declinatione pro activa ut

618   despoliantur eos et corpora nuda relinquont

pro eo quod est spoliant.

> despoliantur *Cancik*: spoliantur *Pomp., Donat.*

Cf. Donat., *GL* IV, p. 394.6–9; *Explan. in Donat., GL* IV, p. 564.

149 Charis., *GL* I, p. 267.9–10 = p. 352 B.

[ut ait Cominianus] soloecismus . . . fit . . . per personas ut

619   vosque Lares tectum nostrum qui funditus curant

147 Sacerdos

synecdoche is an expression saying more or less than the minimum meaning requires . . . from that which is said, the other thing that follows ‹is understood›:

> the king began to stretch both across the trench   617

for "hands" is understood.

148 Pompeius

[solecisms come about] through the types of words, if you use a passive formation in place of an active one, as

> they despoil them and leave their bodies bare   618

for that which it is they spoil.

149 Charisius

[As Cominianus says,] solecism . . . comes about . . . through characterizations, as

> and you, household gods, they[1] who care for our roof   619
> from the foundation

---

[1] The grammarians Donatus (*GL* IV, p. 394.13–14; *Explan. in Don.*, *GL* IV, p. 564.7–9) and Pompeius (*GL* V, p. 237.11–22) cite from an unidentified tragedy a second example of a relative clause with a third-person verb modifying a vocative: *Danai, qui parent Atridis, quam primum arma sumite* ("Danaans, who obey the sons of Atreus, take up arms as soon as possible," *Adesp.* F 155 *TrRF*).

150 Diom., *GL* I, p. 447.3–4

parhomoeon fit cum verba similiter incipiunt ut

620 machina multa minax minitatur maxima muris

  minitatur *Vahlen*: minatur *codd.*

151 *Fragm. de metr.*, *GL* VI, p. 615.17–18

duodecasyllabos spondiazon:

621 olli creterris ex auratis hauserunt

*152 Serv. ad Verg. *Aen.* 6.779

"viden ut geminae stant": "den" naturaliter longa est, bre-
vem tamen eam posuit secutus Ennium, et adeo eius est
immutata natura ut iam ubique brevis inveniatur:

622   viden ⟨ut⟩

suppl. Skutsch

*153 Paul. *Fest.*, p. 51.21–22 L.

CREBRISURO apud Ennium significat vallum crebris suris,
id est palis munitum:

623   crebrisuro

150 Diomedes

parhomoeon comes about when words begin similarly, as

> many a menacing machine menaces much the 620
> muniments[1]

[1] The apparent parody at Catullus 115.8 (*mentula multa minax*) supports identification of the line as Ennian rather than (with Warmington) as a grammarian's invention.

151 *Anonymous metrical treatise*

twelve-syllable spondiazon:[1]

> they drew off from golden bowls 621

[1] Four other Ennian lines of similar metrical shape survive: 1 *Ann.* F 25; 2 *Ann.* F 3.117; 5 *Ann.* F 2; 8 *Ann.* F 12.286.

*152 Servius, *Commentary on Virgil*

"do you see how the twin [crests] stand . . .": *-den* is naturally long. Nevertheless, he made it short following Ennius, and its nature is so changed that it is now found short everywhere:

> do you see ⟨how⟩ 622

*153 Paul the Deacon, *Epitome of Festus*

crebrisuro in Ennius means a rampart thick with stakes, i.e., fortified by poles:

> thick with stakes[1] 623

[1] For *surus* [stake] see Inc. *Ann.* F 80.

441

FRAGMENTA EX ANNALIBUS DUBIA

A small set of quotations, possible quotations, and poetic echoes in ancient sources has sometimes been thought to preserve Ennian verses or Ennian vocabulary derived from the Annals, though editors differ concerning what to

1–2 *CIL* VIII 27790 (= *CLE* 2294)

advena quam lenis celeri vehit unda vegeiia

Idem:

hinc legio stlattis iam transportaverat amne

DOUBTFUL FRAGMENTS OF
THE *ANNALS*

*include under this heading. What follows is Skutsch's col-
lection of such* Dubia. *Of this material, he considered F 7,
11, 13, and 14 the most likely to contain authentic rem-
nants of the* Annals.

1–2 An Inscription (third century AD)

[A mosaic depicts ships arranged in a circular pattern.
There are labels, and some have brief poetic quotations
attached, two of which are possibly Ennian]:

> the foreigner,[1] whom the gentle billow conveys in a
> swift skiff

[The same]:

> from here the legion in transports had by now
> crossed the stream[2]

[1] Perhaps the Great Mother, brought to Rome from Asia Mi-
nor in 205 BC (Liv. 29.10.4–11.8).

[2] The mosaic reads *amne*, most easily understood as *amne‹m›*,
i.e., the accusative object. An ablative is more difficult, perhaps
denoting means with the verb intransitive, i.e. "had crossed via
the stream."

3 Cic. *Tusc.* 1.10

dic quaeso num te illa terrent: triceps apud inferos Cerberus, Cocyti fremitus, transvectio Acherontis, "mento summam attingens aquam, enectus siti" [*Adesp*. F 49 *TrRF*] Tantalus, tum illud quod

> Sisyphus versat
> saxum sudans nitendo neque proficit hilum,

fortasse etiam inexorabiles iudices, Minos et Rhadamantus?

Cf. Non., pp. 121.5 M. = 174 L.; 353.8 M. = 559 L.

4 Cic. *Att.* 2.15.3

ego vero

> in montis patrios et ad incunabula nostra

pergam.

5 Serv. ad Verg. *Aen.* 4.638

sciendum Stoicos dicere unum esse deum cui nomina variantur pro actibus et officiis . . . hinc est Iovis oratio:

> caelicolae, mea membra, dei, quos nostra potestas
> officiis divisa facit

3 Cicero, *Tusculan Disputations*

Please tell me whether those things frighten you: Cerberus, the three-headed dog of the Underworld, Cocytus' roar, the crossing of Acheron, "touching the water's surface with his chin, worn out with thirst" Tantalus, then the fact that

> Sisyphus rolls
> the stone, sweating in his effort, and does not
> advance a jot

perhaps even the pitiless judges, Minos and Rhadamantus?

4 Cicero, *Letters to Atticus*

Well, I shall go off

> to my native hills and cradle of my birth

5 Servius, *Commentary on Virgil*

One must bear in mind that the Stoics say there is one god, whose names vary with his activities and functions ... from this there is the speech of Jupiter:

> heaven-dwelling gods, my limbs, whom our power
> with its duties distributed made[1]

[1] The syntax is difficult and no reading entirely satisfactory.

6 Serv. ad Verg. *Aen.* 3.384

"Trinacria lentandus remus in unda": et quidem lentandus nove verbum fictum putant, sed in Annalibus legitur:

confrictique oleo, lentati et ad arma parati

a verbo lentor.

7 Victorin., *GL* VI, p. 211.18–22

hexameter versus dactylicus . . . in versu duodecim syllabarum species una est. quippe hic sine ulla varietate omnes in se spondeos habet et vocatur spondiazon, ut est

introducuntur legati Minturnenses

quod genus versificationis usque adeo durum est, ut non invenuste Albinus in libro quem de metris scripsit ita posuerit.

Cf. *Fragm. de Spec. hex.*, *GL* VI, p. 634.10–28; Aldhelm. *Ep. ad. Acirc.*, MCH AA 15.84.

6 Servius, *Commentary on Virgil*

"you must bend your oar on the Sicilian sea": and indeed, they think "bend" is a word invented from scratch, but it is read in the *Annals*:

> and rubbed with oil, made flexible and prepared for
>   arms

from the verb "to be bent."

7 Marius Victorinus

the hexameter is a dactylic verse. . . . One kind has twelve syllables in the verse, and indeed, without any variation it contains all spondees and is called a spondiazon, as is

> the envoys from Minturnae are given audience[1]

which kind of versification is so entirely harsh that Albinus,[2] in the book he wrote on meters, not unattractively declared it so.

[1] The verb *introduco* is the technical term for appearing before the Roman Senate. The town of Minturnae on the Appian Way at the border of Latium and Campania sent a delegation to Rome in 207 BC to claim exemption from military service (Liv. 27.38.3–5), one possible context for what may well be an authentic line of Ennius.

[2] The Albinus in question is uncertain. See Kaster 1988, 382–83. Five such twelve-syllable lines are found among the securely attested fragments: Inc. *Ann.* F 31, 117, 157, 286, and 621.

8 Max. Victor., *GL* VI, pp. 216.13–17.4

Ennius quoque ait "vita illa dignus locoque" quasi dignu'
locoque dixerit. similiter Lucilius ait

   tum lateralis dolor, certissimus nuntius mortis

quasi subtractis tribus s litteris.

9 Liv. 22.49.3

tum renuntianti cuidam iussisse consulem ad pedes de-
scendere equites dixisse Hannibalem ferunt:

   quam mallem vinctos mihi traderet

10 Cic. *De or.* 3.167

"Africa terribili tremit horrida terra tumultu" [9 *Ann.* F 7];
pro Afris est sumpta Africa, neque factum est verbum ut

      mare saxifragis undis

neque translatum ut "mollitur mare" [Pac. *Trag.* 77 R.²⁻³]
. . .

---

1 The phrase may well be anapestic and, like Cicero's other
counterexample, taken from Pacuvius.

8 Maximus Victorinus

Ennius too, says "deserving that life and station," as if he had said "deservin' station." Similarly, Lucilius says,[1]

> then pain in the side, a most certain harbinger of
> death

as if with three *s*'s taken away.

[1] The first phrase quoted by Victorinus is attested for Lucilius by Cicero, Quintilian, and Nonius (150 M. = 173 W.). Marx then attributes the second quotation to Lucilius as well (1314 M., not in W.), but the names of the two poets may have been reversed in transmission. At issue is the failure of final -*s* to make position in early Latin verse.

9 Livy, *History of Rome*

Then to someone announcing that the consul had ordered his cavalry to dismount,[1] they report that Hannibal said:

> how I would have preferred that he hand them to me
> in chains

[1] The consul is L. Aemilius Paullus, who fell at Cannae. Cf. Plut. *Fab.* 16.5.

10 Cicero, *On the Orator*

"Africa, shuddering, trembles with a terrible tumult" [9 *Ann.* F 7], for "Africans" is substituted "Africa." The word is neither manufactured, like

> the sea with rock-breaking waves[1]

nor metaphorical, like "the sea is softened" [Pac. *Trag.* 77 R.[2-3]] . . .

11 Paul. *Fest.*, p. 31.22–24 L.

BELLICREP(AM)

saltationem dicebant quando cum armis saltabant, quod a
Romulo institutum est ne simile pateretur quod fecerat
ipse cum a ludis Sabinorum virgines rapuit.

12 Paul. *Fest.*, p. 108.13–20 L.

LIBYCUS campus in agro Argeo . . . LEPARESES Liparitani
cives id est Liparenses. LABES macula in vestimento . . .
LATRARE Ennius pro poscere posuit [cf. Inc. *Ann.* F 34].

13 Gloss. Verg. *Aen.* 12.19, ap. Casp. Barthium, *Adversa-
riorum libri* LX (Francofurti 1624) XXXIII 13

O praestans animi iuvenis

est prudens senis dictum . . . est vero ex † seno Ennius
translatum.

ex † seno Ennius *codd.*: *fortasse* ex somnis Ennii *Vahlen*

14 Varro, *Rust.* 2.4

sed quis

e portu post Italico

prodit ac de suillo pecore expedit?

---

1 Skutsch 1978 argues for the attribution of this phrase to
Ennius.

11 Paul the Deacon, *Epitome of Festus*

> war-rattling[1]

is what they used to call the dance when they danced in
armor, which was instituted by Romulus, so he would not
endure something like what he himself had done when he
abducted the Sabine girls from the games.

[1] The word may be Ennian, but the accusative case is certain
only for Festus.

12 Paul the Deacon, *Epitome of Festus*

The Libyan Field is in Argive territory . . . The Lepareses
are the citizens of Lipari, i.e., Liparians. *labes* is a stain on
a garment . . . *latrare* Ennius employed for "to request"
[cf. Inc. *Ann.* F 34].[1]

[1] Skutsch prints *Lepareses* as an Ennian word and considers
labes possibly Ennian, but the pattern of Festus' citations makes
these attributions uncertain.

13 Anonymous gloss on Virgil, *Aeneid*

> O youth, outstanding in spirit

this is the judicious saying of an old man [Latinus] . . . it
is in fact taken from [?] Ennius.

14 Varro, *On Agriculture*

But who sails

> eventually from an Italian port

and expounds on swine?[1]

CONCORDANCES

CONCORDANCE 1
FRL—Vahlen[2]—Warmington

FRL	Vahlen[2]	Warmington
1	1	1
2	5	4
3	6	5
4	8	6
5	69	65
6–7	13–14	11–12
8–10	10–12	7–10
11	15	13
12–13	3–4	2–3
14	17	15
15–16	18–19	18–19
17	20	22–23
18	21	20
19	22	21
20	23	24
21	25	26
22	24	25
23–24	26–27	27–28
25	28	29
26	54	51
27	29	59
28–29	30–31	16–17
30	34	30

CONCORDANCE 1

FRL	Vahlen[2]	Warmington
31	33	31
32	32	78
33	102	79
34–50	35–51	32–48
51	60	57
52	61	58
53	64	62
54–55	65–66	63–64
56	58	56
57	59	55
58–59	52–53	49–50
60	55	52
61–62	56–57	53–54
63–64	67	68–69
65	68	71
66–68	70–72	72–74
69–70	73–74	75–76
71	75	77
72–91	77–96	80–100
92	97	101
93	76	104
94–95	99–100	102–3
96	105	106
97	98	105
98	101	108
99	104	111
100	117	116
101	106	110
102–3	107–8	112–13
104	109	109

FRL	Vahlen[2]	Warmington
105–9	110–14	117–21
110–11	115–16	114–15
112	118	p. 564
113	119	124
114–15	120–21	125–26
116–18	122–24	127–29
119	125	130
120	126	139
121	127	525
122	136	135
123	129	132
124	137	140
125–26	138–39	141–42
127	143	149
128–29	144–45	146–47
130	134	134
131	130	137
132	133	133
133	132	131
134	128	122
135	131	136
136	135	138
137	149	154
138	150	155
139–40	147–48	151–52
141	151	156
142	152	159
143–44	153–54	160–61
145	159	162
146	146	150

FRL	Vahlen[2]	Warmington
147	155	157
148	156	158
149	158	163
150	157	123
151	161	164
152	162	165
153	163	166
154–55	501–2	468–69
156	500	467
157	169	p. 446 no. 2
158	170	474
159	166	167
160	167	170
161	172	168
162	171	169
163	173	171
164	174	173
165	177	178
166	178	172
167	179	174
168	182	179
169	186	180
170–72	183–85	526–28
173–74	416–17	425–26
175–79	187–91	181–85
180–82	192–93	p. 454 nos. 21–22
183–90	194–201	186–93
191–94	208–10	200–202
195–96	205–6	198–99
197–98	180–81	175–76

FRL	Vahlen[2]	Warmington
199–200	202–3	194–95
201	204	196
202	207	197
203–4	175–76	207–8
205	211	205
206–7	213–14	231–32
208–9	215–16	232–34
210	217	235
211–12	218–19	229–30
213	222	271
214	221	237
215	265	316
216	223	238
217	225	248
218	230	245
219	231	246
220–21	521–22	260–61
222	260	255
223–24	262–63	239–40
225–26	266–67	258–59
227–28	164–65	251–52
229	276	p. 448 no. 5
230	256	244
231	524	544
232	258	253
233	257	254
234–35	280–81	276–77
236–37	232–33	256–57
238	252	247
239	253	250

CONCORDANCE 1

FRL	Vahlen[2]	Warmington
240–41	62–63	60–61
242	224	204
243–44	254–55	242–43
245	261	241
246	259	228
247–53	268–73	262–68
254–55	294	295
256–57	*Var.* 4–5	*Scipio* 8–9
258–60	287–89	284–86
261	278	274
262	279	275
263	277	283
264	282	279
265	283	278
266	284	281
267	285	280
268–86	234–51	210–27
287	286	282
288	292	294
289	298	290
290	295	287
291	296	289
292	297	288
293	299	291
294–96	227–29	297–99
297	290	269
298	300	307
299	301	296
300–301	319–20	318–19
302	302	546

FRL	Vahlen[2]	Warmington
303	325	270
304–8	303–8	300–305
309	310	306
310	311	p. 448 no. 4
311	323	317
312–13	312–13	313–14
314	314	315
315	315	308
316	316	312
317–18	317–18	320–21
319–20	321–22	310–11
321	324	309
322–23	326–27	322–23
324	329	325
325	330	p. 564
326–28	343–45	333–35
329	331	326
330–31	332–33	337–38
332–34	340–42	339–41
335	338	330
336	334	331
337–39	335–37	327–29
340–42	—	—
343	348	345
344+45	358–59	349–50
346	328	324
347	346–47	336
348	339	332
349	349	343–44
350	351	342

FRL	Vahlen[2]	Warmington
351	353	p. 454 no. 23
352	354	13
353	355	346
354	366	359
355	363	356
356	364	357
357, 459–60	356–57	347–48
358	365	351
359–60	360–61	354–55
361	352	352
362	362	353
363–65	370–72	360–62
366–68	367–69	363–65
369	378	369
370	606	p. 442 no. 30
371–73	381–83	366–68
374	380	370
375	389	377
376	386	374
377–78	384–85	372–73
379–80	387–88	375–76
381	390	p. 141n
382–83	391–92	378–79
384	393	380
385–86	394–95	381–82
387	396	383
388	397	384
389–90	398–99	385–86
391–98	401–8	409–16
399–400	409	387

FRL	Vahlen[2]	Warmington
401	425	391
402	426	p. 562
403	410	390
404–5	411–12	393–94
406	413	392
407	423	396
408	421	397
409	422	422
410	414	423
411	415	417
412	427	405
413	428	408
414	433	400
415–16	434–35	401–2
417	418	424
418	419	371
419	420	398
420	424	395
421	429	407
422	430	406
423	431	399
424	432	418
425–26	436–37	403–4
427	438	203
428	442	433
429	440	427
430	441	428
431	439	429
432–34	443–45	430–32
435–36	446–47	434–35

FRL	Vahlen[2]	Warmington
437–38	450–51	436–38
439	452	429
440	454	440
441	453	439
442	7	p. 430n
443	160	475
444	456	p. 448 no. 8
445	491	292
446–47	457–58	450–51
448	264	70
449	617	p. 456 no. 25
450	459	487
451	140	143
452	141	144
453	142	145
454	526	*Plays* 395–96
455	168	506
456	373	209
457	488	542
458	564	p. 436 no. 13
459–60	356–57	348
461	455	555
462	226	177
463–64	484–85	443–44
465	486	445
466	479	447
467	480	441
468	495	524
469–70	561–62	547–48
471	503	358

FRL	Vahlen[2]	Warmington
472	220	236
473	293	p. 562
474–75	274–75	272–73
476	535	554
477	496	543
478	523	—
479	507	493
480	587	509
481	584	464
482	379	551
483–84	472–73	501–2
485–86	519–20	499–500
487	2	p. 462 no. 43
488–89	461–62	419–20
490	350	344
491	460	455
492	463	462
493	464	463
494–95	465–66	471–72
496–97	467–68	458–59
498	103	p. 462 no. 40
499	469	480
500–501	470–71	p. 432 nos. 3–4
502	474	513
503	475	p. 563
504	477	148
505	478	442
506	481	446
507	482	537
508	483	538

CONCORDANCE 1

FRL	Vahlen[2]	Warmington
509	487	531
510	489	564
511	490	565
512	492	533
513	493	485
514	494	486
515–16	497–98	534–35
517	499	539
518	309	540
519	400	491
520–21	448–49	514–15
522–23	374–75	388–89
524	376	p. 434 nos. 8–9
525	377	p. 434 no. 10
526	504	249
527	505	490
528	506	492
529	508	483
530	509	p. 440 no. 22
531	510	498
532	511	552
533	512	460
534	513	550
535–39	514–18	517–21
540	525	484
541	527	454
542	528	p. 432 no. 7
543	529	p. 458 no. 30
544	530	488
545	531	421

FRL	Vahlen[2]	Warmington
546	532	479
547	533	p. 460 no. 38
548	534	530
549	536	478
550	537	529
551–52	538–39	481–82
553	540	457
554	541	p. 450 no. 11
555–56	542–43	452–53
557	544	494
558	545	557
559	546	470
560–61	547–48	p. 434 nos. 8–9
562	549	478
563	550	489
564–65	551–52	504–5
566–67	553	516
568	554	510
569	555	456
570	556	563
571	557	559
572	558	558
573	559	476
574	560	549
575	—	—
576	563	p. 436 no. 12
577	565	477
578	566	532
579	567	545
580	568	p. 460 no. 37

CONCORDANCE 1

FRL	Vahlen[2]	Warmington
581	569	541
582	570	495
583	571	511
584	572	507–8
585	574	p. 460 no. 33
586	575	p. 460 no. 34
587	576	p. 460 no. 35
588	577	p. 460 no. 36
589	578	461
590	579	p. 440 no. 21
591	580	449
592	581	448
593	582	p. 430 no. 18
594	585	465
595	586	466
596	588	p. 440 no. 19
597	589	497
598	590	p. 563
599	591–92	522
600	593	556
601	594	561
602	596	536
603	597	523
604	598	p. 442 no. 26
605	599	473
606	600	560
607	601	496
608	602	p. 563
609	603	p. 562
610	605	p. 562

FRL	Vahlen[2]	Warmington
611	607	512
612	608	503
613–14	611–12	p. 440 no. 20
615	613	153
616	—	p. 562
617	618	p. 454 no. 19
618	619	p. 452 no. 18
619	620	p. 450 no. 12
620	621	p. 456 no. 24
621	624	p. 462 no. 39
622	*Inc.* 28	p. 563
623	*Inc.* 35	p. 563

469

CONCORDANCE 2
Vahlen[2]—*FRL*—Warmington

Vahlen[2]	*FRL*	Warmington
1	1	1
2	487	p. 462 no. 43
3–4	12–13	2–3
5	2	4
6	3	5
7	442	p. 430n
8	4	6
10–12	8–10	7–10
13–14	6–7	11–12
15	11	13
17	14	15
18–19	15–16	18–19
20	17	22–23
21	18	20
22	19	21
23	20	24
24	22	25
25	21	26
26–27	23–24	27–28
28	25	29
29	27	59
30–31	28–29	16–17
32	32	78
33	31	31
34	30	30
35–51	34–50	32–48
52–53	58–59	49–50

Vahlen[2]	FRL	Warmington
54	26	51
55	60	52
56–57	61–62	53–54
58	56	56
59	57	55
60	51	57
61	52	58
62–63	240–41	60–61
64	53	62
65–66	54–55	63–64
67	63	68–69
68	65	71
69	5	65
70–72	66–68	72–74
73–74	69–70	75–76
75	71	77
76	93	104
77–96	72–91	80–100
97	92	101
98	97	105
99–100	94–95	102–3
101	98	108
102	33	79
103	498	p. 462 no. 40
104	99	111
105	96	106
106	101	110
107–8	102–3	112–13
109	104	93
110–14	105–9	117–21

Vahlen[2]	*FRL*	Warmington
115–16	110–11	114–15
117	100	116
118	112	p. 564
119	113	124
120–21	114–15	125–26
122–24	116–18	127–29
125	119	130
126	120	139
127	121	525
128	134	122
129	123	132
130	131	137
131	135	136
132	133	131
133	132	133
134	130	134
135	136	138
136	122	135
137	124	140
138–39	125–26	141–42
140	451	143
141	452	144
142	453	145
143	127	149
144–45	128–29	146–47
146	146	150
147–48	139–40	151–52
149	137	154
150	138	155
151	141	156

Vahlen[2]	*FRL*	Warmington
152	142	159
153–54	143–44	160–61
155	147	157
156	148	158
157	150	123
158	149	163
159	145	162
160	443	475
161	151	164
162	152	165
163	153	166
164–65	227–28	251–52
166	159	167
167	160	170
168	455	506
169	157	p. 446 no. 2
170	158	474
171	162	169
172	161	168
173	163	171
174	164	173
175–76	203–4	207–8
177	165	178
178	166	172
179	167	174
180–81	197–98	175–76
182	168	179
183–85	170–72	526–28
186	169	180
187–91	175–79	181–85

CONCORDANCE 2

Vahlen[2]	*FRL*	Warmington
192–93	180–82	p. 454 nos. 21–22
194–201	183–90	186–93
202–3	199–200	194–95
204	201	196
205–6	195–96	198–99
207	202	197
208–10	191–94	200–2
211	205	205
213–14	206–7	231–32
215–16	208–9	232–34
217	210	235
218–19	211–12	229–30
220	472	236
221	214	237
222	213	271
223	216	238
224	242	204
225	217	248
226	462	177
227–29	294–96	297–99
230	218	245
231	219	246
232–33	236–37	256–57
234–51	268–86	210–27
252	238	247
253	239	250
254–55	243–44	242–43
256	230	244
257	233	254
258	232	253

Vahlen[2]	FRL	Warmington
259	246	228
260	222	255
261	245	241
262–63	223–24	239–40
264	448	70
265	215	316
266–67	225–26	258–59
268–73	247–53	262–68
274–75	474–75	272–73
276	229	p. 448 no. 5
277	263	283
278	261	274
279	262	275
280–81	234–35	276–77
282	264	279
283	265	278
284	266	281
285	267	280
286	287	282
287–89	258–60	284–86
290	297	269
292	288	294
293	473	p. 562
294	254–55	295
295	290	287
296	291	289
297	292	288
298	289	290
299	293	291
300	298	307

CONCORDANCE 2

Vahlen[2]	*FRL*	Warmington
301	299	296
302	302	546
303–8	304–8	300–305
309	518	540
310	309	306
311	310	p. 448 no. 4
312–13	312–13	313–14
314	314	315
315	315	308
316	316	312
317–18	317–18	320–21
319–20	300–301	318–19
321–22	319–20	310–11
323	311	317
324	321	309
325	303	270
326–27	322–23	322–23
328	346	324
329	324	325
330	325	p. 564
331	329	326
332–33	330–31	337–38
334	336	331
335–37	337–39	327–29
338	335	330
339	348	332
340–42	332–34	339–41
343–45	326–28	333–35
346–47	347	336
348	343	345

Vahlen[2]	FRL	Warmington
349	349	343–44
350	490	344
351	350	342
352	361	352
353	351	p. 454 no. 23
354	352	13
355	353	346
356–57	357, 459–60	347–48
358–59	344 + 45	349–50
360–61	359–60	354–55
362	362	353
363	355	356
364	356	357
365	358	351
366	354	359
367–69	366–68	363–65
370–72	363–65	360–62
373	456	209
374–75	522–23	388–89
376	524	p. 434 nos. 8–9
377	525	p. 434 no. 10
378	369	369
379	482	551
380	374	370
381–83	371–73	366–68
384–85	377–78	372–73
386	376	374
387–88	379–80	375–76
389	375	377
390	381	p. 141n

Vahlen[2]	FRL	Warmington
391–92	382–83	378–79
393	384	380
394–95	385–86	381–82
396	387	383
397	388	384
398–99	389–90	385–86
400	519	491
401–8	391–98	409–16
409	399–400	387
410	403	390
411–12	404–5	393–94
413	406	392
414	410	423
415	411	417
416–17	173–74	425–26
418	417	424
419	418	371
420	419	398
421	408	397
422	409	422
423	407	396
424	420	395
425	401	391
426	402	p. 562
427	412	405
428	413	408
429	421	407
430	422	406
431	423	399
432	424	418

Vahlen[2]	*FRL*	Warmington
433	414	400
434–35	415–16	401–2
436–37	425–26	403–4
438	427	203
439	431	429
440	429	427
441	430	428
442	428	433
443–45	432–34	430–32
446–47	435–36	434–35
448–49	520–21	514–15
450–51	437–38	436–38
452	439	429
453	441	439
454	440	440
455	461	555
456	444	p. 448 no. 8
457–58	446–47	450–51
459	450	487
460	491	455
461–62	488–89	419–20
463	492	462
464	493	463
465–66	494–95	471–72
467–68	496–97	458–59
469	499	480
470–71	500–501	p. 432 nos. 3–4
472–73	483–84	501–2
474	502	513
475–76	503	p. 563

CONCORDANCE 2

Vahlen[2]	FRL	Warmington
477	504	148
478	505	442
479	466	447
480	467	441
481	506	446
482	507	537
483	508	538
484–85	463–64	443–44
486	465	445
487	509	531
488	457	542
489	510	564
490	511	565
491	445	292
492	512	533
493	513	485
494	514	486
495	468	524
496	477	543
497–98	515–16	534–35
499	517	539
500	156	467
501–2	154–55	468–69
503	471	358
504	526	249
505	527	490
506	528	492
507	479	493
508	529	483
509	530	p. 440 no. 22

480

Vahlen[2]	FRL	Warmington
510	531	498
511	532	552
512	533	460
513	534	550
514–18	535–39	517–21
519–20	485–86	499–500
521–22	220–21	260–61
523	478	—
524	231	544
525	540	484
526	454	*Plays* 395–96
527	541	454
528	542	p. 432 no. 7
529	543	p. 458 no. 30
530	544	488
531	545	421
532	546	479
533	547	p. 460 no. 38
534	548	530
535	476	554
536	549	478
537	550	529
538–39	551–52	481–82
540	553	457
541	554	p. 450 no. 11
542–43	555–56	452–53
544	557	494
545	558	557
546	559	470
547–48	560–61	p. 434 nos. 8–9

Vahlen[2]	FRL	Warmington
549	562	478
550	563	489
551–52	564–65	504–5
553	566–67	516
554	568	510
555	569	456
556	570	563
557	571	559
558	572	558
559	573	476
560	574	549
561–62	469–70	547–48
563	576	p. 436 no. 12
564	458	p. 436 no. 13
565	577	477
566	578	532
567	579	545
568	580	p. 460 no. 37
569	581	541
570	582	495
571	583	511
572	584	507–8
574	585	p. 460 no. 33
575	586	p. 460 no. 34
576	587	p. 460 no. 35
577	588	p. 460 no. 36
578	589	461
579	590	p. 440 no. 21
580	591	449
581	592	448

Vahlen[2]	FRL	Warmington
582–83	593	p. 438 no. 18
584	481	464
585	594	465
586	595	466
587	480	509
588	596	p. 440 no. 19
589	597	497
590	598	p. 563
591–92	599	522
593	600	556
594	601	561
595	—	562
596	602	536
597	603	523
598	604	p. 442 no. 26
599	605	473
600	606	560
601	607	496
602	608	p. 563
603	609	p. 562
605	610	p. 562
606	370	p. 442 no. 30
607	611	512
608	612	503
611–12	613–14	p. 440 no. 20
613	615	153
617	449	p. 456 no. 25
618	617	p. 454 no. 19
619	618	p. 452 no. 18
620	619	p. 450 no. 12

CONCORDANCE 2

Vahlen[2]	*FRL*	Warmington
621	620	p. 456 no. 24
624	621	p. 462 no. 39
Var. 4–5	256–57	*Scipio* 8–9
Inc. 28	622	p. 563
Inc. 35	623	p. 563
—	340–42	—
—	575	—
—	616	p. 562

CONCORDANCE 3
Warmington—*FRL*—Vahlen[2]

Warmington	*FRL*	Vahlen[2]
1	1	1
2–3	12–13	3–4
4	2	5
5	3	6
6	4	8
7–10	8–10	10–12
11–12	6–7	13–14
13	11, 352	15, 354
14	*Sat.* 19	16
15	14	17
16–17	28–29	30–31
18–19	15–16	18–19
20	18	21
21	19	22
22–23	17	20
24	20	23
25	22	24
26	21	25
27–28	23–24	26–27
29	25	28
30	30	34
31	31	33
32–48	34–50	35–51
49–50	58–59	52–53
51	26	54
52	60	55
53–54	61–62	56–57

CONCORDANCE 3

Warmington	*FRL*	Vahlen[2]
55	57	59
56	56	58
57	51	60
58	52	61
59	27	29
60–61	240–41	62–63
62	53	64
63–64	54–55	65–66
65	5	69
68–69	63–64	67
70	448	264
71	65	68
72–74	66–68	70–72
75–76	69–70	73–74
77	71	75
78	32	32
79	33	102
80–100	72–91	77–96
101	92	97
102–3	94–95	99–100
104	93	76
105	97	98
106	96	105
108	98	101
109	104	109
110	101	106
111	99	104
112–13	102–3	107–8
114–15	110–11	115–16
116	100	117

Warmington	*FRL*	Vahlen[2]
117–21	105–9	110–14
122	134	128
123	150	157
124	113	119
125–26	114–15	120–21
127–29	116–18	122–24
130	119	125
131	133	132
132	123	129
133	132	133
134	130	134
135	122	136
136	135	131
137	131	130
138	136	135
139	120	126
140	124	137
141–42	125–26	138–39
143	451	140
144	452	141
145	453	142
146–47	128–29	144–45
148	504	477
149	127	143
150	146	146
151–52	139–40	147–48
153	615	613
154	137	149
155	138	150
156	141	151

CONCORDANCE 3

Warmington	*FRL*	Vahlen[2]
157	147	155
158	148	156
159	142	152
160–61	143–44	153–54
162	145	159
163	149	158
164	151	161
165	152	162
166	153	163
167	159	166
168	161	172
169	162	171
170	160	167
171	163	173
172	166	178
173	164	174
174–76	167, 197–98	179, 180–81
177	462	226
178	165	177
179	168	182
180	169	186
181–85	175–79	187–91
186–93	183–90	194–201
194–95	199–200	202–3
196	201	204
197	202	207
198–99	195–96	205–6
200–202	191–94	208–10
203	427	438
204	242	224

Warmington	*FRL*	Vahlen[2]
205	205	211
207–8	203–4	175–76
209	456	373
210–27	268–86	234–51
228	246	259
229–30	211–12	218–19
231–32	206–7	213–14
232–34	208–9	215–16
235	210	217
236	472	230
237	214	221
238	216	223
239–40	223–24	262–63
241	245	261
242–43	243–44	254–55
244	230	256
245	218	230
246	219	231
247	238	252
248	217	225
249	526	504
250	239	253
251–52	227–28	164–65
253	232	258
254	233	257
255	222	260
256–57	236–37	232–33
258–59	225–26	266–67
260–61	220–21	521–22
262–68	247–53	268–73

CONCORDANCE 3

Warmington	*FRL*	Vahlen[2]
269	297	290
270	303	325
271	213	222
272–73	474–75	274–75
274	261	278
275	262	279
276–77	234–35	280–81
278	265	283
279	264	282
280	267	285
281	266	284
282	287	286
283	263	277
284–86	258–60	287–89
287	290	295
288	292	297
289	291	296
290	289	298
291	293	299
292	445	491
293	—	291
294	288	292
295	254–55	294
296	299	301
297–99	294–96	227–29
300–305	304–8	303–7
306	309	310
307	298	300
308	315	315
309	321	324

Warmington	*FRL*	Vahlen[2]
310–11	319–20	321–22
312	316	316
313–14	312–13	312–13
315	314	314
316	215	265
317	311	323
318–19	300–301	319–20
320–21	317–18	317–18
322–23	322–23	326–27
324	346	328
325	324	329
326	329	331
327–29	337–39	335–37
330	335	338
331	336	334
332	348	339
333–35	326–28	343–45
336	347	346
337–38	330–31	332–33
339–41	332–34	340–42
342	350	351
343–44	349, 490	350
345	343	348
346	353	355
347–48	357, 459–60	356–57
349–50	369	378
351	358	365
352	361	352
353	362	362
354–55	359–60	360–61

CONCORDANCE 3

Warmington	*FRL*	Vahlen[2]
356	355	363
357	356	364
358	471	503
359	354	366
360–62	363–65	370–72
363–65	366–68	363–65
366–68	371–73	366–68
369	369	378
370	374	380
371	418	419
372–73	377–78	384–85
374	376	386
375–76	379–80	387–88
377	375	389
378–79	382–83	391–92
380	384	393
381–82	385–86	394–95
383	387	396
384	388	397
385–86	389–90	398–99
387	399–400	409
388–89	522–23	374–75
390	403	410
391	401	425
392	406	413
393–94	404–5	411–12
395	420	424
396	407	423
397	408	421
398	419	420

Warmington	*FRL*	Vahlen[2]
399	423	431
400	414	433
401–2	415–16	434–35
403–4	425–26	436–37
405	412	427
406	422	430
407	421	429
408	413	428
409–16	391–98	401–8
417	411	415
418	424	432
419–20	488–89	461–62
421	545	531
422	409	422
423	410	414
424	417	418
425–26	173–74	416–17
427	429	440
428	430	441
429	431	439
430–32	432–34	443–45
433	428	442
434–35	435–36	446–47
436–38	437–39	450–52
439	441	453
440	440	454
441	467	480
442	505	478
443–44	463–64	484–85
445	465	486

CONCORDANCE 3

Warmington	*FRL*	Vahlen[2]
446	506	481
447	466	479
448	592	581
449	591	580
450–51	446–47	457–58
452–53	555–56	542–43
454	541	527
455	491	460
456	569	555
457	553	540
458–59	496–97	467–68
460	533	512
461	589	578
462	492	463
463	493	464
464	481	584
465	594	585
466	595	586
467	156	500
468–69	154–55	501–2
470	559	546
471–72	494–95	465–66
473	605	599
474	158	170
475	443	160
476	573	559
477	577	565
478	562	549
479	546	532
480	499	469

494

Warmington	*FRL*	Vahlen[2]
481–82	551–52	538–39
483	529	508
484	540	525
485	513	493
486	514	494
487	450	459
488	544	530
489	563	550
490	527	505
491	519	400
492	528	506
493	479	507
494	557	544
495	582	570
496	607	601
497	597	589
498	531	510
499–500	485–86	519–20
501–2	483–84	472–73
503	612	608
504–5	564–65	551–52
506	455	168
507–8	584	572
509	480	587
510	568	554
511	583	571
512	611	607
513	502	474
514–15	520–21	448–49
516	566–67	553

Warmington	*FRL*	Vahlen[2]
517–21	535–39	514–18
522	599	591–92
523	603	597
524	468	495
525	121	127
526–28	170–72	183–85
529	550	537
530	548	534
531	509	487
532	578	566
533	512	492
534–35	515–16	497–98
536	602	596
537	507	482
538	508	483
539	517	499
540	518	309
541	581	569
542	457	488
543	477	496
544	231	524
545	579	567
546	302	302
547–48	469–70	561–62
549	574	560
550	534	513
551	482	379
552	532	511
553	549	536
554	476	535

Warmington	*FRL*	Vahlen[2]
555	461	455
556	600	593
557	558	545
558	572	558
559	571	557
560	606	600
561	601	594
562	—	595
563	570	556
564	510	489
565	511	490
Plays 395–96	454	526
Scipio 8–9	256–57	*Var.* 4–5
p. 430n	442	7
p. 432 nos. 3–4	500–501	470–71
p. 432 no. 7	542	528
p. 434 nos. 8–9	524	376
p. 434 nos. 8–9	560–61	547–48
p. 434 no. 10	525	377
p. 436 nos. 12–13	458	564
p. 436 nos. 12–13	576, 458	563, 564
p. 438 no. 18	593	582
p. 440 no. 19	596	588
p. 440 no. 20	613–14	611–12
p. 440 no. 21	590	579
p. 440 no. 22	530	509
p. 442 no. 26	604	598
p. 442 no. 30	370	606
p. 446 no. 2	157	169
p. 448 no. 4	310	311

CONCORDANCE 3

Warmington	*FRL*	Vahlen[2]
p. 448 no. 5	229	276
p. 448 no. 8	444	456
p. 450 no. 11	554	541
p. 450 no. 12	619	620
p. 452 no. 18	618	619
p. 454 no. 19	617	618
p. 454 nos. 21–22	180–82	192–93
p. 454 no. 23	353	351
p. 456 no. 24	620	621
p. 456 no. 25	449	617
p. 458 no. 30	543	529
p. 460 no. 33	585	574
p. 460 no. 34	586	575
p. 460 no. 35	587	576
p. 460 no. 36	588	577
p. 460 no. 37	580	568
p. 460 no. 38	547	533
p. 462 no. 39	621	624
p. 462 no. 40	498	103
p. 462 no. 43	487	2
p. 563	622	*Inc.* 28
p. 563	623	*Inc.* 35
p. 564	112	118
p. 564	325	330
—	340–42	—
—	478	523
—	575	—